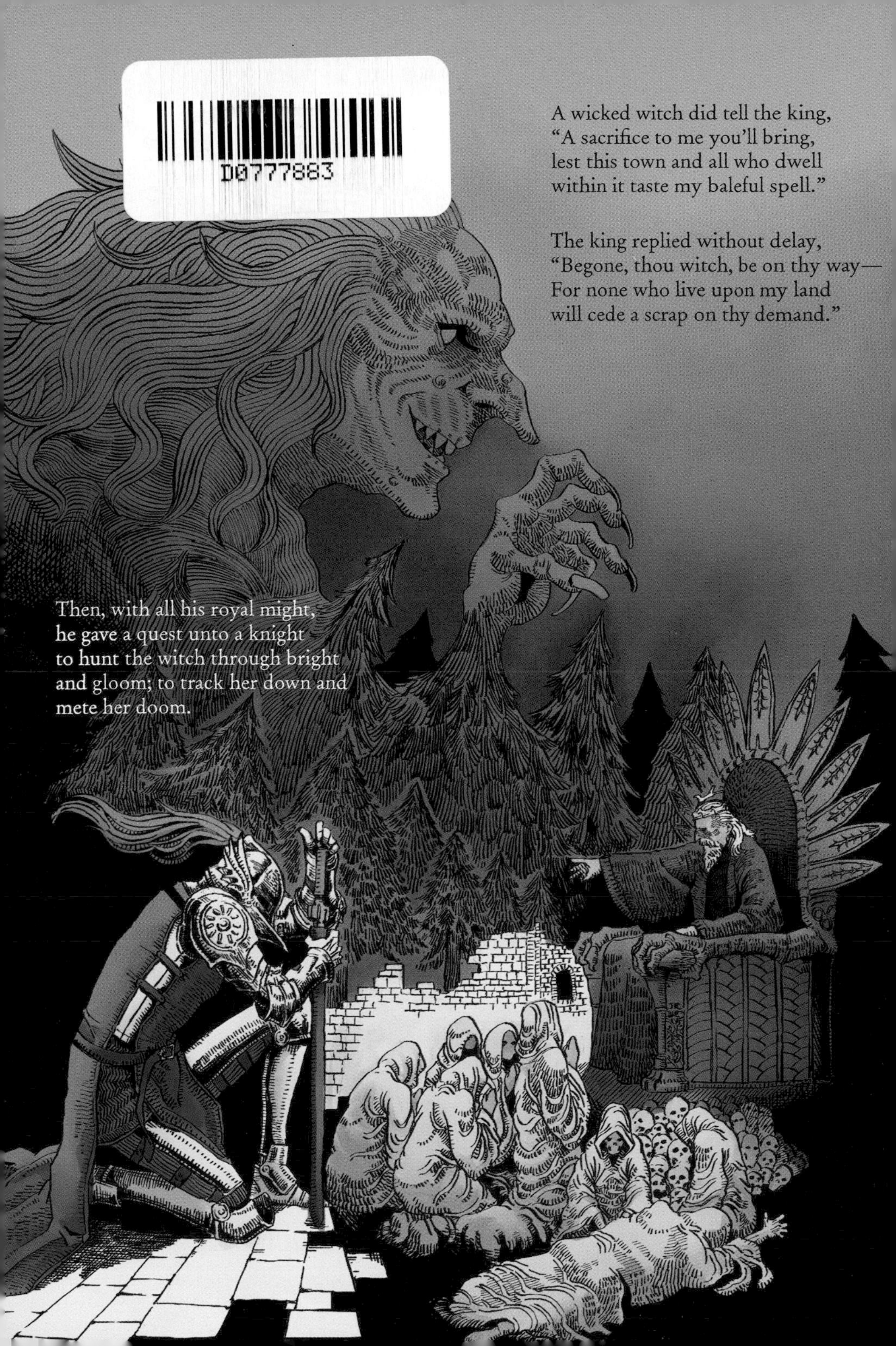

A wicked witch did tell the king,
"A sacrifice to me you'll bring,
lest this town and all who dwell
within it taste my baleful spell."

The king replied without delay,
"Begone, thou witch, be on thy way—
For none who live upon my land
will cede a scrap on thy demand."

Then, with all his royal might,
he gave a quest unto a knight
to hunt the witch through bright
and gloom; to track her down and
mete her doom.

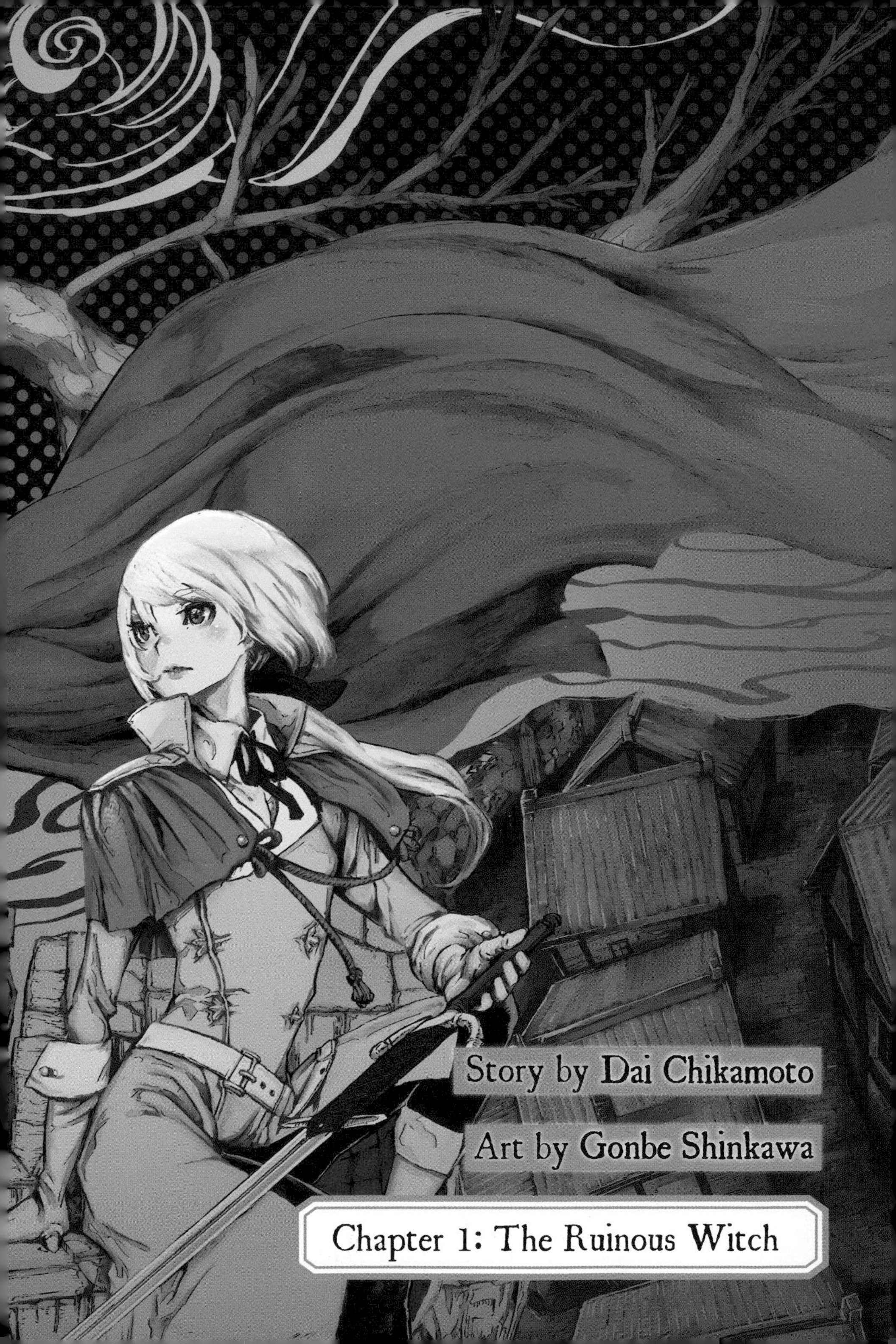

Story by Dai Chikamoto

Art by Gonbe Shinkawa

Chapter 1: The Ruinous Witch

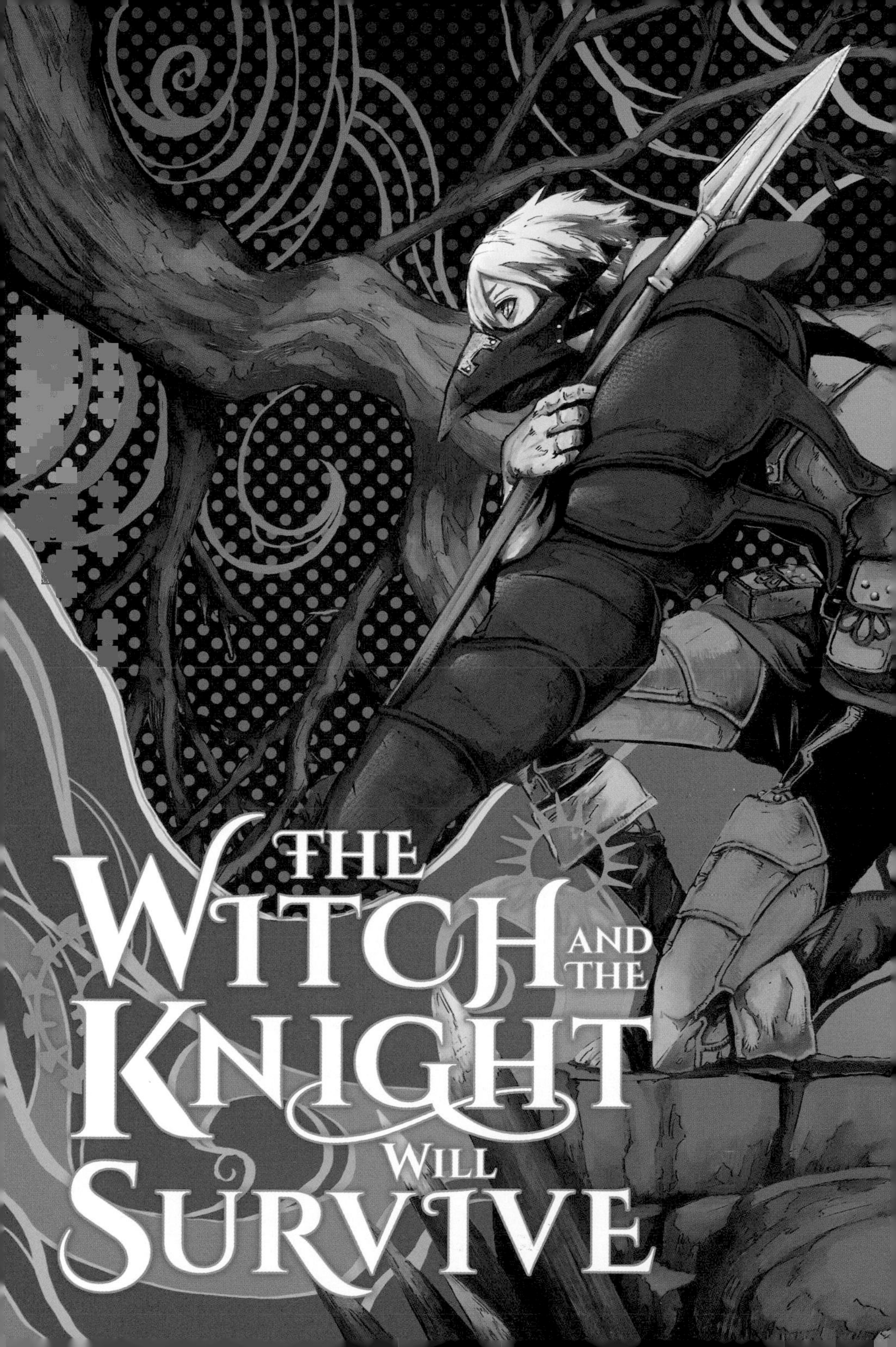
THE WITCH AND THE KNIGHT WILL SURVIVE

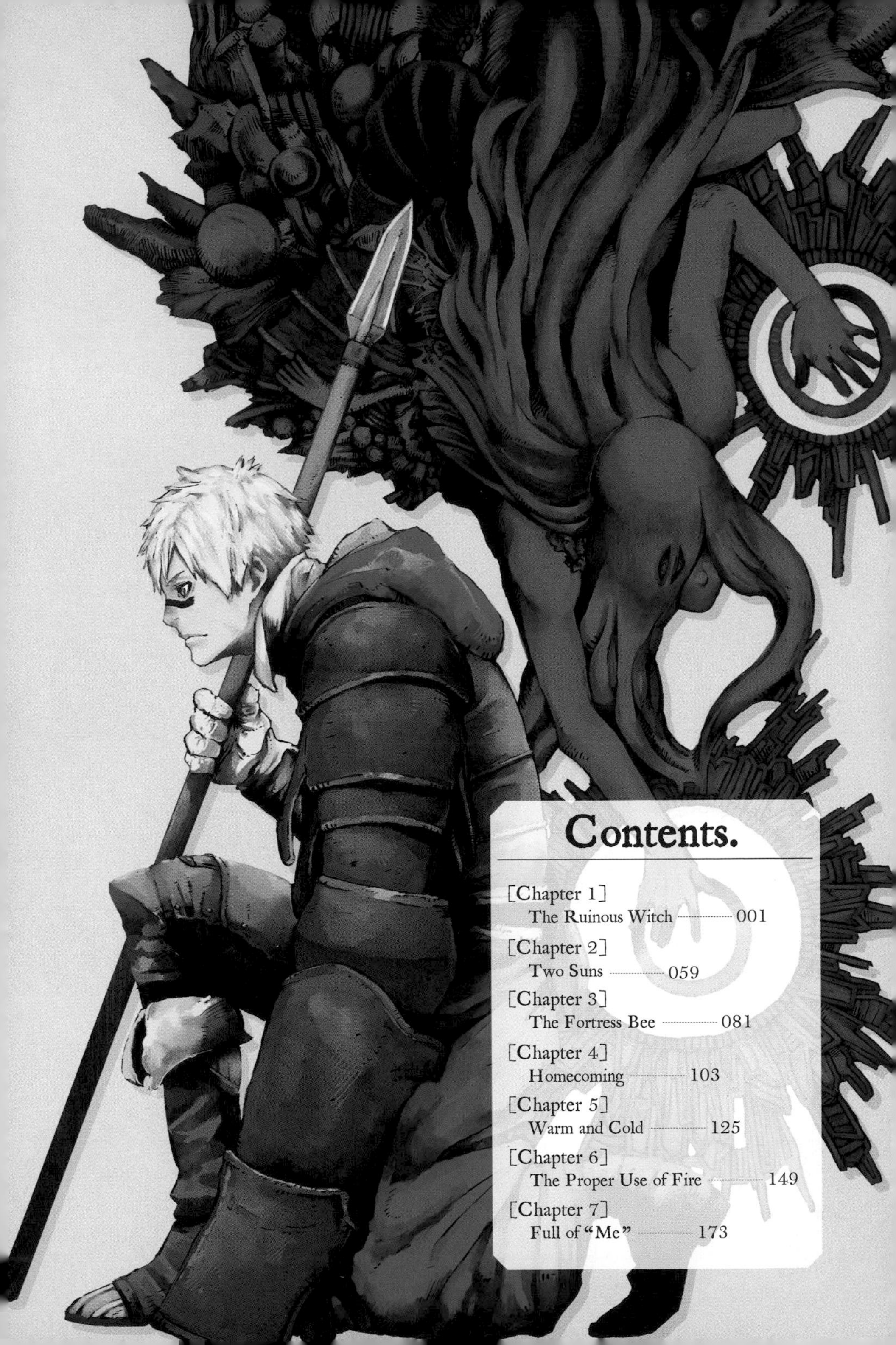

Contents.

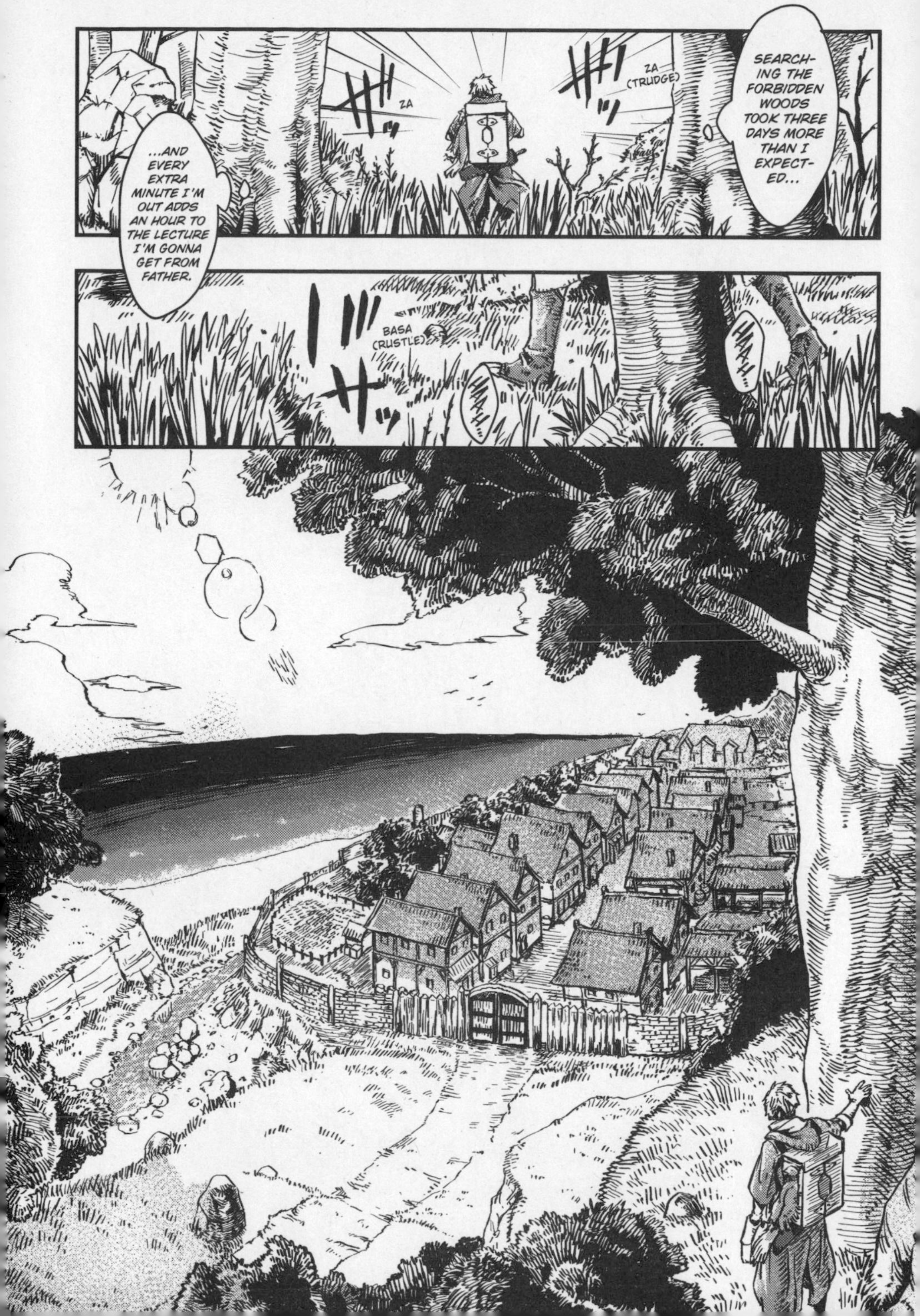
SEARCH-ING THE FORBIDDEN WOODS TOOK THREE DAYS MORE THAN I EXPECT-ED...
ZA (TRUDGE)
ZA
...AND EVERY EXTRA MINUTE I'M OUT ADDS AN HOUR TO THE LECTURE I'M GONNA GET FROM FATHER.
HAAH
HAAH
BASA (RUSTLE)

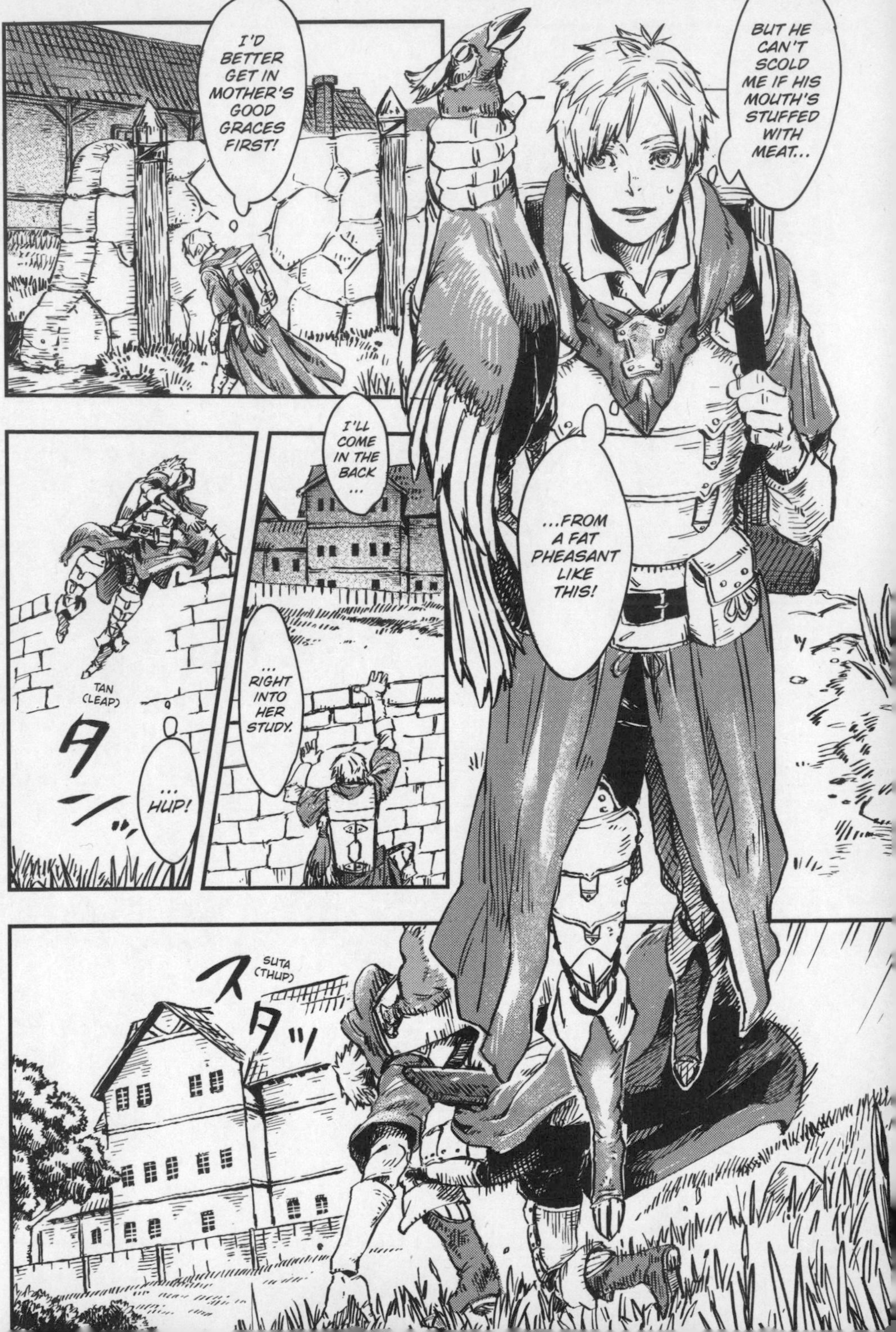
BUT HE CAN'T SCOLD ME IF HIS MOUTH'S STUFFED WITH MEAT...
...FROM A FAT PHEASANT LIKE THIS!
I'D BETTER GET IN MOTHER'S GOOD GRACES FIRST!
I'LL COME IN THE BACK...
...RIGHT INTO HER STUDY.
TAN (LEAP)
タン
...HUP!
SUTA (THUP)
スタッ

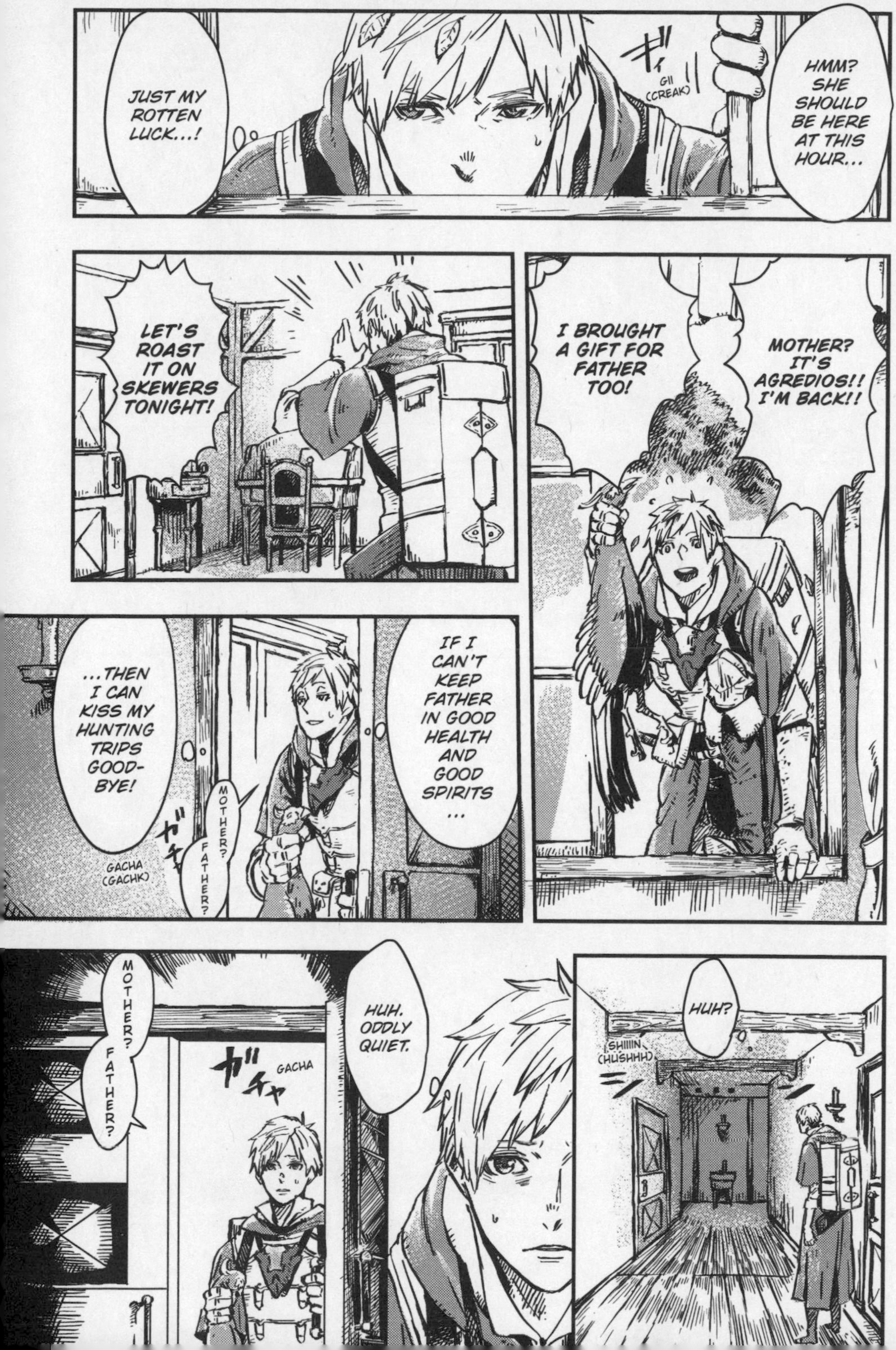
HMM? SHE SHOULD BE HERE AT THIS HOUR...
GII (CREAK)
JUST MY ROTTEN LUCK...!
MOTHER? IT'S AGREDIOS!! I'M BACK!!
I BROUGHT A GIFT FOR FATHER TOO!
LET'S ROAST IT ON SKEWERS TONIGHT!
IF I CAN'T KEEP FATHER IN GOOD HEALTH AND GOOD SPIRITS...
MOTHER? FATHER?
GACHA (GACHK)
...THEN I CAN KISS MY HUNTING TRIPS GOOD-BYE!
HUH?
SHIIIN (HUSHHH)
HUH. ODDLY QUIET.
GACHA
MOTHER? FATHER?

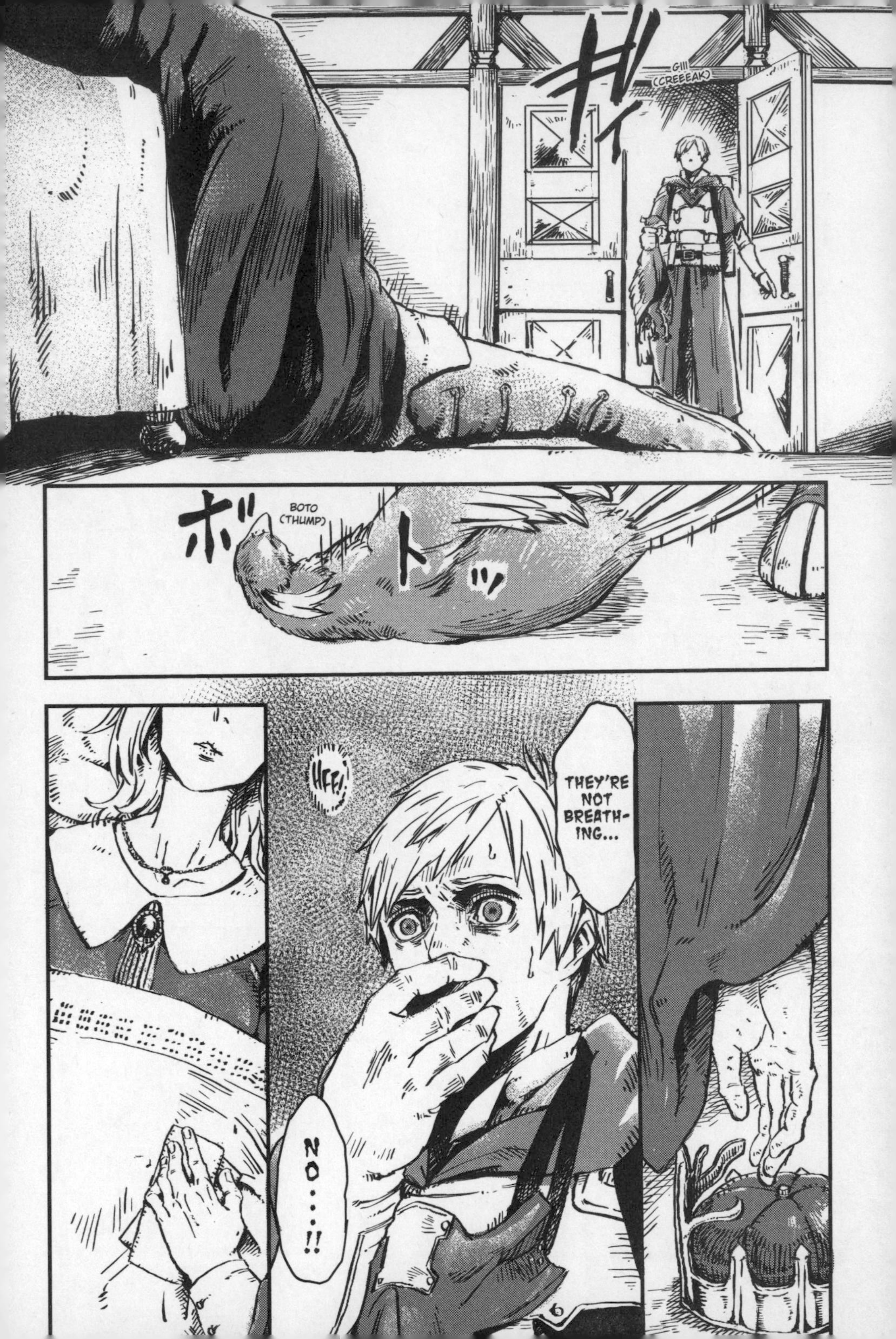
ギィ
GIII (CREEEAK)
ボトッ
BOTO (THUMP)
HFF!
THEY'RE NOT BREATHING...
NO...!!

WHY...!?
HFF
HFF
WHAT'S GOING ON...!?
WHAT'S THIS... ... IN HIS HAND ...?
LETTERS?
TO ME... ...AND GRIAMELDA ...?
DEAREST AGREDIOS...
BAAN (BANG)
DA (DASH)

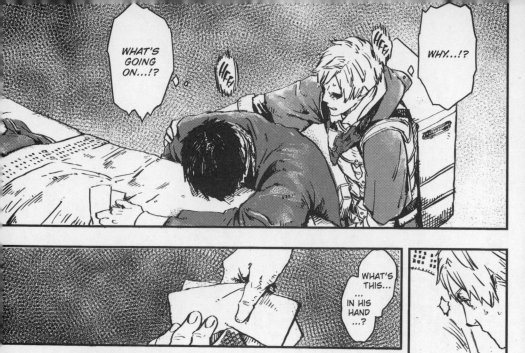

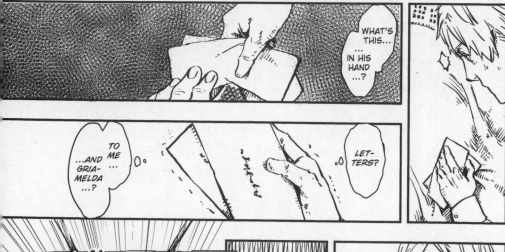

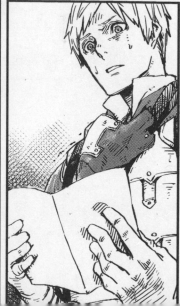

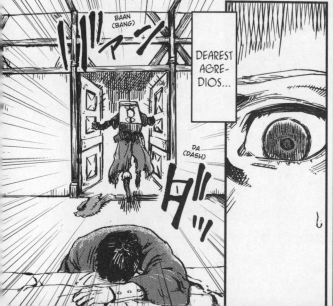

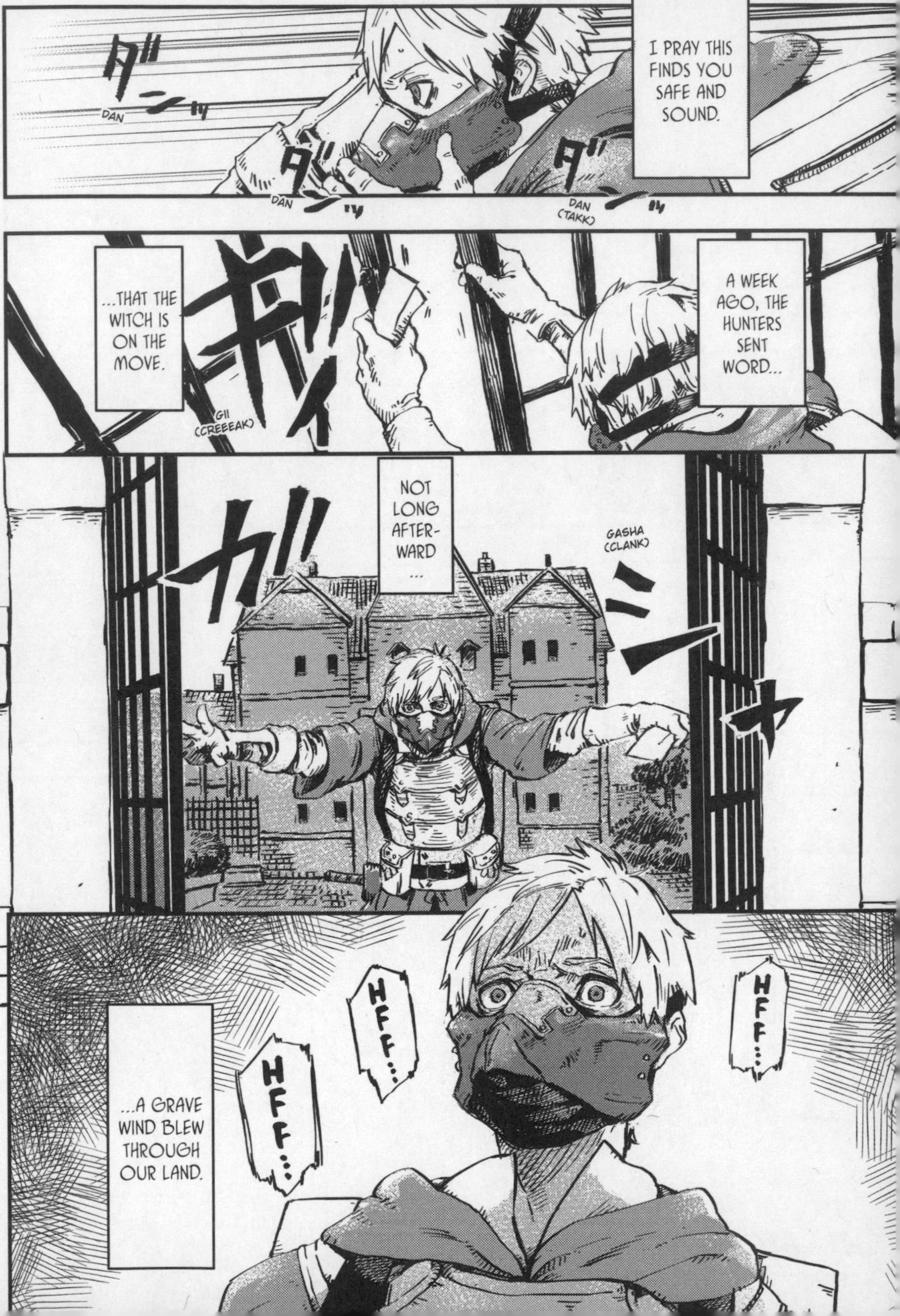
I PRAY THIS FINDS YOU SAFE AND SOUND.
DAN (TAKK)
DAN
DAN
A WEEK AGO, THE HUNTERS SENT WORD...
...THAT THE WITCH IS ON THE MOVE.
GII (CREEEAK)
NOT LONG AFTER-WARD ...
GASHA (CLANK)
HFF...
HFF...
HFF...
...A GRAVE WIND BLEW THROUGH OUR LAND.

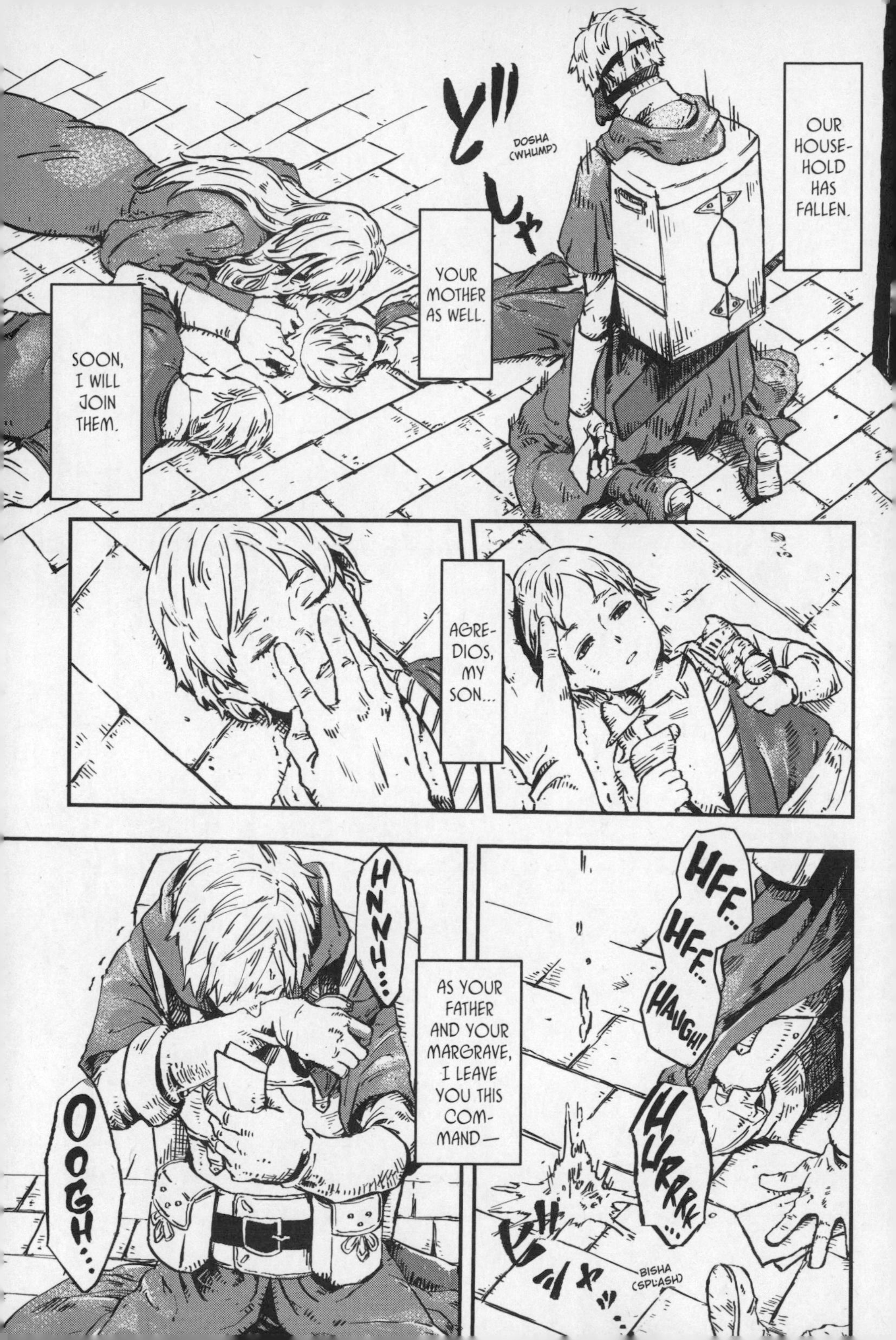

OUR HOUSE-HOLD HAS FALLEN.
どしゃ
DOSHA (WHUMP)
YOUR MOTHER AS WELL.
SOON, I WILL JOIN THEM.
AGRE-DIOS, MY SON...
HFF... HFF... HAUGH!
HURRRK...
びしゃっ
BISHA (SPLASH)
AS YOUR FATHER AND YOUR MARGRAVE, I LEAVE YOU THIS COM-MAND—
HNNH...
OOGH...

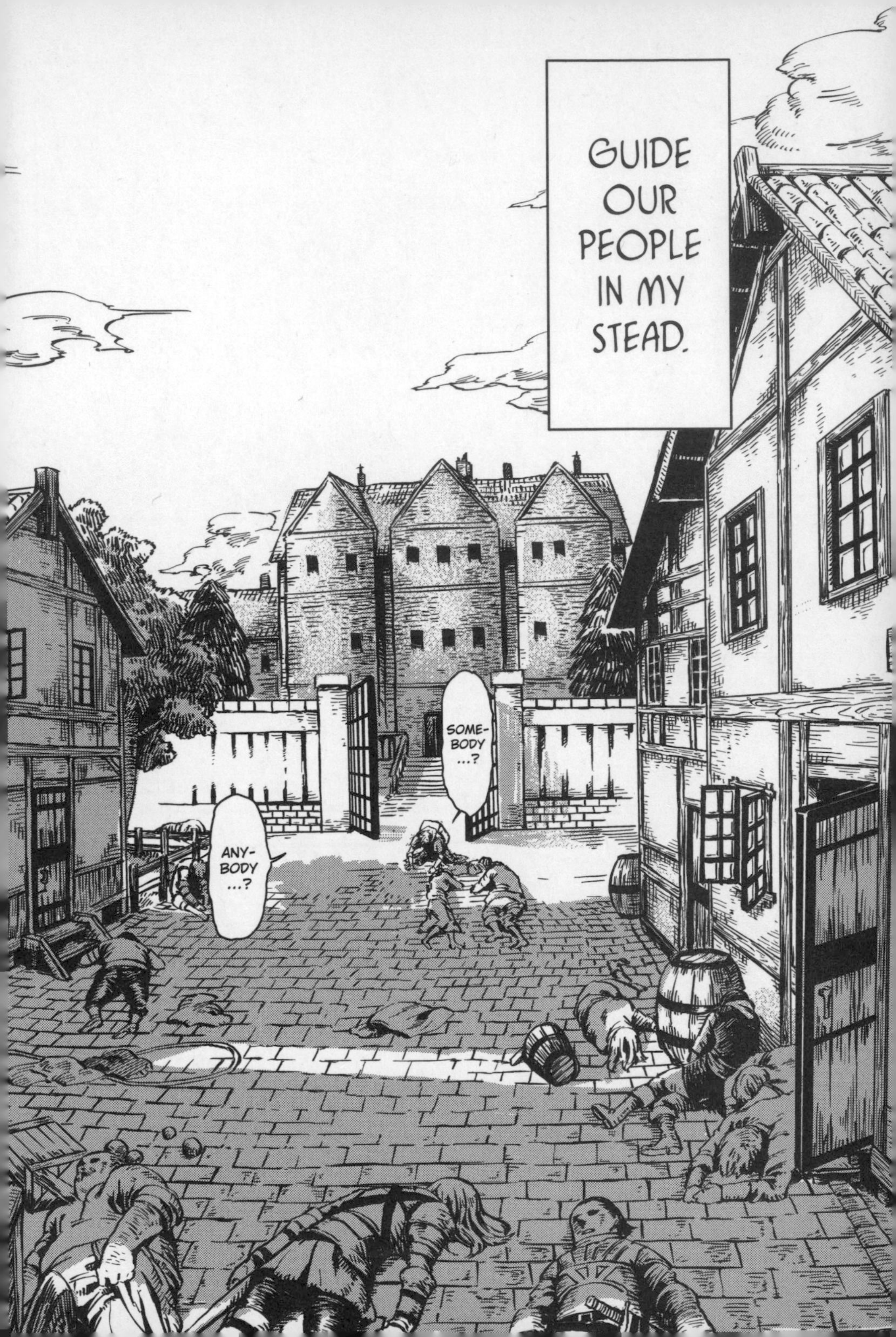
GUIDE OUR PEOPLE IN MY STEAD.
SOME-BODY ...?
ANY-BODY ...?

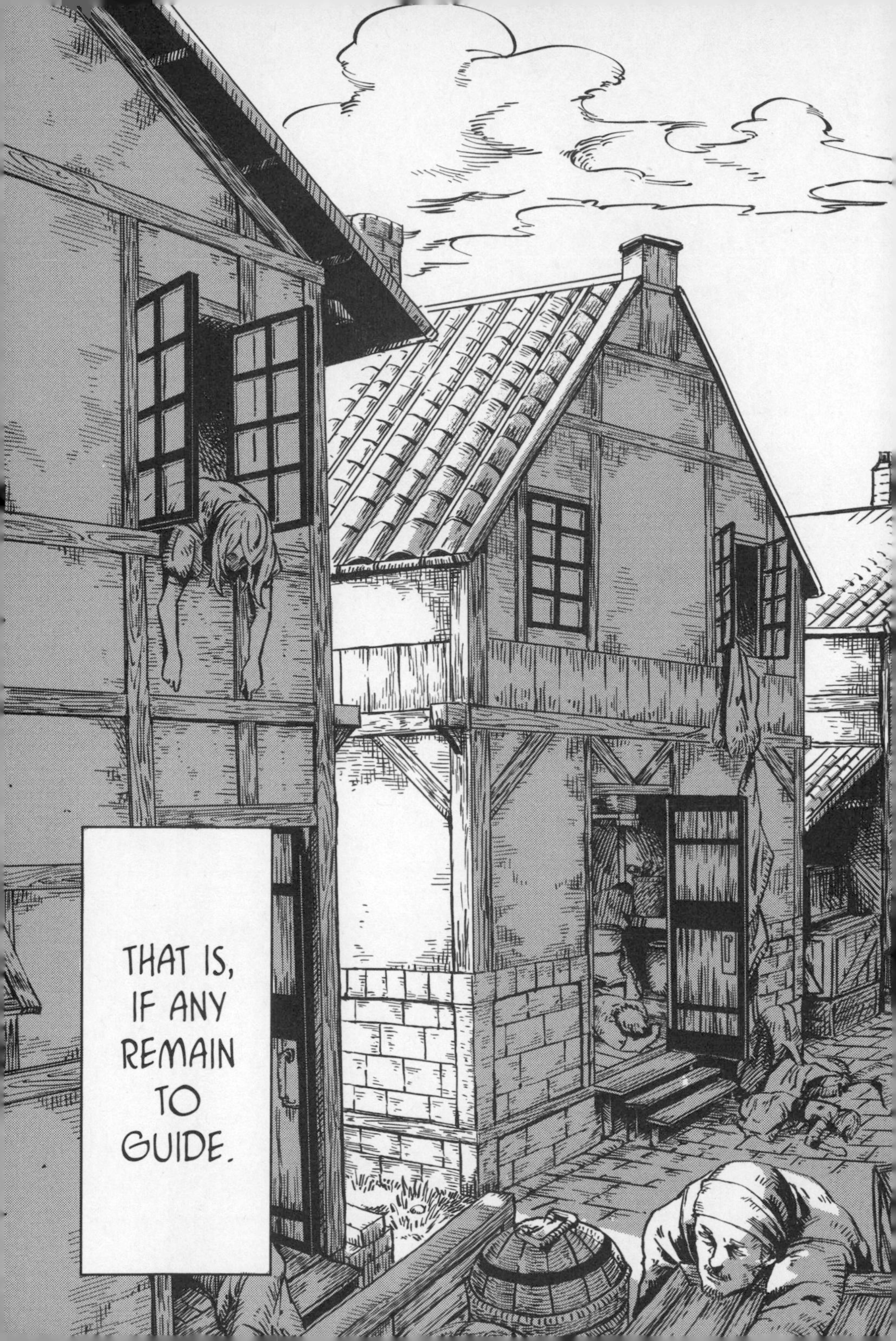
THAT IS, IF ANY REMAIN TO GUIDE.

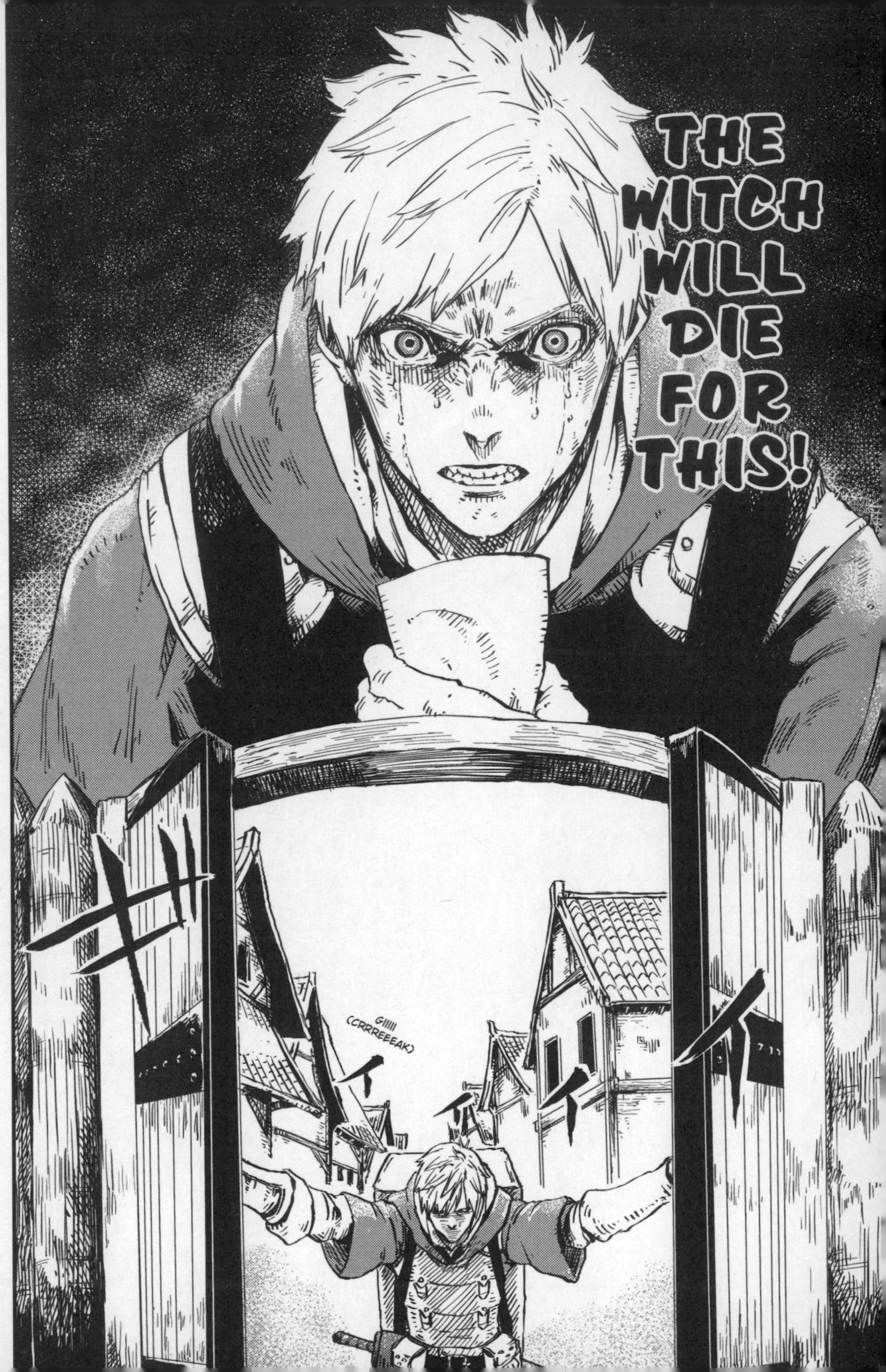
THE WITCH WILL DIE FOR THIS!
GIIII (CRRREEEAK)

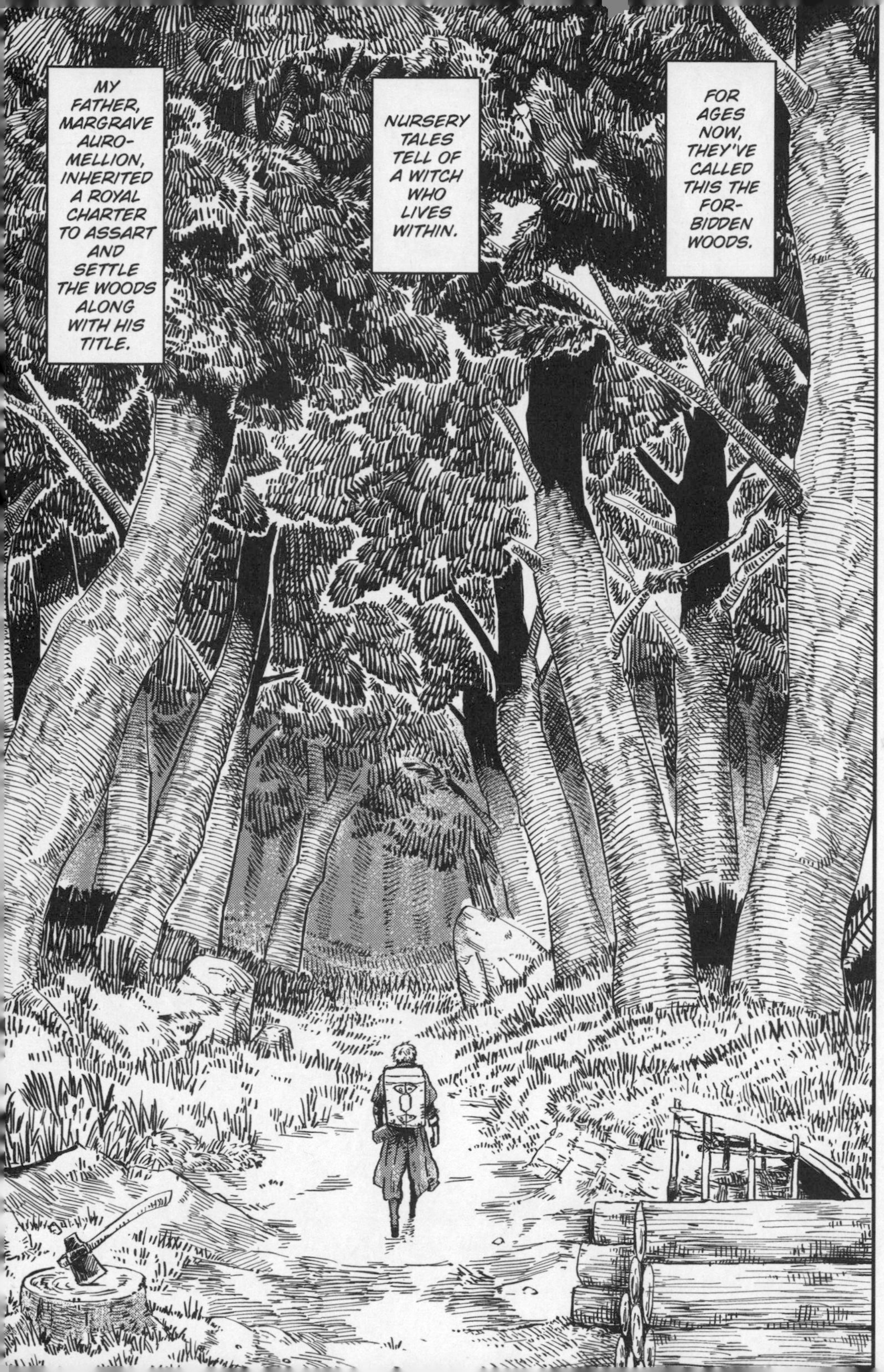
FOR AGES NOW, THEY'VE CALLED THIS THE FOR-BIDDEN WOODS.
NURSERY TALES TELL OF A WITCH WHO LIVES WITHIN.
MY FATHER, MARGRAVE AURO-MELLION, INHERITED A ROYAL CHARTER TO ASSART AND SETTLE THE WOODS ALONG WITH HIS TITLE.

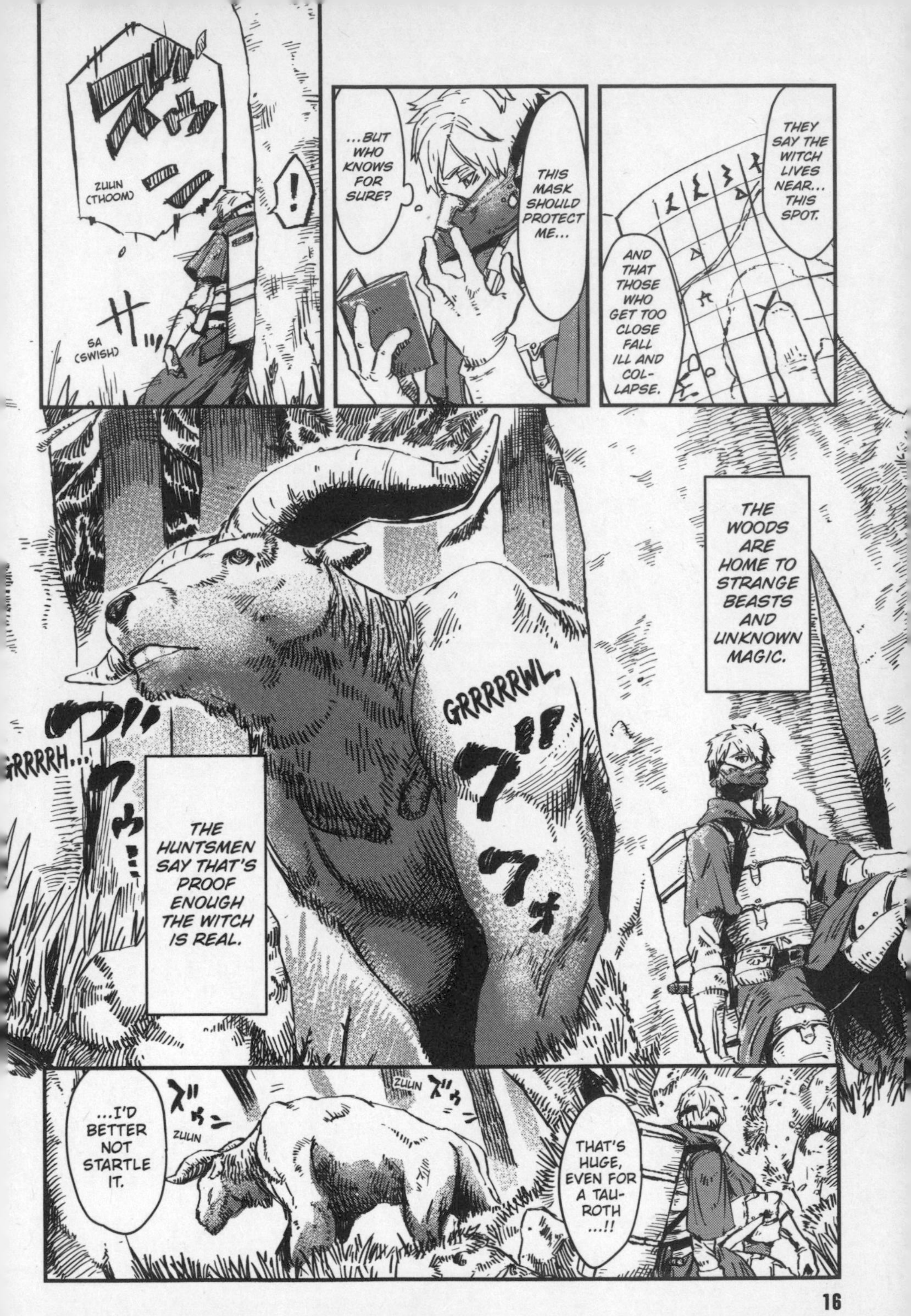
THEY SAY THE WITCH LIVES NEAR... THIS SPOT.
AND THAT THOSE WHO GET TOO CLOSE FALL ILL AND COL-LAPSE.
THIS MASK SHOULD PROTECT ME...
...BUT WHO KNOWS FOR SURE?
ZUUN (THOOM)
!
SA (SWISH)
THE WOODS ARE HOME TO STRANGE BEASTS AND UNKNOWN MAGIC.
GRRRRRWL.
GRRRRH...
THE HUNTSMEN SAY THAT'S PROOF ENOUGH THE WITCH IS REAL.
THAT'S HUGE, EVEN FOR A TAU-ROTH ...!!
ZUUN
ZUUN
...I'D BETTER NOT STARTLE IT.

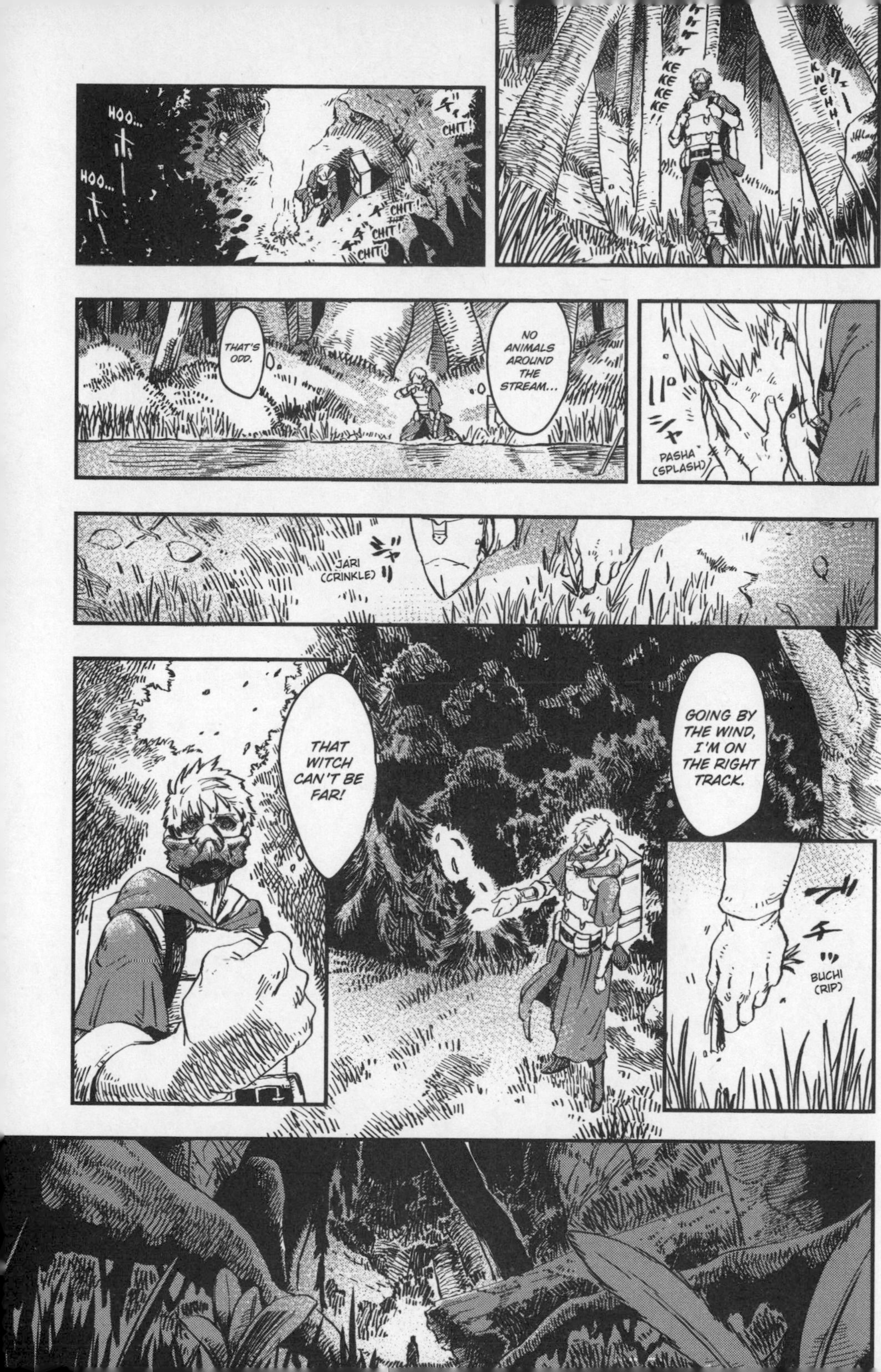
KEKEKEKE!!
KWEHH!
HOO...
HOO...
CHIT!
CHIT!
CHIT!
CHIT!
PASHA (SPLASH)
NO ANIMALS AROUND THE STREAM...
THAT'S ODD.
JARI (CRINKLE)
GOING BY THE WIND, I'M ON THE RIGHT TRACK.
BUCHI (RIP)
THAT WITCH CAN'T BE FAR!

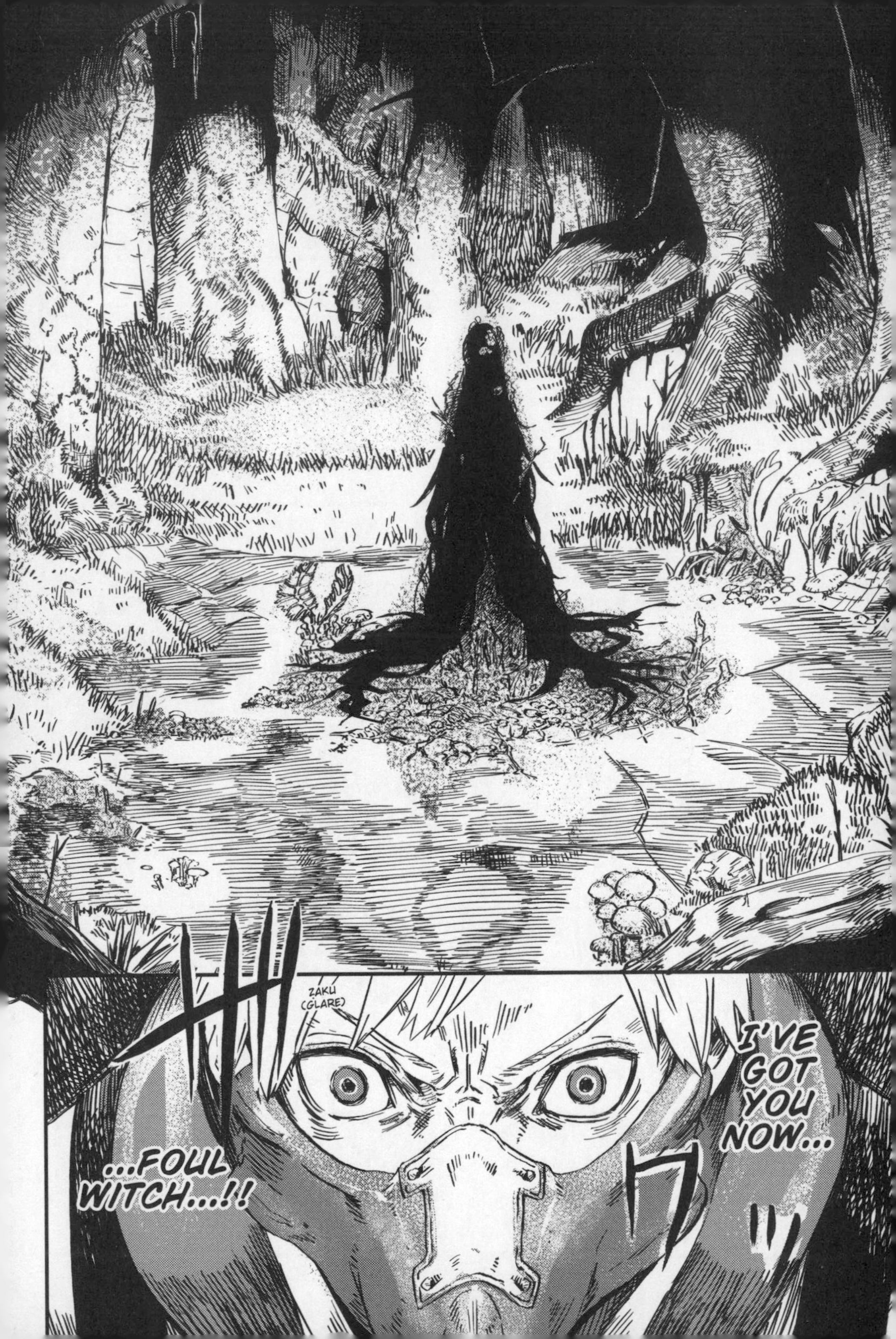
I'VE GOT YOU NOW...
ZAKU (GLARE)
...FOUL WITCH...!!

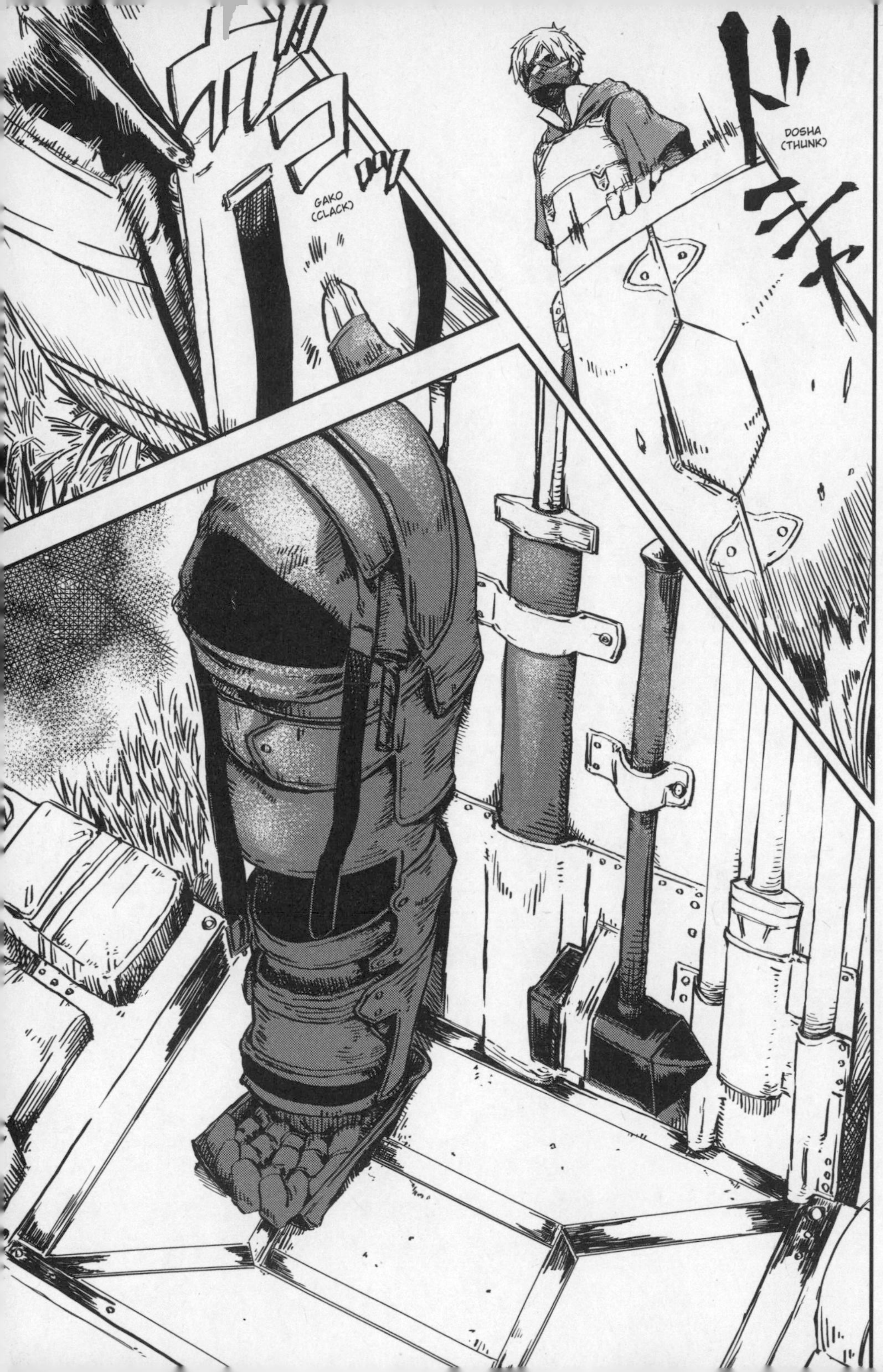
DOSHA
(THUNK)
GAKO
(CLACK)

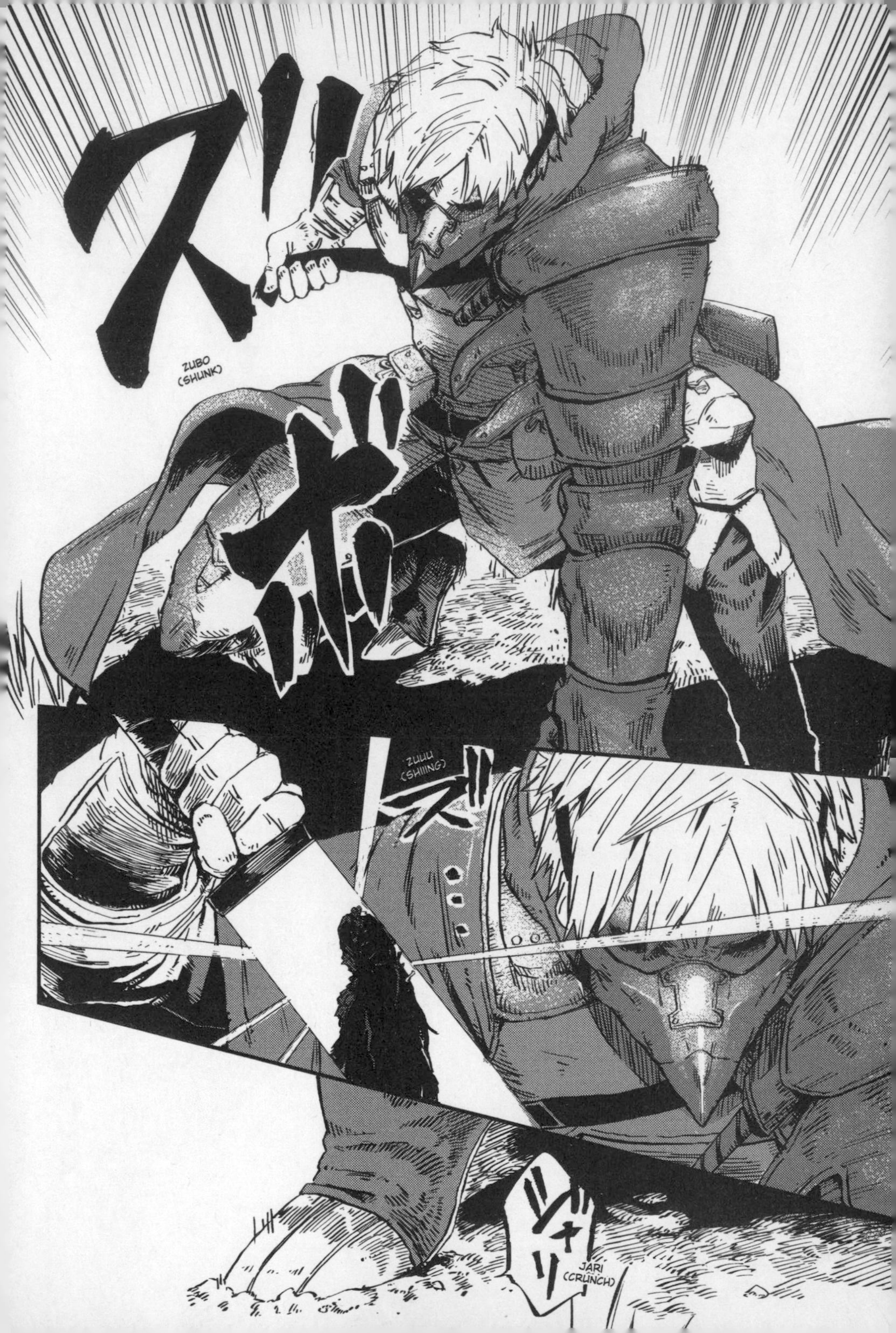
ズボ
ZUBO (SHUNK)
ズ…
ZUUU (SHIIING)
ジャリ
JARI (CRUNCH)

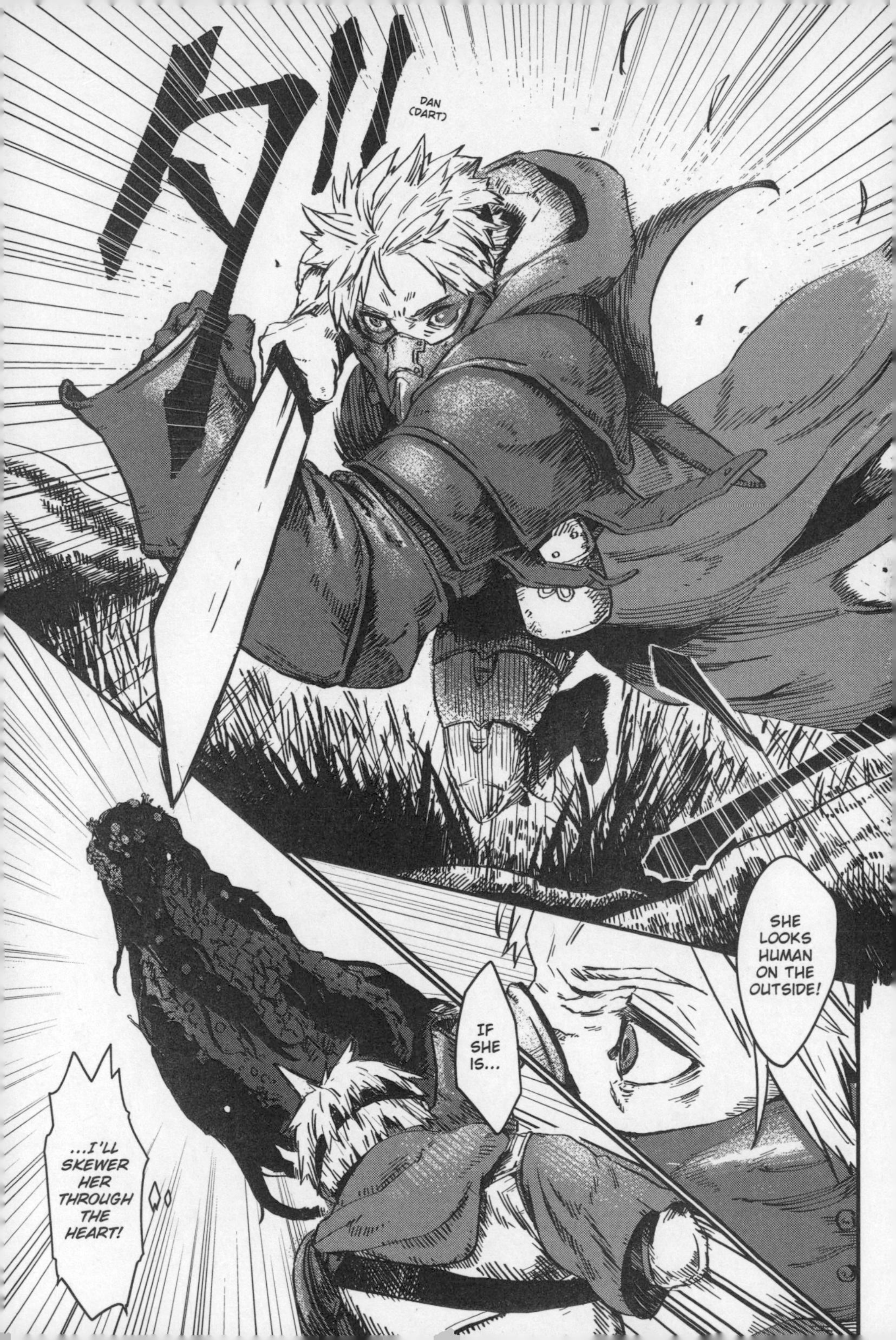
DAN (DART)
SHE LOOKS HUMAN ON THE OUTSIDE!
IF SHE IS...
...I'LL SKEWER HER THROUGH THE HEART!

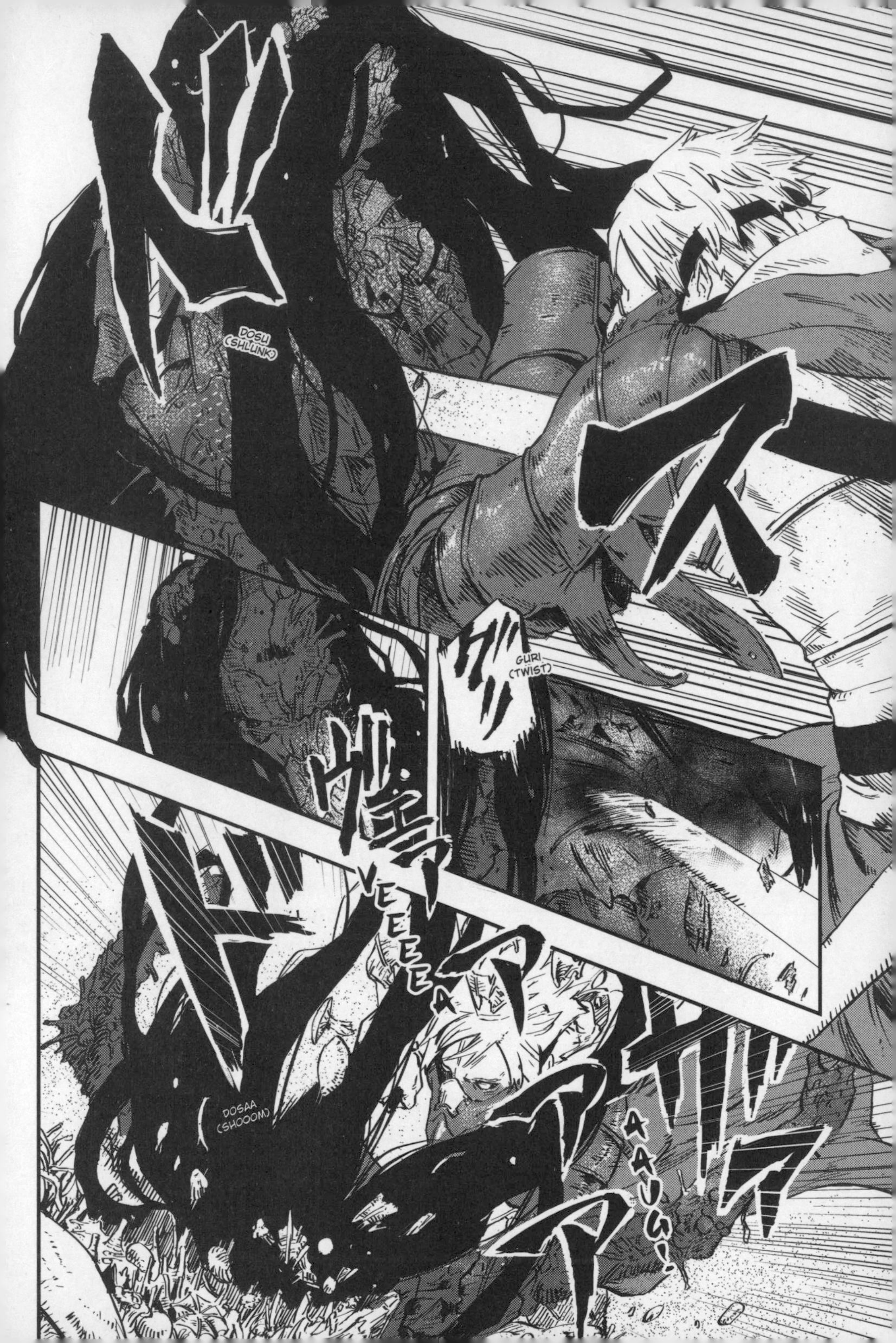
DOSU (SHLUNK)
GURI (TWIST)
VEEEEA
DOSAA (SHOOOM)
AAUGI!

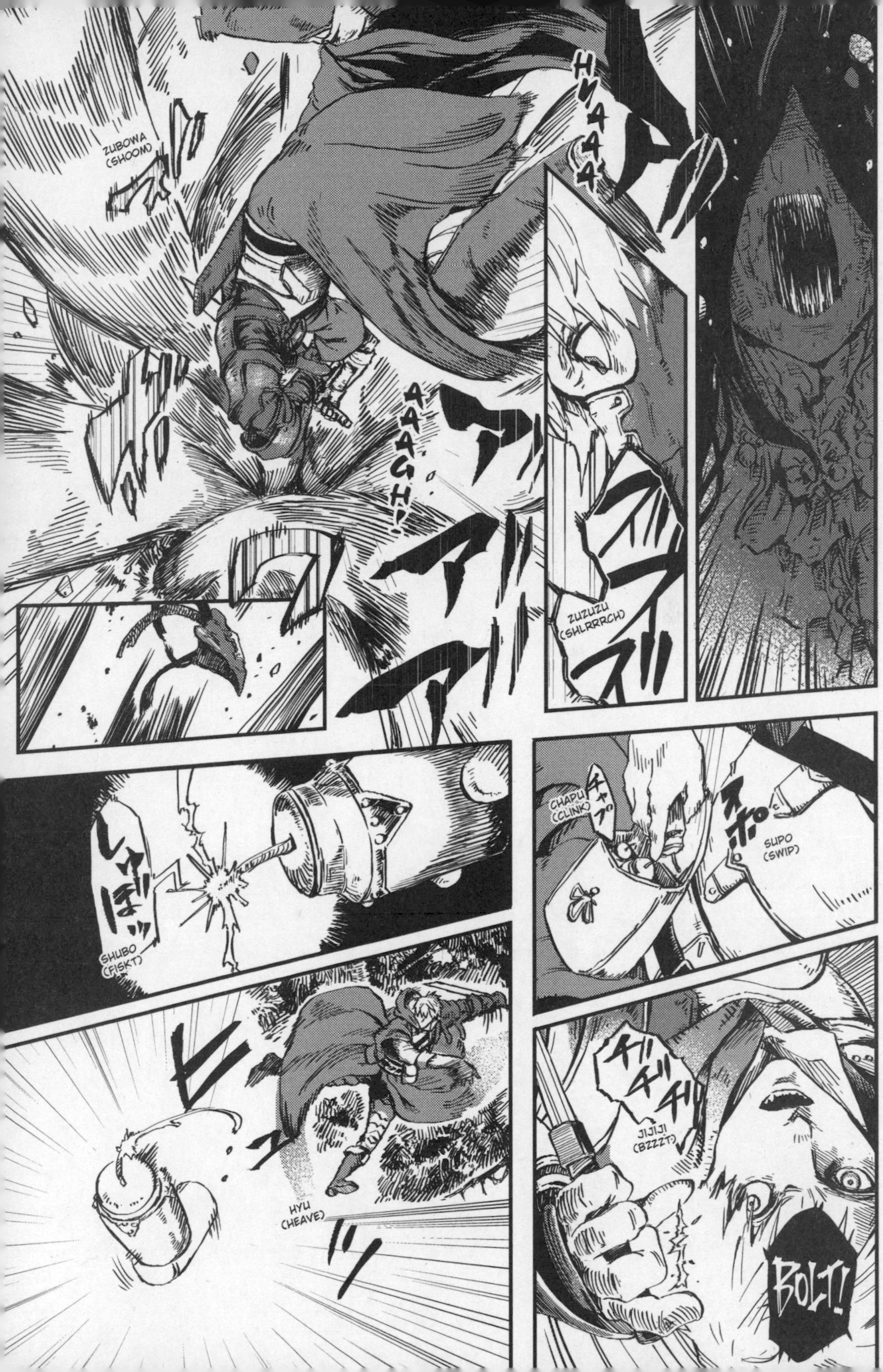

ZUZUZU (SHLRRRCH)
HYAAAAA
AAAAGH!
ZUBOWA (SHOOM)
CHAPU (CLINK)
SUPO (SWIP)
SHUBO (FISKT)
JIJIJI (BZZZT)
BOLT!
HYU (HEAVE)

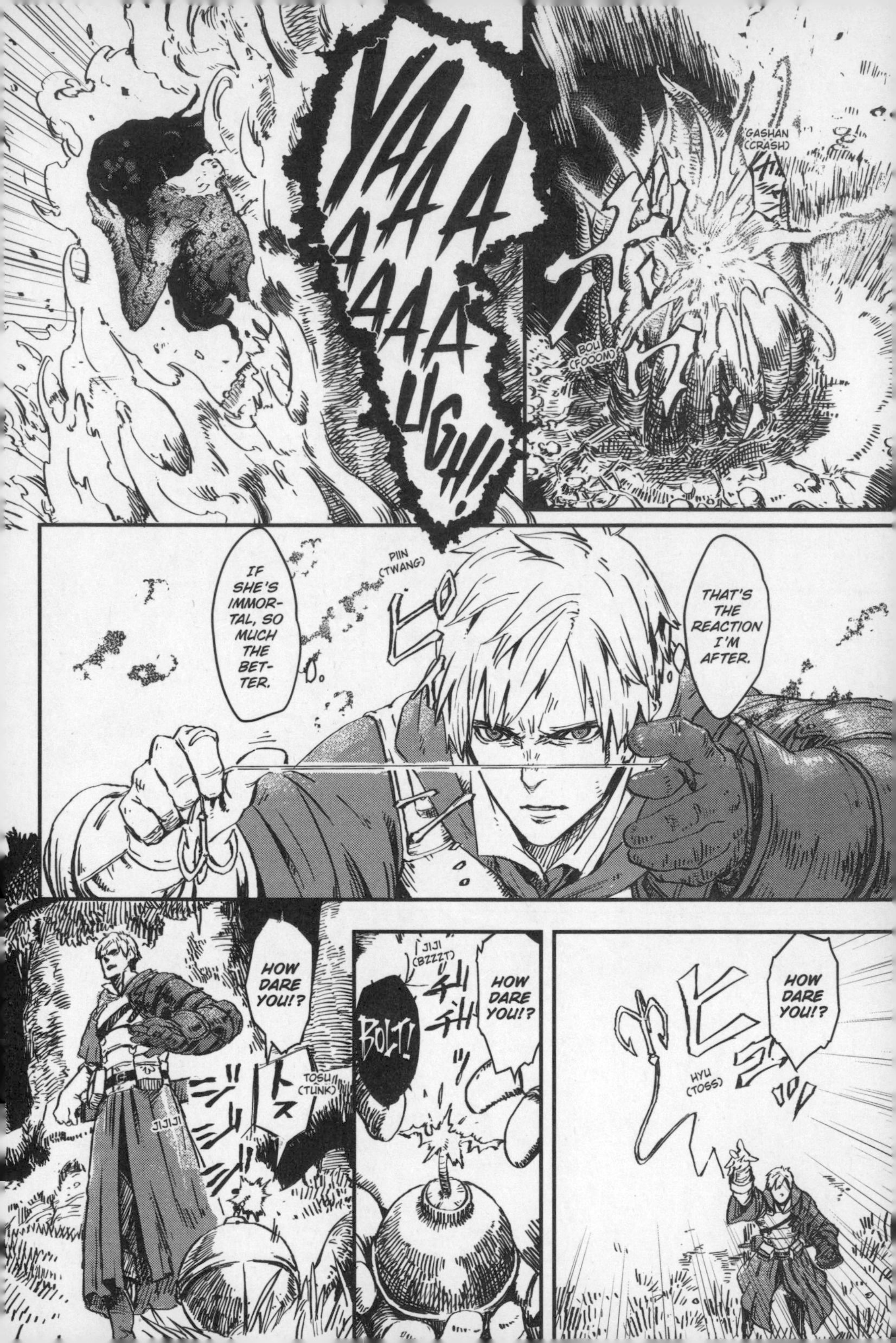
GASHAN (CRASH)
BOU (FOOOM)
YAAAAAAAAAUGH!!
THAT'S THE REACTION I'M AFTER.
PIIN (TWANG)
IF SHE'S IMMORTAL, SO MUCH THE BETTER.
HOW DARE YOU!?
HYU (TOSS)
JIJI (BZZZT)
HOW DARE YOU!?
BOLT!
HOW DARE YOU!?
TOSU (TUNK)
JIJIJI

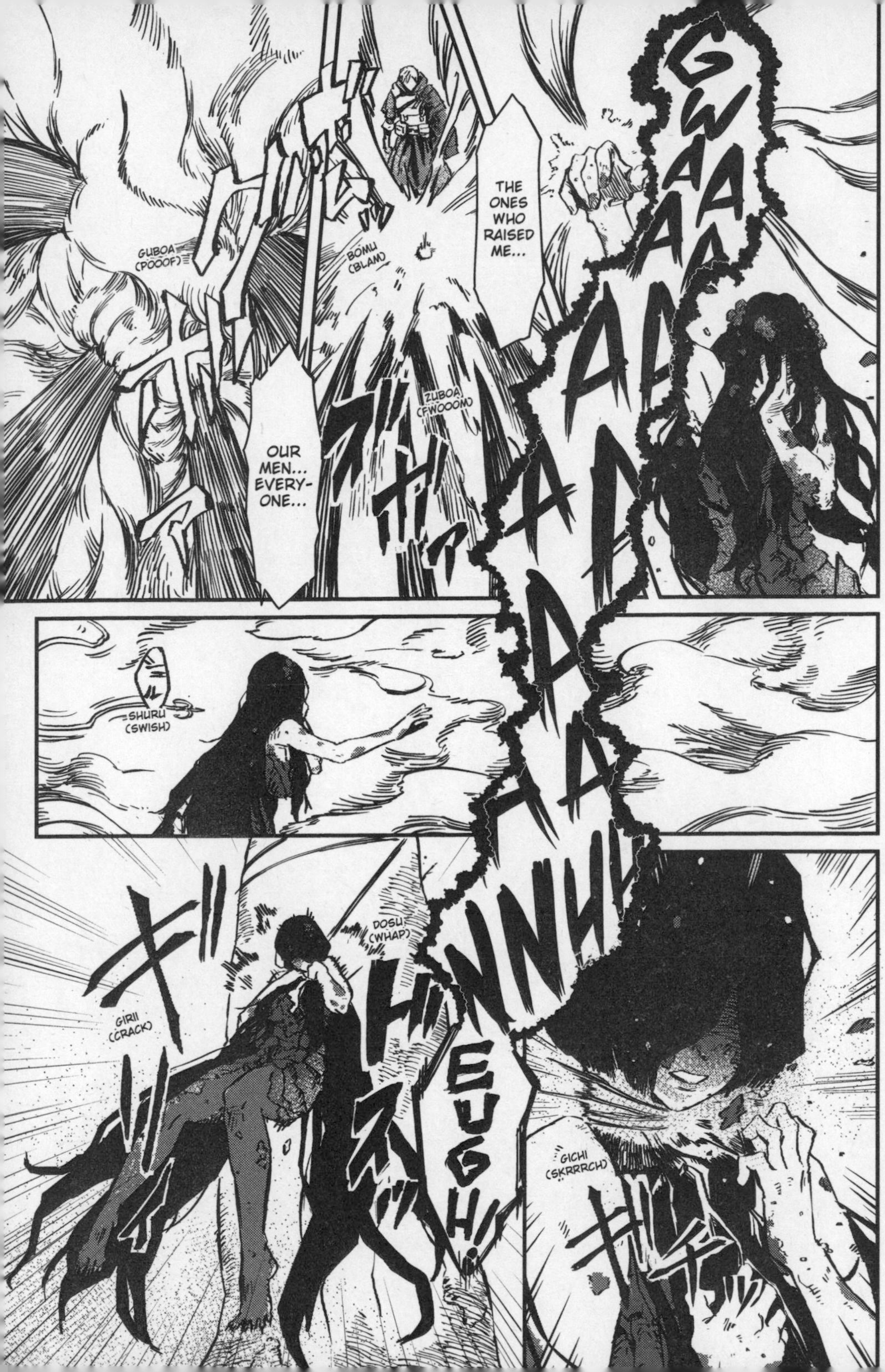
GWAAAAAAAAAAAAAAHNNNUU
THE ONES WHO RAISED ME...
BOMU (BLAM)
GUBOA (POOOF)
ZUBOA (FWOOOM)
OUR MEN... EVERY-ONE...
SHURU (SWISH)
GICHI (SKRRRCH)
DOSU (WHAP)
GIRII (CRACK)
EUGH!!

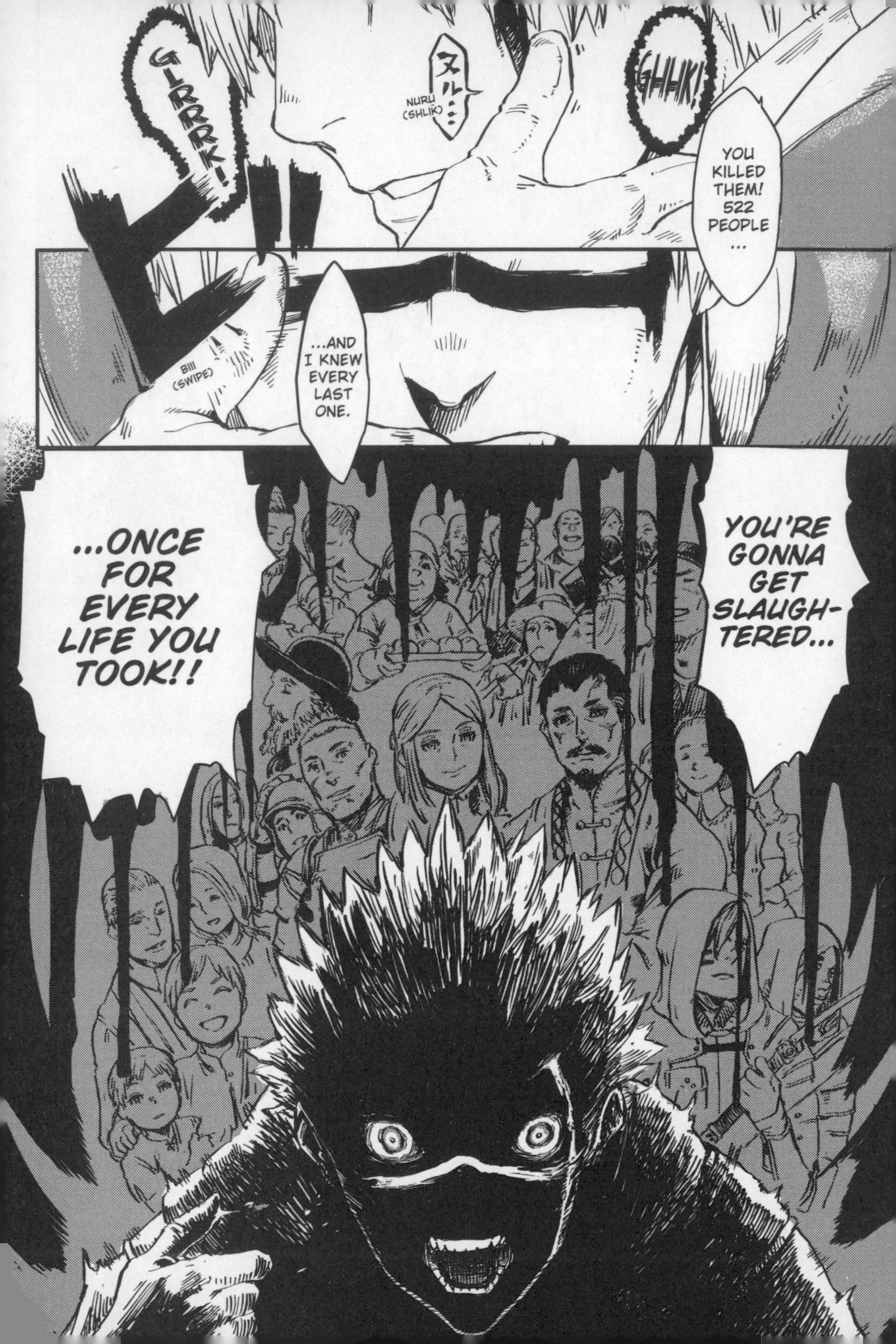
GHHK!
ヌル…
NURU (SHLIK)
GIRRRK!
YOU KILLED THEM! 522 PEOPLE ...
...AND I KNEW EVERY LAST ONE.
BIII (SWIPE)
YOU'RE GONNA GET SLAUGHTERED...
...ONCE FOR EVERY LIFE YOU TOOK!!

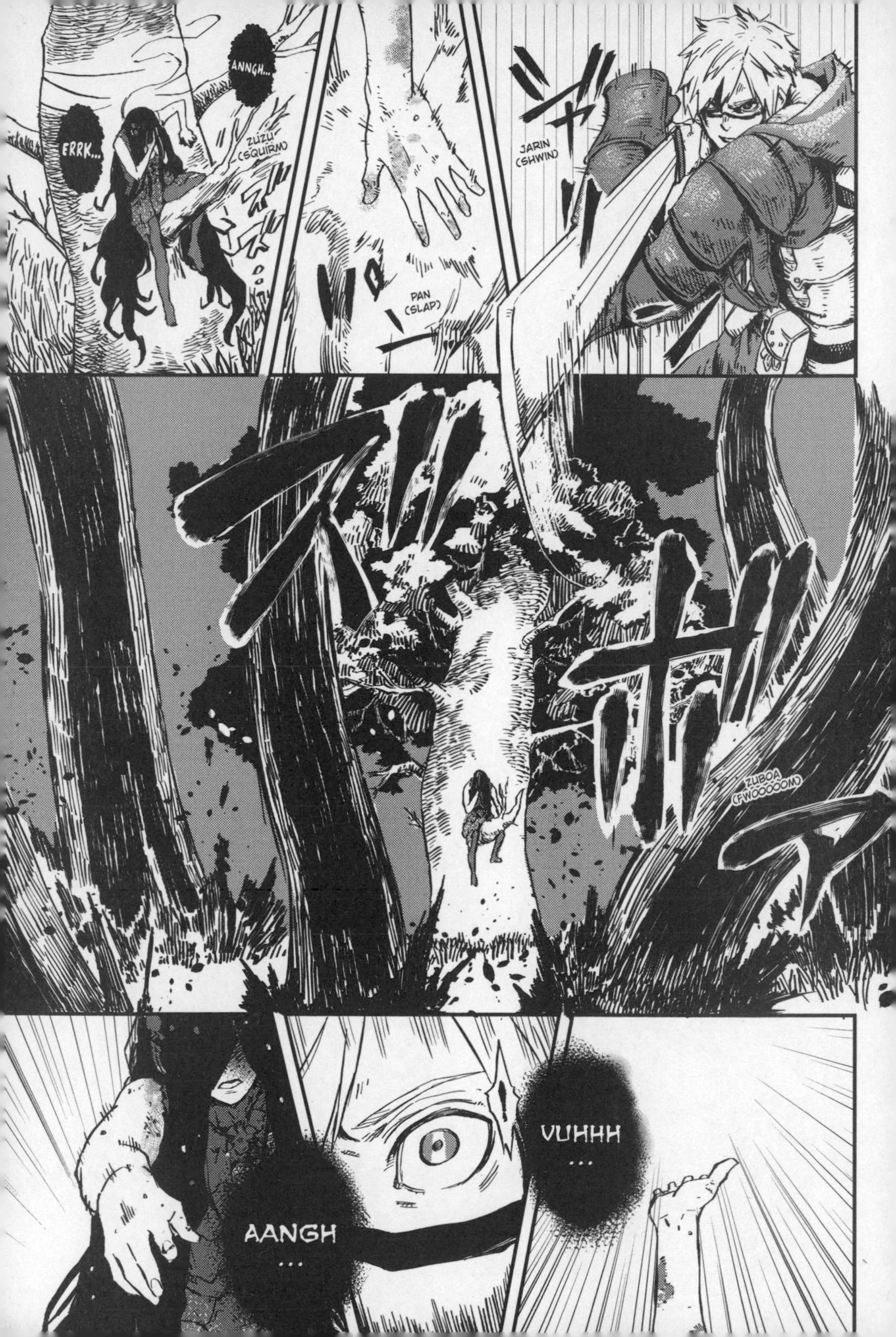
JARIN (SHWIN)
PAN (SLAP)
ANNGH...
ZUZU (SQUIRM)
ERRK...
ZUBOA (FWOOOOOM)
VUHHH ...
AANGH ...

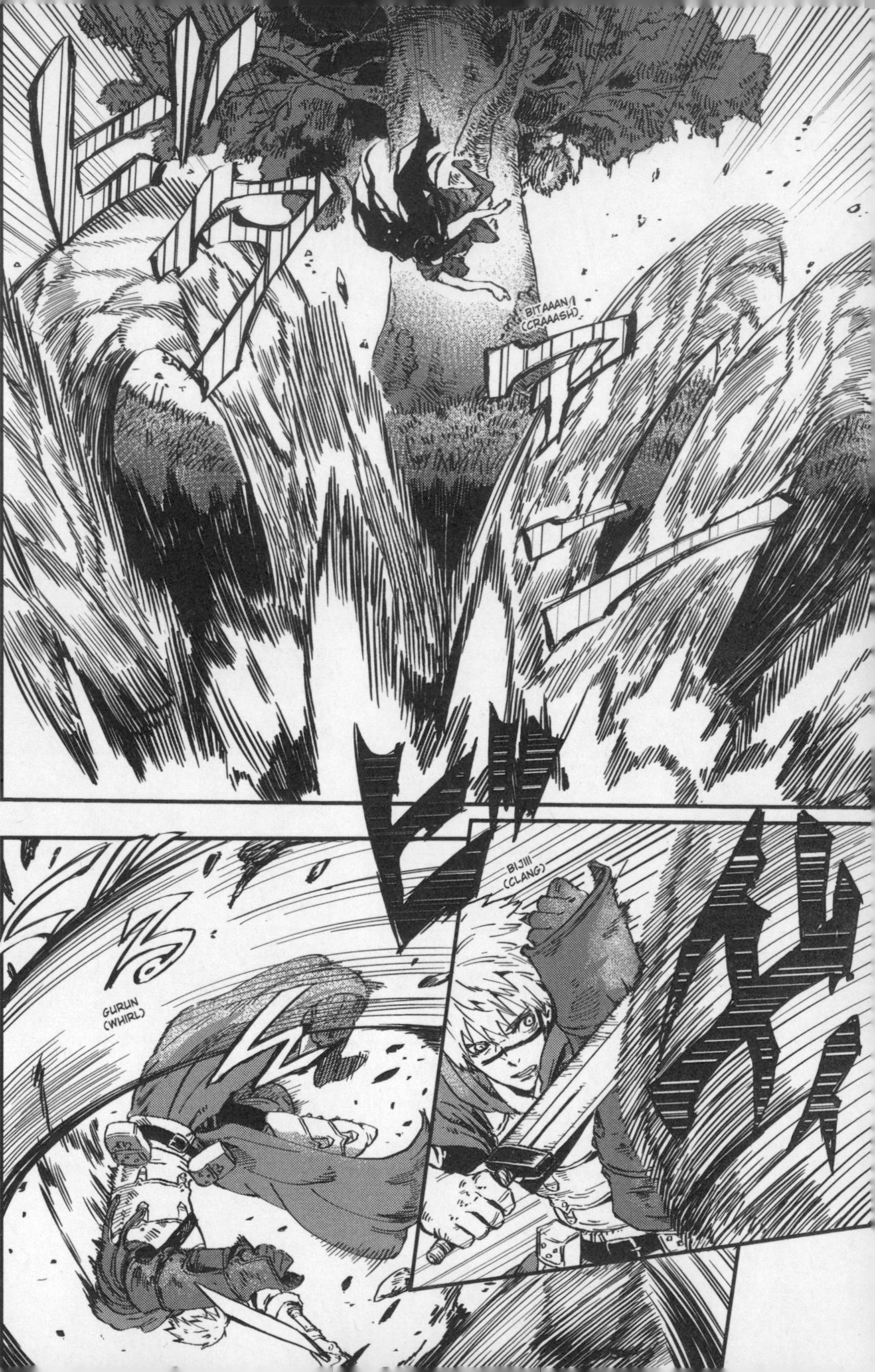
BITAAAN!!
(CRAAASH)
BIJIII
(CLANG)
GURUN
(WHIRL)

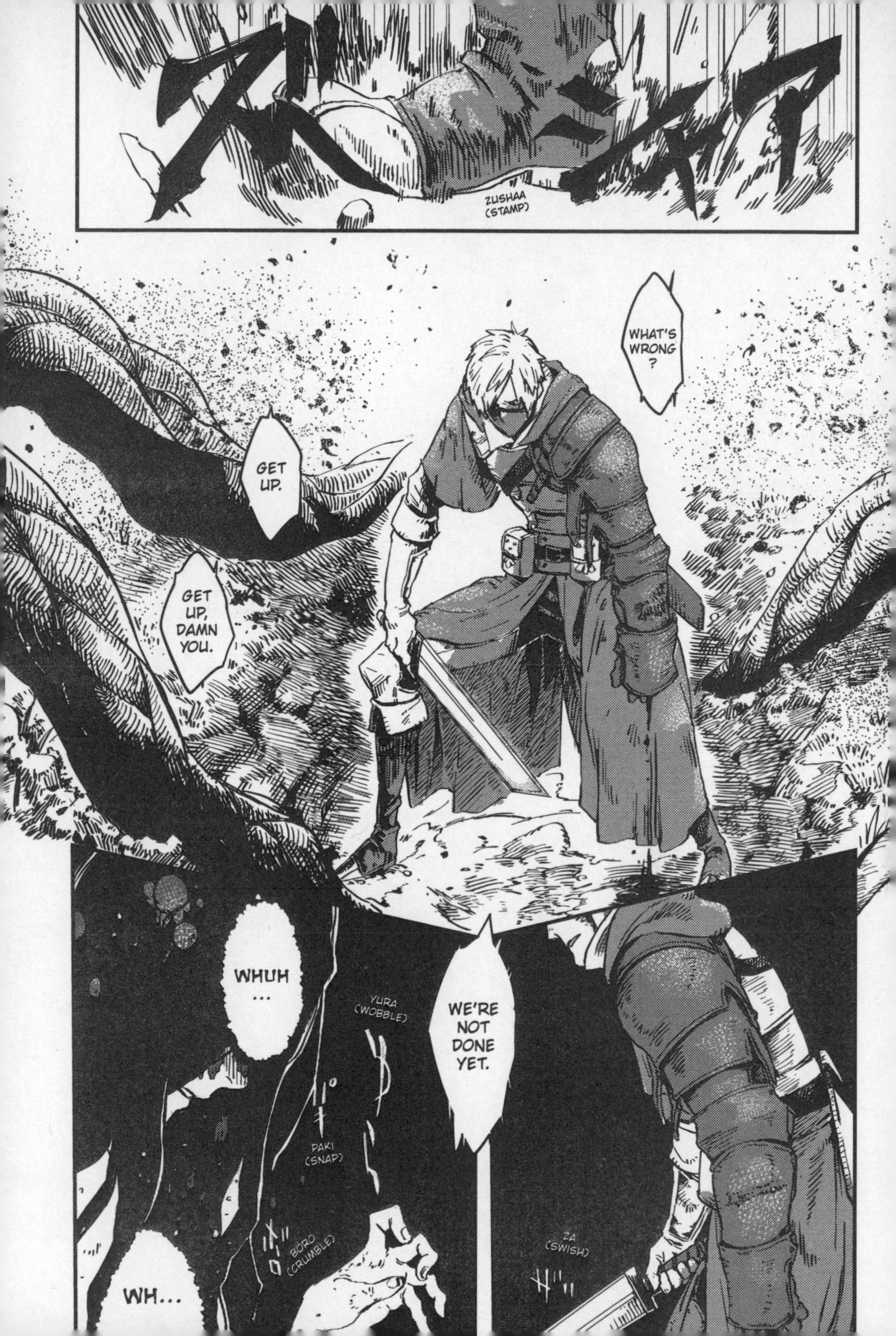
ZUSHAA (STAMP)
WHAT'S WRONG?
GET UP.
GET UP, DAMN YOU.
WE'RE NOT DONE YET.
ZA (SWISH)
WHUH...
YURA (WOBBLE)
PAKI (SNAP)
BORO (CRUMBLE)
WH...

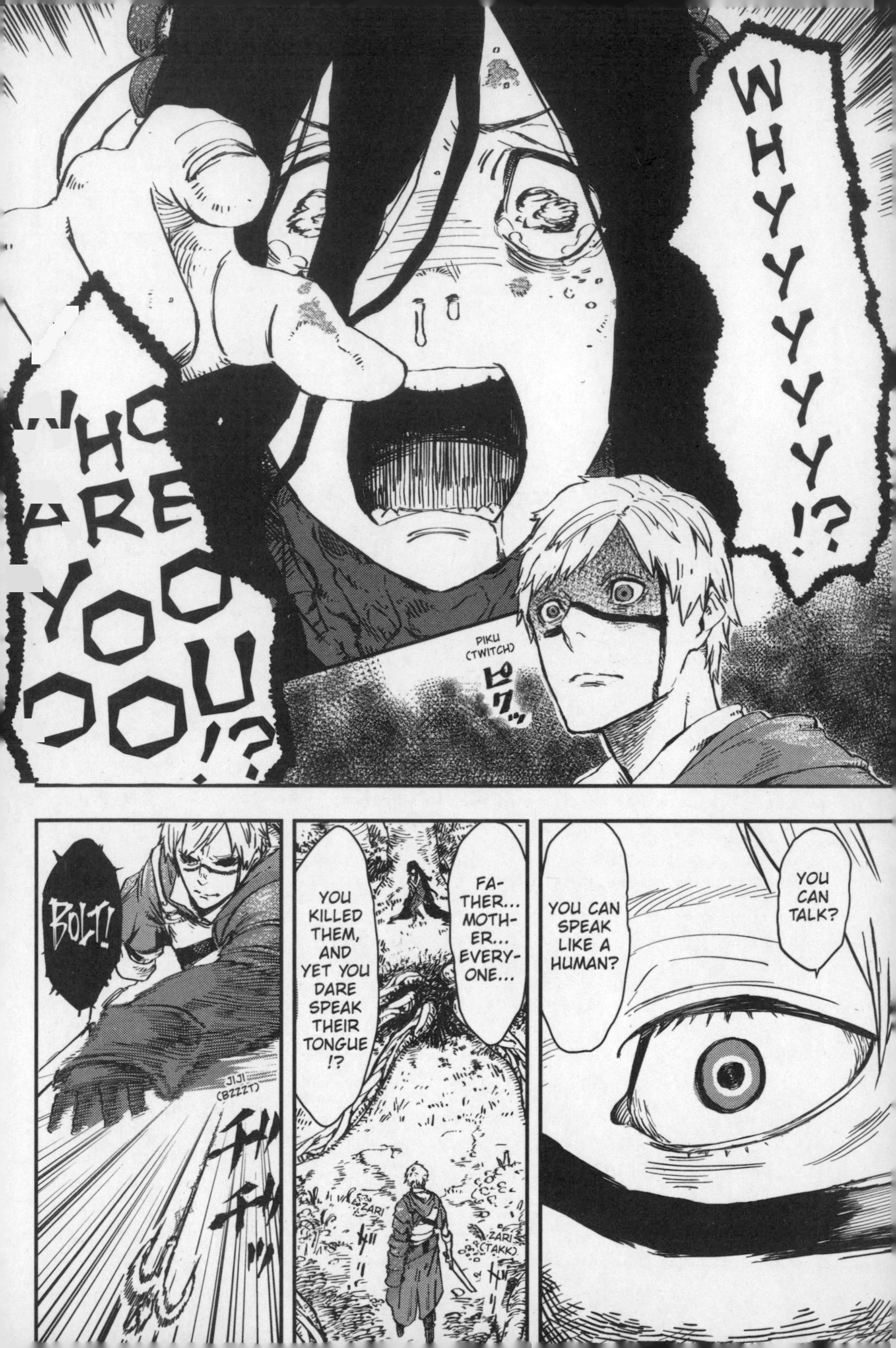
WHYYYYY!?
WHO ARE YOOOU!?
PIKU (TWITCH)
ピクッ
YOU CAN TALK?
YOU CAN SPEAK LIKE A HUMAN?
FA-THER... MOTH-ER... EVERY-ONE...
YOU KILLED THEM, AND YET YOU DARE SPEAK THEIR TONGUE!?
ZARI
ZARI (TAKK)
BOLT!
JIJI (BZZZT)

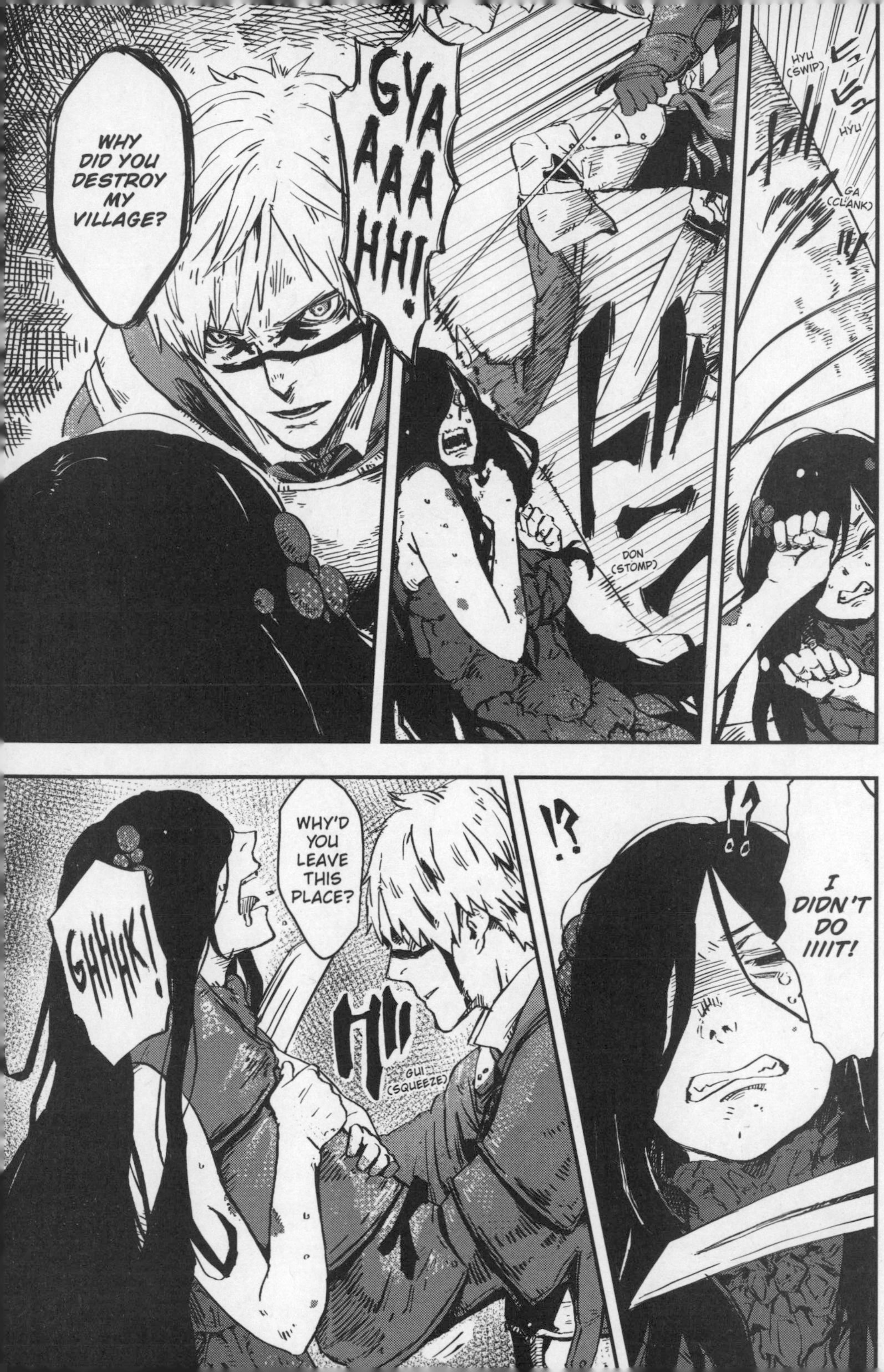
HYU (SWIP)
HYU
GA (CLANK)
GYAAAAAHH!
DON (STOMP)
WHY DID YOU DESTROY MY VILLAGE?
!?
I DIDN'T DO IIIIT!
WHY'D YOU LEAVE THIS PLACE?
GUI (SQUEEZE)
GHHHK!

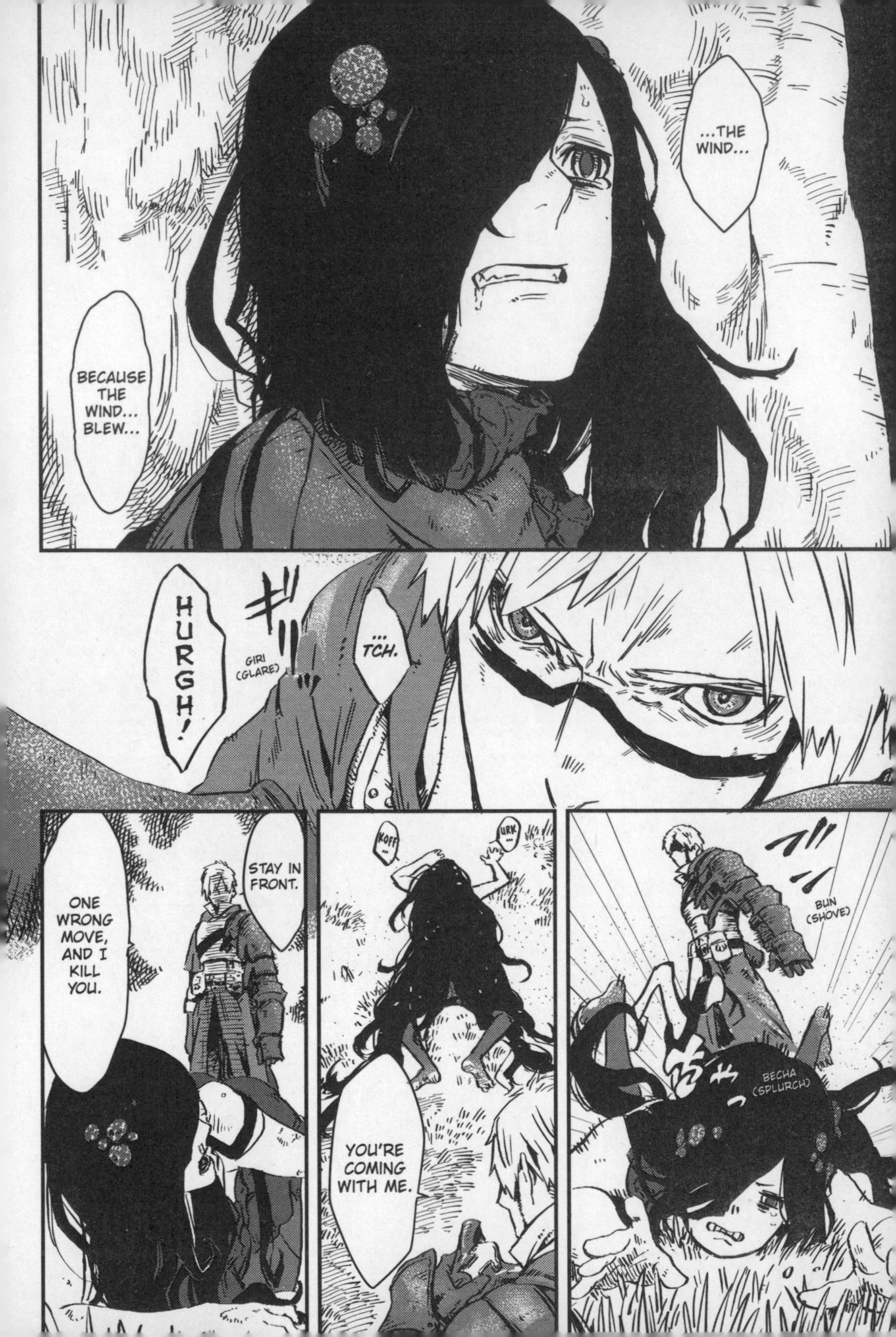
...THE WIND...
BECAUSE THE WIND... BLEW...
... TCH.
GIRI (GLARE)
HURGH!
BUN (SHOVE)
BECHA (SPLURCH)
URK
KOFF...
YOU'RE COMING WITH ME.
STAY IN FRONT.
ONE WRONG MOVE, AND I KILL YOU.

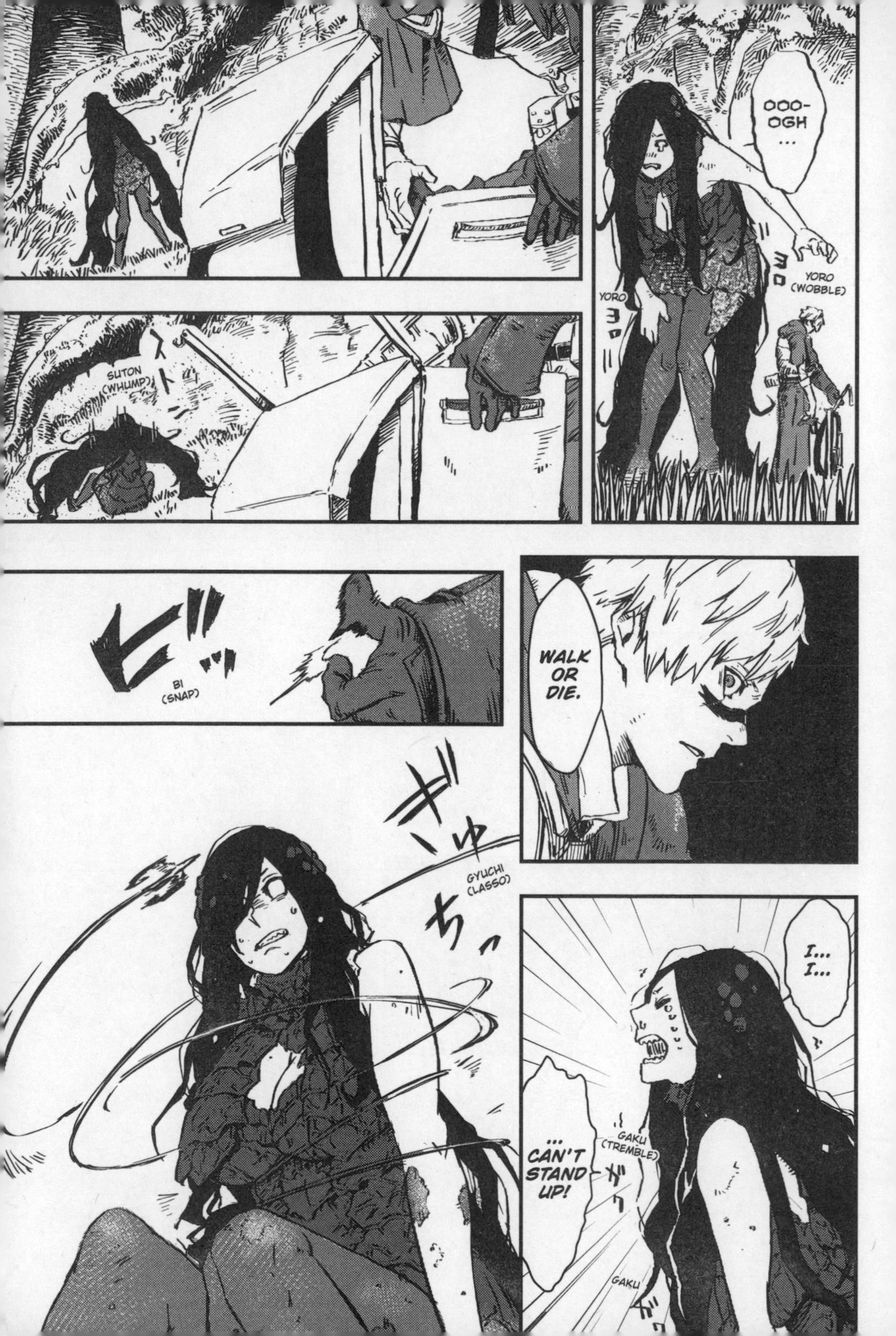
OOO-OGH ...
YORO (WOBBLE)
YORO
SUTON (WHUMP)
WALK OR DIE.
BI (SNAP)
I... I...
...CAN'T STAND UP!
GAKU (TREMBLE)
GAKU
GYUCHI (LASSO)

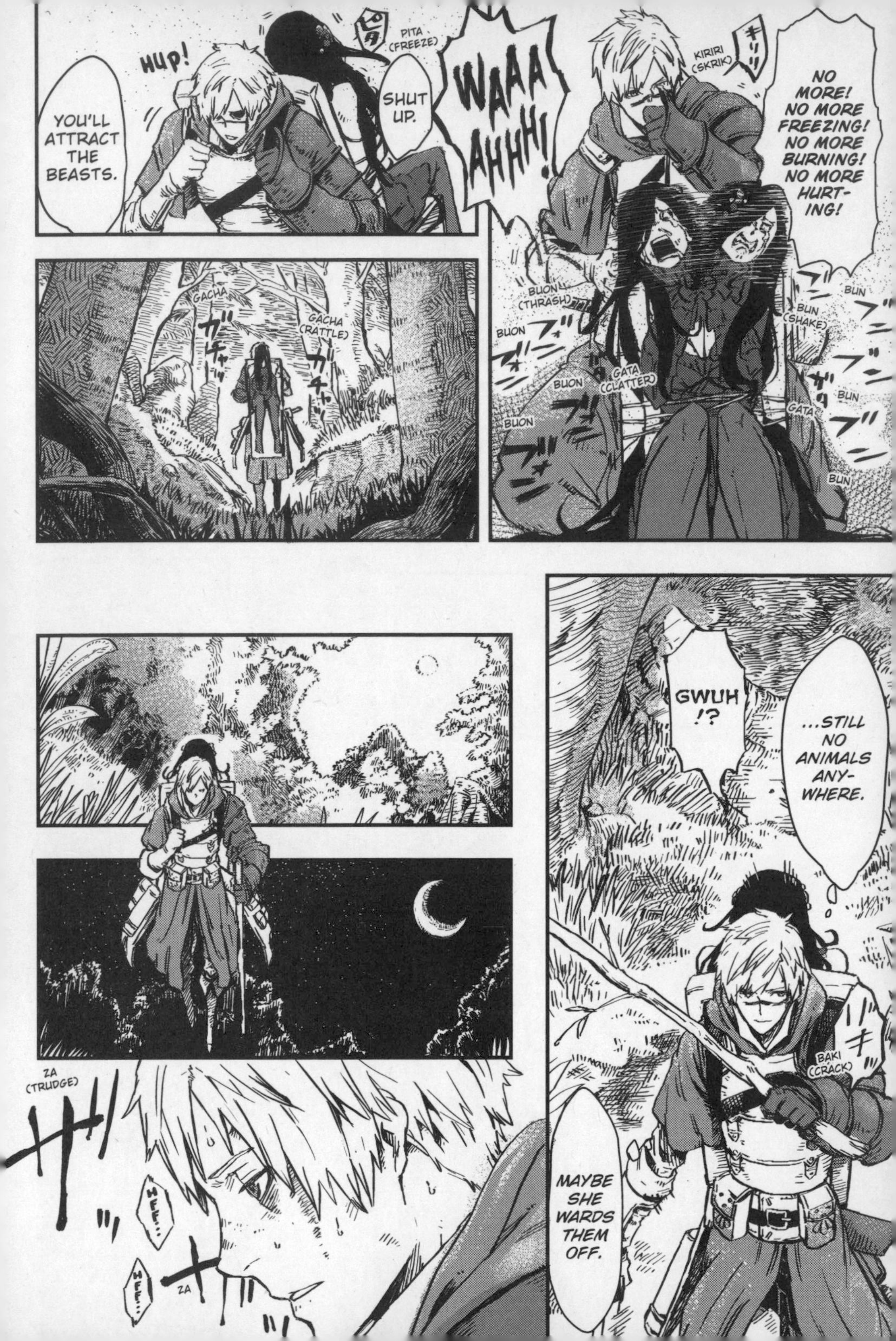
KIRIRI (SKRIK)
WAAA AHHH!
NO MORE! NO MORE FREEZING! NO MORE BURNING! NO MORE HURT-ING!
BUON (THRASH)
BUN (SHAKE)
BUN
BUON
BUON
GATA (CLATTER)
BUON
BUN
GATA
BUN
PITA (FREEZE)
SHUT UP.
HUP!
YOU'LL ATTRACT THE BEASTS.
GACHA
GACHA (RATTLE)
...STILL NO ANIMALS ANY-WHERE.
GWUH !?
BAKI (CRACK)
MAYBE SHE WARDS THEM OFF.
ZA (TRUDGE)
HEF...
HEF...
ZA

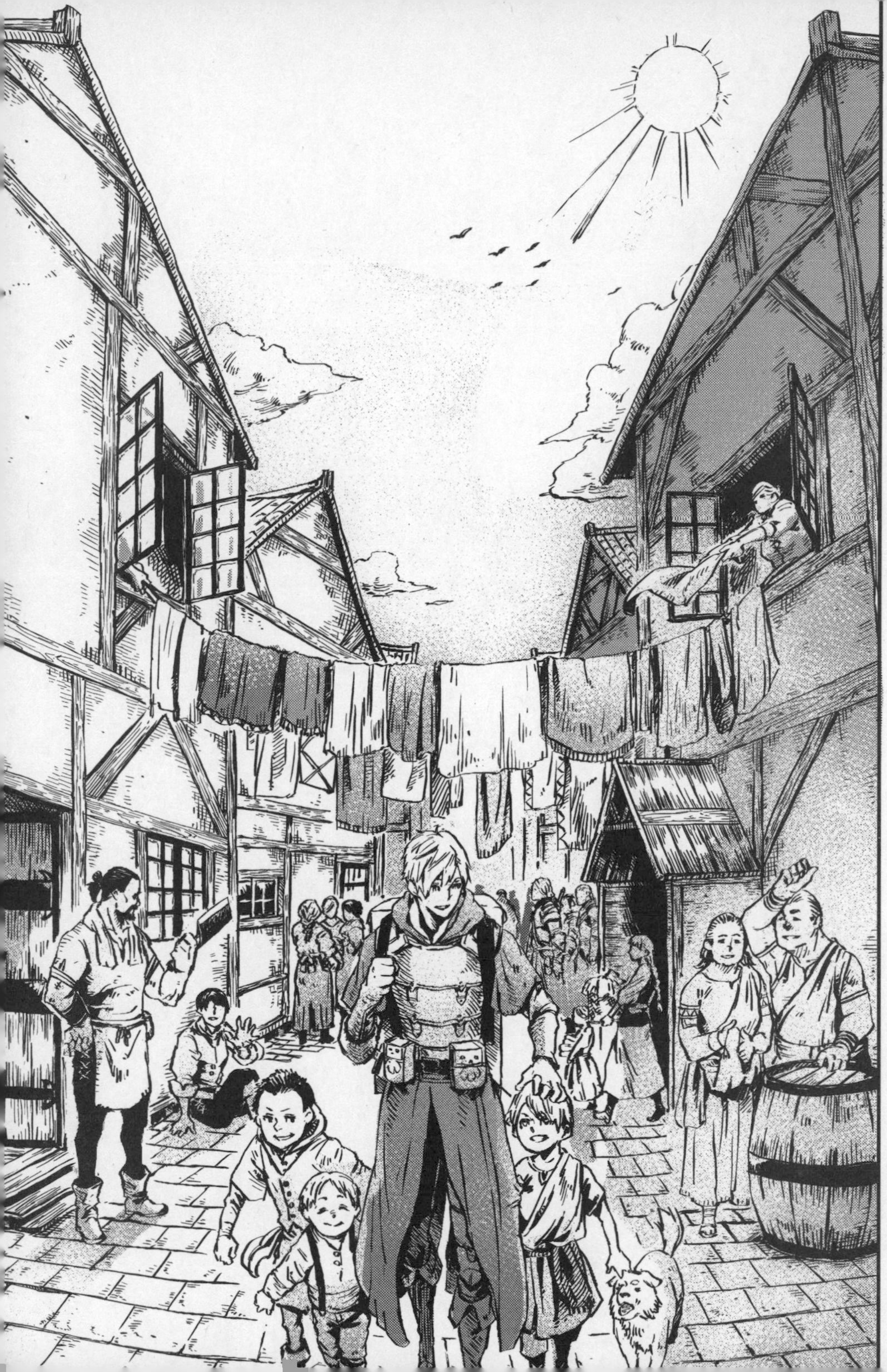

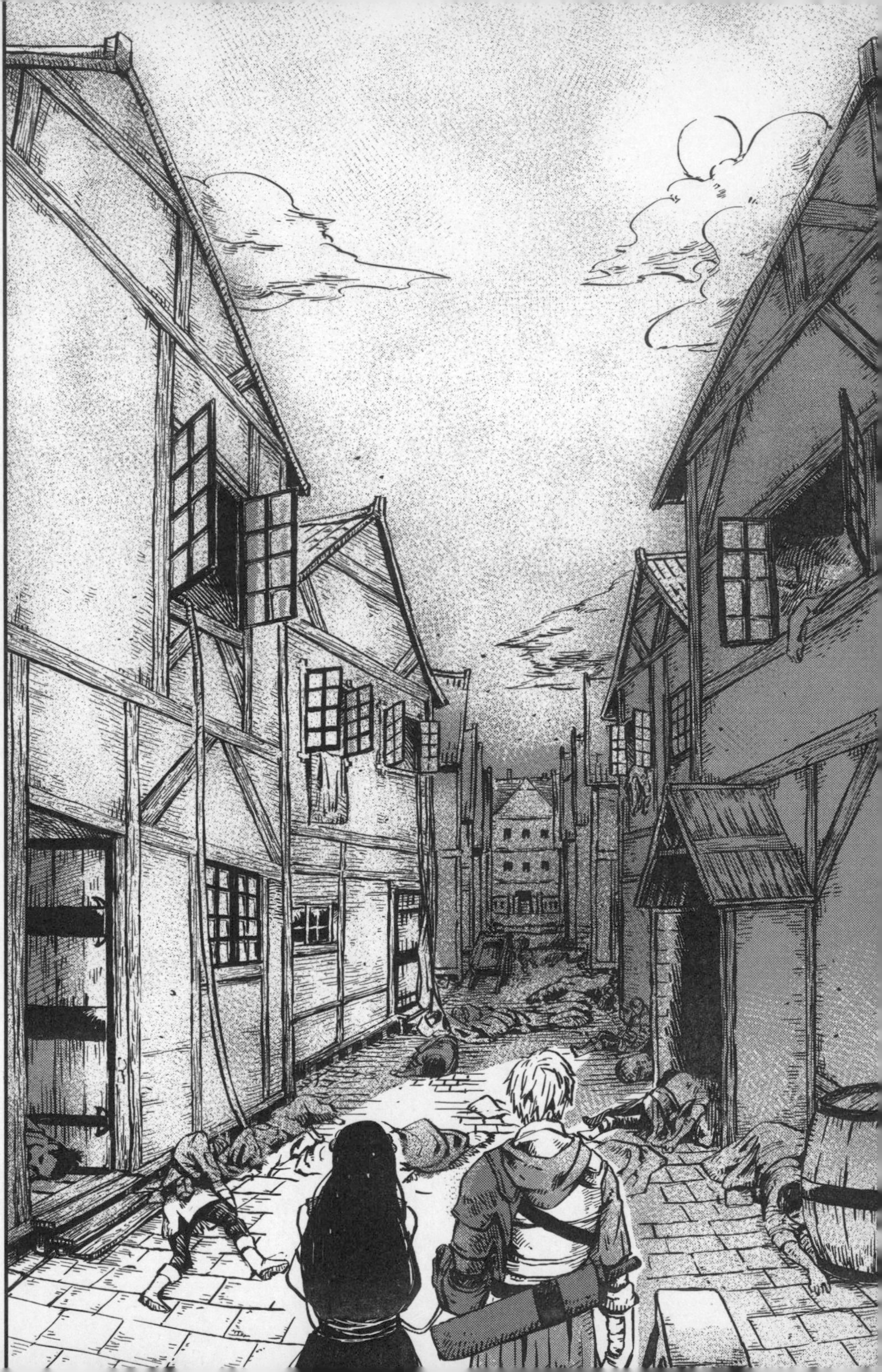

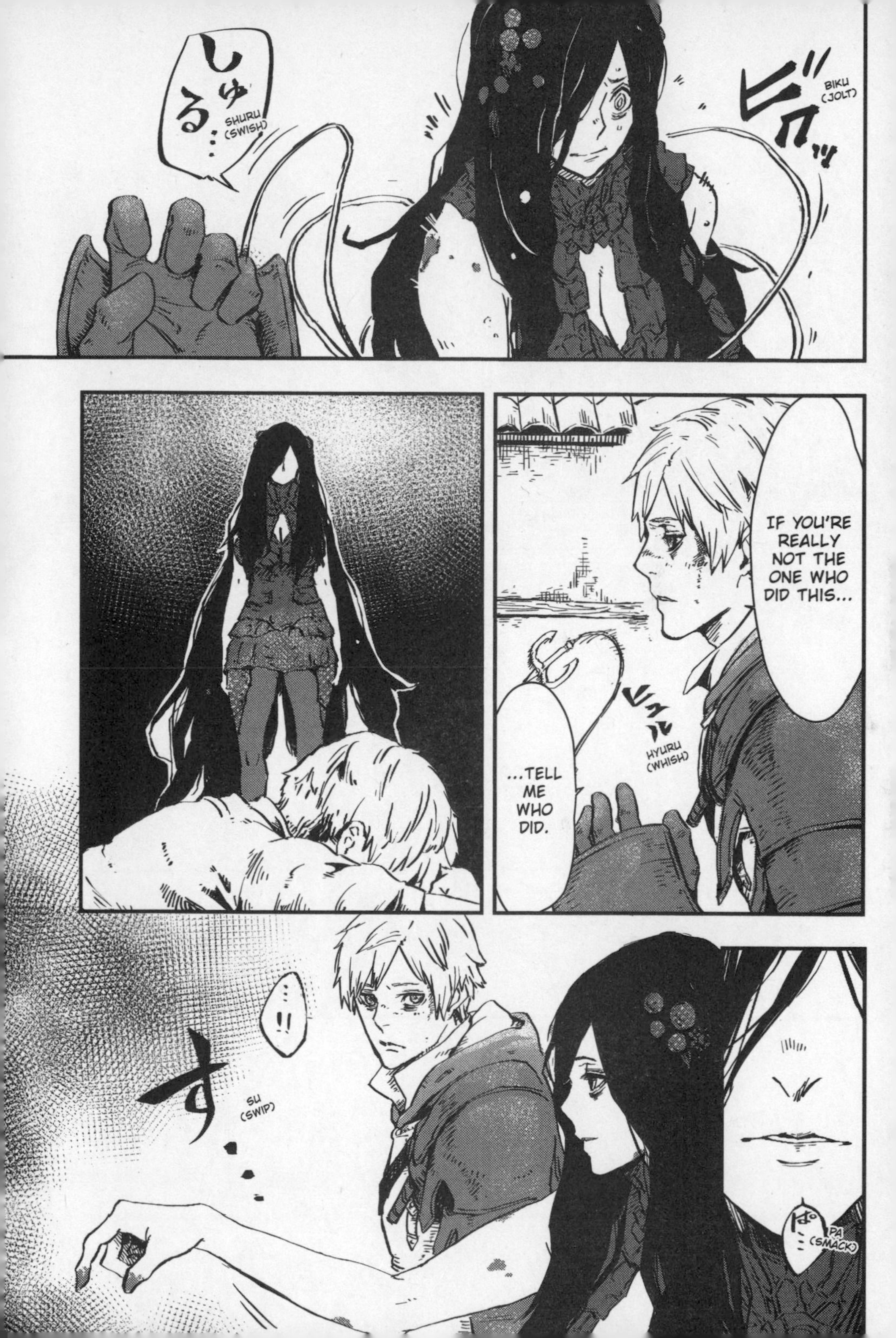

ビクッ
BIKU (JOLT)
しゅる…
SHURU (SWISH)
IF YOU'RE REALLY NOT THE ONE WHO DID THIS...
ヒュル
HYURU (WHISH)
...TELL ME WHO DID.
ぱっ
PA (SMACK)
...!!
す
SU (SWIP)

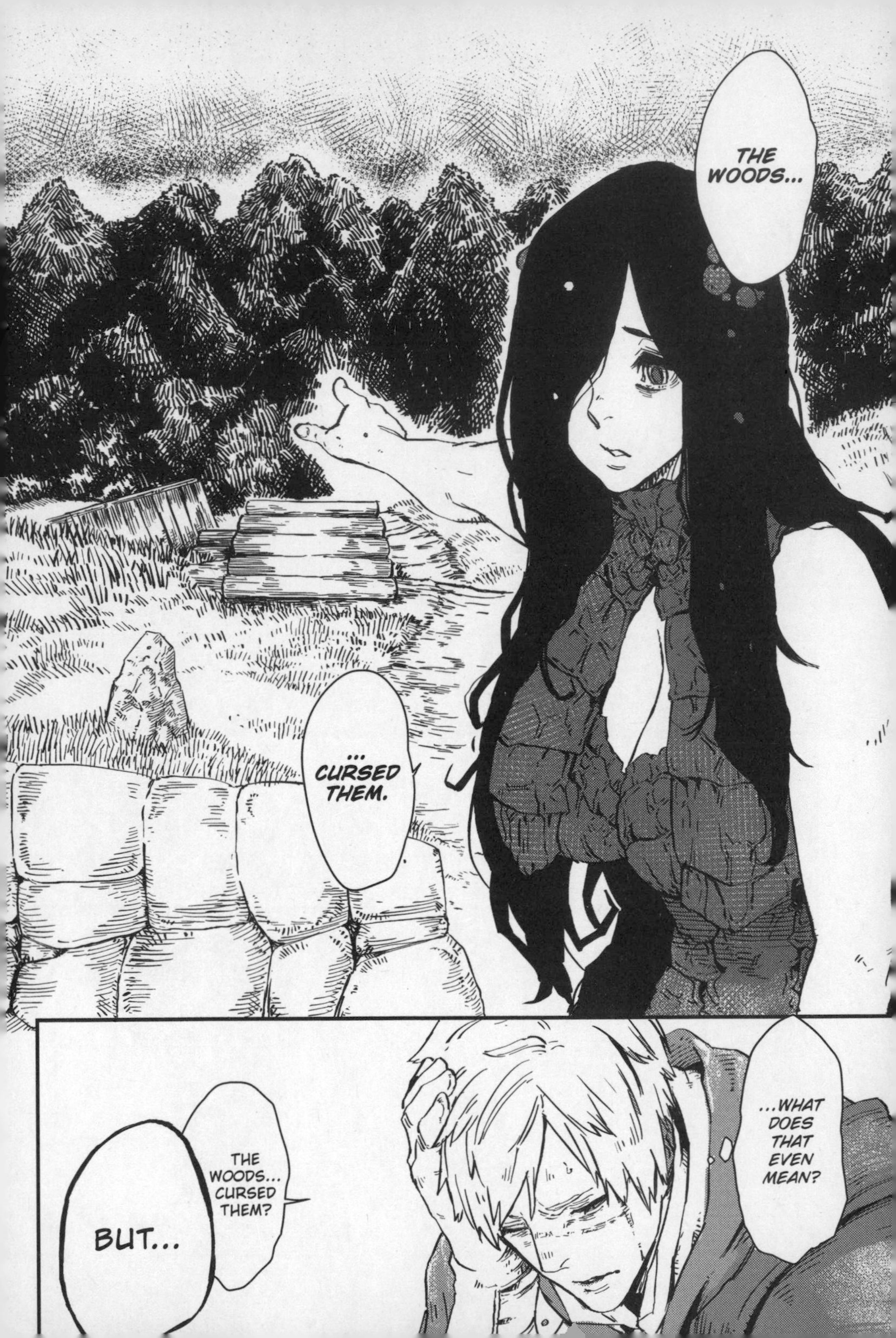
THE WOODS...
...CURSED THEM.
...WHAT DOES THAT EVEN MEAN?
THE WOODS... CURSED THEM?
BUT...

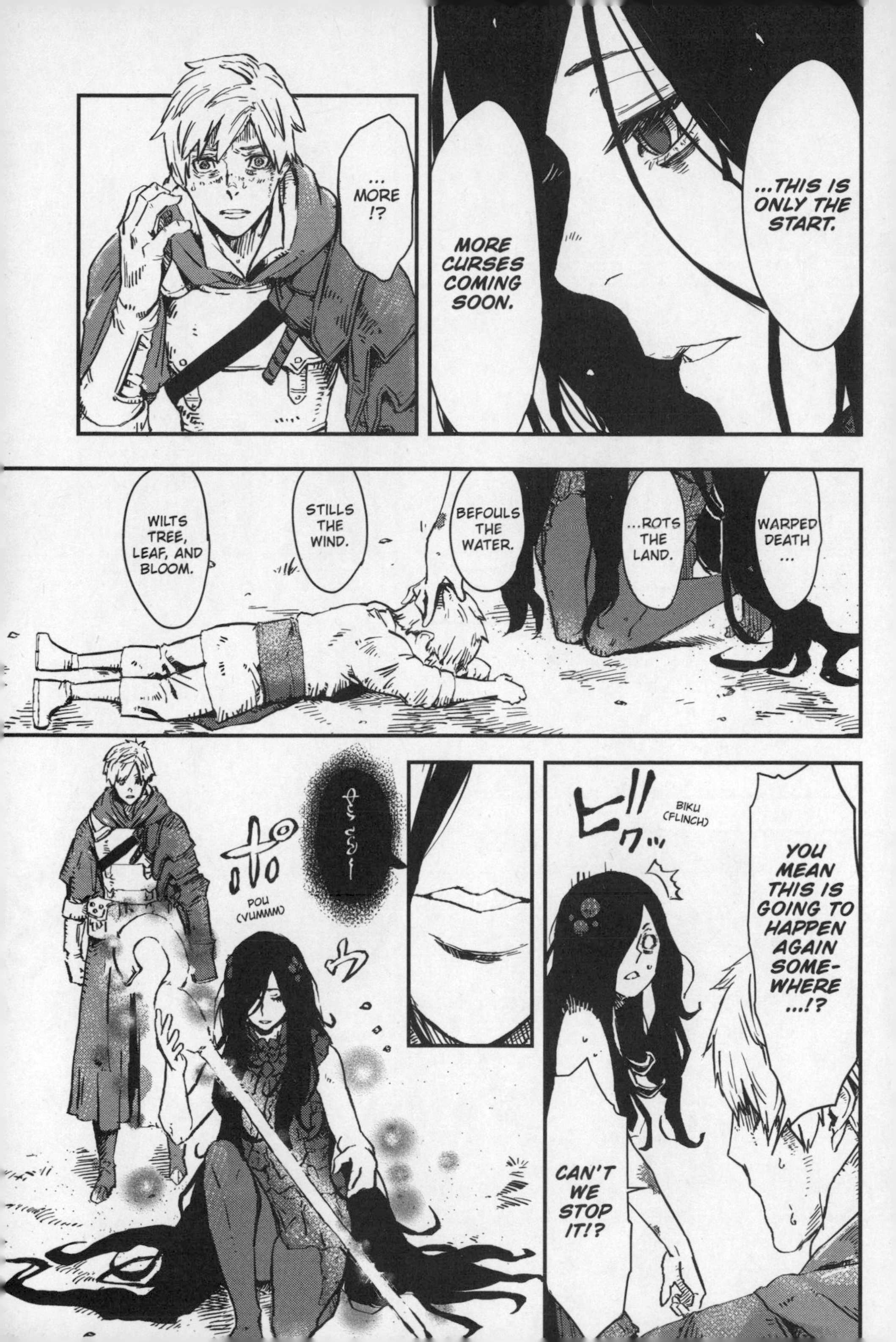
...THIS IS ONLY THE START.
MORE CURSES COMING SOON.
...MORE!?
WARPED DEATH...
...ROTS THE LAND.
BEFOULS THE WATER.
STILLS THE WIND.
WILTS TREE, LEAF, AND BLOOM.
BIKU (FLINCH)
YOU MEAN THIS IS GOING TO HAPPEN AGAIN SOMEWHERE...!?
CAN'T WE STOP IT!?
POU (VUMMM)

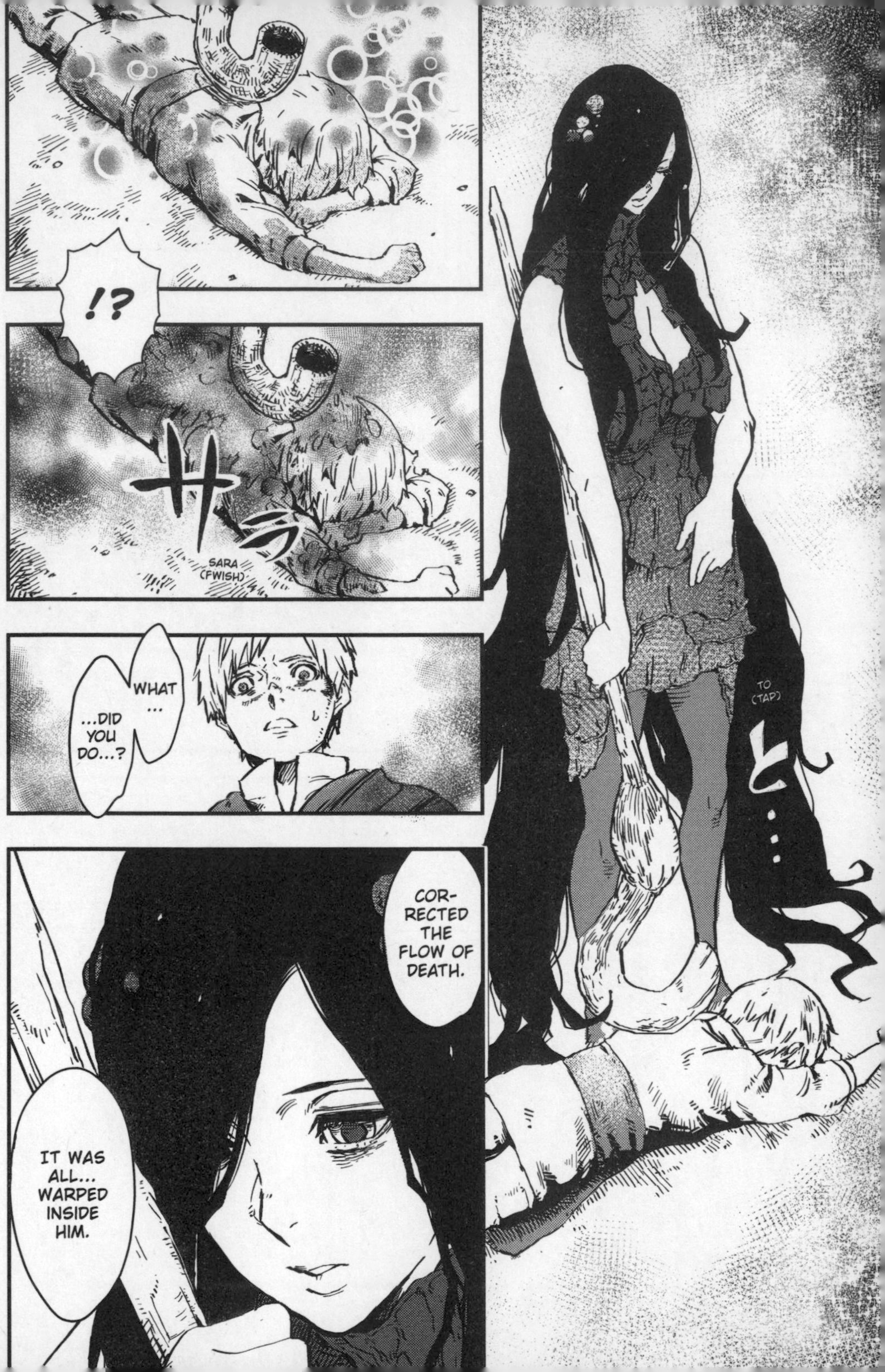
TO (TAP)
!?
SARA (FWISH)
WHAT... ...DID YOU DO...?
COR-RECTED THE FLOW OF DEATH.
IT WAS ALL... WARPED INSIDE HIM.

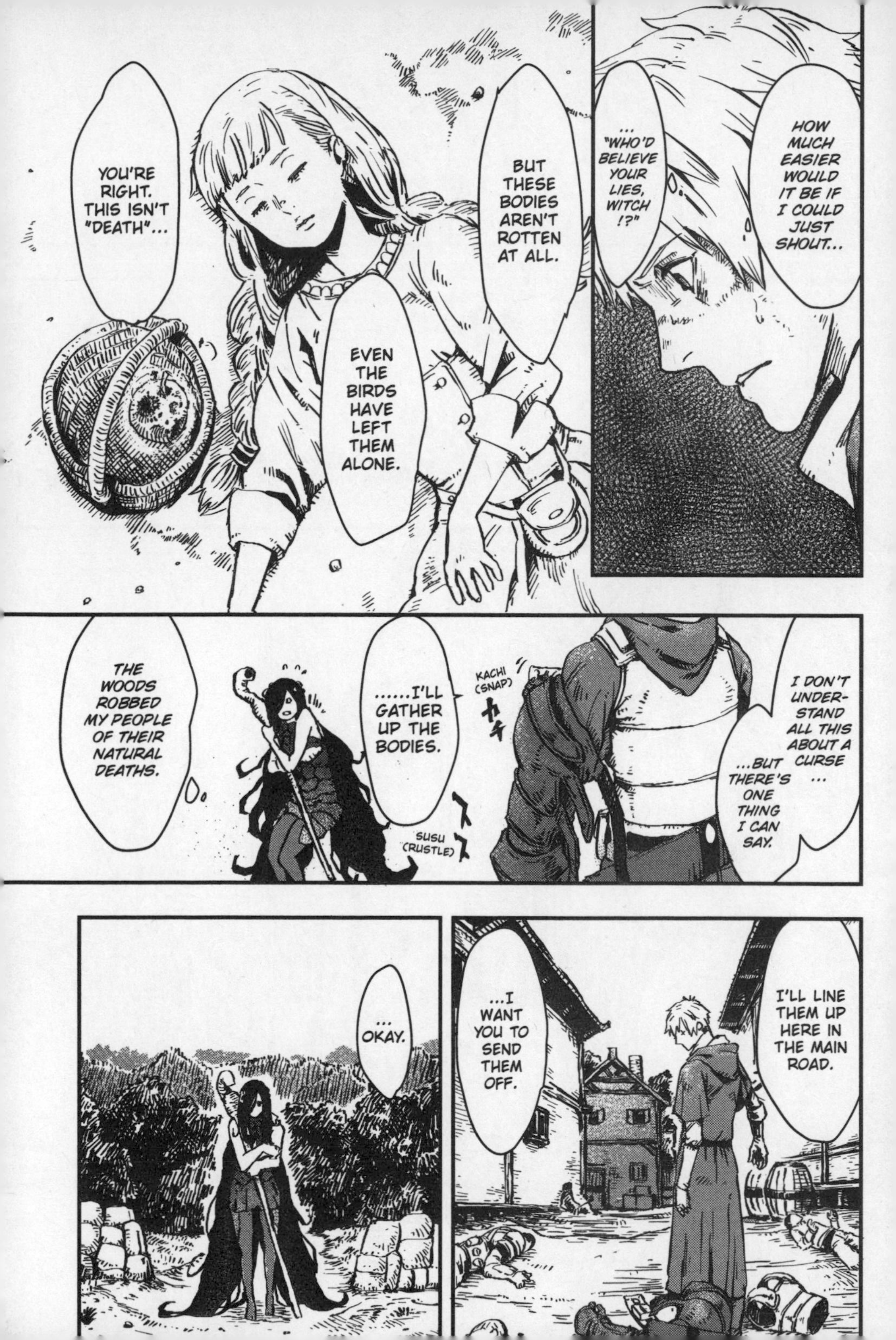
HOW MUCH EASIER WOULD IT BE IF I COULD JUST SHOUT...
..."WHO'D BELIEVE YOUR LIES, WITCH!?"
BUT THESE BODIES AREN'T ROTTEN AT ALL.
EVEN THE BIRDS HAVE LEFT THEM ALONE.
YOU'RE RIGHT. THIS ISN'T "DEATH"...
I DON'T UNDERSTAND ALL THIS ABOUT A CURSE...
...BUT THERE'S ONE THING I CAN SAY.
KACHI (SNAP)
カチ
......I'LL GATHER UP THE BODIES.
SUSU (RUSTLE)
スス
THE WOODS ROBBED MY PEOPLE OF THEIR NATURAL DEATHS.
I'LL LINE THEM UP HERE IN THE MAIN ROAD.
...I WANT YOU TO SEND THEM OFF.
... OKAY.

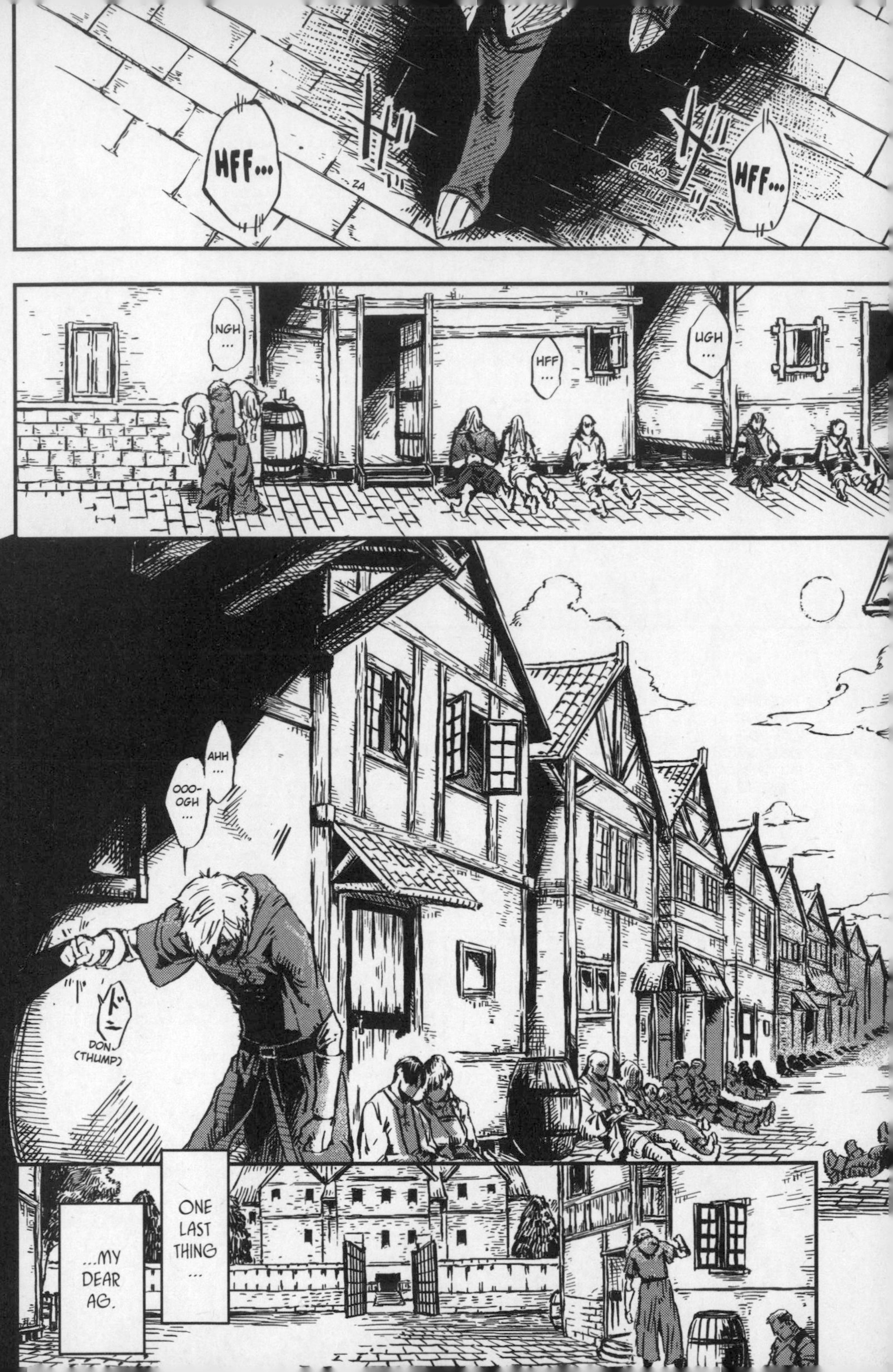
HFF...
ZA
(TAKK)
HFF...
ZA
UGH
...
HFF
...
NGH
...
AHH
...
OOO-
OGH
...
DON
(THUMP)
ONE LAST THING ...
...MY DEAR AG.

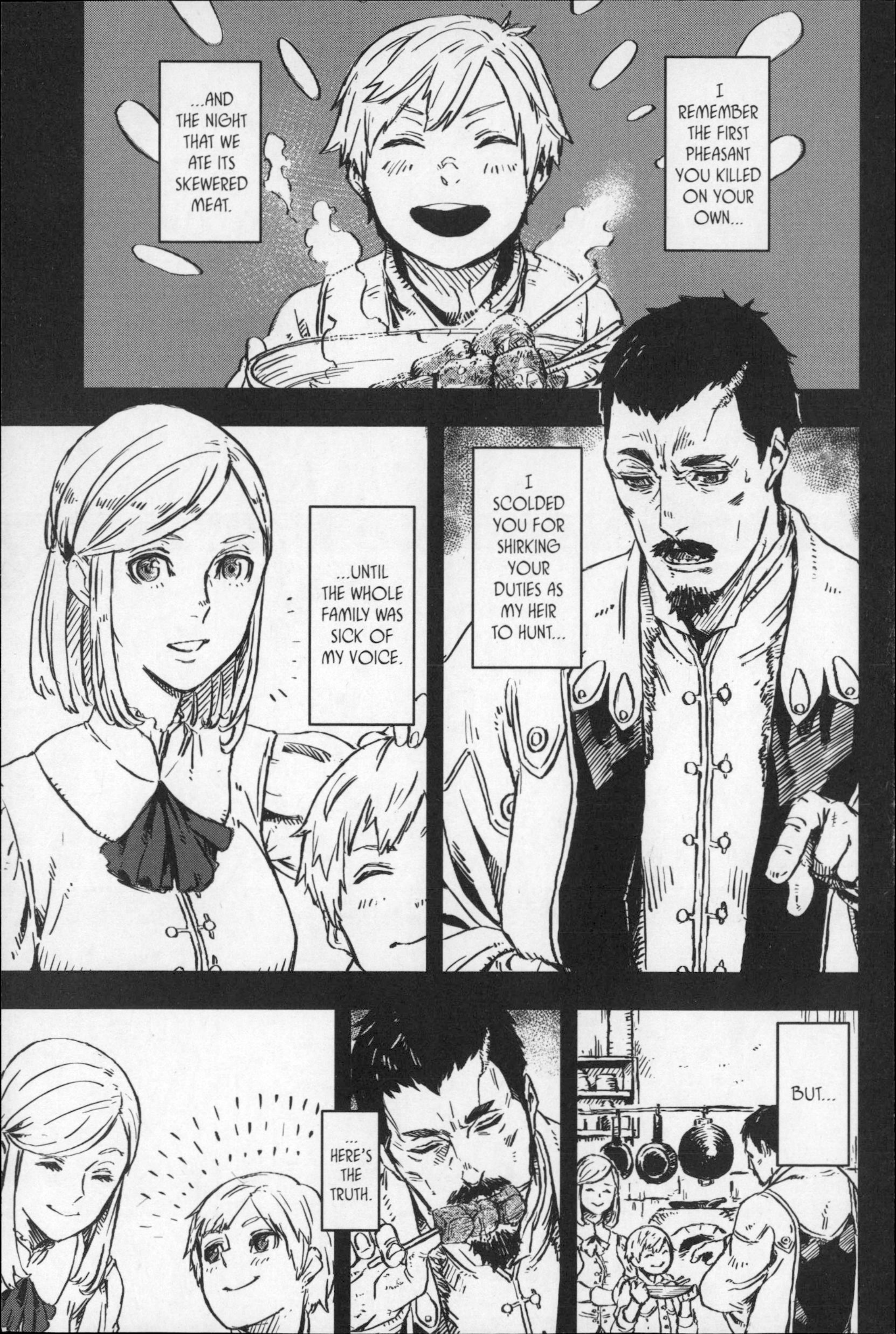
I REMEMBER THE FIRST PHEASANT YOU KILLED ON YOUR OWN...
...AND THE NIGHT THAT WE ATE ITS SKEWERED MEAT.
I SCOLDED YOU FOR SHIRKING YOUR DUTIES AS MY HEIR TO HUNT...
...UNTIL THE WHOLE FAMILY WAS SICK OF MY VOICE.
BUT...
...HERE'S THE TRUTH.

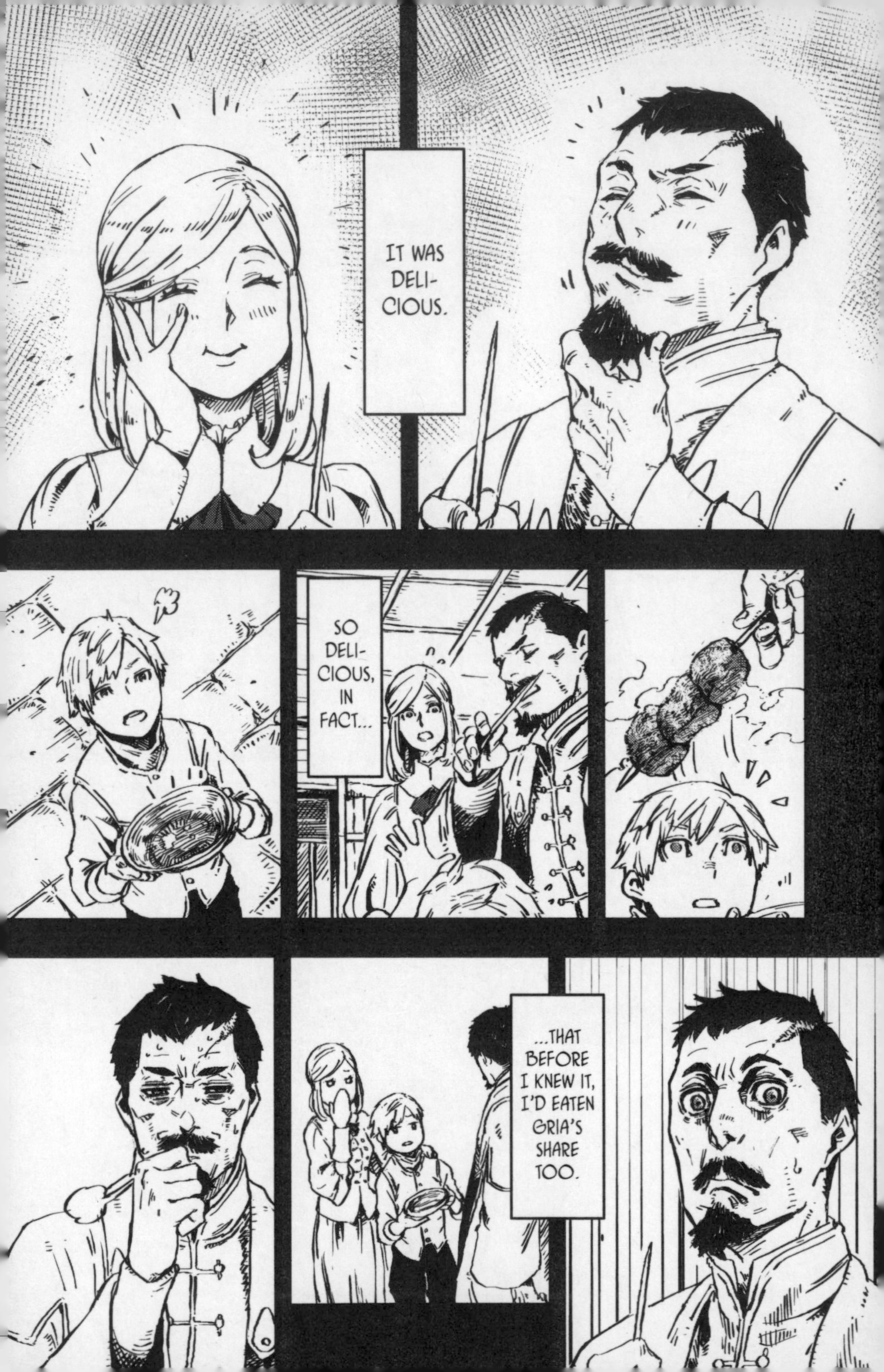
IT WAS DELI-CIOUS.
SO DELI-CIOUS, IN FACT...
...THAT BEFORE I KNEW IT, I'D EATEN GRIA'S SHARE TOO.

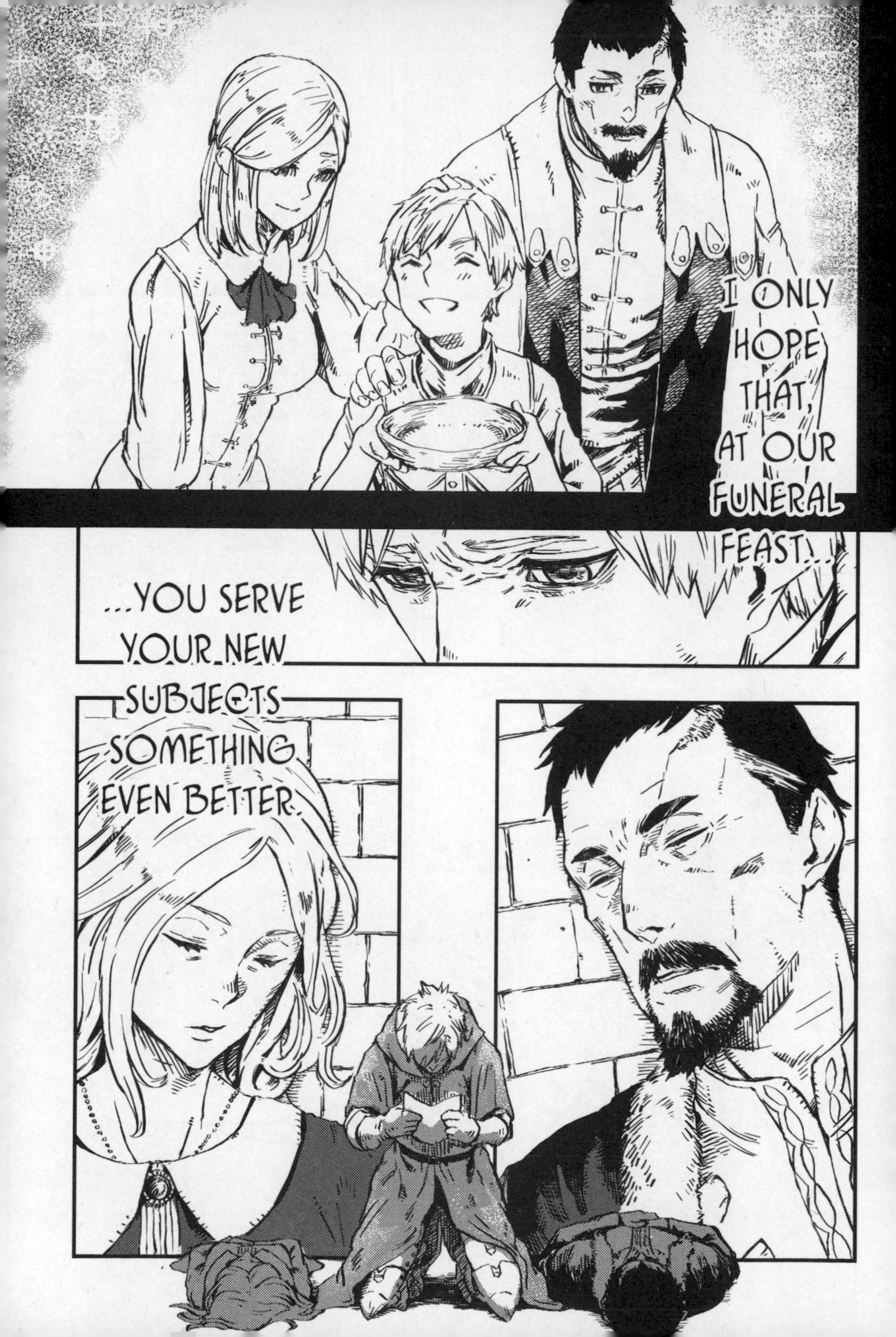
I ONLY HOPE THAT, AT OUR FUNERAL FEAST...
...YOU SERVE YOUR NEW SUBJECTS SOMETHING EVEN BETTER.

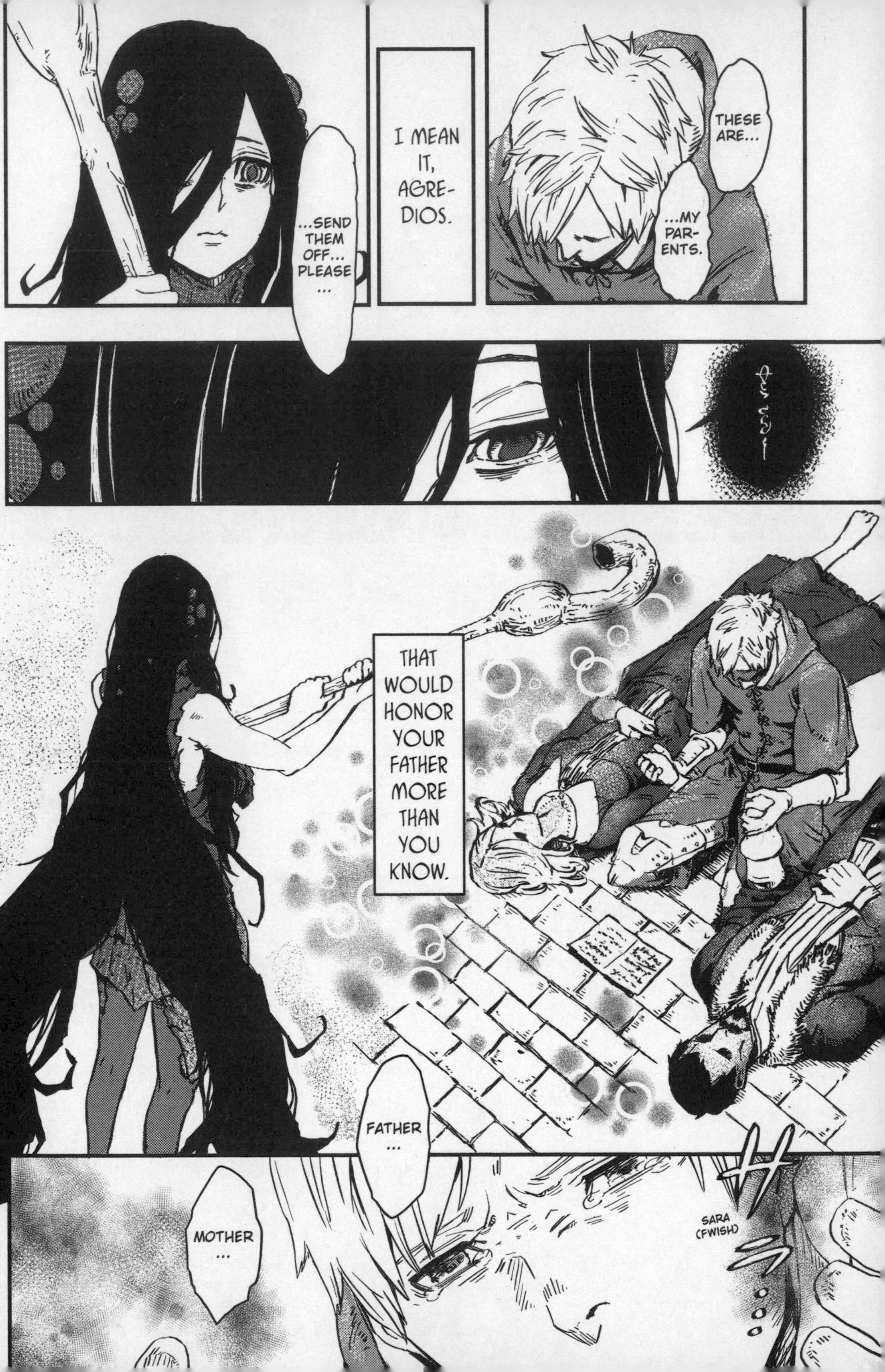
THESE ARE...
...MY PAR-ENTS.
I MEAN IT, AGRE-DIOS.
...SEND THEM OFF... PLEASE ...
THAT WOULD HONOR YOUR FATHER MORE THAN YOU KNOW.
FATHER ...
SARA (FWISH)
MOTHER ...

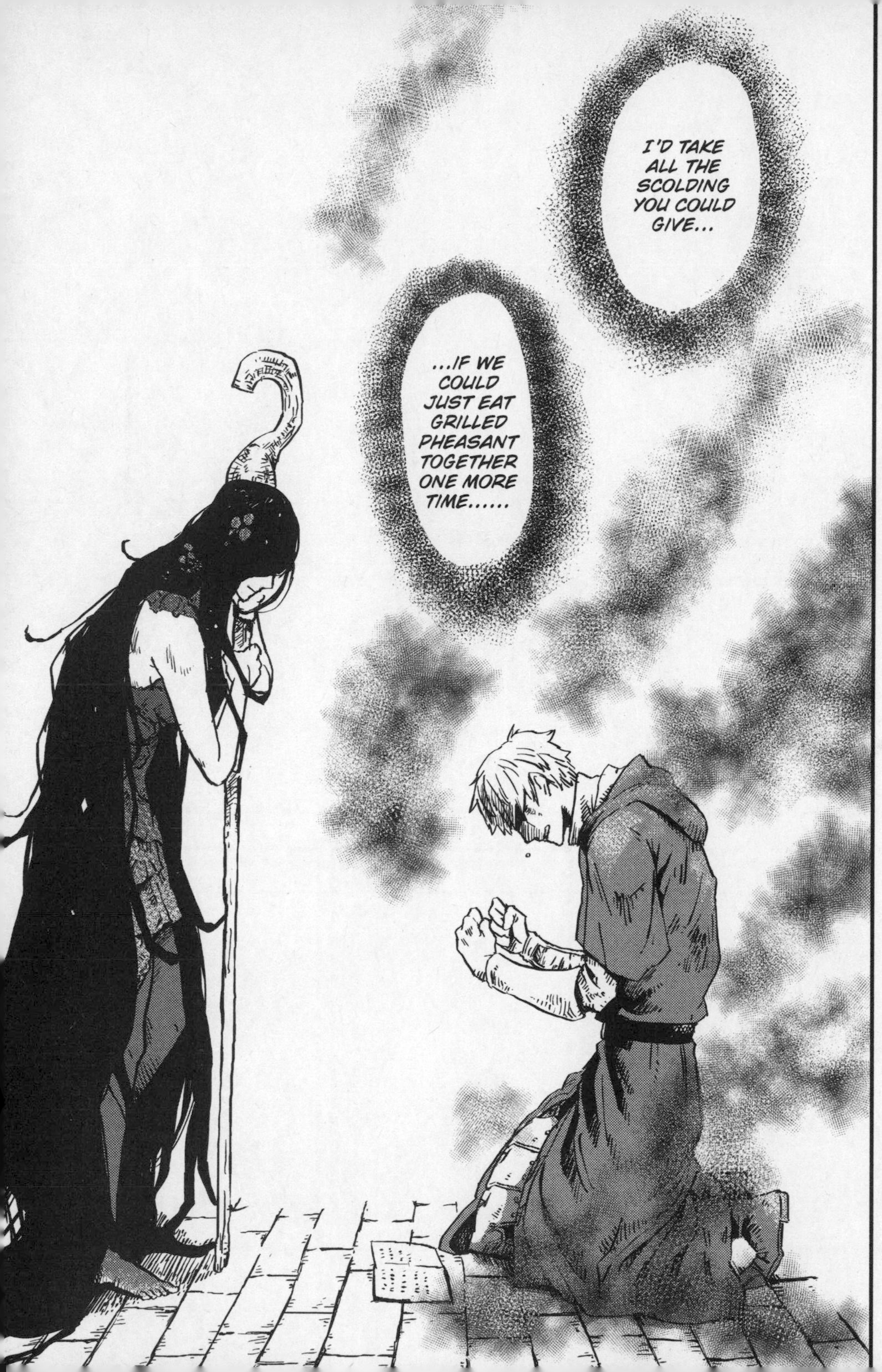
I'D TAKE ALL THE SCOLDING YOU COULD GIVE...
...IF WE COULD JUST EAT GRILLED PHEASANT TOGETHER ONE MORE TIME......

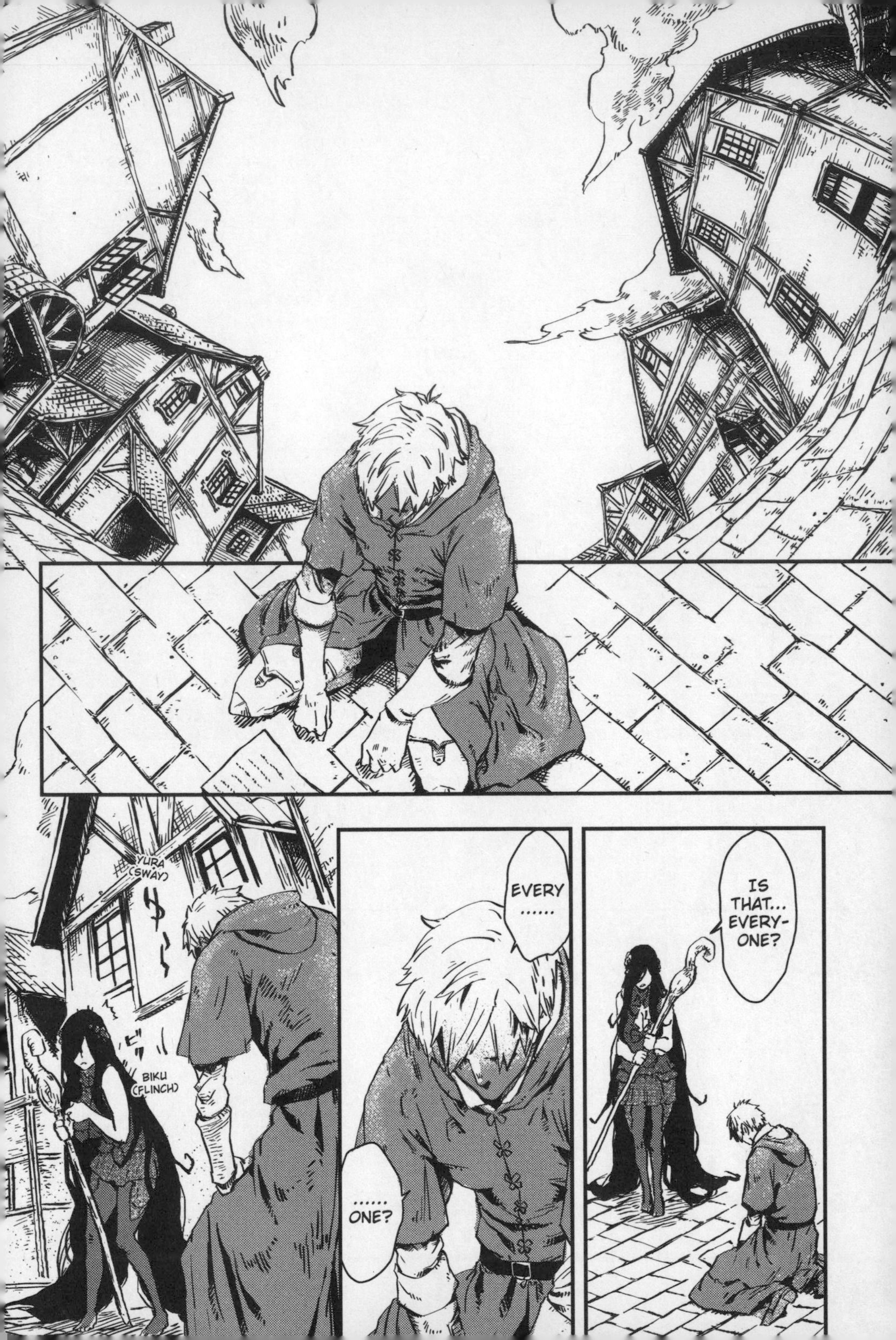
IS THAT... EVERY-ONE?
EVERY ......
...... ONE?
YURA (SWAY)
BIKU (FLINCH)

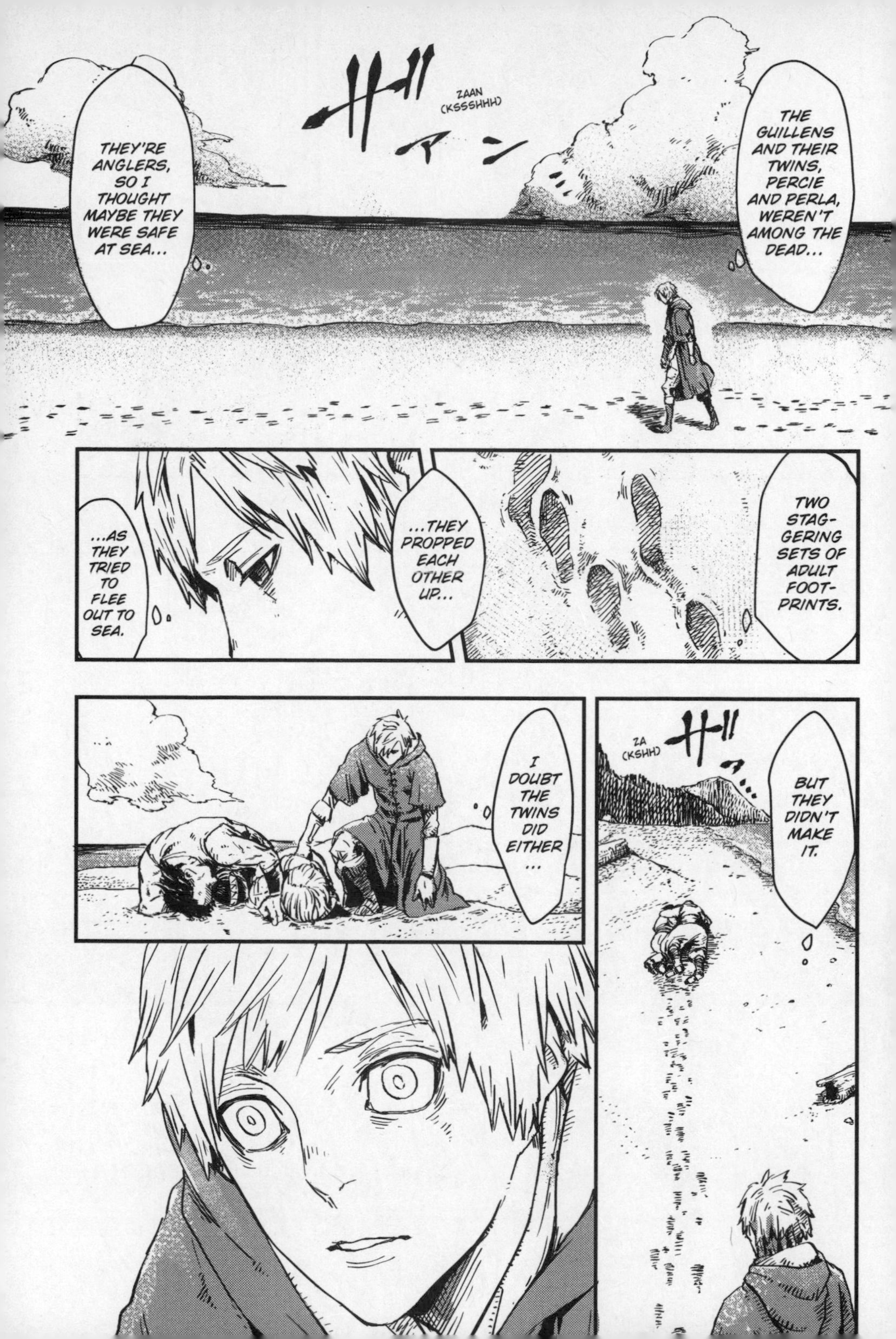
THE GUILLENS AND THEIR TWINS, PERCIE AND PERLA, WEREN'T AMONG THE DEAD...
ZAAN (KSSSHHH)
THEY'RE ANGLERS, SO I THOUGHT MAYBE THEY WERE SAFE AT SEA...
TWO STAG-GERING SETS OF ADULT FOOT-PRINTS.
...THEY PROPPED EACH OTHER UP...
...AS THEY TRIED TO FLEE OUT TO SEA.
ZA (KSHH)
BUT THEY DIDN'T MAKE IT.
I DOUBT THE TWINS DID EITHER...

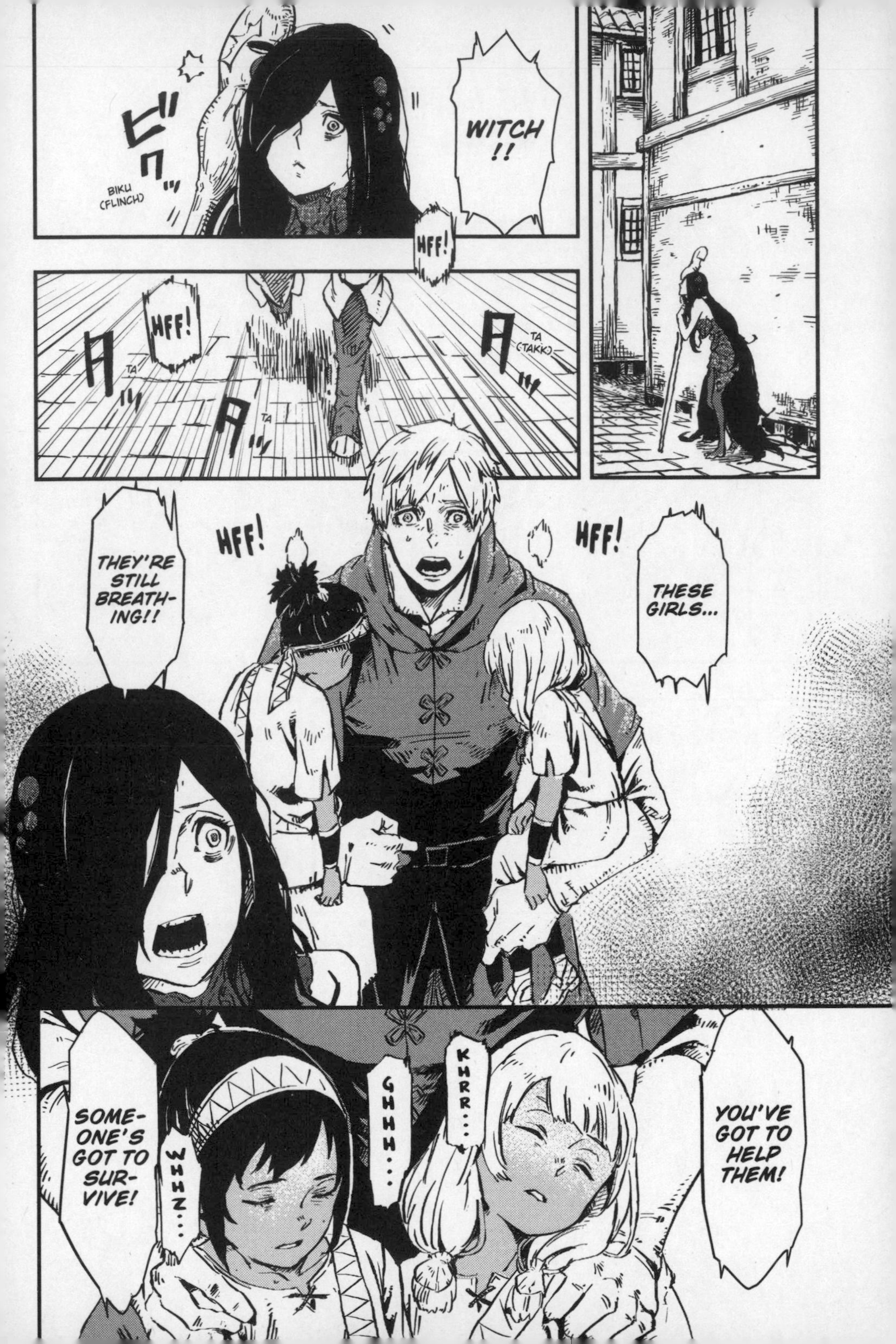
WITCH!!
BIKU (FLINCH)
HFF!
TA (TAKK)
HFF!
TA
TA
THESE GIRLS...
HFF!
HFF!
THEY'RE STILL BREATHING!!
YOU'VE GOT TO HELP THEM!
KHRR...
GHHH...
WHHZ...
SOME-ONE'S GOT TO SUR-VIVE!

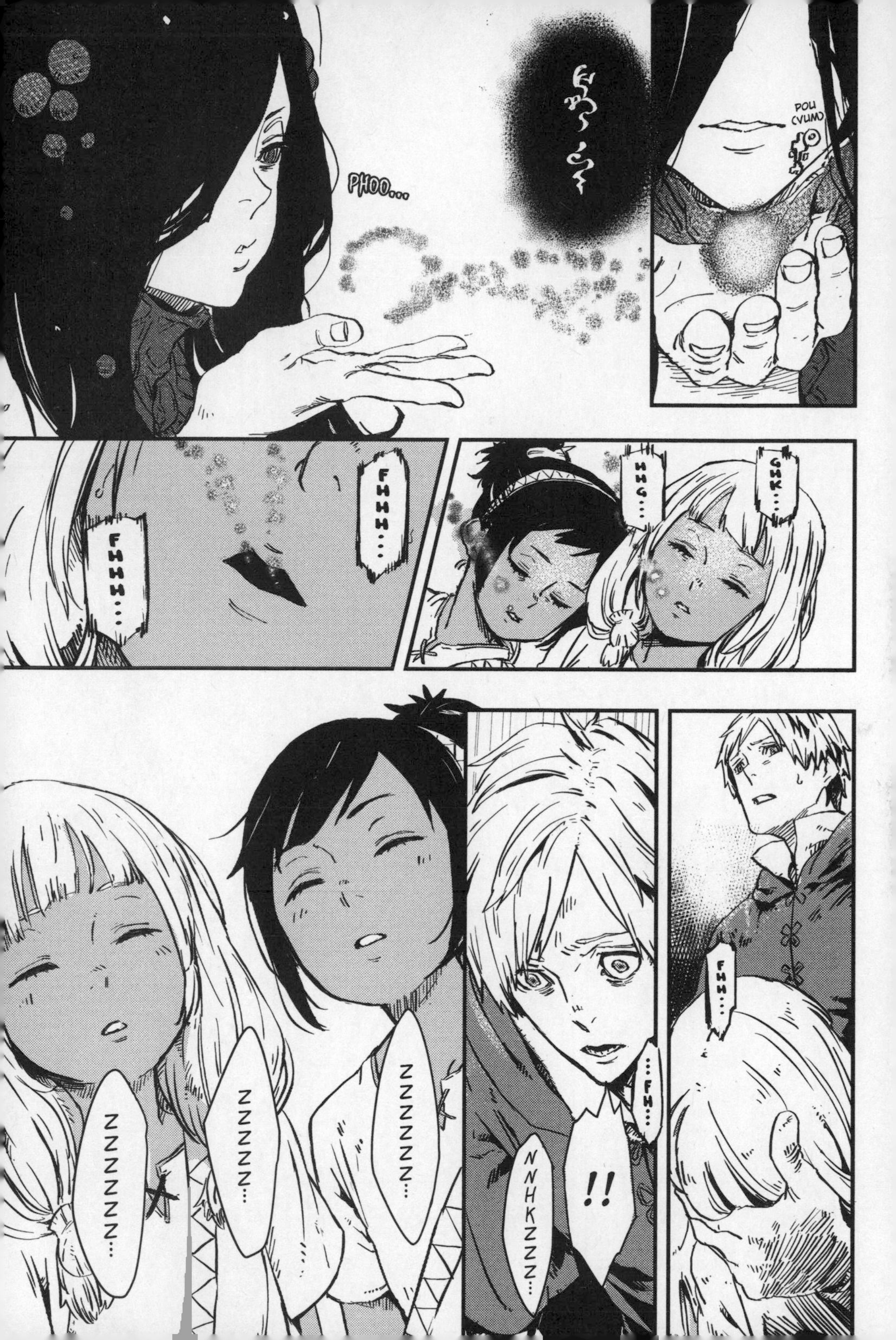

POU (VUM)
PHOO...
GHK...
HHG...
FHHH...
FHHH...
FHH...
...FH...
!!
NNHKZZZ...
ZZZZZZ...
ZZZZZ...
ZZZZZZ...

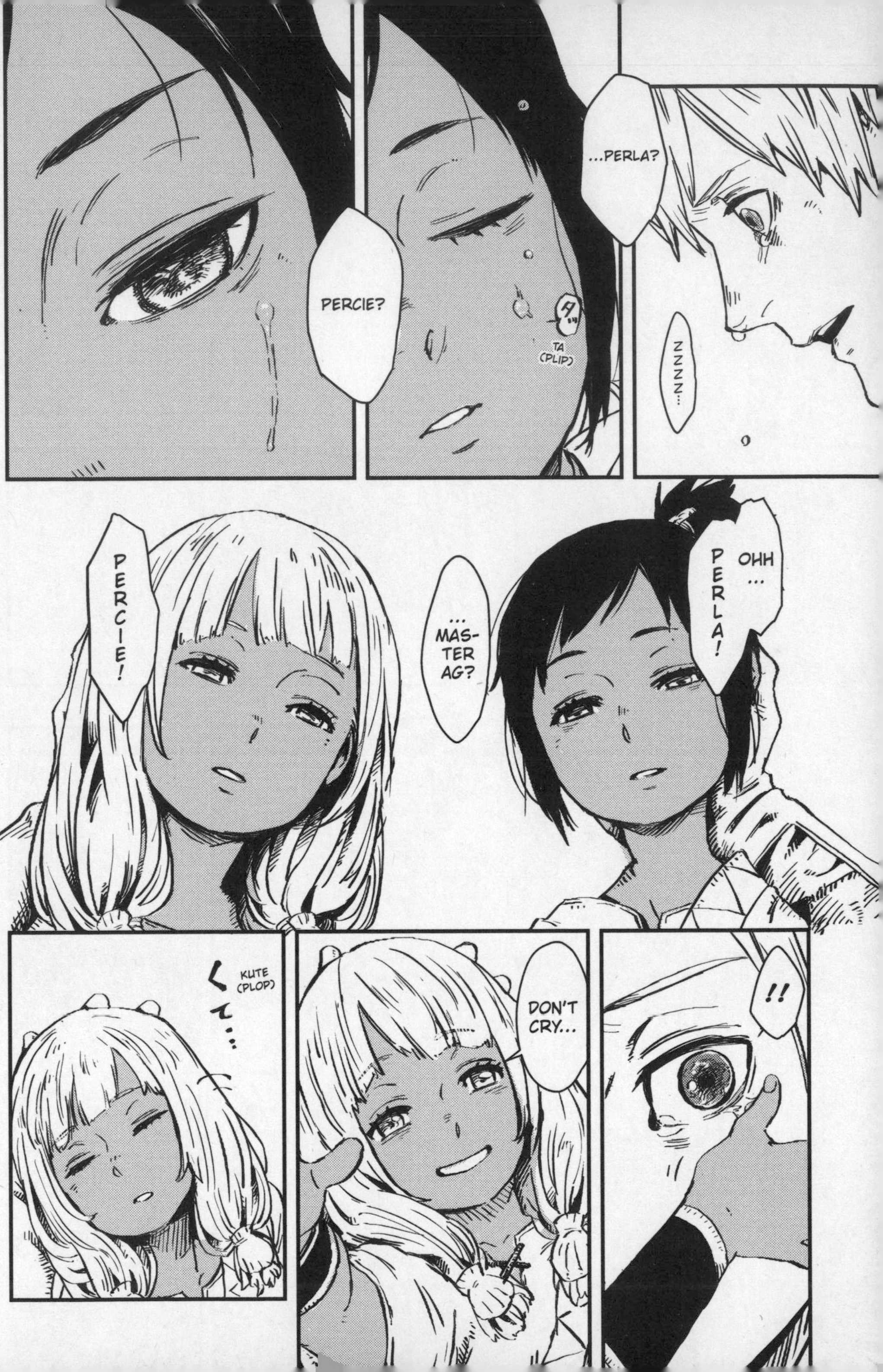
...PERLA?
ZZZZ...
PERCIE?
タ
TA (PLIP)
OHH... PERLA!
...MASTER AG?
PERCIE!
!!
DON'T CRY...
くて..
KUTE (PLOP)

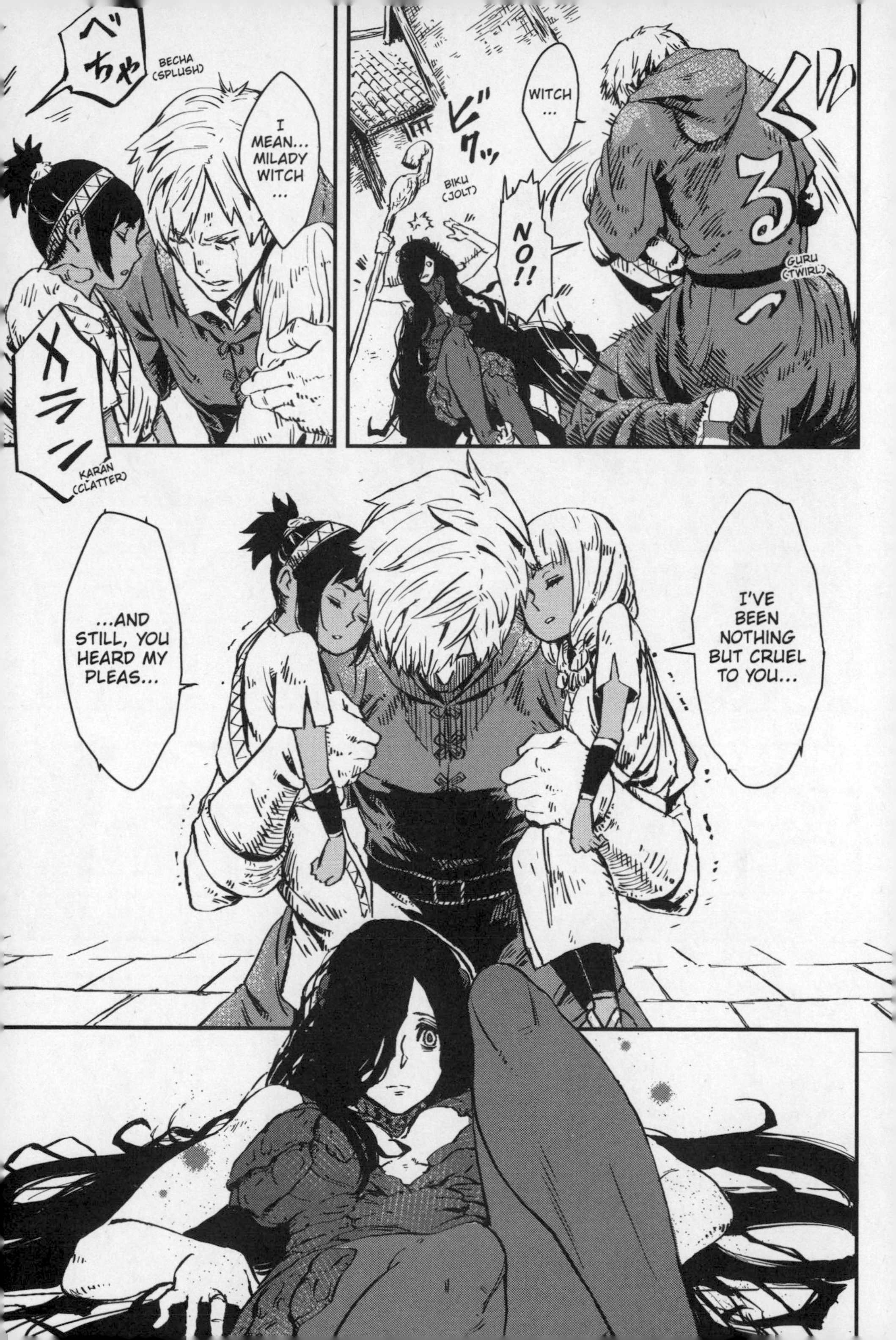
WITCH...
BIKU (JOLT)
NO!!
GURU (TWIRL)
BECHA (SPLUSH)
I MEAN... MILADY WITCH...
KARAN (CLATTER)
I'VE BEEN NOTHING BUT CRUEL TO YOU...
...AND STILL, YOU HEARD MY PLEAS...

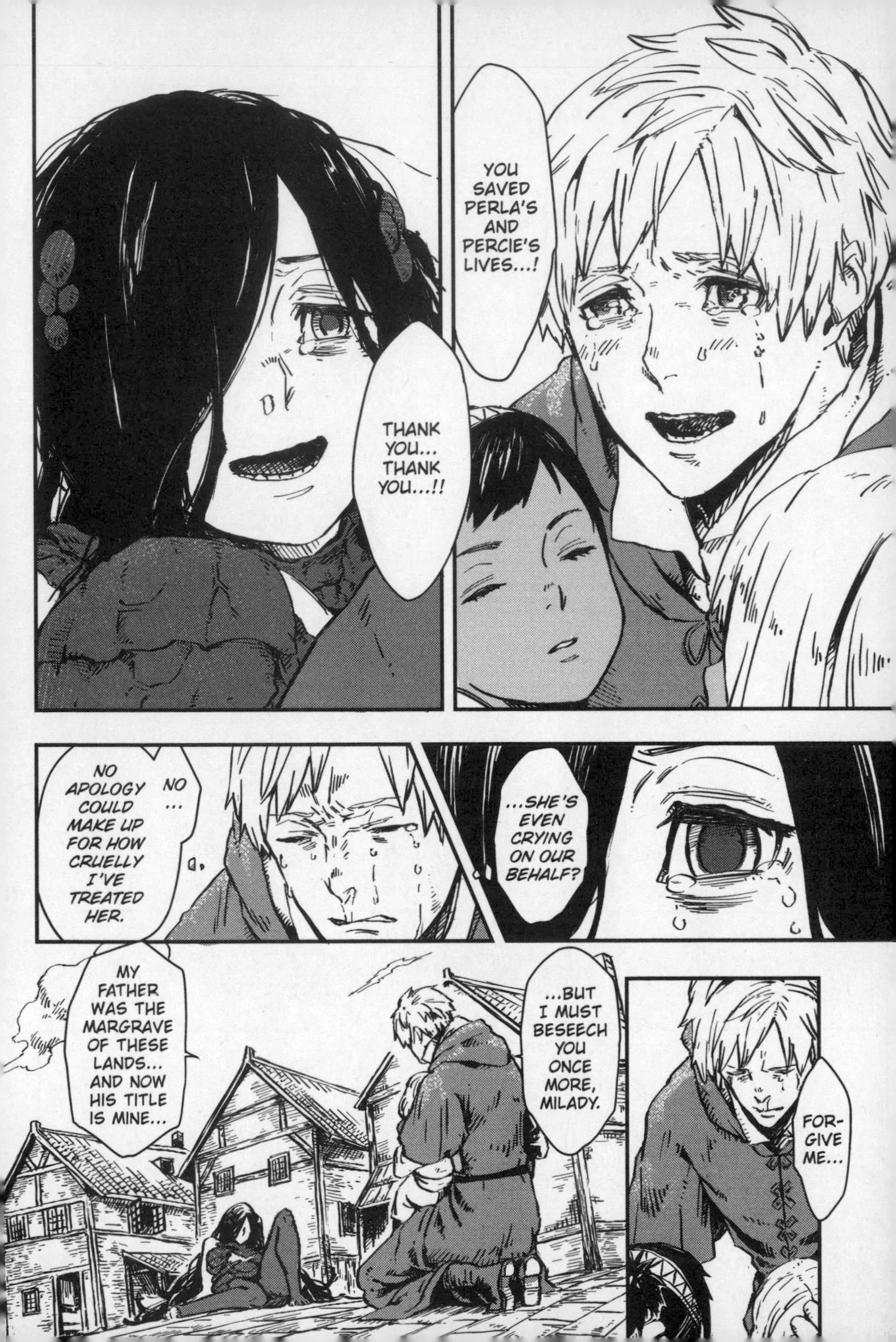
YOU SAVED PERLA'S AND PERCIE'S LIVES...!
THANK YOU... THANK YOU...!!
...SHE'S EVEN CRYING ON OUR BEHALF?
NO...
NO APOLOGY COULD MAKE UP FOR HOW CRUELLY I'VE TREATED HER.
FOR-GIVE ME...
...BUT I MUST BESEECH YOU ONCE MORE, MILADY.
MY FATHER WAS THE MARGRAVE OF THESE LANDS... AND NOW HIS TITLE IS MINE...

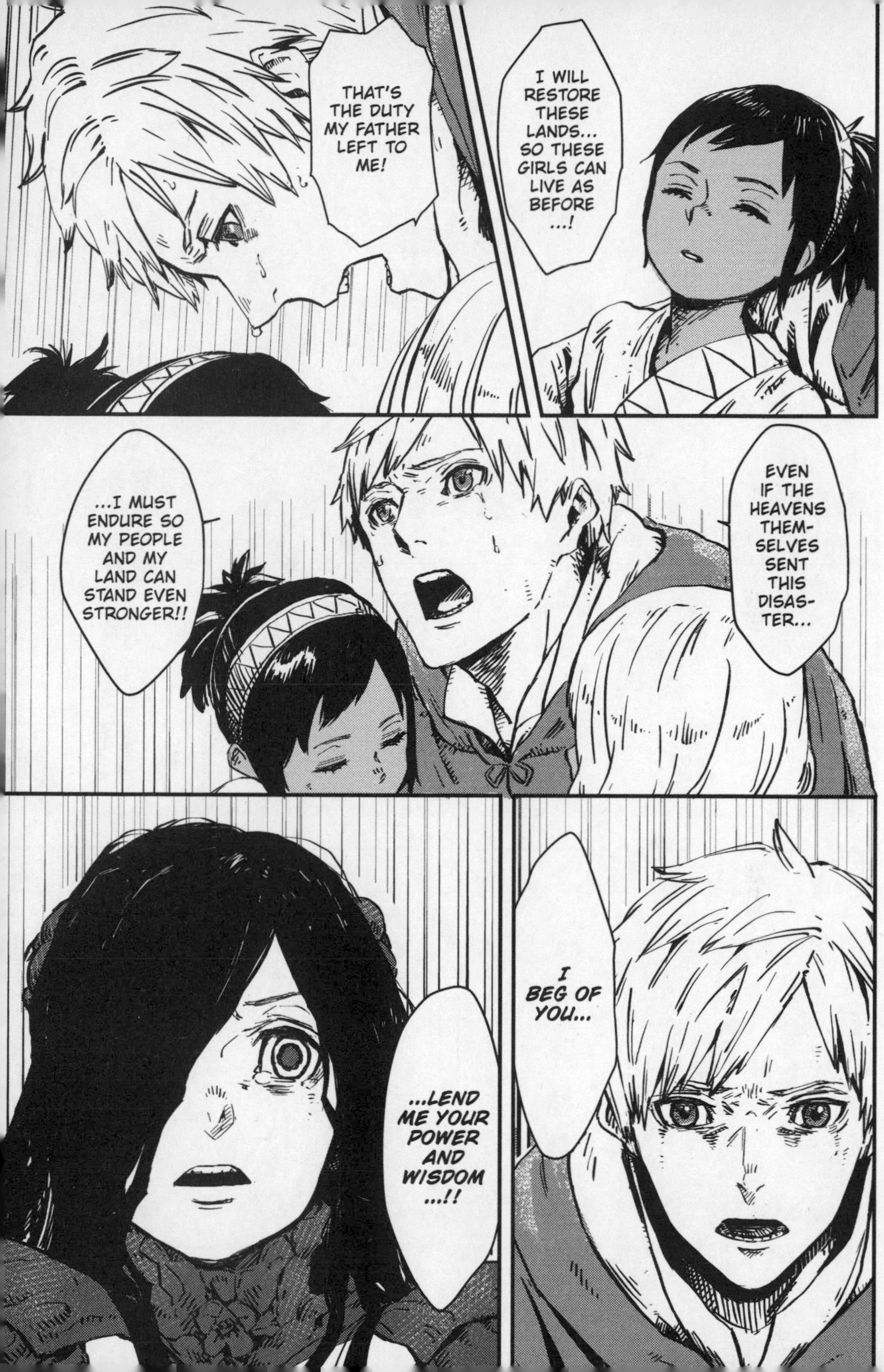
I WILL RESTORE THESE LANDS... SO THESE GIRLS CAN LIVE AS BEFORE ...!
THAT'S THE DUTY MY FATHER LEFT TO ME!
EVEN IF THE HEAVENS THEM-SELVES SENT THIS DISAS-TER...
...I MUST ENDURE SO MY PEOPLE AND MY LAND CAN STAND EVEN STRONGER!!
I BEG OF YOU...
...LEND ME YOUR POWER AND WISDOM ...!!

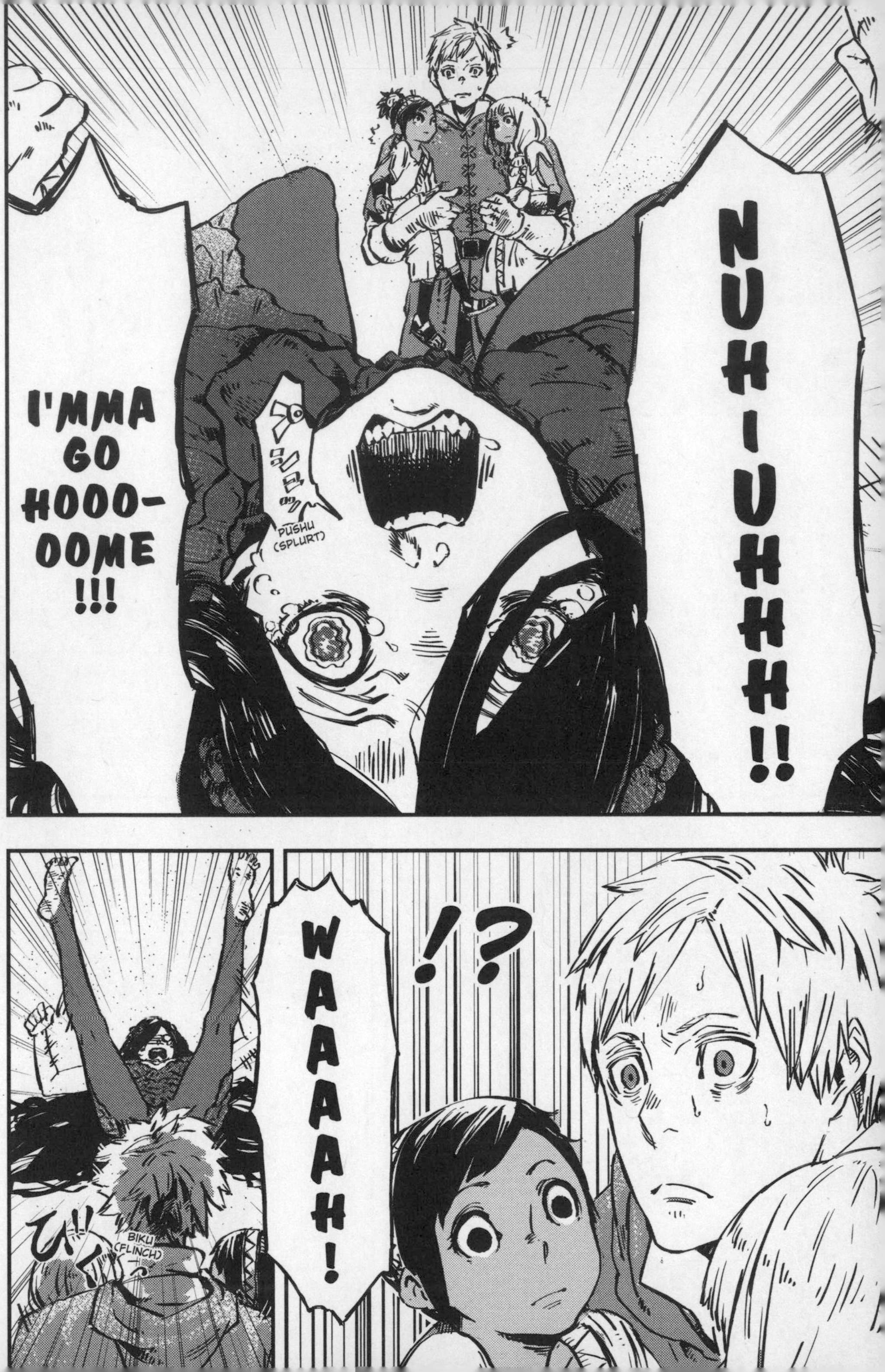
NUH-UHHHH!!
I'MMA GO HOOOO-OOME!!!
PUSHU (SPLURT)
!?
WAAAAH!
BIKU (FLINCH)

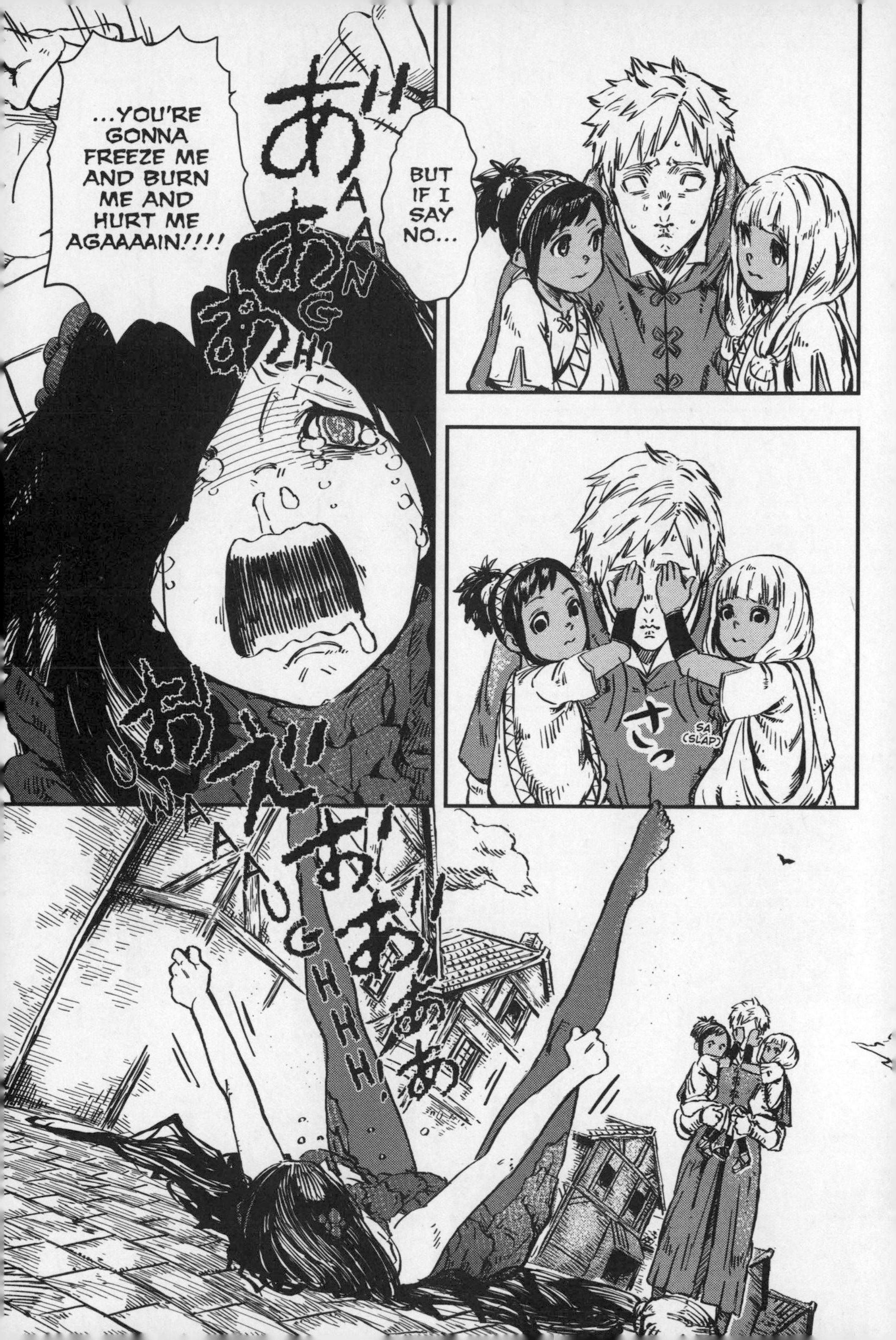
BUT IF I SAY NO...
...YOU'RE GONNA FREEZE ME AND BURN ME AND HURT ME AGAAAAIN!!!!
AAANGH!
さっ
SA (SLAP)
WAAAUGHHH!!

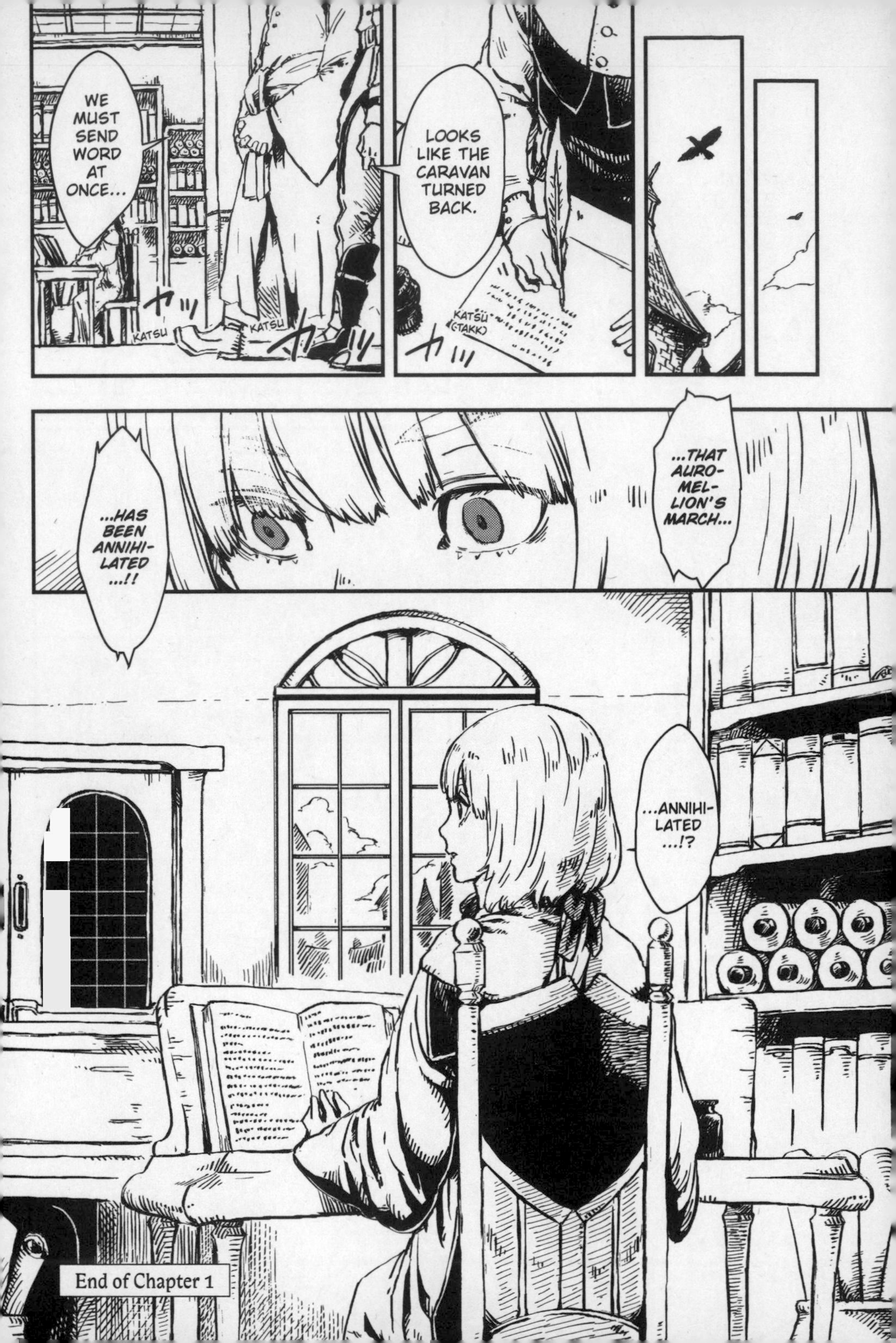
LOOKS LIKE THE CARAVAN TURNED BACK.
KATSU (-TAKK)
WE MUST SEND WORD AT ONCE...
KATSU
KATSU
...THAT AURO-MEL-LION'S MARCH...
...HAS BEEN ANNIHI-LATED ...!!
...ANNIHI-LATED ...!?
End of Chapter 1

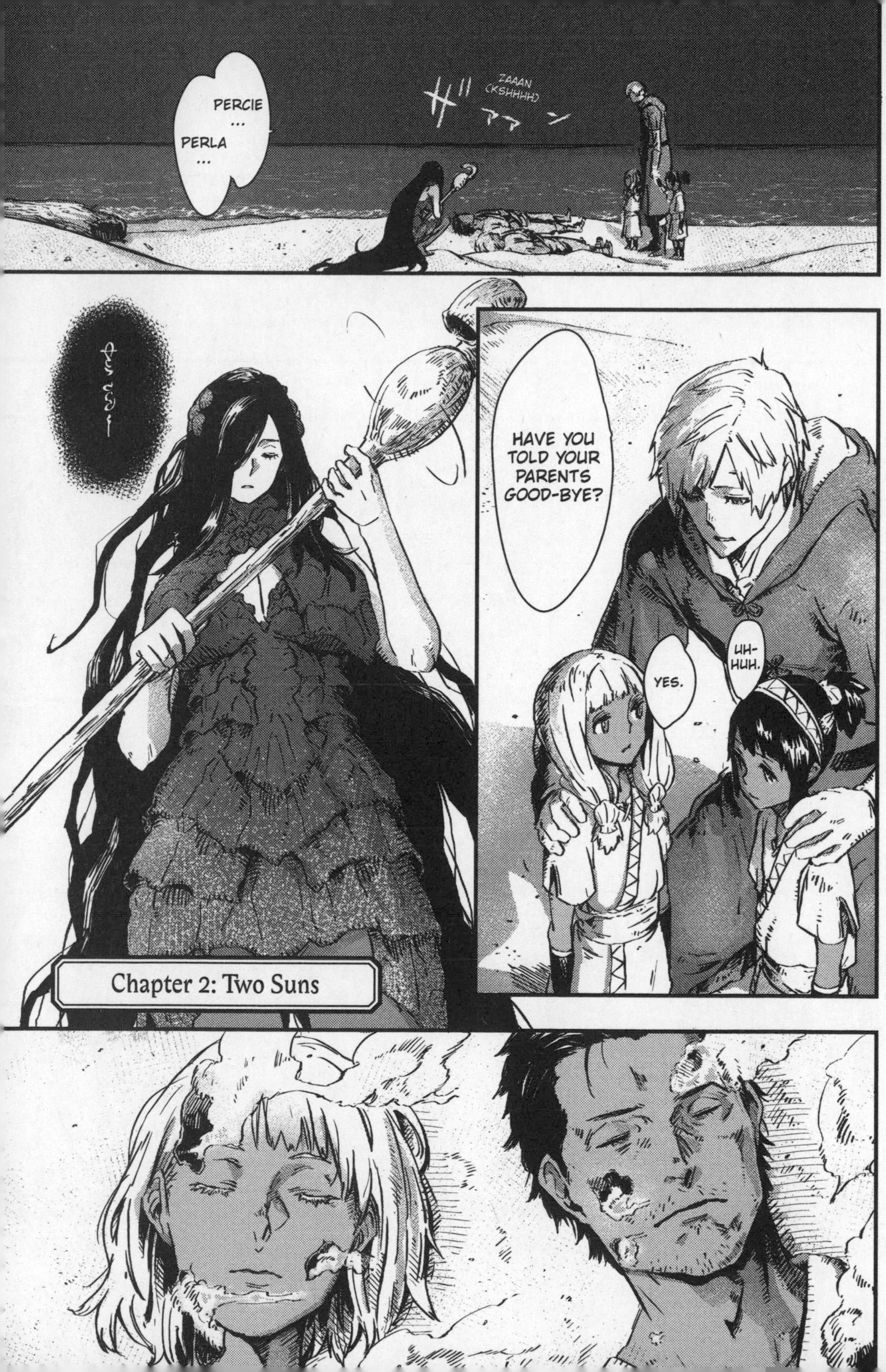
ZAAAN (KSHHHH)
PERCIE ... PERLA ...
HAVE YOU TOLD YOUR PARENTS GOOD-BYE?
UH-HUH.
YES.
Chapter 2: Two Suns

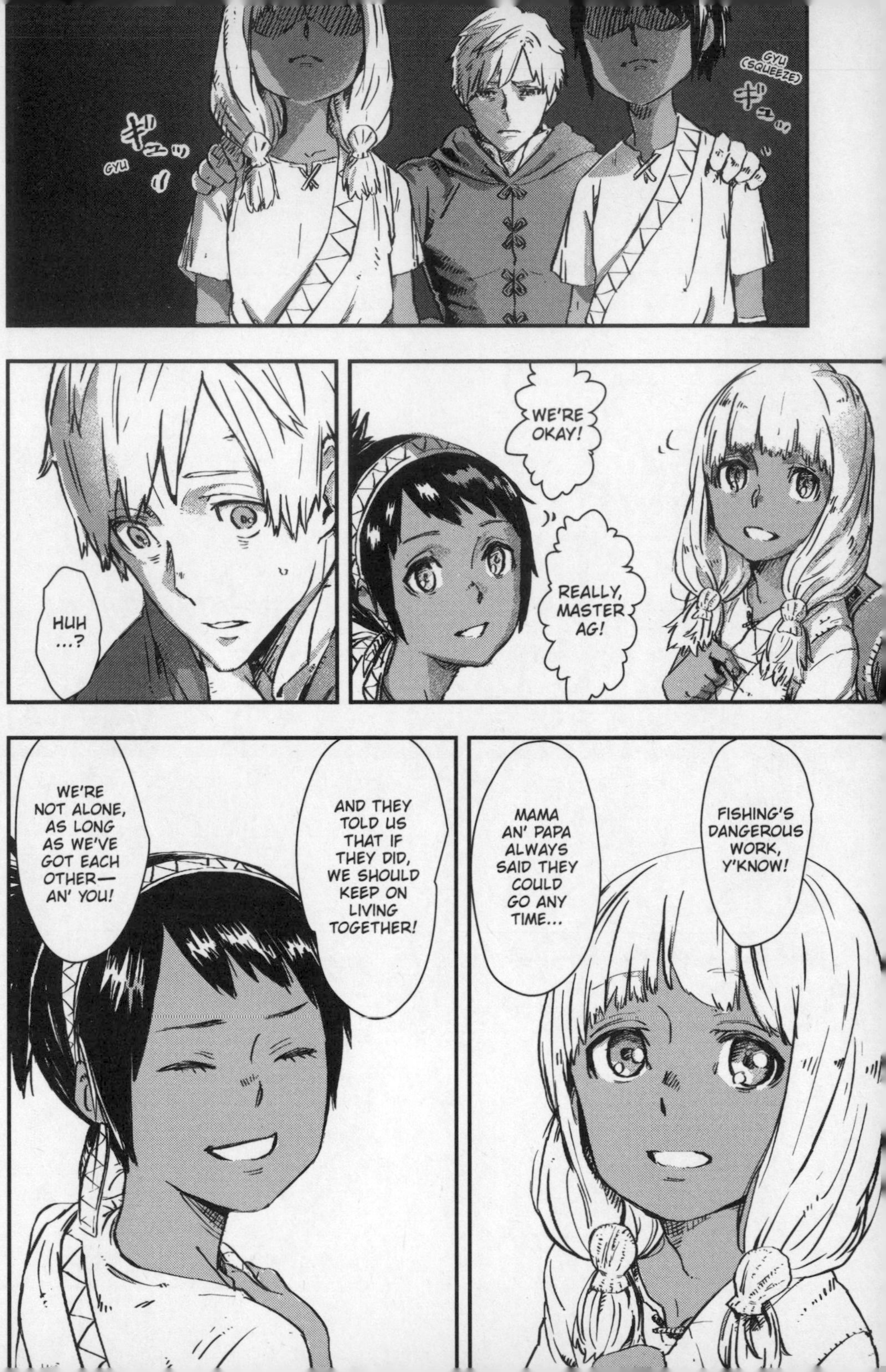
GYU (SQUEEZE)
ギュッ
ギュッ
GYU
WE'RE OKAY!
REALLY, MASTER AG!
HUH ...?
FISHING'S DANGEROUS WORK, Y'KNOW!
MAMA AN' PAPA ALWAYS SAID THEY COULD GO ANY TIME...
AND THEY TOLD US THAT IF THEY DID, WE SHOULD KEEP ON LIVING TOGETHER!
WE'RE NOT ALONE, AS LONG AS WE'VE GOT EACH OTHER— AN' YOU!

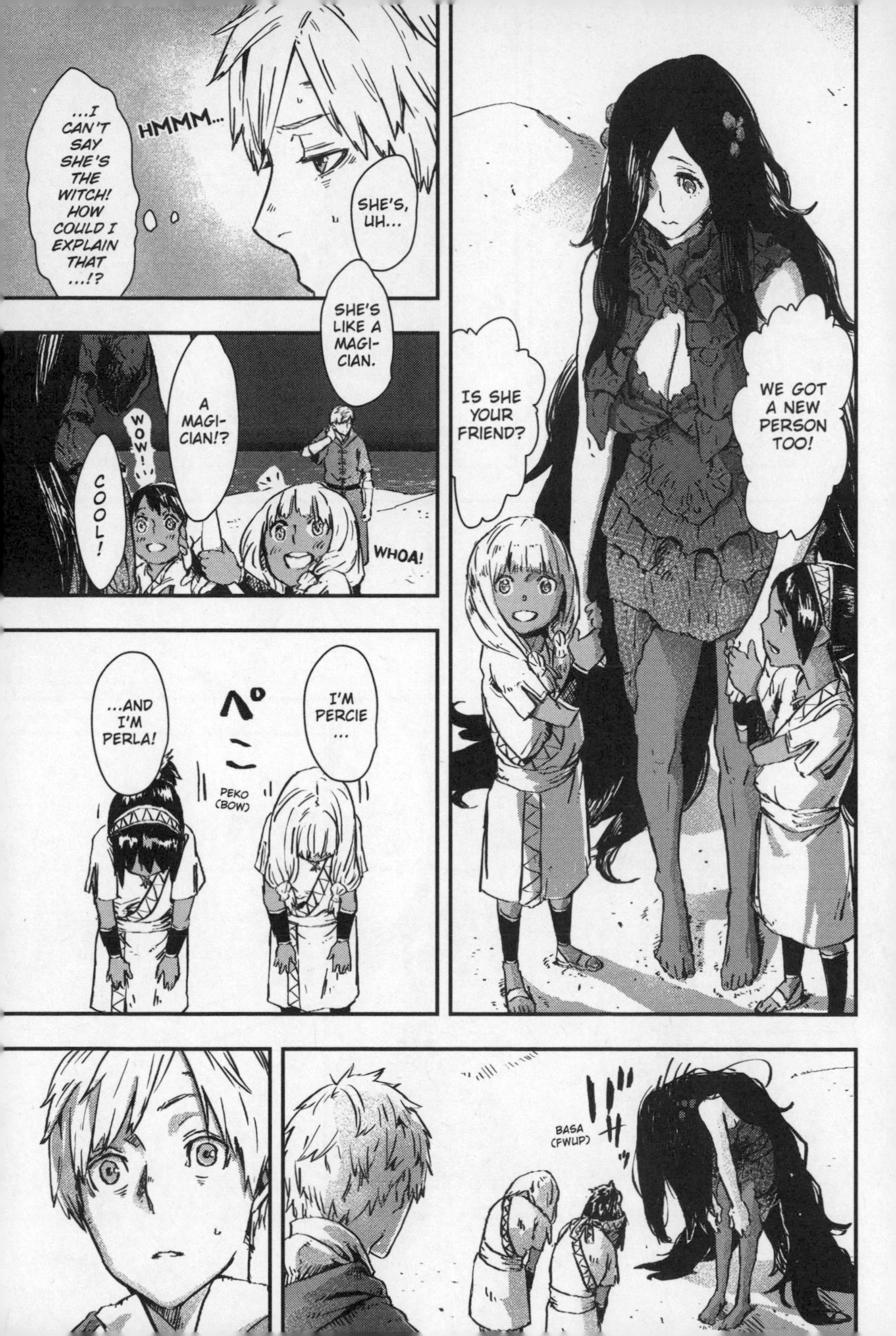
WE GOT A NEW PERSON TOO!
IS SHE YOUR FRIEND?
SHE'S, UH...
HMMM...
...I CAN'T SAY SHE'S THE WITCH! HOW COULD I EXPLAIN THAT ...!?
SHE'S LIKE A MAGICIAN.
WHOA!
A MAGICIAN!?
WOW!!
COOL!
I'M PERCIE ...
PEKO (BOW)
...AND I'M PERLA!
BASA (FWUP)

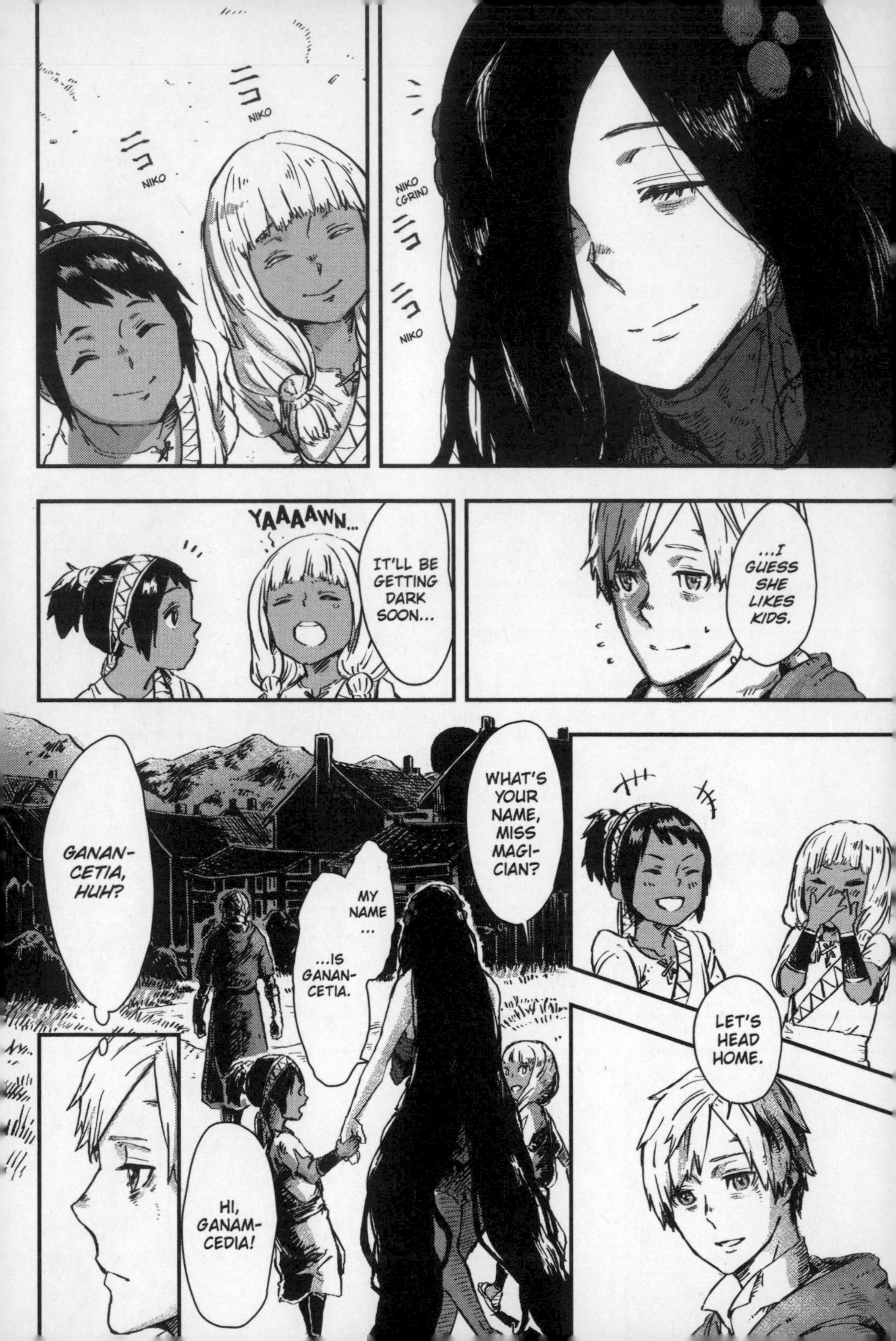
NIKO (GRIN)
NIKO
NIKO
NIKO
...I GUESS SHE LIKES KIDS.
YAAAAWN...
IT'LL BE GETTING DARK SOON...
LET'S HEAD HOME.
WHAT'S YOUR NAME, MISS MAGICIAN?
MY NAME...
...IS GANANCETIA.
HI, GANAMCEDIA!
GANANCETIA, HUH?

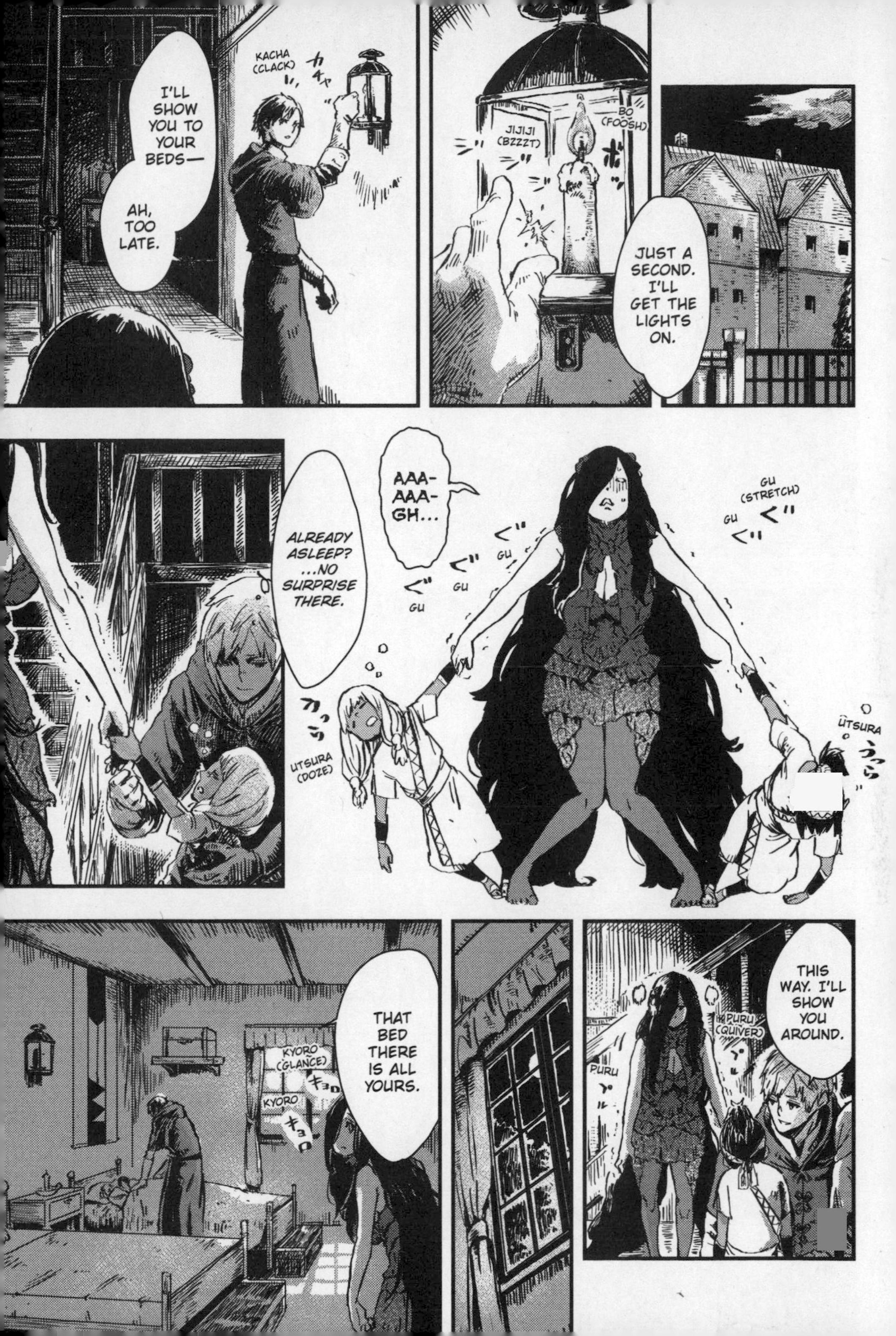
JUST A SECOND. I'LL GET THE LIGHTS ON.
BO (FOOSH)
JIJIJI (BZZZT)
KACHA (CLACK)
I'LL SHOW YOU TO YOUR BEDS—
AH, TOO LATE.
AAA-AAAGH...
GU (STRETCH)
GU
GU
GU
GU
UTSURA
UTSURA (DOZE)
ALREADY ASLEEP? ...NO SURPRISE THERE.
THIS WAY. I'LL SHOW YOU AROUND.
PURU (QUIVER)
PURU
THAT BED THERE IS ALL YOURS.
KYORO (GLANCE)
KYORO

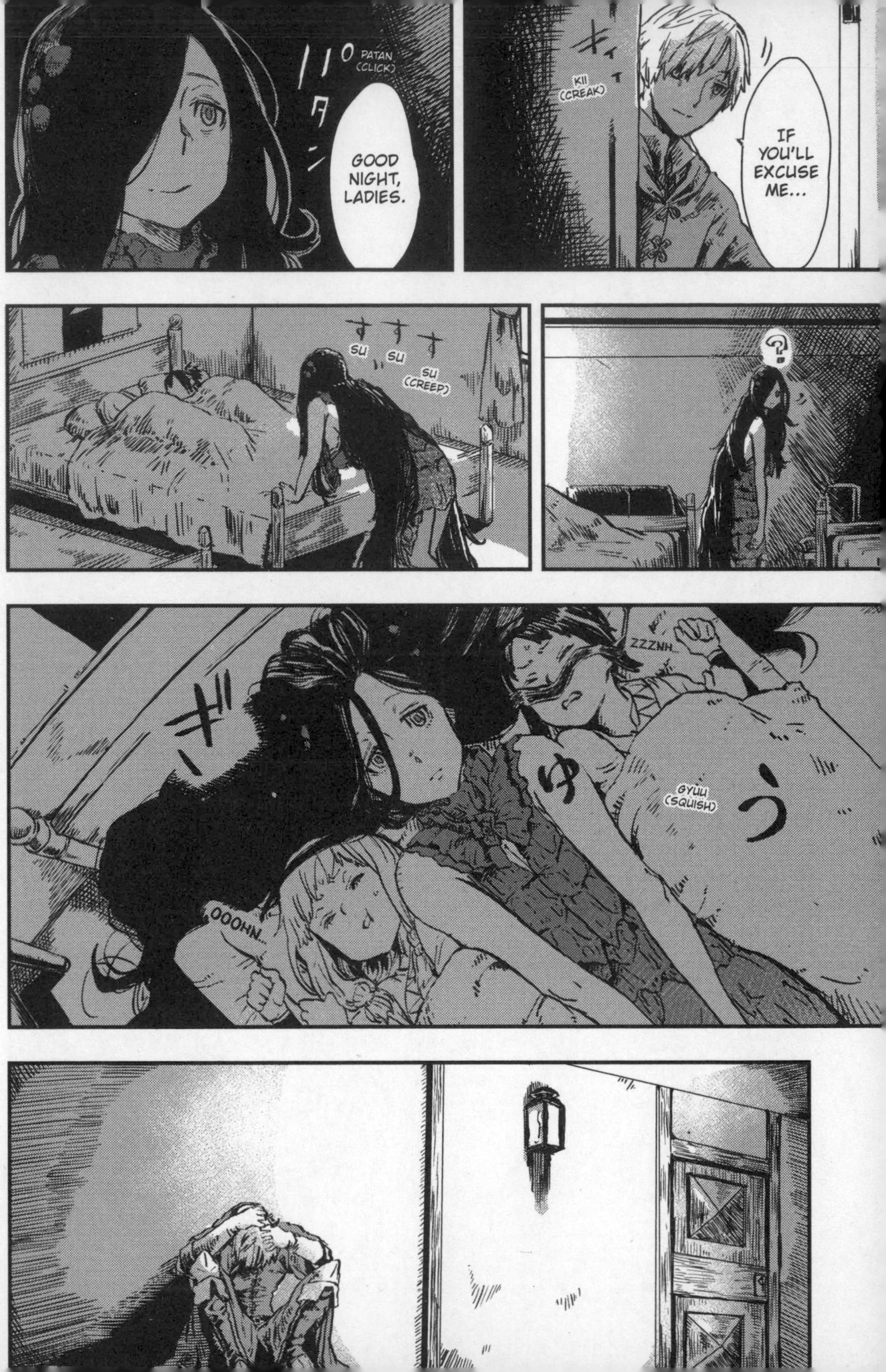
KII (CREAK)
IF YOU'LL EXCUSE ME...
PATAN (CLICK)
GOOD NIGHT, LADIES.
?
SU SU SU (CREEP)
ZZZNH...
GYUU (SQUISH)
OOOHN...

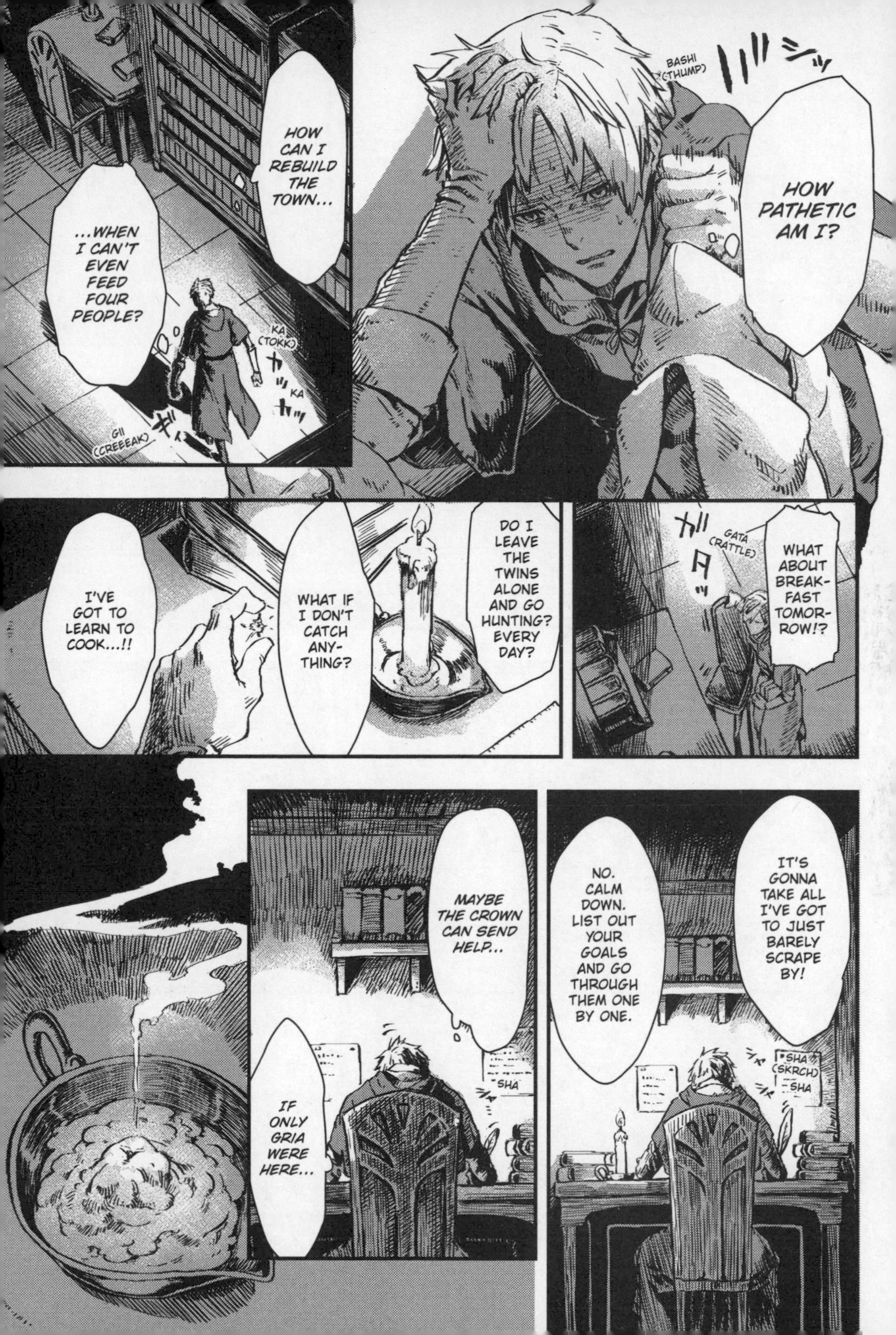
BASHI (THUMP)
HOW PATHETIC AM I?
HOW CAN I REBUILD THE TOWN...
...WHEN I CAN'T EVEN FEED FOUR PEOPLE?
KA (TOKK)
KA
GII (CREEEAK)
GATA (RATTLE)
WHAT ABOUT BREAK-FAST TOMOR-ROW!?
DO I LEAVE THE TWINS ALONE AND GO HUNTING? EVERY DAY?
WHAT IF I DON'T CATCH ANY-THING?
I'VE GOT TO LEARN TO COOK...!!
IT'S GONNA TAKE ALL I'VE GOT TO JUST BARELY SCRAPE BY!
NO. CALM DOWN. LIST OUT YOUR GOALS AND GO THROUGH THEM ONE BY ONE.
SHA (SKRCH)
SHA
MAYBE THE CROWN CAN SEND HELP...
SHA
IF ONLY GRIA WERE HERE...

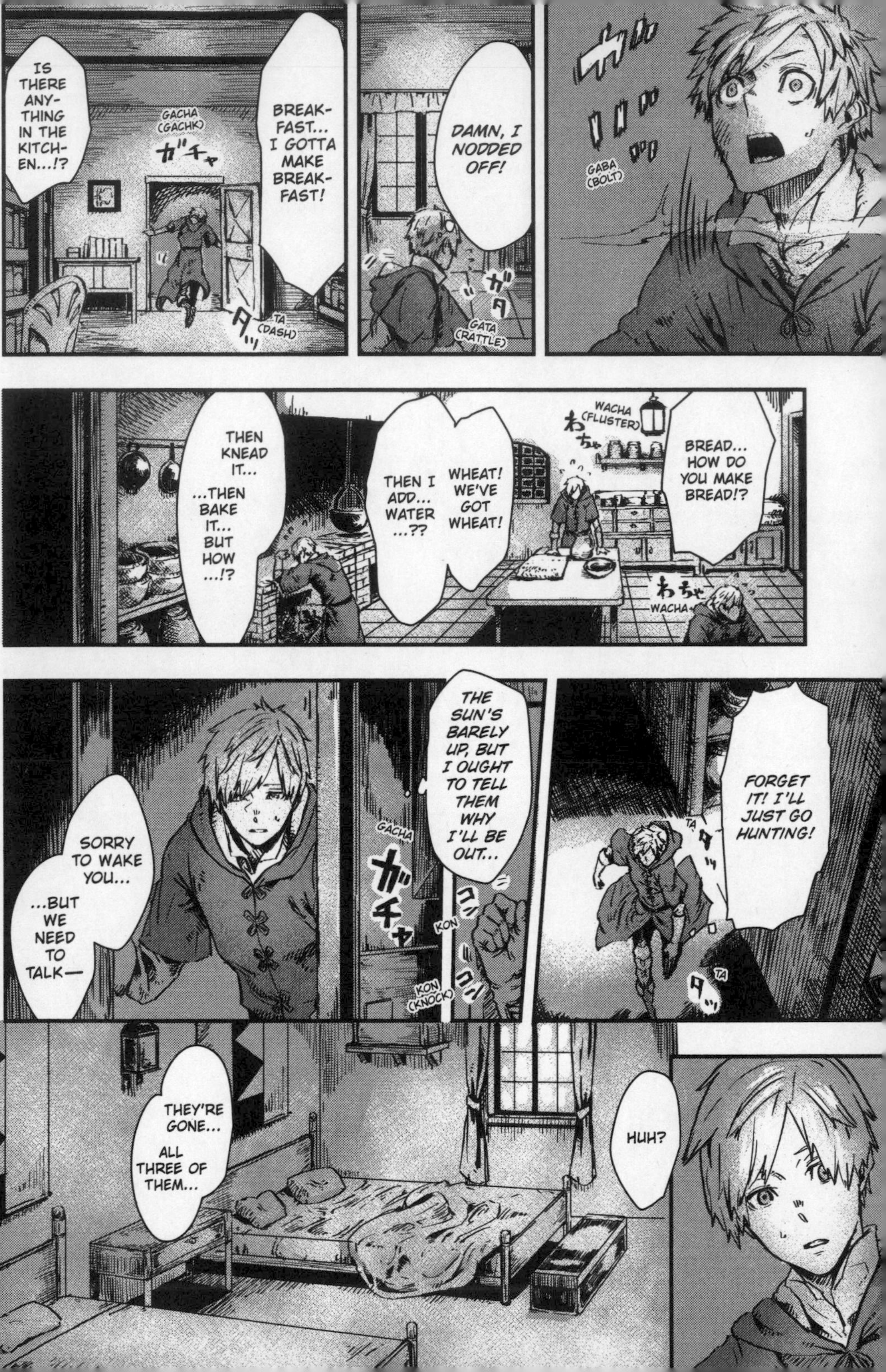
GABA (BOLT)
DAMN, I NODDED OFF!
GATA (RATTLE)
BREAK-FAST... I GOTTA MAKE BREAK-FAST!
IS THERE ANY-THING IN THE KITCH-EN...!?
GACHA (GACHK)
TA (DASH)
BREAD... HOW DO YOU MAKE BREAD!?
WACHA (FLUSTER)
WACHA
WHEAT! WE'VE GOT WHEAT!
THEN I ADD... WATER ...??
THEN KNEAD IT...
...THEN BAKE IT... BUT HOW ...!?
FORGET IT! I'LL JUST GO HUNTING!
TA
TA
THE SUN'S BARELY UP, BUT I OUGHT TO TELL THEM WHY I'LL BE OUT...
KON
KON (KNOCK)
GACHA
SORRY TO WAKE YOU...
...BUT WE NEED TO TALK—
HUH?
THEY'RE GONE...
ALL THREE OF THEM...

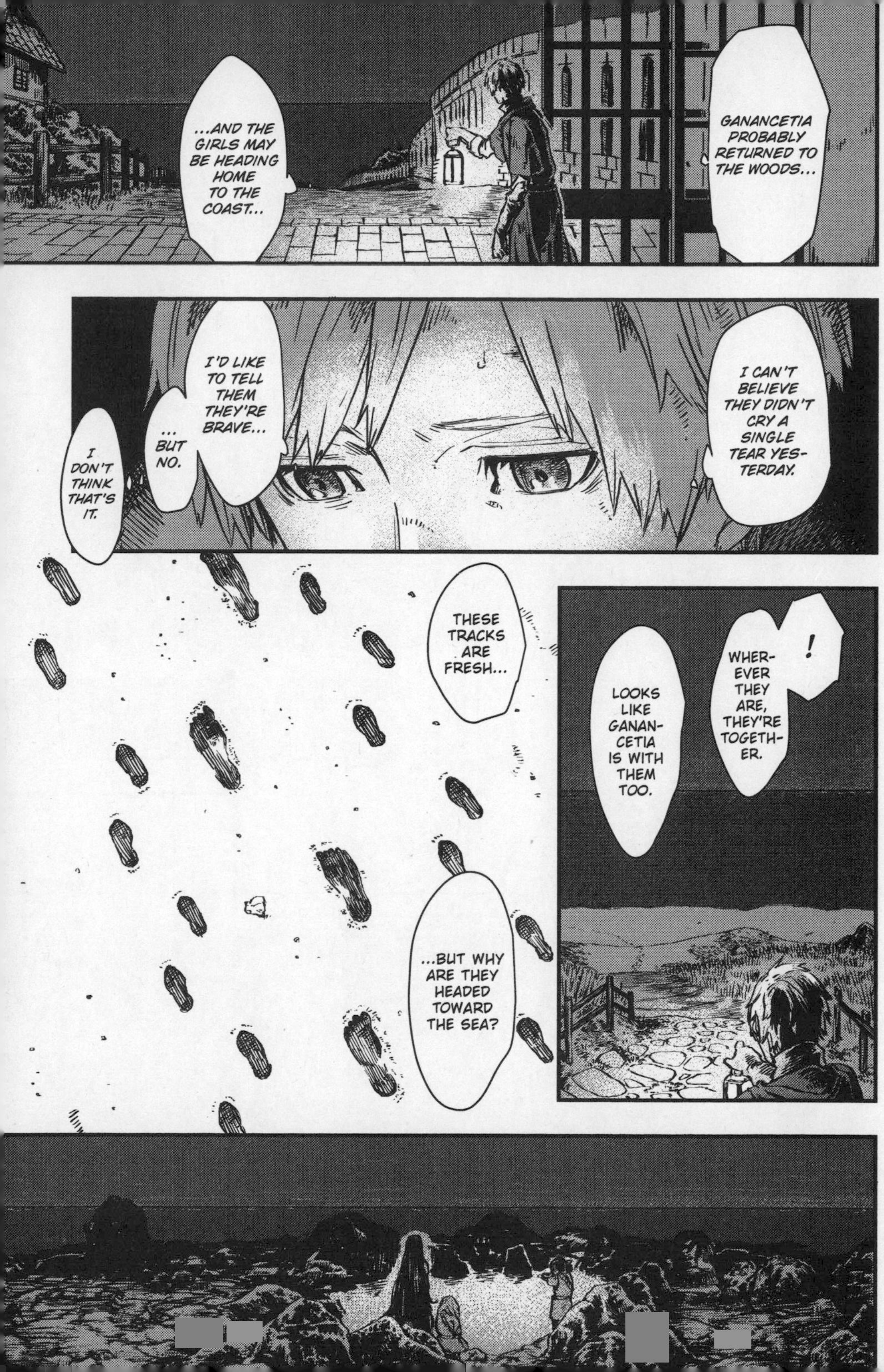
GANANCETIA PROBABLY RETURNED TO THE WOODS...
...AND THE GIRLS MAY BE HEADING HOME TO THE COAST...
I CAN'T BELIEVE THEY DIDN'T CRY A SINGLE TEAR YES-TERDAY.
I'D LIKE TO TELL THEM THEY'RE BRAVE...
...BUT NO.
I DON'T THINK THAT'S IT.
!
WHER-EVER THEY ARE, THEY'RE TOGETH-ER.
LOOKS LIKE GANAN-CETIA IS WITH THEM TOO.
THESE TRACKS ARE FRESH...
...BUT WHY ARE THEY HEADED TOWARD THE SEA?

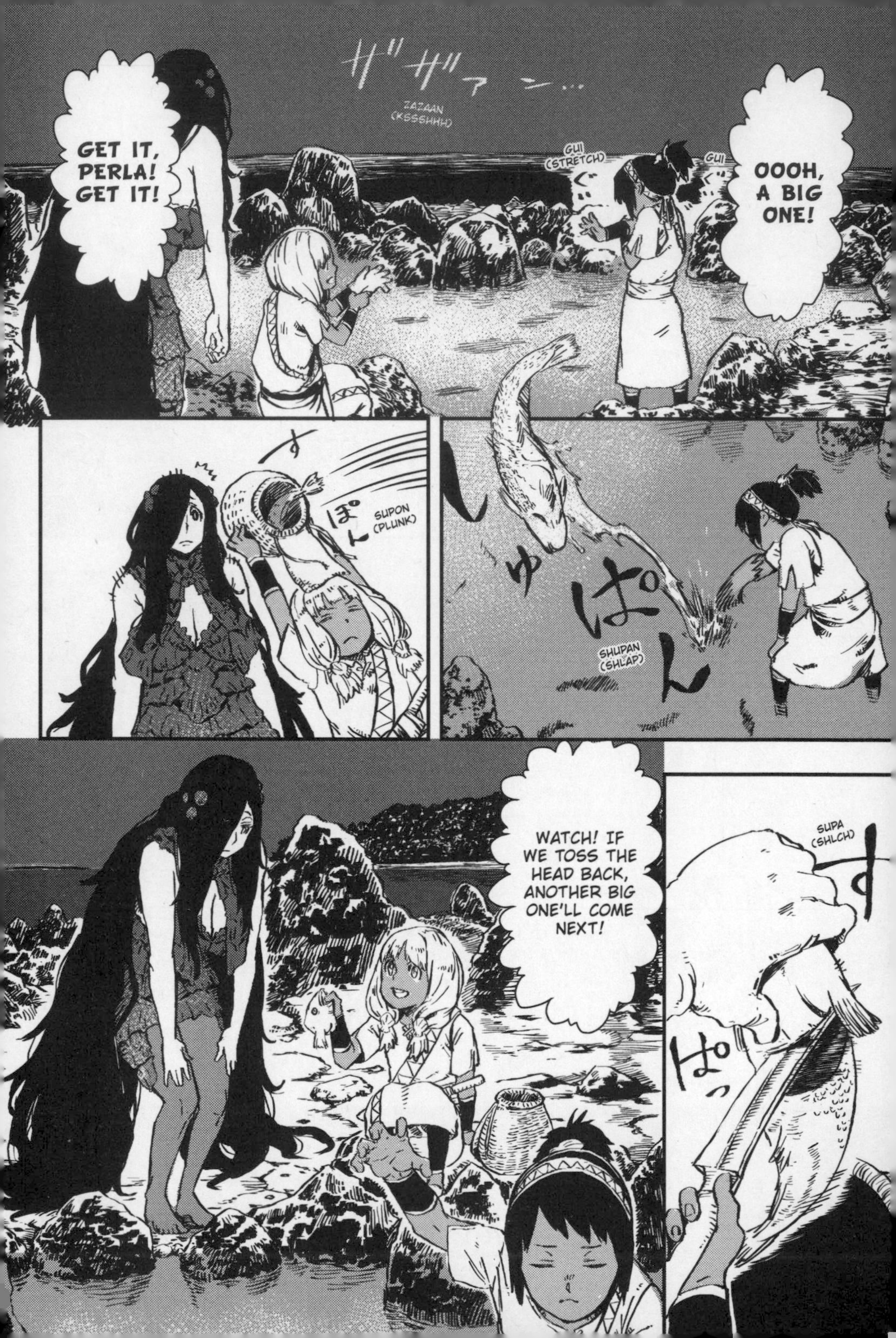

ザザァ〜ン…
ZAZAAN (KSSSHHH)
OOOH, A BIG ONE!
GUI
GUI (STRETCH)
GET IT, PERLA! GET IT!
SHUPAN (SHLAP)
SUPON (PLUNK)
SUPA (SHLCH)
WATCH! IF WE TOSS THE HEAD BACK, ANOTHER BIG ONE'LL COME NEXT!

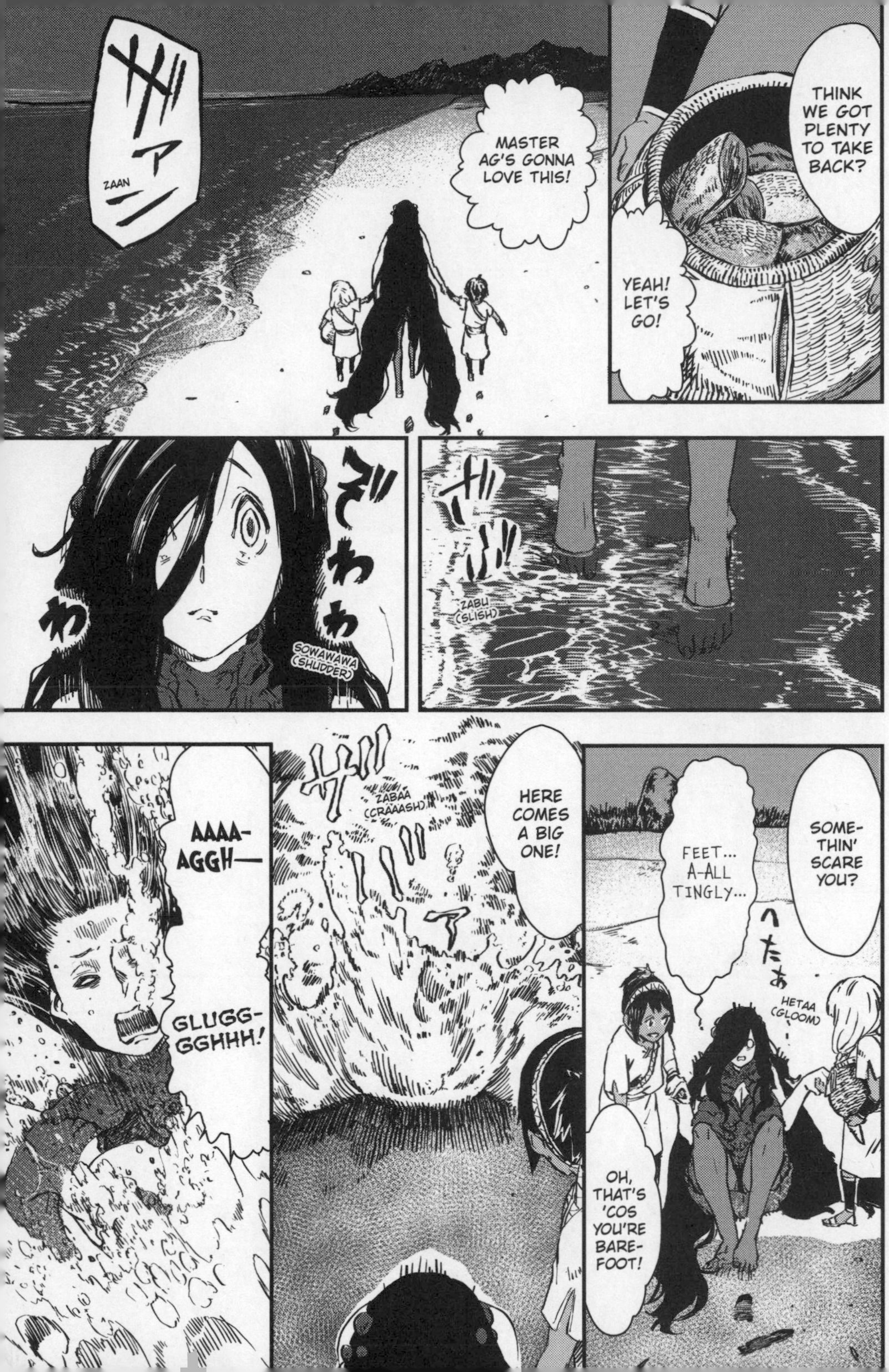
THINK WE GOT PLENTY TO TAKE BACK?
YEAH! LET'S GO!
MASTER AG'S GONNA LOVE THIS!
ZAAN
ZABU (SLISH)
SOWAWAWA (SHUDDER)
SOME-THIN' SCARE YOU?
FEET... A-ALL TINGLY...
HETAA (GLOOM)
OH, THAT'S 'COS YOU'RE BARE-FOOT!
HERE COMES A BIG ONE!
ZABAA (CRÄAASH)
AAAA-AGGH—
GLUGG-GGHHH!

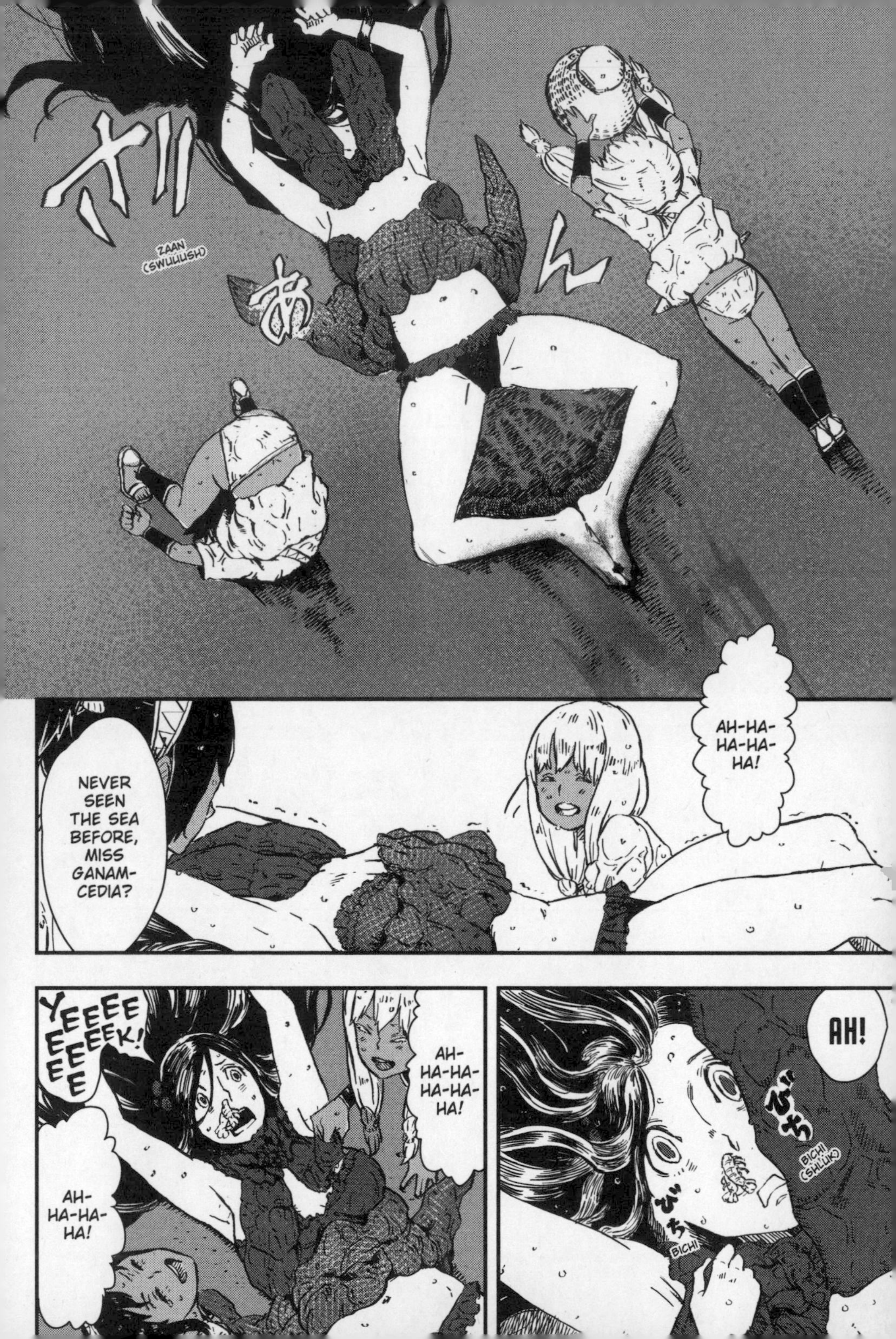
ZAAN (SWUUUSH)
AH-HA-HA-HA-HA!
NEVER SEEN THE SEA BEFORE, MISS GANAM-CEDIA?
AH!
BICHI (SHLUK)
BICHI
AH-HA-HA-HA-HA-HA!
YEEEEEEEEEK!
AH-HA-HA-HA!

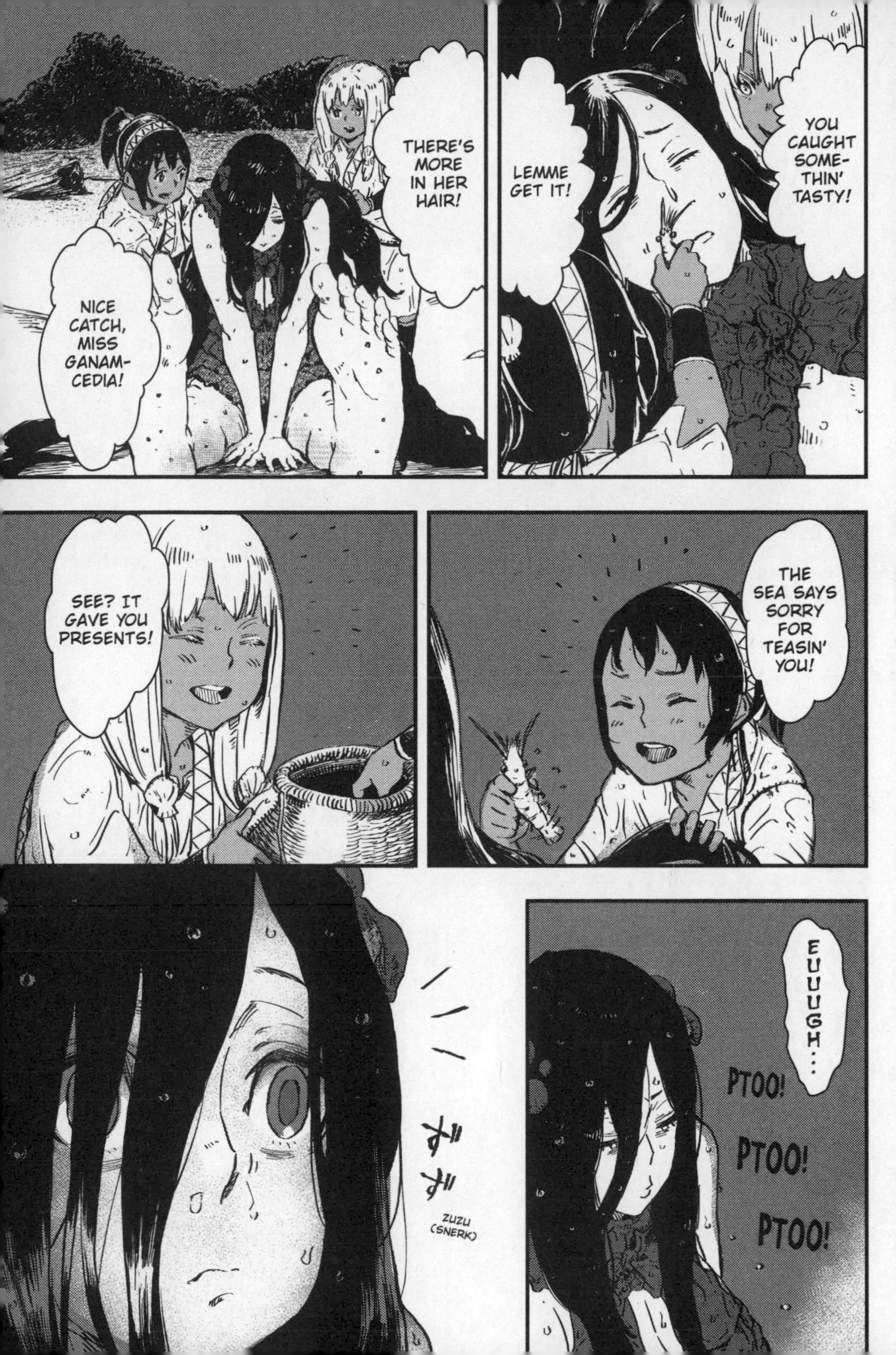
YOU CAUGHT SOMETHIN' TASTY!
LEMME GET IT!
THERE'S MORE IN HER HAIR!
NICE CATCH, MISS GANAMCEDIA!
THE SEA SAYS SORRY FOR TEASIN' YOU!
SEE? IT GAVE YOU PRESENTS!
EUUUGH...
PTOO!
PTOO!
PTOO!
ずず
ZUZU (SNERK)

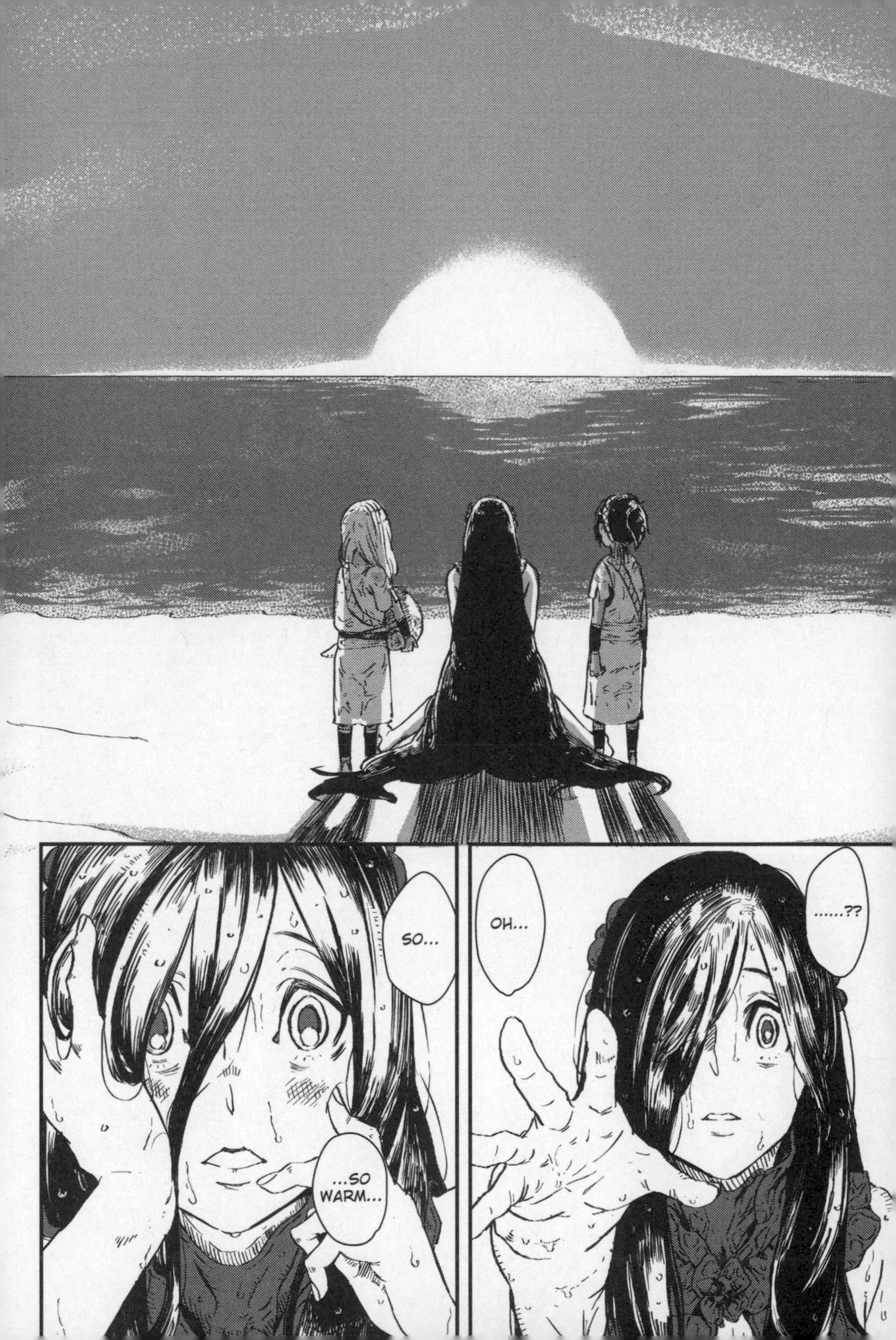

......??
OH...
SO...
...SO WARM...

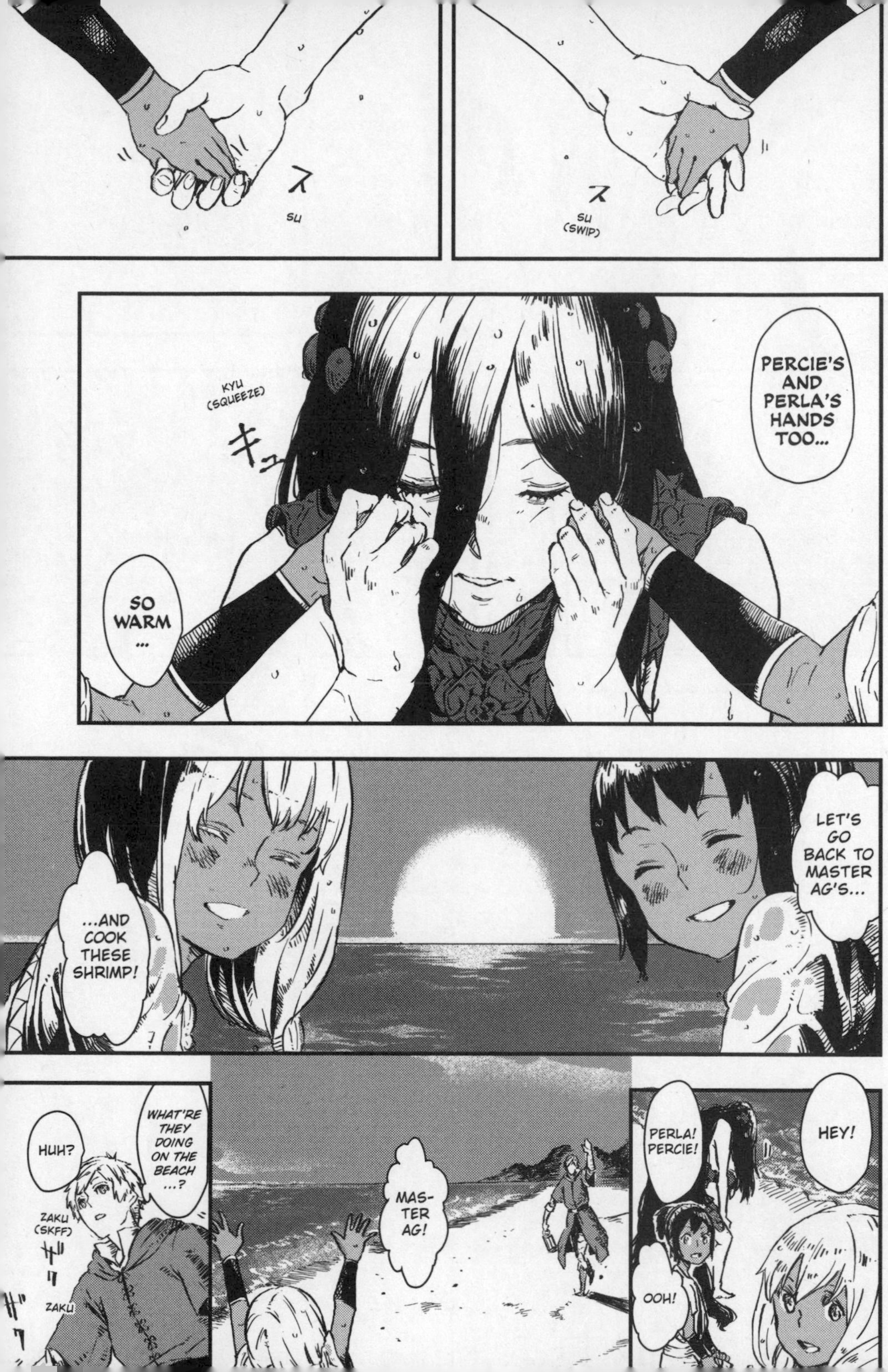

ス
SU (SWIP)
ス
SU
PERCIE'S AND PERLA'S HANDS TOO...
KYU (SQUEEZE)
キュ
SO WARM ...
LET'S GO BACK TO MASTER AG'S...
...AND COOK THESE SHRIMP!
HEY!
PERLA! PERCIE!
OOH!
MAS-TER AG!
WHAT'RE THEY DOING ON THE BEACH ...?
HUH?
ZAKU (SKFF)
ザッ
ZAKU
ザッ

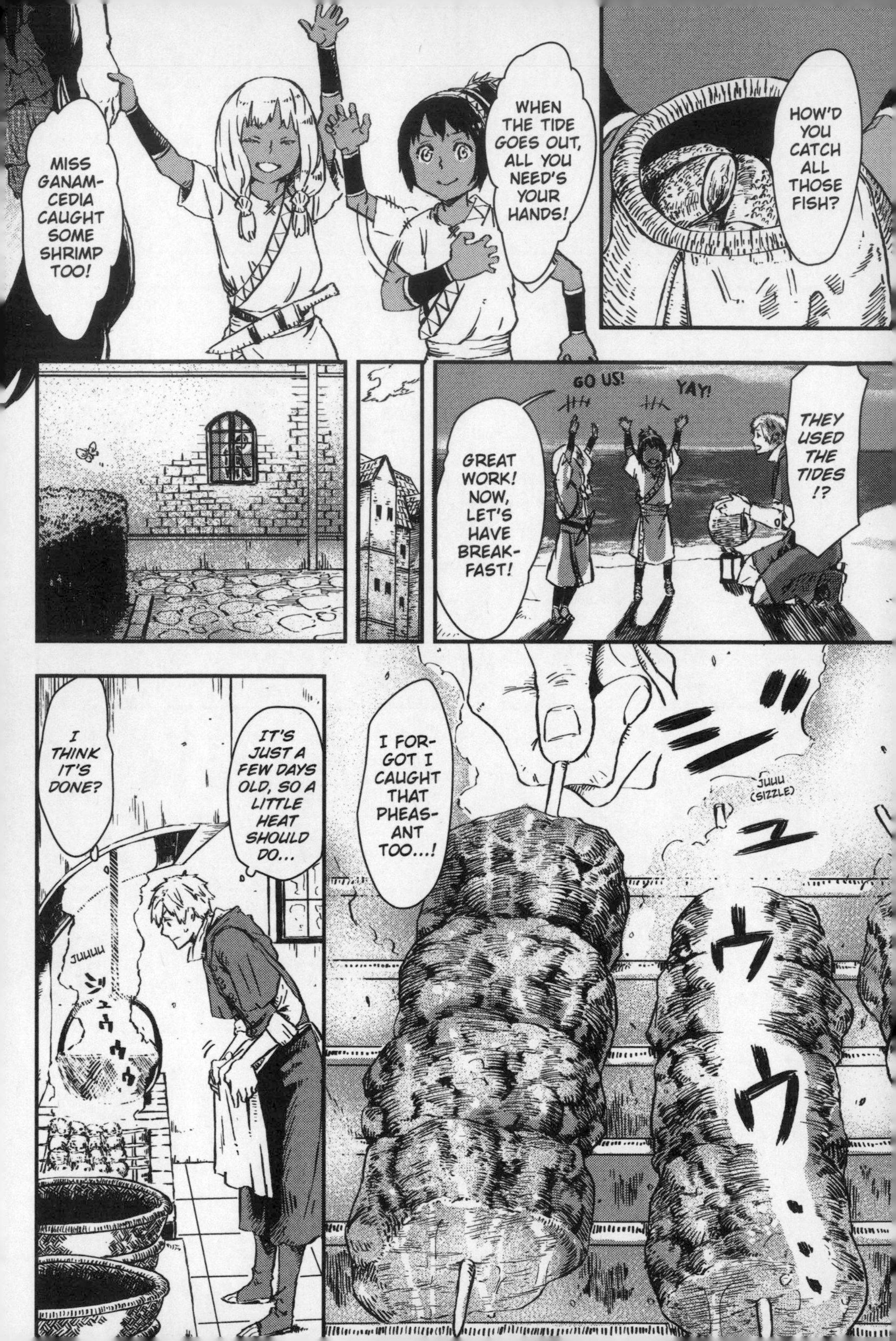
HOW'D YOU CATCH ALL THOSE FISH?
WHEN THE TIDE GOES OUT, ALL YOU NEED'S YOUR HANDS!
MISS GANAMCEDIA CAUGHT SOME SHRIMP TOO!
THEY USED THE TIDES !?
YAY!
GO US!
GREAT WORK! NOW, LET'S HAVE BREAKFAST!
JUUU (SIZZLE)
I FORGOT I CAUGHT THAT PHEASANT TOO...!
IT'S JUST A FEW DAYS OLD, SO A LITTLE HEAT SHOULD DO...
I THINK IT'S DONE?
JUUUU

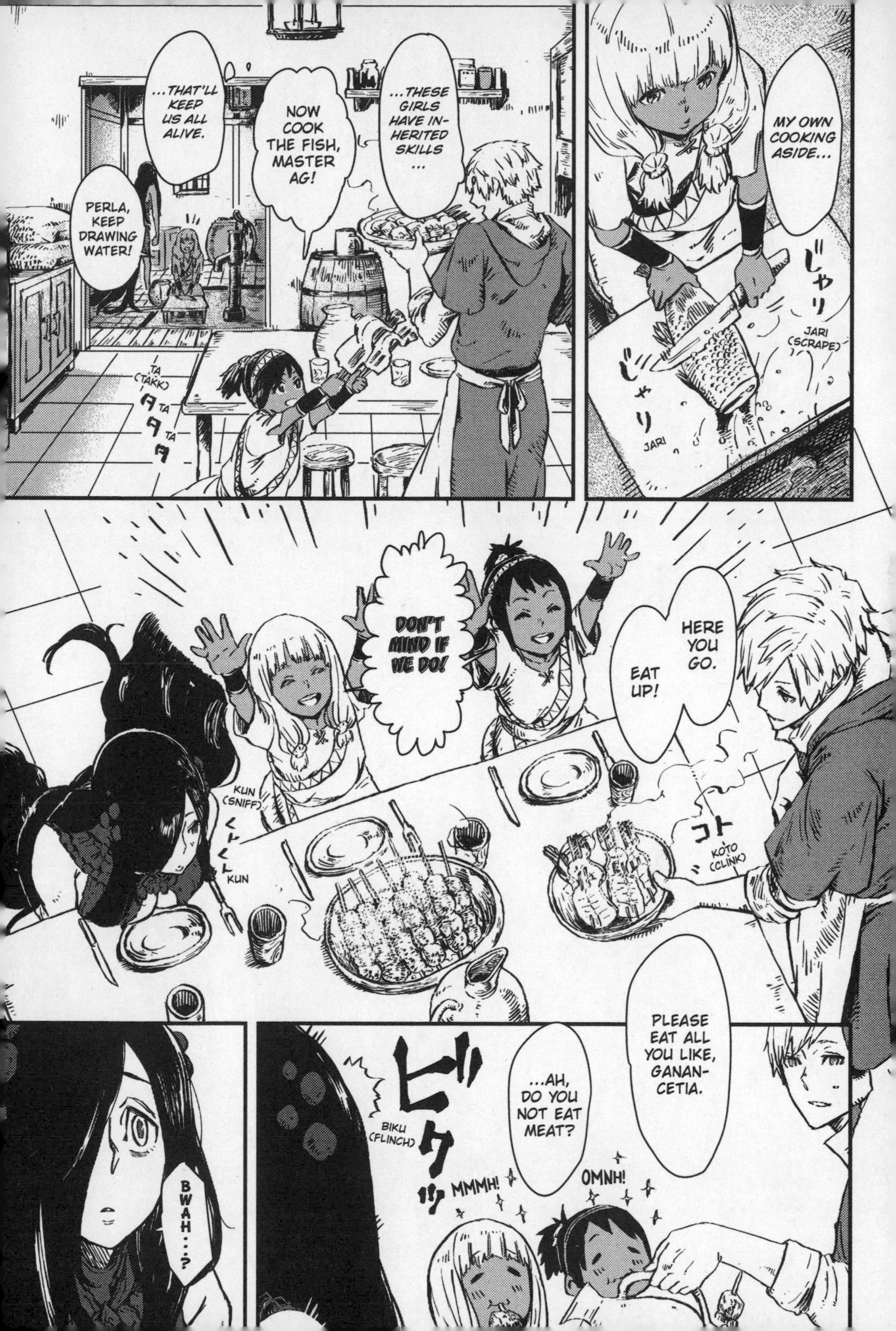

MY OWN COOKING ASIDE...
じゃり
JARI (SCRAPE)
じゃり
JARI
...THESE GIRLS HAVE IN-HERITED SKILLS...
NOW COOK THE FISH, MASTER AG!
...THAT'LL KEEP US ALL ALIVE.
PERLA, KEEP DRAWING WATER!
TA (TAKK)
タ TA
タ TA
タ
HERE YOU GO.
EAT UP!
DON'T MIND IF WE DO!
コト
KOTO (CLINK)
KUN (SNIFF)
くんくん
KUN
PLEASE EAT ALL YOU LIKE, GANAN-CETIA.
...AH, DO YOU NOT EAT MEAT?
OMNH!
MMMH!
ビクッ
BIKU (FLINCH)
BWAH...?

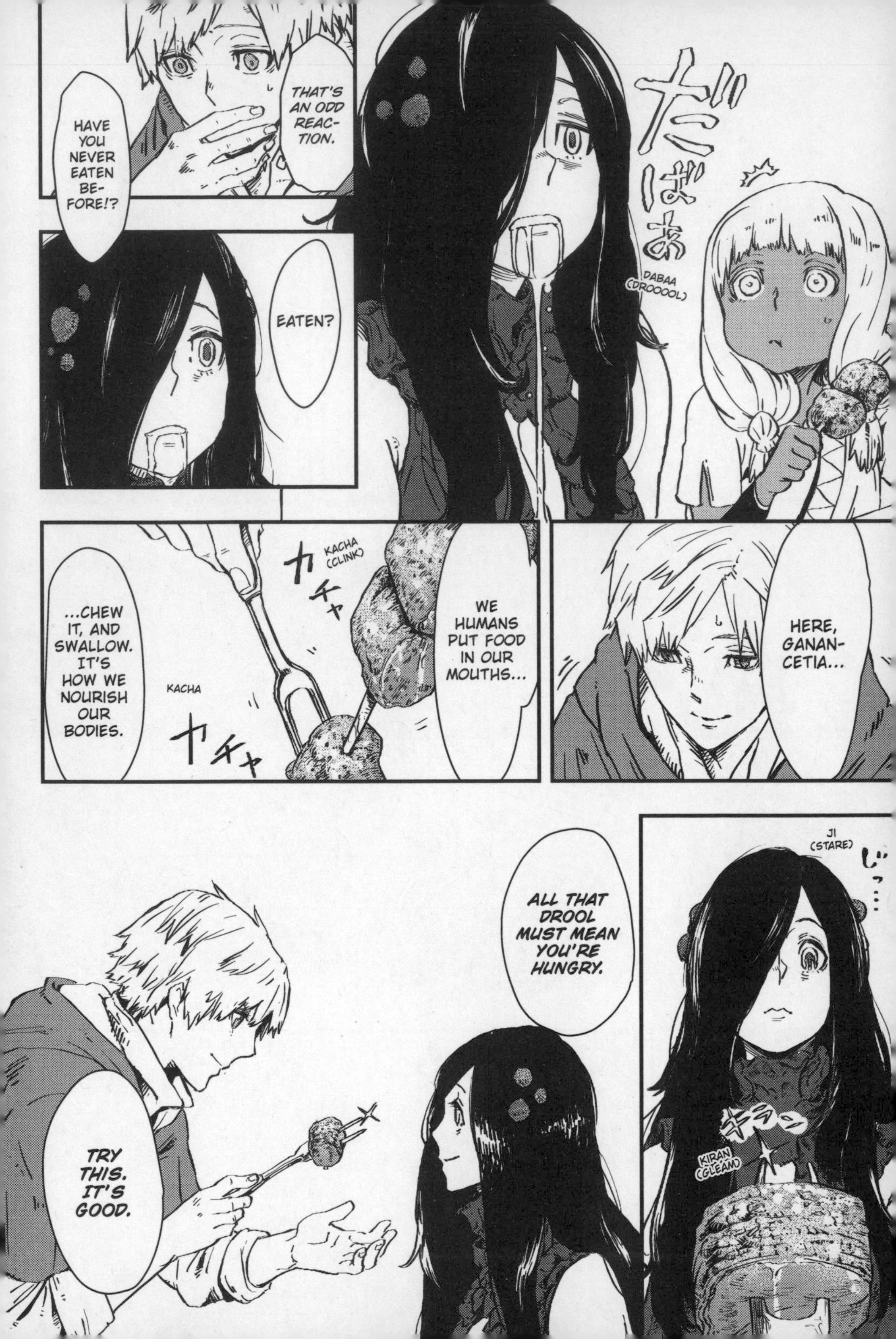
だばぁ
DABAA (DROOOOL)
THAT'S AN ODD REACTION.
HAVE YOU NEVER EATEN BEFORE!?
EATEN?
HERE, GANANCETIA...
WE HUMANS PUT FOOD IN OUR MOUTHS...
カチャ
KACHA (CLINK)
カチャ
KACHA
...CHEW IT, AND SWALLOW. IT'S HOW WE NOURISH OUR BODIES.
じっ…
JI (STARE)
キラン
KIRAN (GLEAM)
ALL THAT DROOL MUST MEAN YOU'RE HUNGRY.
TRY THIS. IT'S GOOD.

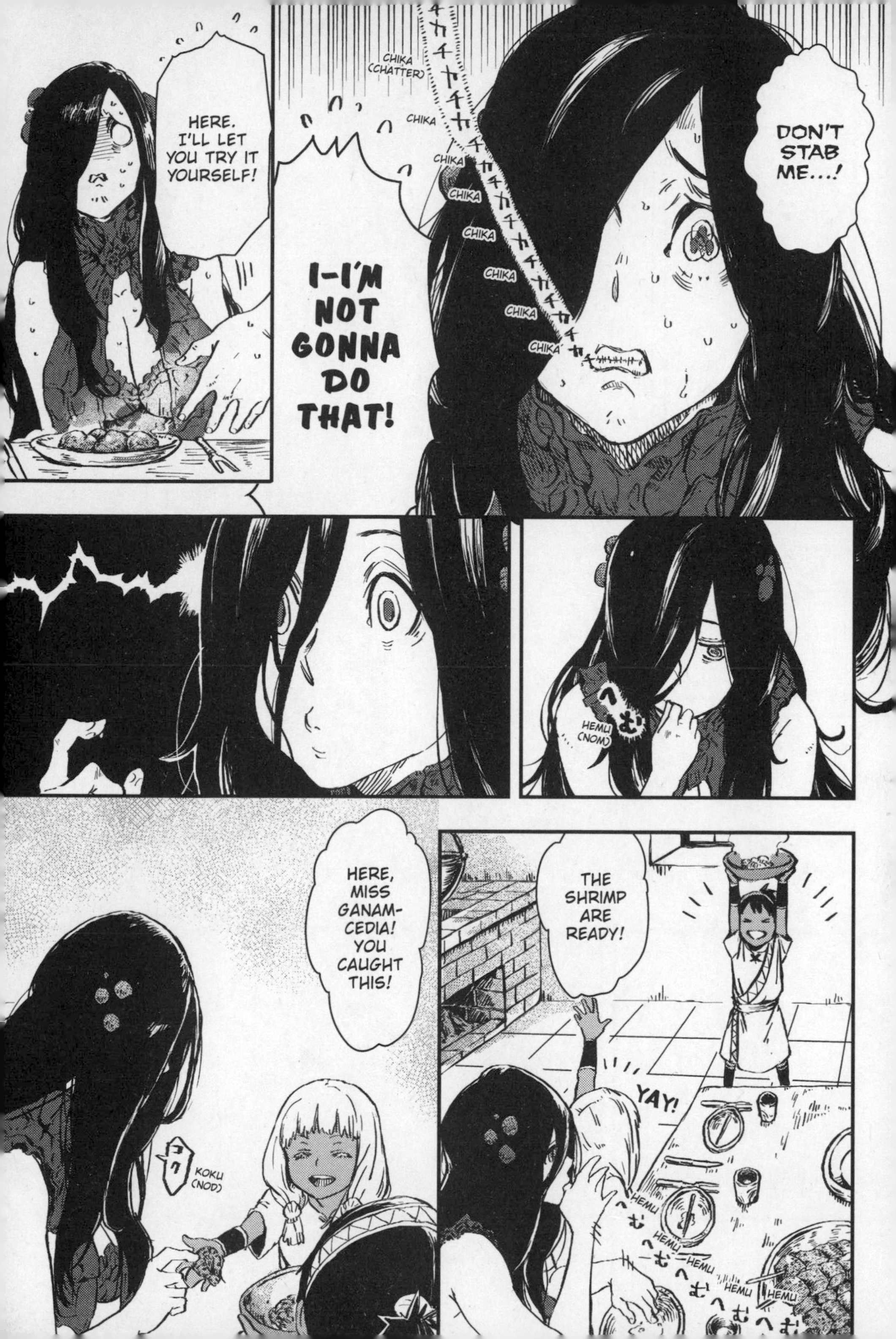

DON'T STAB ME...!
CHIKA (CHATTER)
CHIKA
CHIKA
CHIKA
CHIKA
CHIKA
CHIKA
CHIKA
I-I'M NOT GONNA DO THAT!
HERE. I'LL LET YOU TRY IT YOURSELF!
HEMU (NOM)
THE SHRIMP ARE READY!
YAY!
HEMU
HEMU
HEMU
HEMU
HEMU
HERE, MISS GANAM-CEDIA! YOU CAUGHT THIS!
KOKU (NOD)

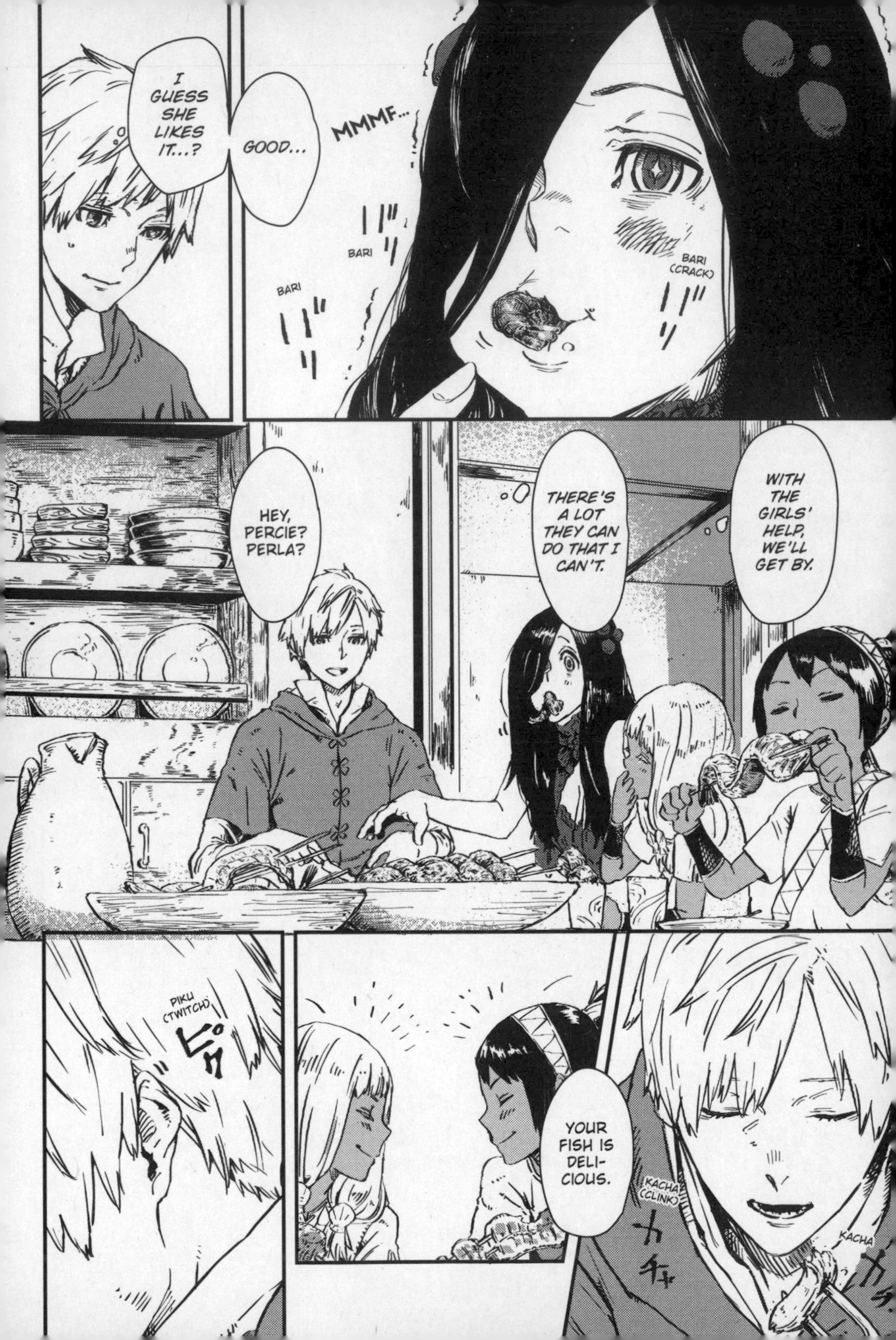
MMMF...
BARI (CRACK)
BARI
BARI
GOOD...
I GUESS SHE LIKES IT...?
WITH THE GIRLS' HELP, WE'LL GET BY.
THERE'S A LOT THEY CAN DO THAT I CAN'T.
HEY, PERCIE? PERLA?
KACHA
KACHA (CLINK)
YOUR FISH IS DELI-CIOUS.
PIKU (TWITCH)

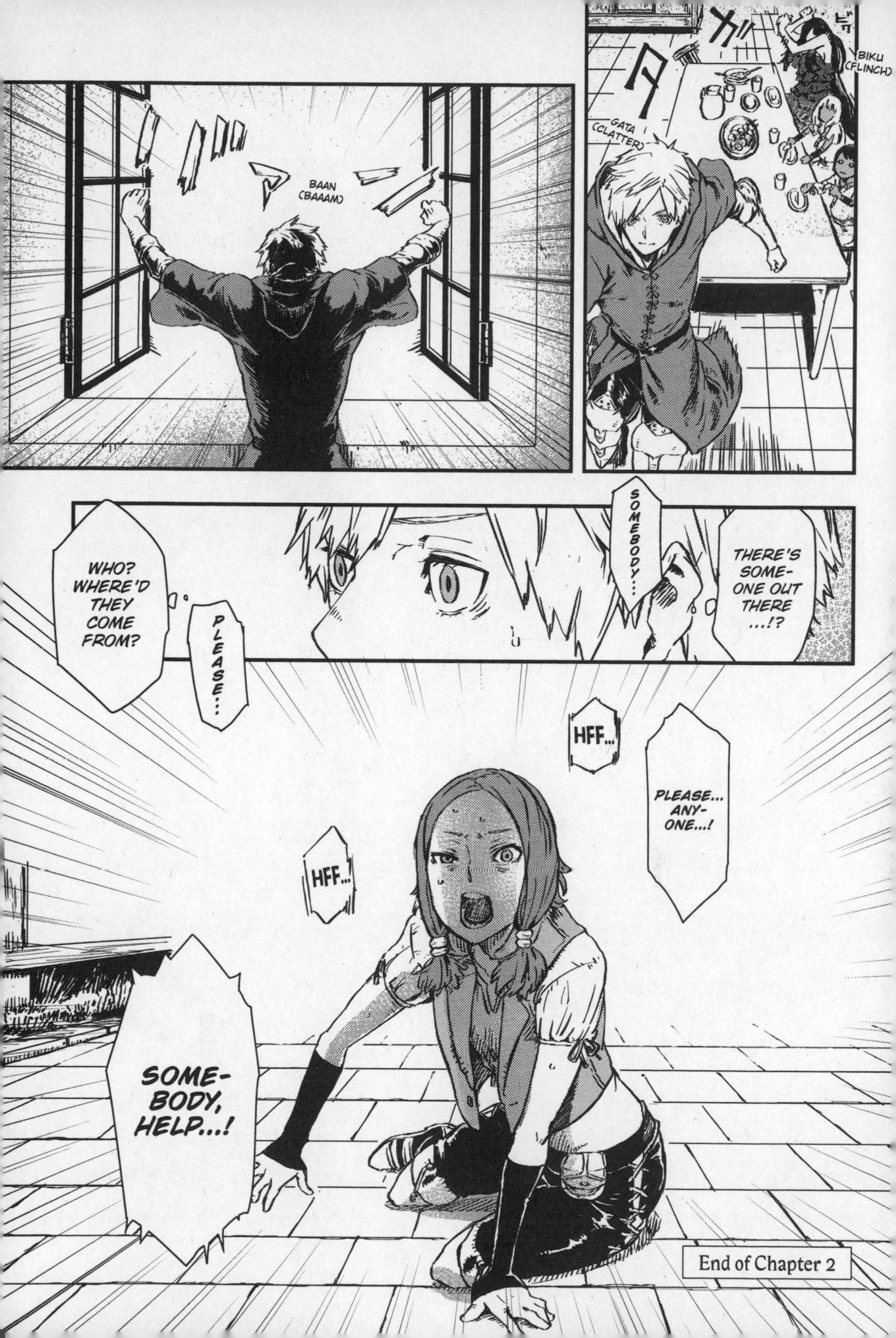
BIKU (FLINCH)
GATA (CLATTER)
BAAN (BAAAM)
THERE'S SOME-ONE OUT THERE ...!?
SOMEBODY...
PLEASE...
WHO? WHERE'D THEY COME FROM?
PLEASE... ANY-ONE...!
HFF...
HFF...
SOME-BODY, HELP...!
End of Chapter 2

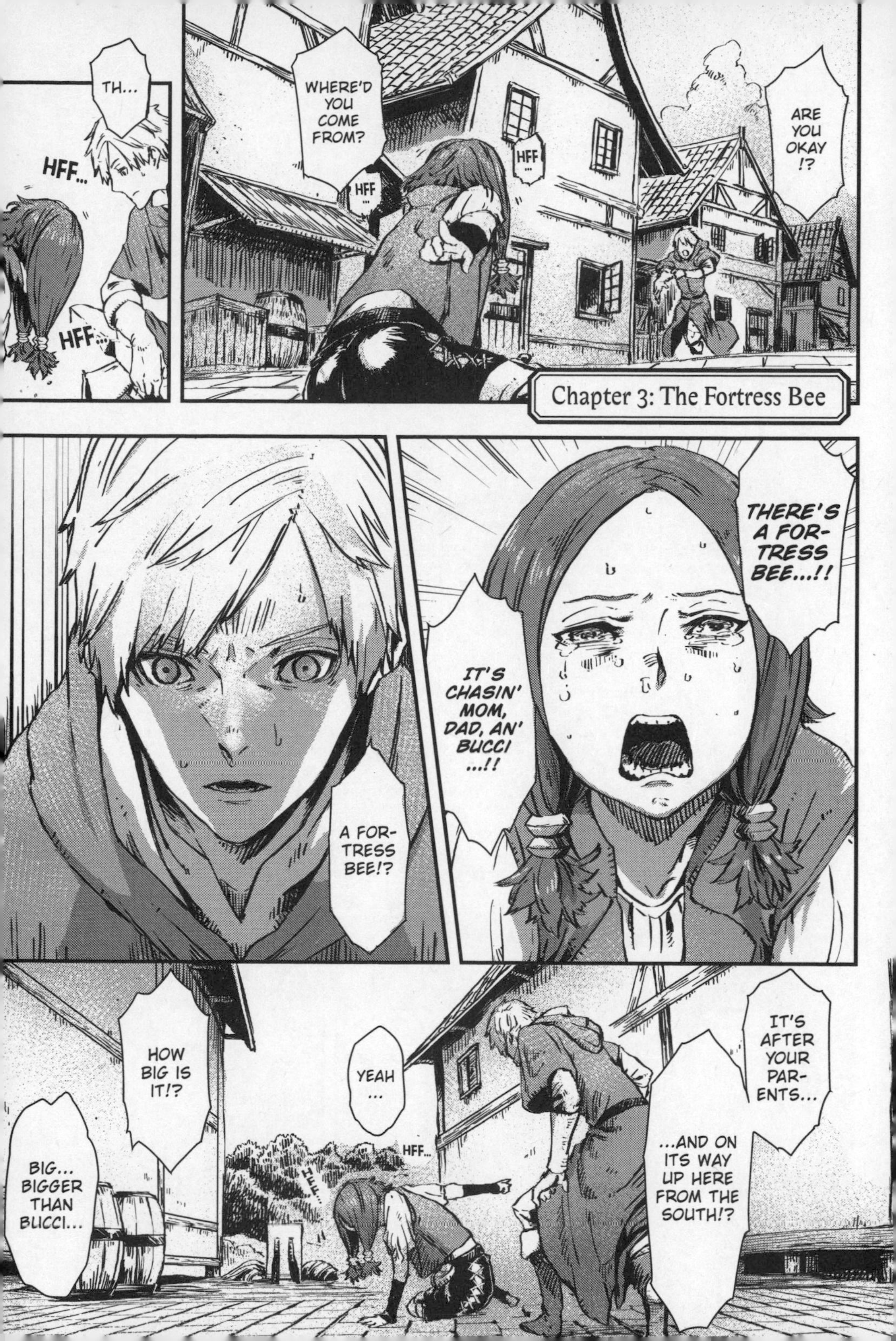
ARE YOU OKAY!?
HFF...
HFF...
WHERE'D YOU COME FROM?
Chapter 3: The Fortress Bee
TH...
HFF...
HFF...
THERE'S A FORTRESS BEE...!!
IT'S CHASIN' MOM, DAD, AN' BUCCI...!!
A FORTRESS BEE!?
IT'S AFTER YOUR PARENTS...
...AND ON ITS WAY UP HERE FROM THE SOUTH!?
YEAH...
HFF...
HFF...
HOW BIG IS IT!?
BIG... BIGGER THAN BUCCI...

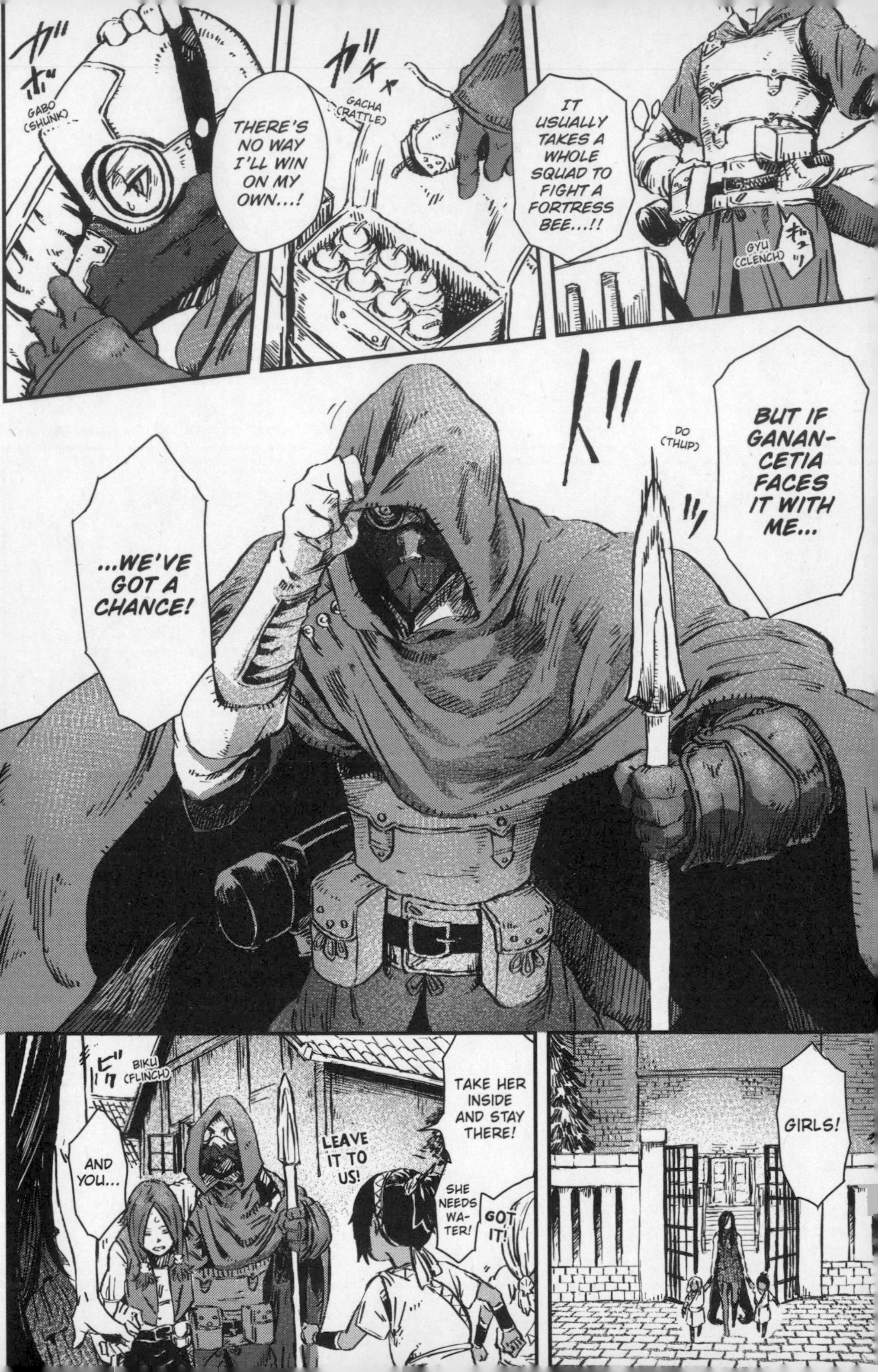
IT USUALLY TAKES A WHOLE SQUAD TO FIGHT A FORTRESS BEE...!!
GYU (CLENCH)
GACHA (RATTLE)
THERE'S NO WAY I'LL WIN ON MY OWN...!
GABO (SHUNK)
BUT IF GANAN-CETIA FACES IT WITH ME...
DO (THUP)
...WE'VE GOT A CHANCE!
GIRLS!
TAKE HER INSIDE AND STAY THERE!
SHE NEEDS WA-TER!
GOT IT!
LEAVE IT TO US!
BIKU (FLINCH)
AND YOU...

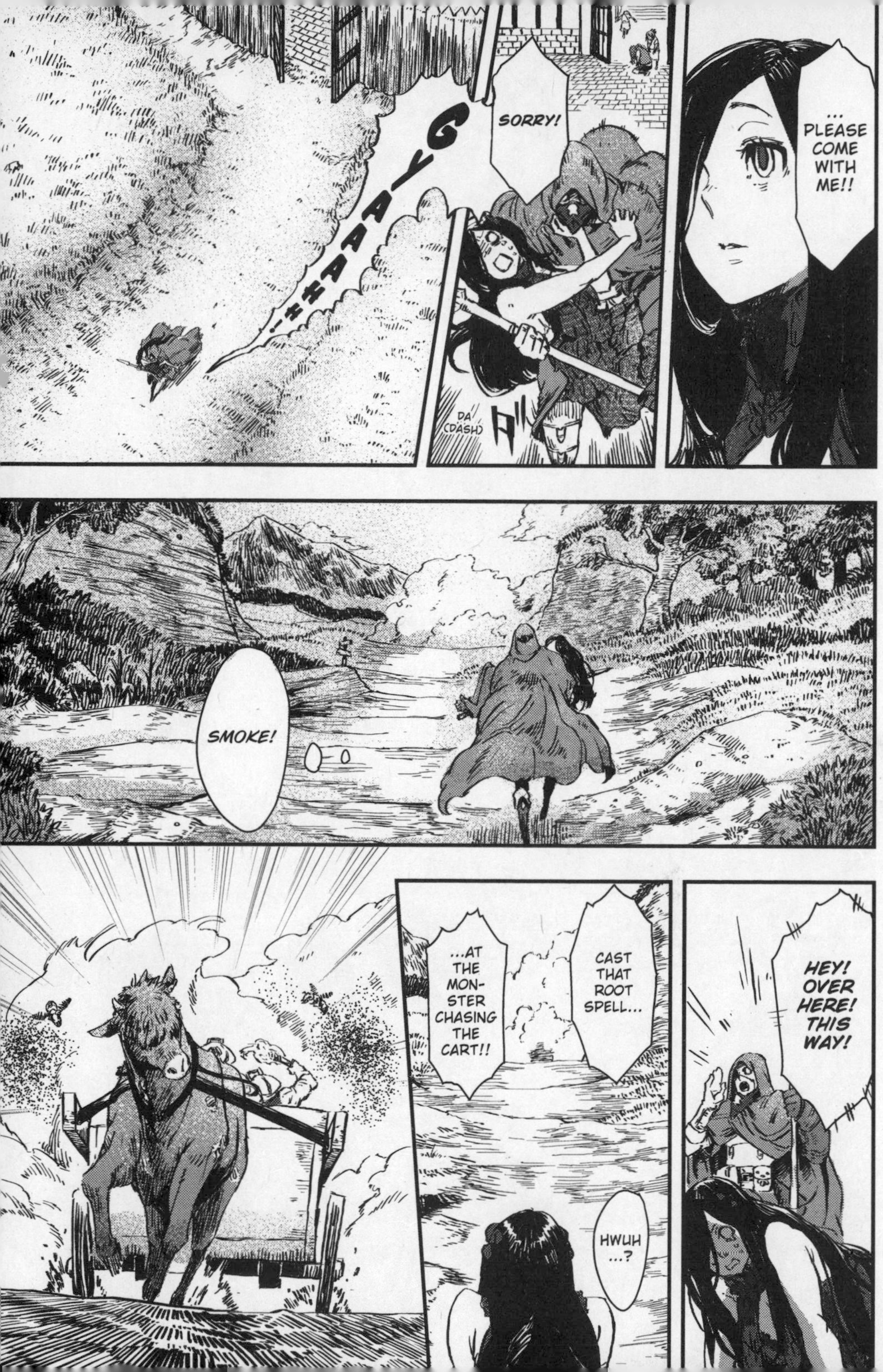
...PLEASE COME WITH ME!!
SORRY!
GYAAAHH!
DA (DASH)
SMOKE!
HEY! OVER HERE! THIS WAY!
CAST THAT ROOT SPELL...
...AT THE MON-STER CHASING THE CART!!
HWUH ...?

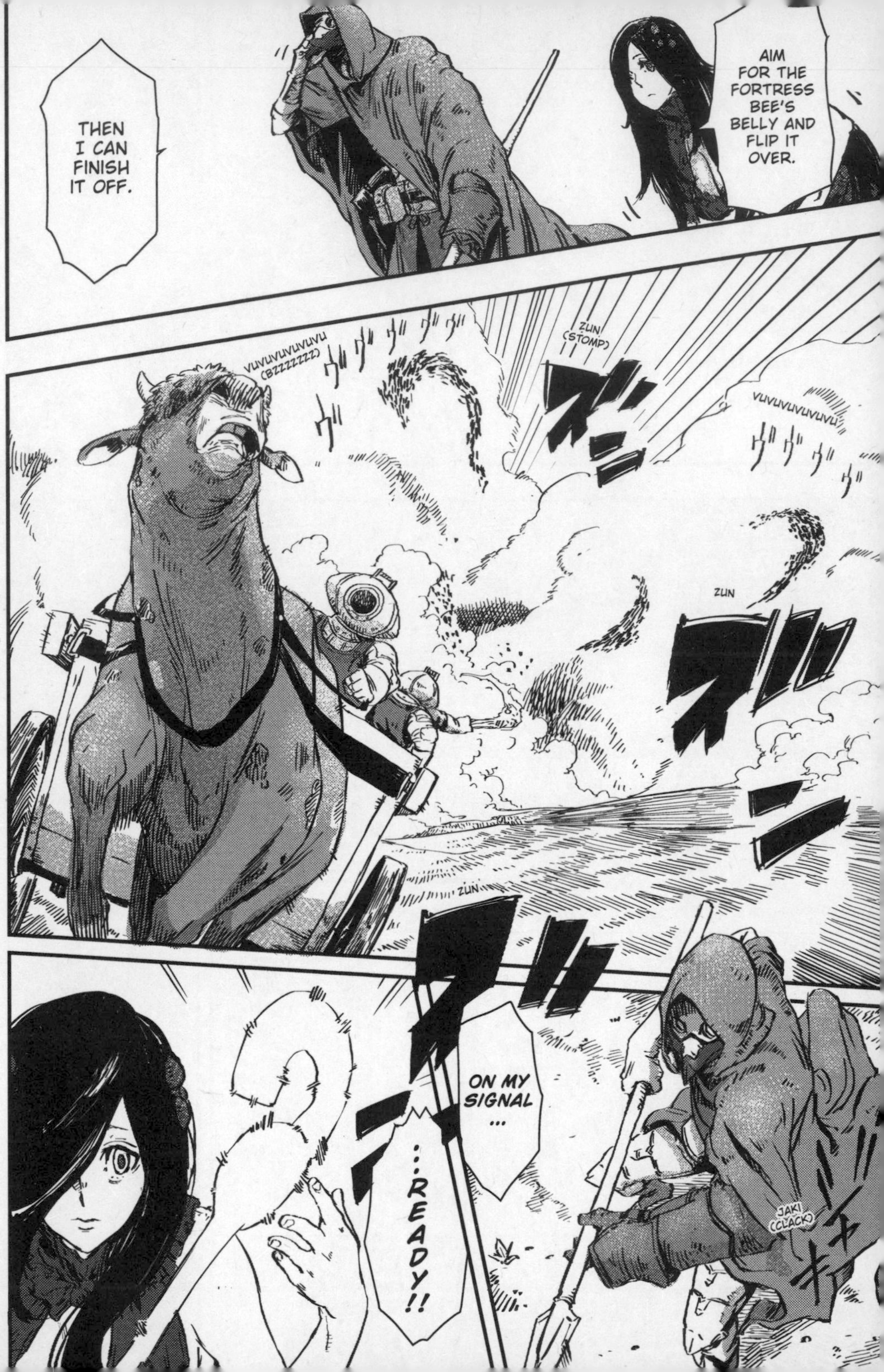
AIM FOR THE FORTRESS BEE'S BELLY AND FLIP IT OVER.
THEN I CAN FINISH IT OFF.
ZUN (STOMP)
VUVUVUVUVUVU
VUVUVUVUVUVU (BZZZZZZZ)
ZUN
ZUN
JAKI (CLACK)
ON MY SIGNAL ...
...READY!!

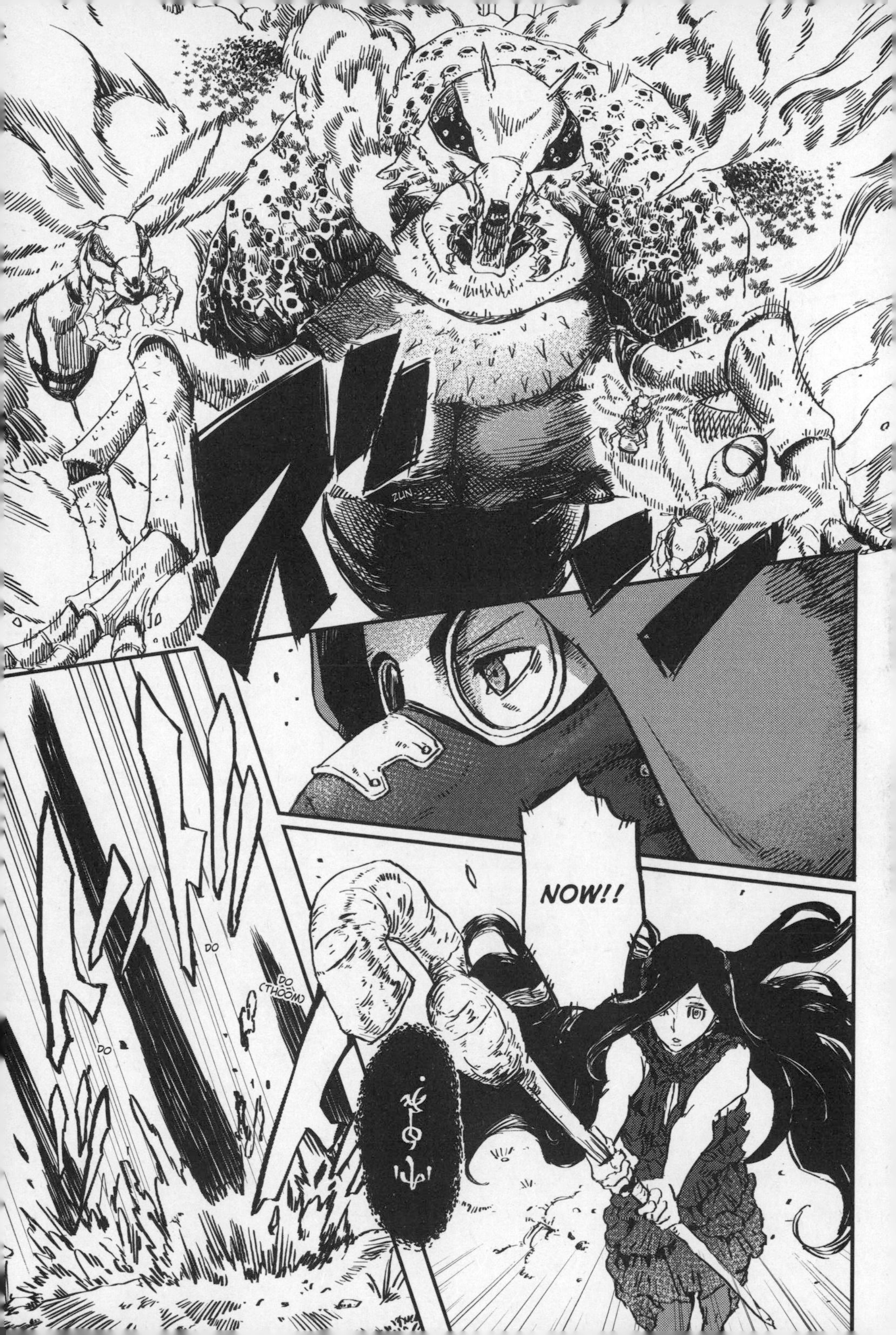
ZUN
NOW!!
DO
DO (THOOM)
DO

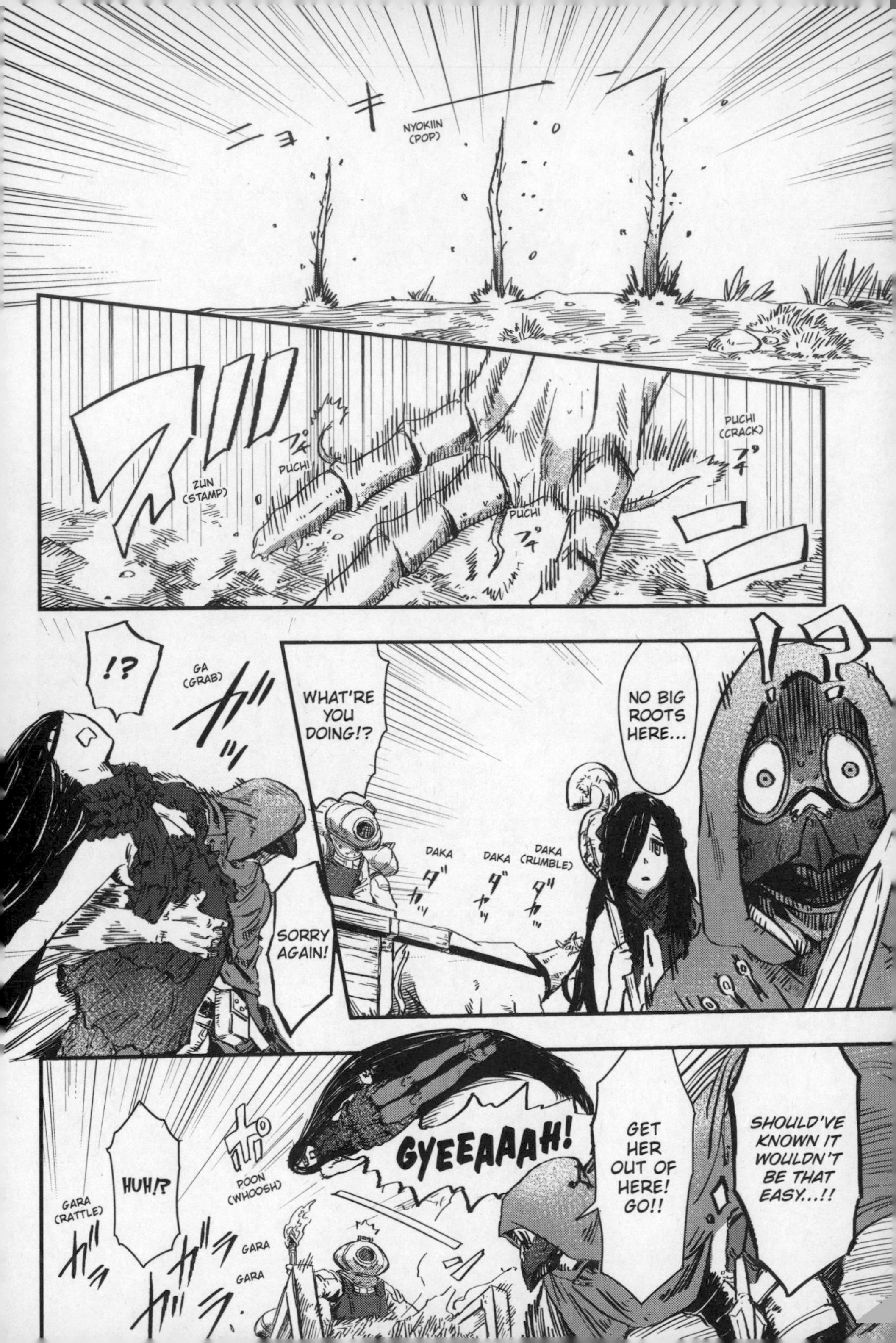
NYOKIIN (POP)
PUCHI (CRACK)
PUCHI
PUCHI
ZUN (STAMP)
!?
NO BIG ROOTS HERE...
DAKA (RUMBLE)
DAKA
DAKA
WHAT'RE YOU DOING!?
SORRY AGAIN!
GA (GRAB)
!?
SHOULD'VE KNOWN IT WOULDN'T BE THAT EASY...!!
GET HER OUT OF HERE! GO!!
GYEEAAAH!
POON (WHOOSH)
HUH!?
GARA
GARA
GARA (RATTLE)

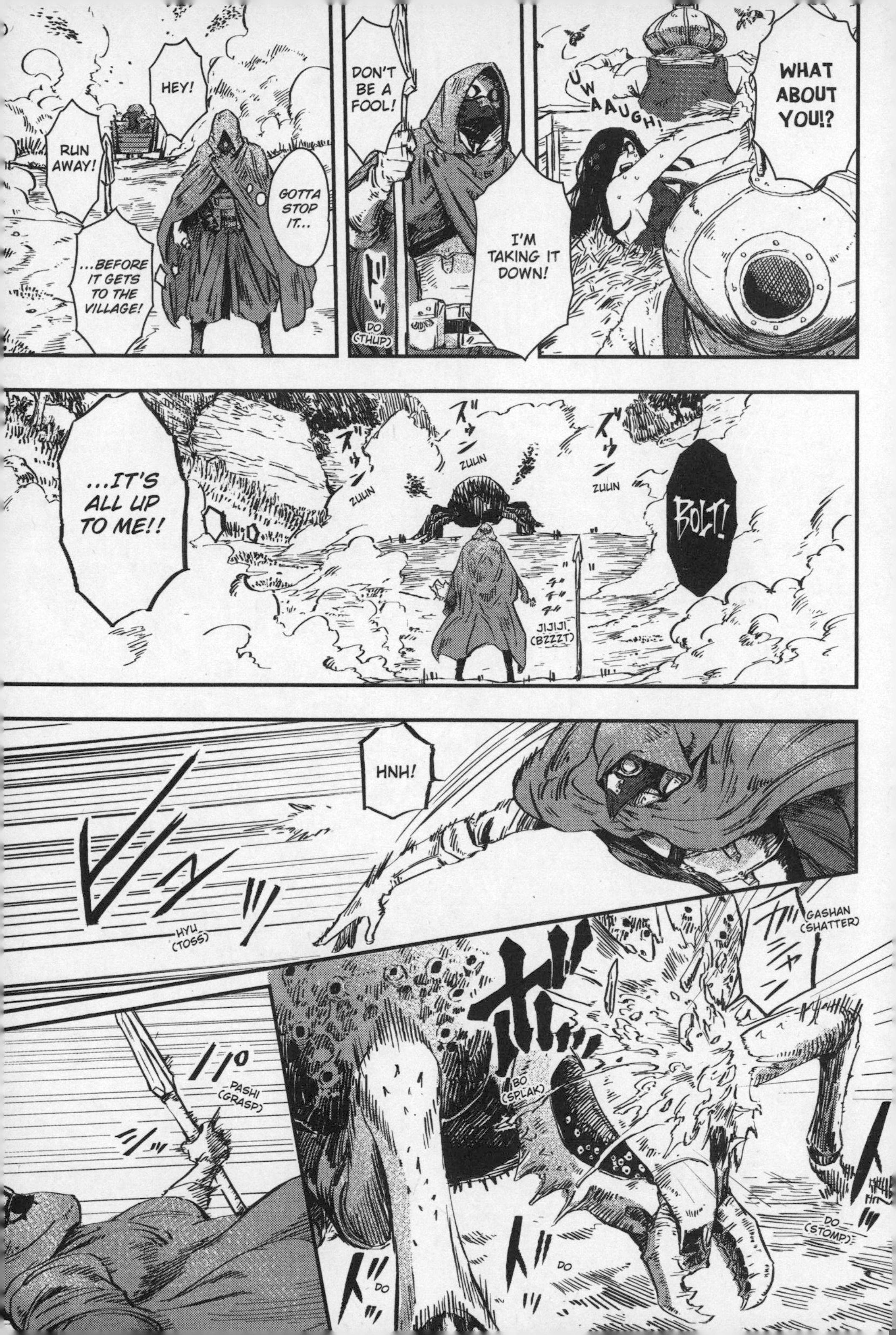
WHAT ABOUT YOU!?
UWAAUGH!
DON'T BE A FOOL!
I'M TAKING IT DOWN!
DO (THUP)
HEY!
GOTTA STOP IT...
RUN AWAY!
...BEFORE IT GETS TO THE VILLAGE!
BOLT!
ZUUN
ZUUN
ZUUN
JIJIJI (BZZZT)
...IT'S ALL UP TO ME!!
HNH!
GASHAN (SHATTER)
HYU (TOSS)
DO (STOMP)
BO (SPLAK)
DO
DO
PASHI (GRASP)

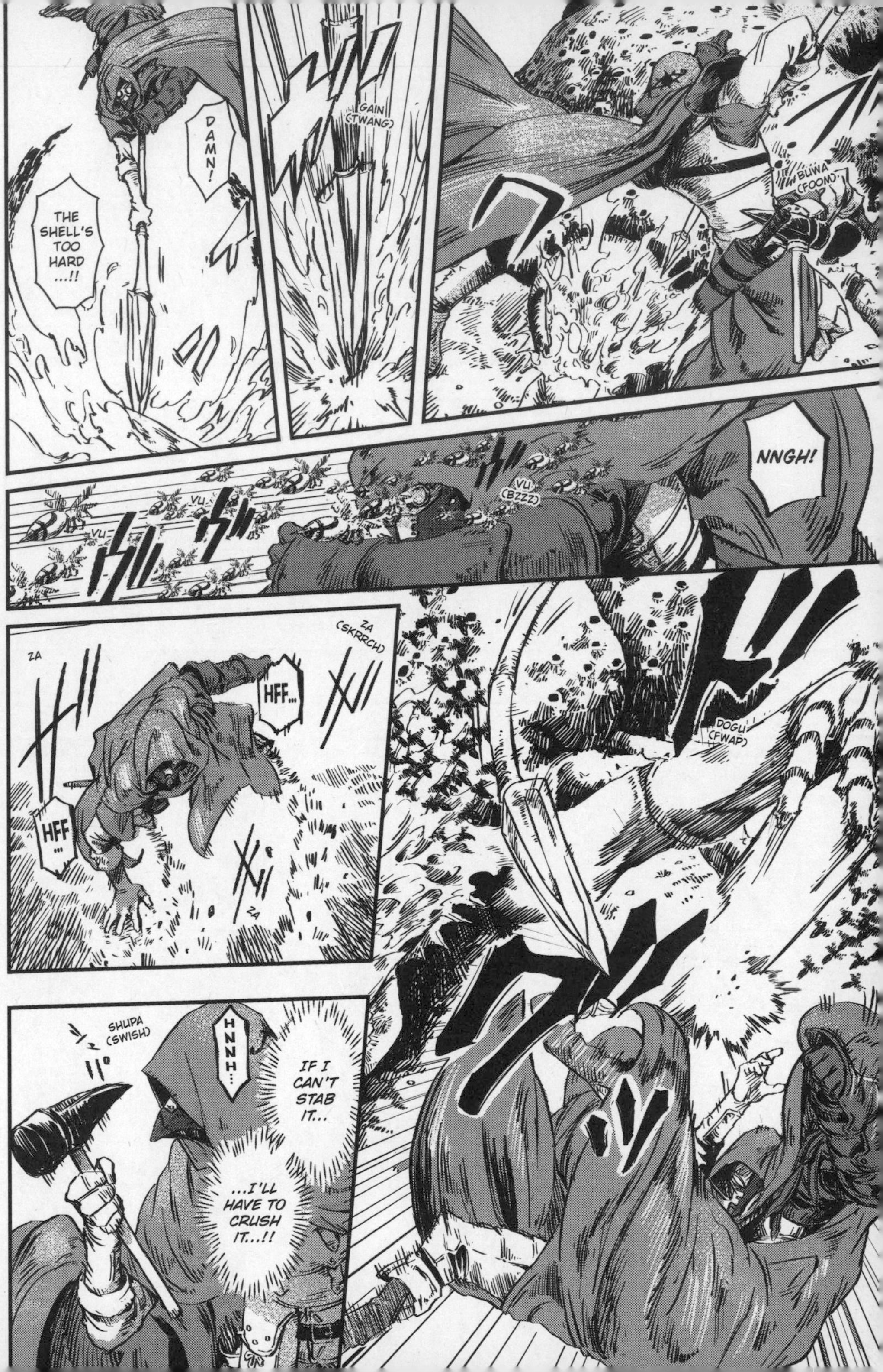
BUWA (FOOM)
GAIN (TWANG)
DAMN!
THE SHELL'S TOO HARD ...!!
NNGH!
VU (BZZZ)
VU
VU
DOGU (FWAP)
ZA (SKRRCH)
HFF...
ZA
HFF...
ZA
HNNH...
IF I CAN'T STAB IT...
...I'LL HAVE TO CRUSH IT...!!
SHUPA (SWISH)

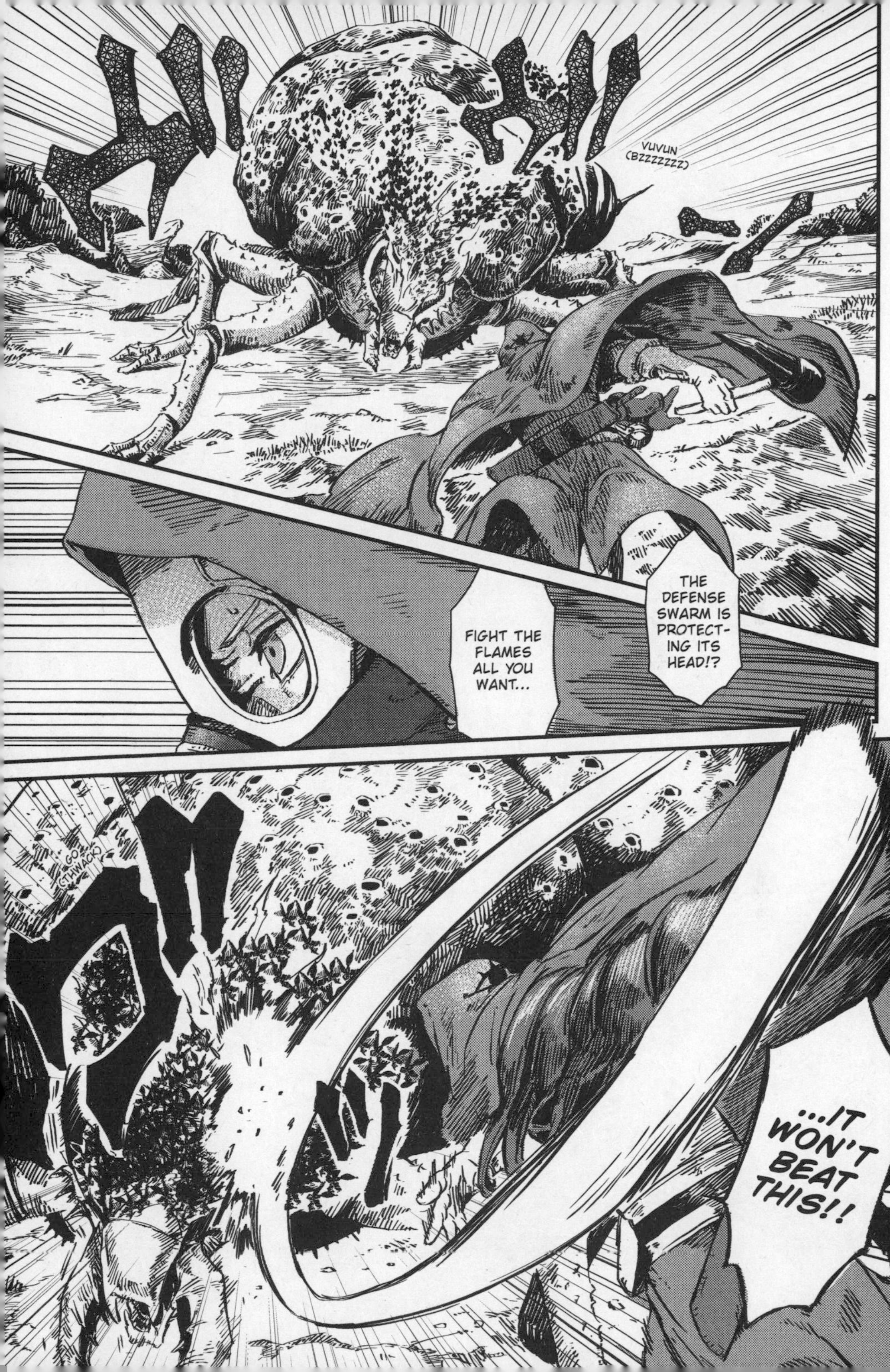
VUVUN
(BZZZZZZZ)
THE DEFENSE SWARM IS PROTECTING ITS HEAD!?
FIGHT THE FLAMES ALL YOU WANT...
GO
(THWACK)
...IT WON'T BEAT THIS!!

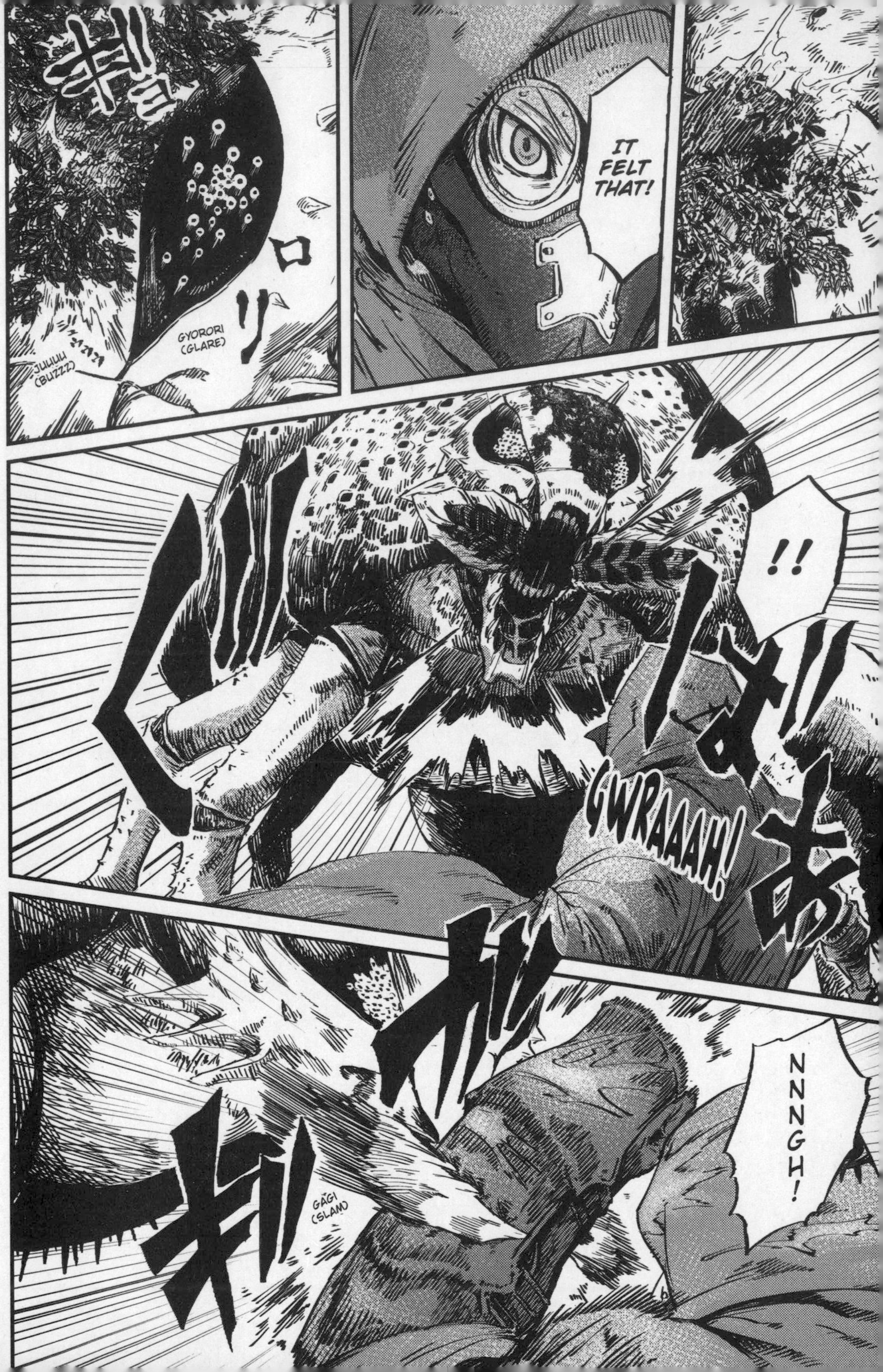
IT FELT THAT!
GYORORI (GLARE)
JUUUU (BUZZZ)
!!
GWRAAAH!
NNNGH!
GAGI (SLAM)

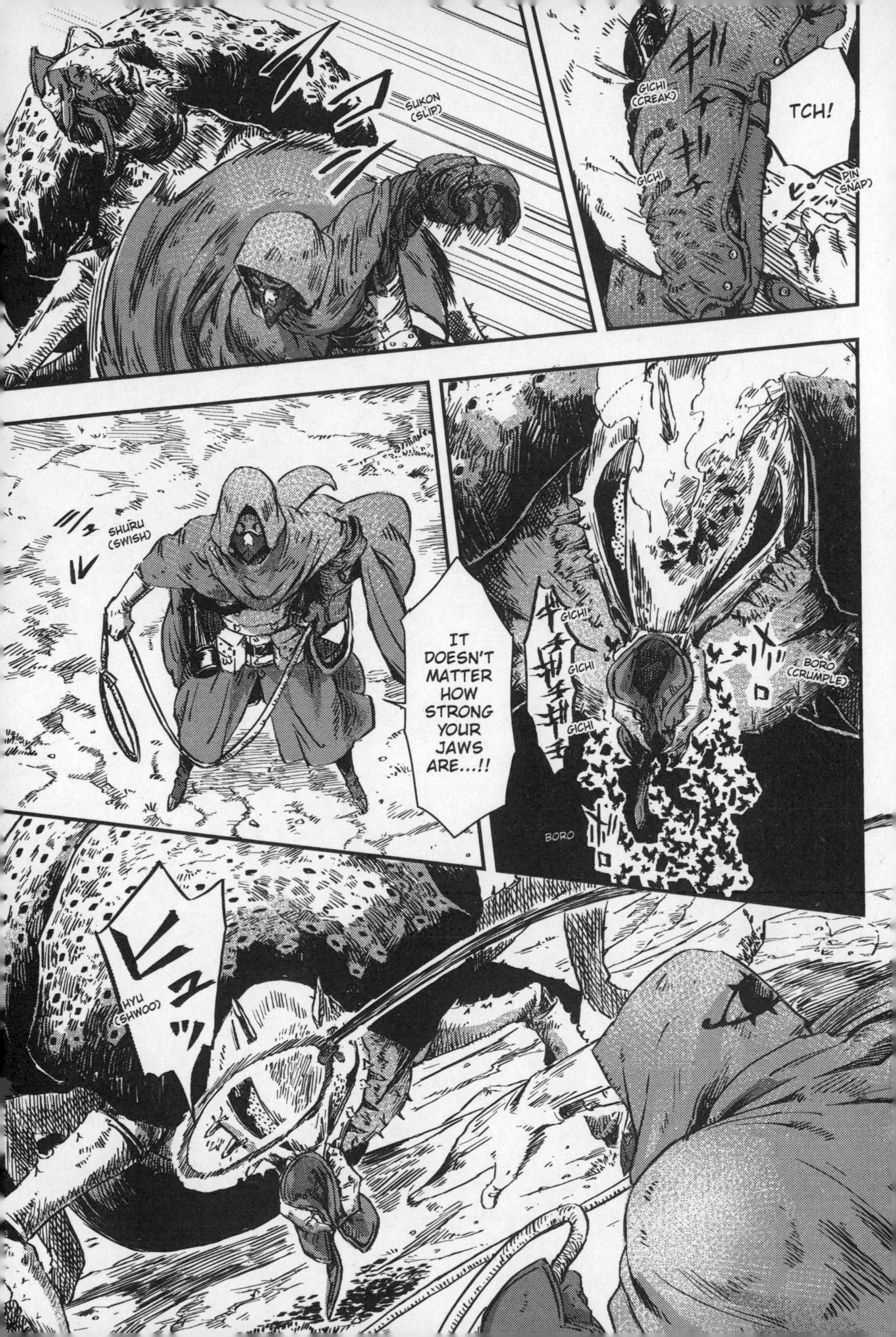
TCH!
GICHI (CREAK)
GICHI
PIN (SNAP)
SLIKON (SLIP)
BORO (CRUMPLE)
GICHI
GICHI
GICHI
BORO
IT DOESN'T MATTER HOW STRONG YOUR JAWS ARE...!!
SHURU (SWISH)
HYU (SHWOO)

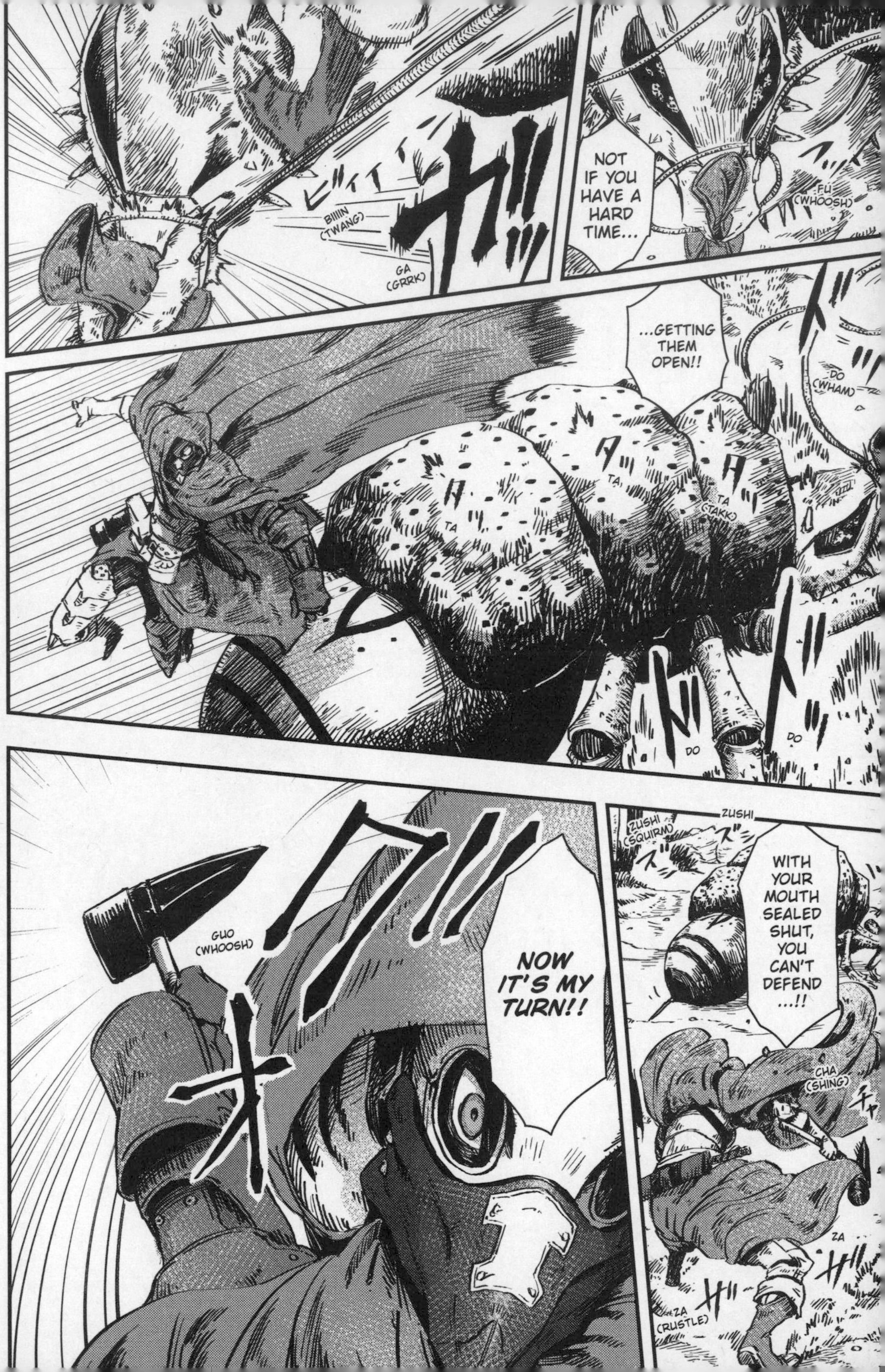
NOT IF YOU HAVE A HARD TIME...
FU (WHOOSH)
BIIIN (TWANG)
GA (GRRK)
...GETTING THEM OPEN!!
DO (WHAM)
TA (TAKK)
TA
TA
DO
DO
ZUSHI
ZUSHI (SQUIRM)
WITH YOUR MOUTH SEALED SHUT, YOU CAN'T DEFEND ...!!
CHA (SHING)
ZA
ZA (RUSTLE)
GUO (WHOOSH)
NOW IT'S MY TURN!!

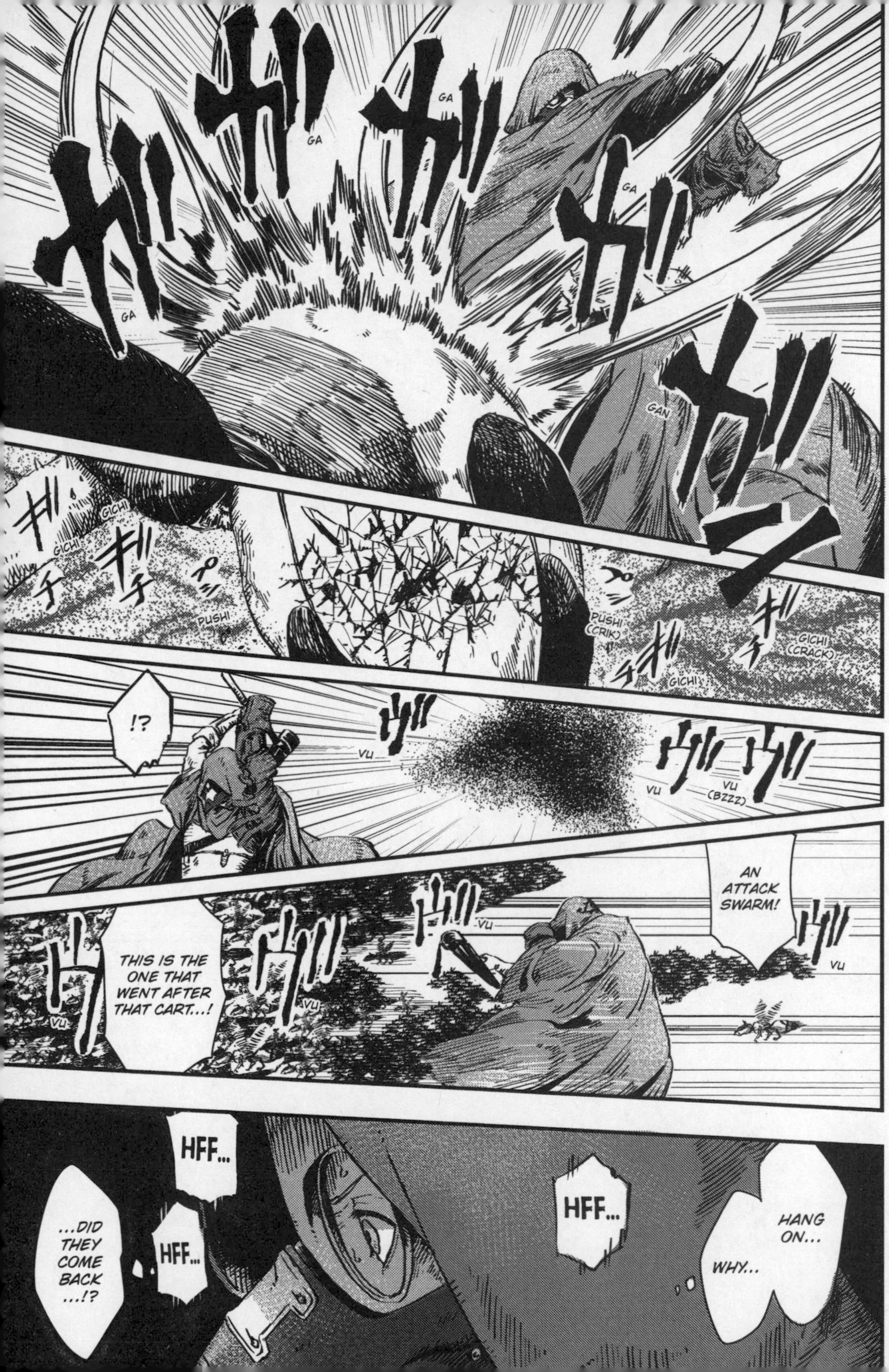
GAN
GA
GA
GA
GA
GICHI (CRACK)
GICHI
PUSHI (CRIK)
PUSHI
GICHI
GICHI
VU (BZZZ)
VU
VU
!?
VU
AN ATTACK SWARM!
VU
VU
THIS IS THE ONE THAT WENT AFTER THAT CART...!
VU
HANG ON...
WHY...
HFF...
HFF...
HFF...
...DID THEY COME BACK ...!?

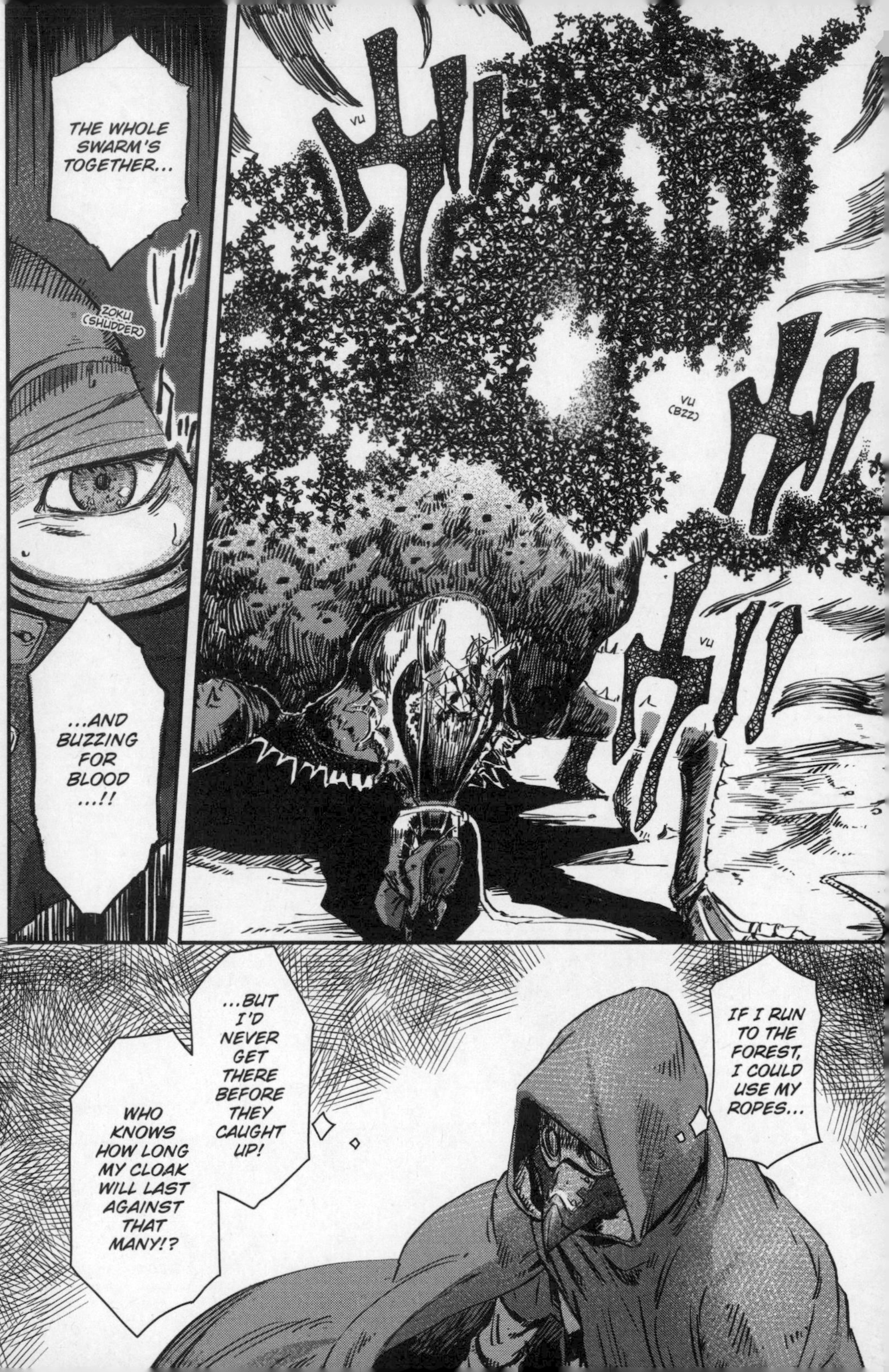
VU
VU (BZZ)
VU
THE WHOLE SWARM'S TOGETHER...
ZOKU (SHUDDER)
...AND BUZZING FOR BLOOD ...!!
IF I RUN TO THE FOREST, I COULD USE MY ROPES...
...BUT I'D NEVER GET THERE BEFORE THEY CAUGHT UP!
WHO KNOWS HOW LONG MY CLOAK WILL LAST AGAINST THAT MANY!?

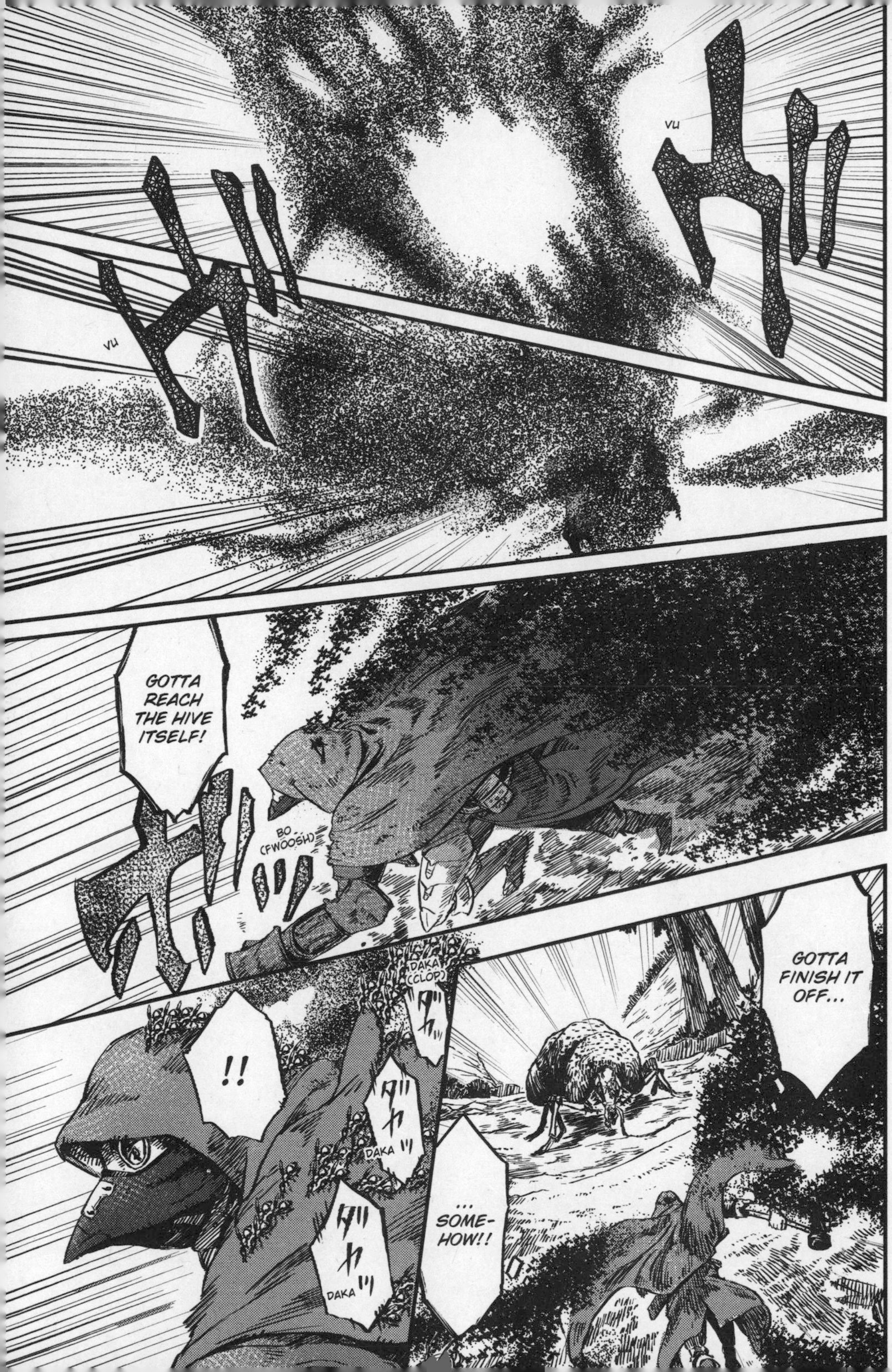
VU
VU
GOTTA REACH THE HIVE ITSELF!
BO (FWOOSH)
GOTTA FINISH IT OFF...
DAKA (CLOP)
...SOME-HOW!!
DAKA
!!
DAKA

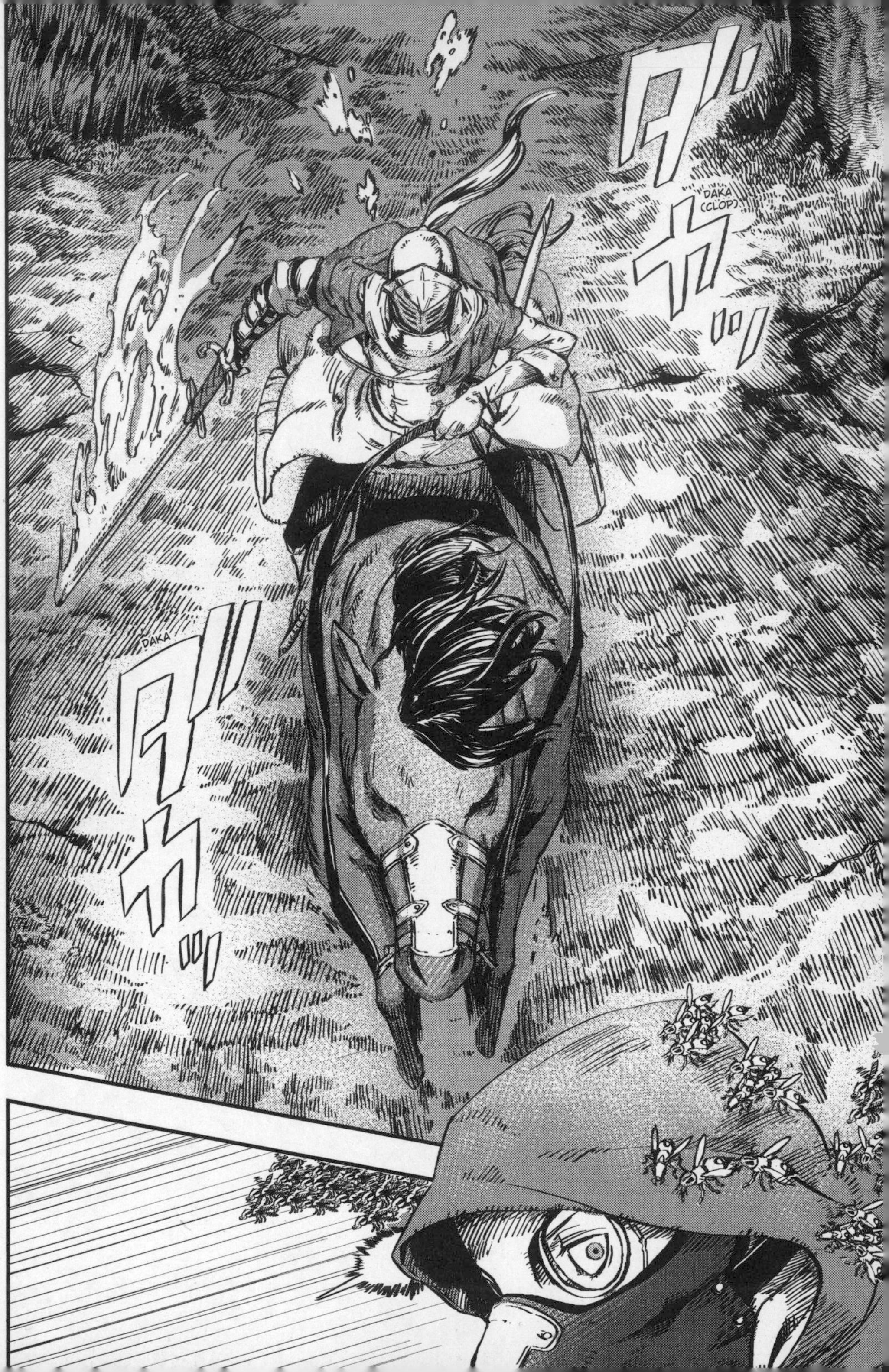
ダカッ
DAKA (CLOP)
DAKA
ダカッ

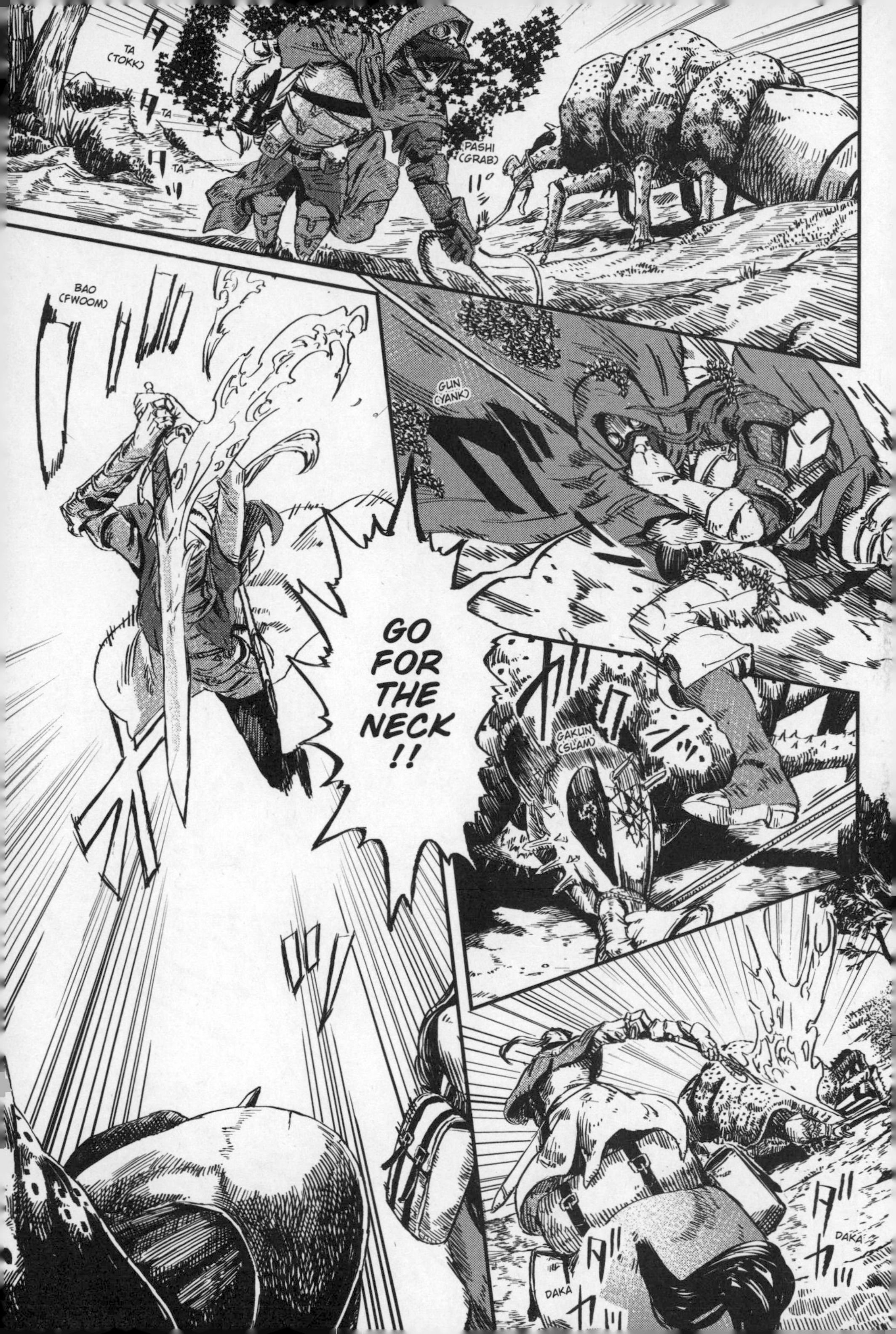
PASHI (GRAB)
TA (TOKK)
TA
TA
GUN (YANK)
GAKUN (SLAM)
BAO (FWOOM)
GO FOR THE NECK!!
DAKA
DAKA

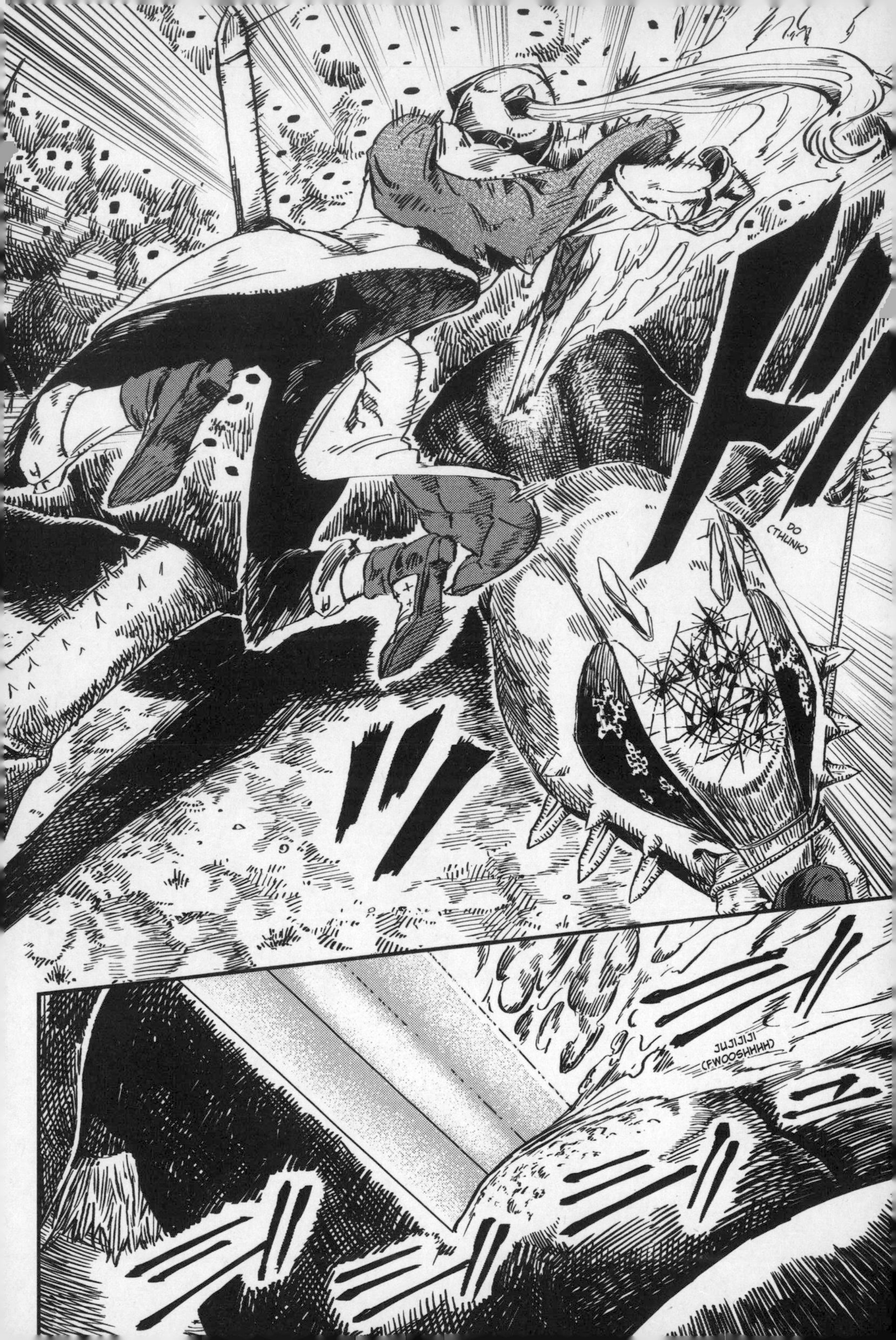
DO
(THUNK)
JUJIJIJI
(FWOOSHHHH)

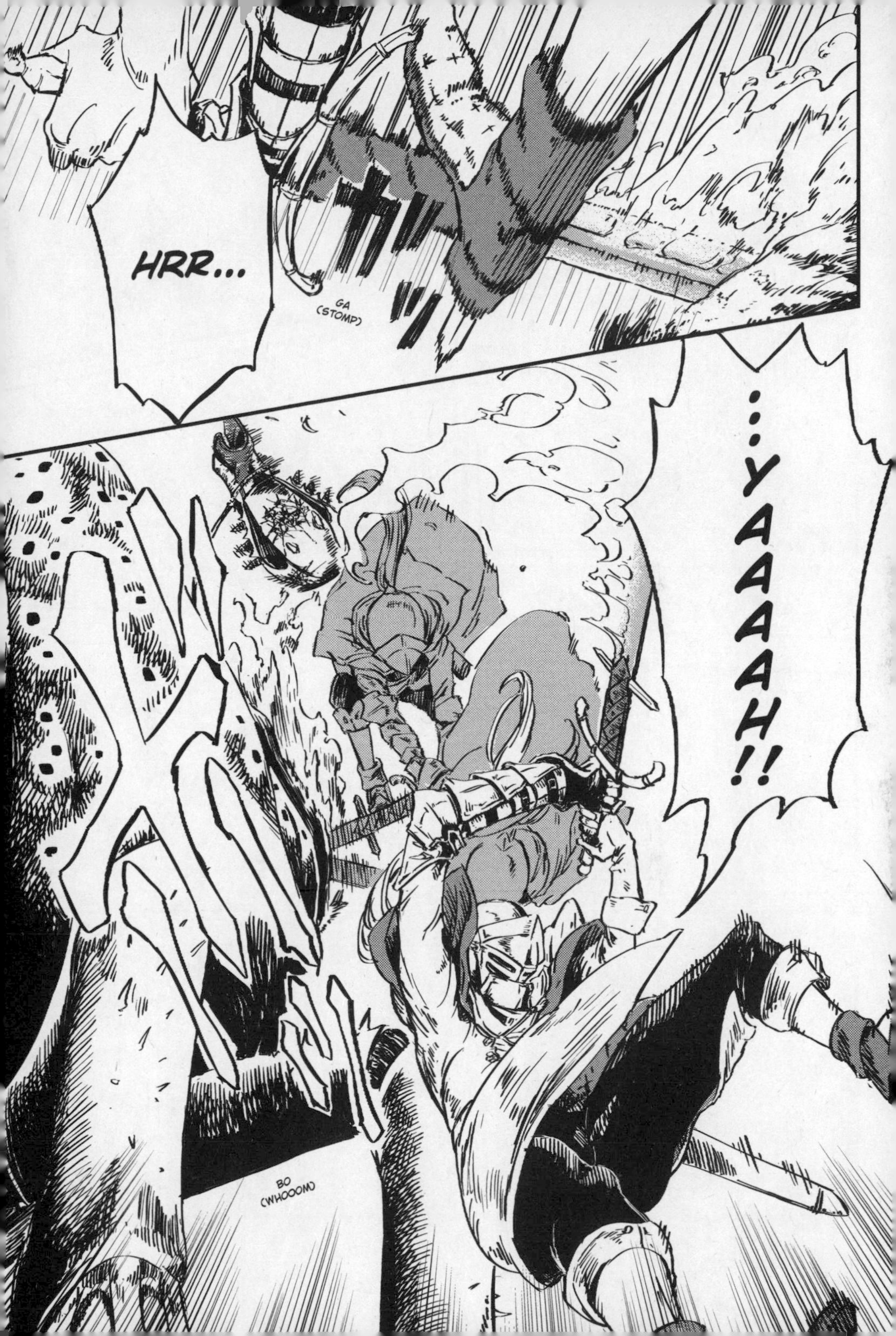
HRR...
GA
(STOMP)
...YAAAAAH!!
BO
(WHOOOM)

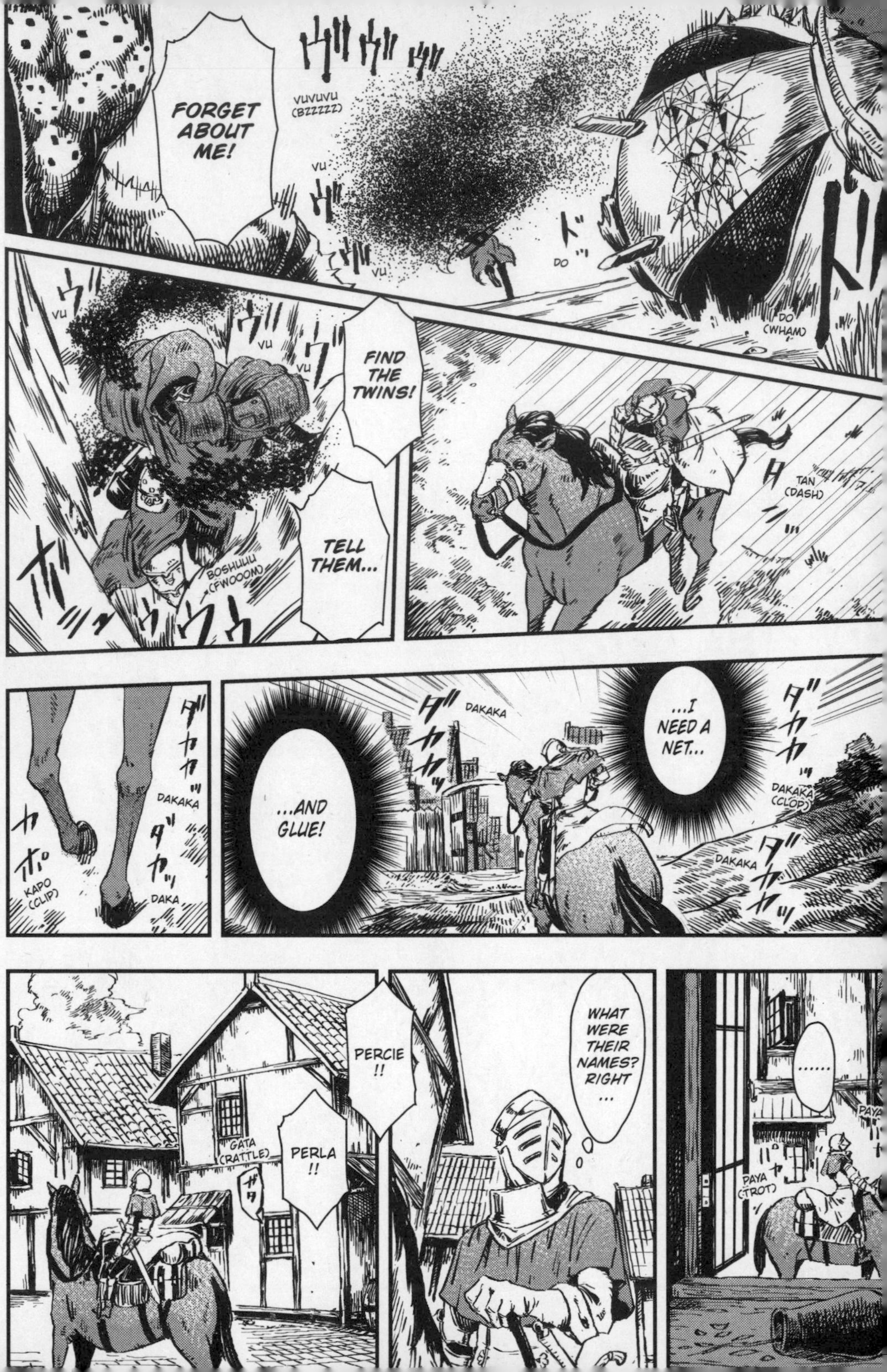
DO (WHAM)
DO
VUVUVU (BZZZZZ)
FORGET ABOUT ME!
VU
VU
TAN (DASH)
FIND THE TWINS!
VU
VU
VU
TELL THEM...
BOSHUUU (FWOOOM)
DAKAKA (CLOP)
...I NEED A NET...
DAKAKA
DAKAKA
...AND GLUE!
DAKAKA
KAPO (CLIP)
DAKA
......
PAYA
PAYA (TROT)
WHAT WERE THEIR NAMES? RIGHT...
PERCIE!!
GATA (RATTLE)
PERLA!!

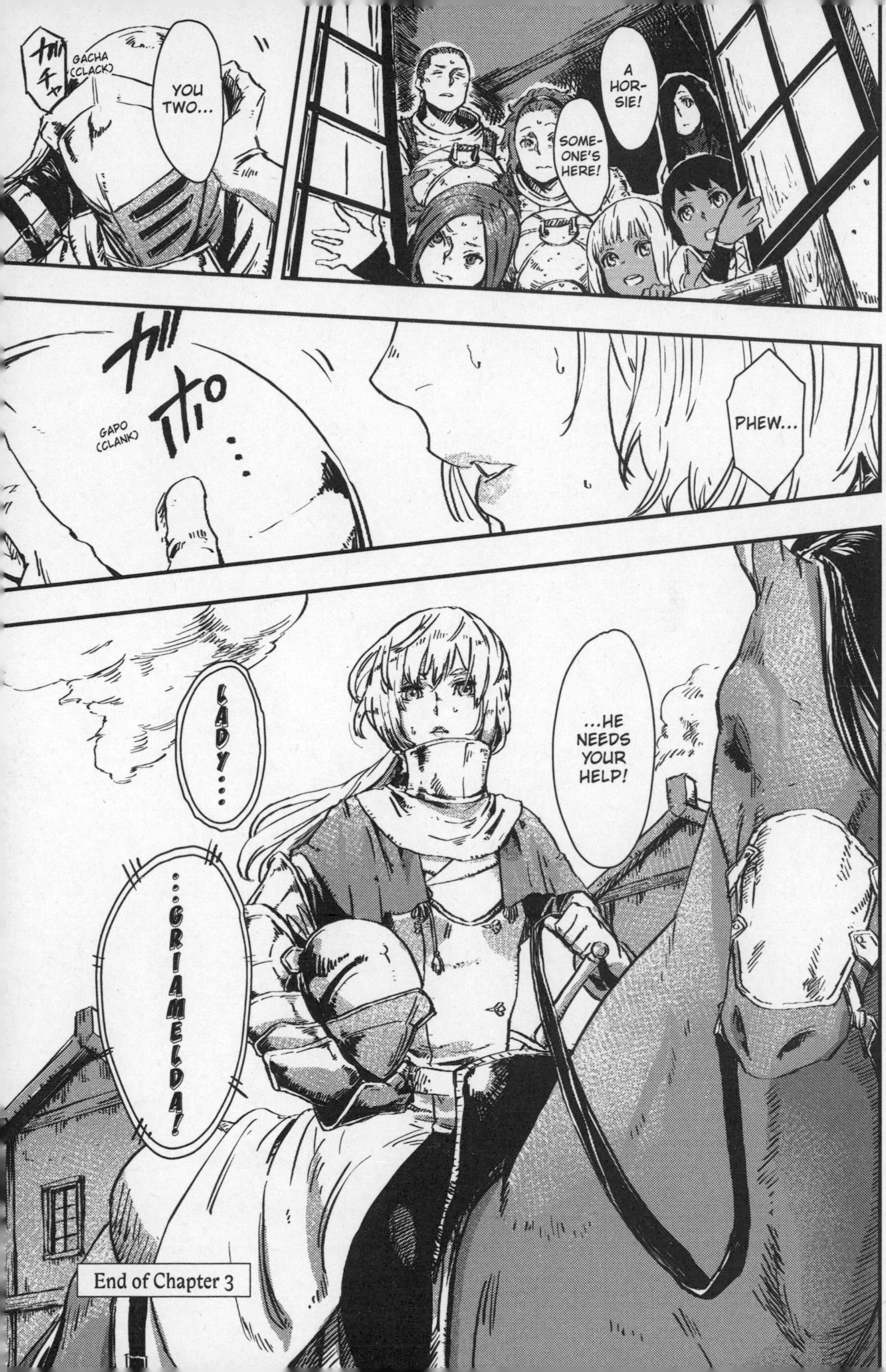
A HOR-SIE!
SOME-ONE'S HERE!
YOU TWO...
カチャ
GACHA (CLACK)
PHEW...
GAPO (CLANK)
...
...HE NEEDS YOUR HELP!
LADY...
...GRIAMELDA!

End of Chapter 3

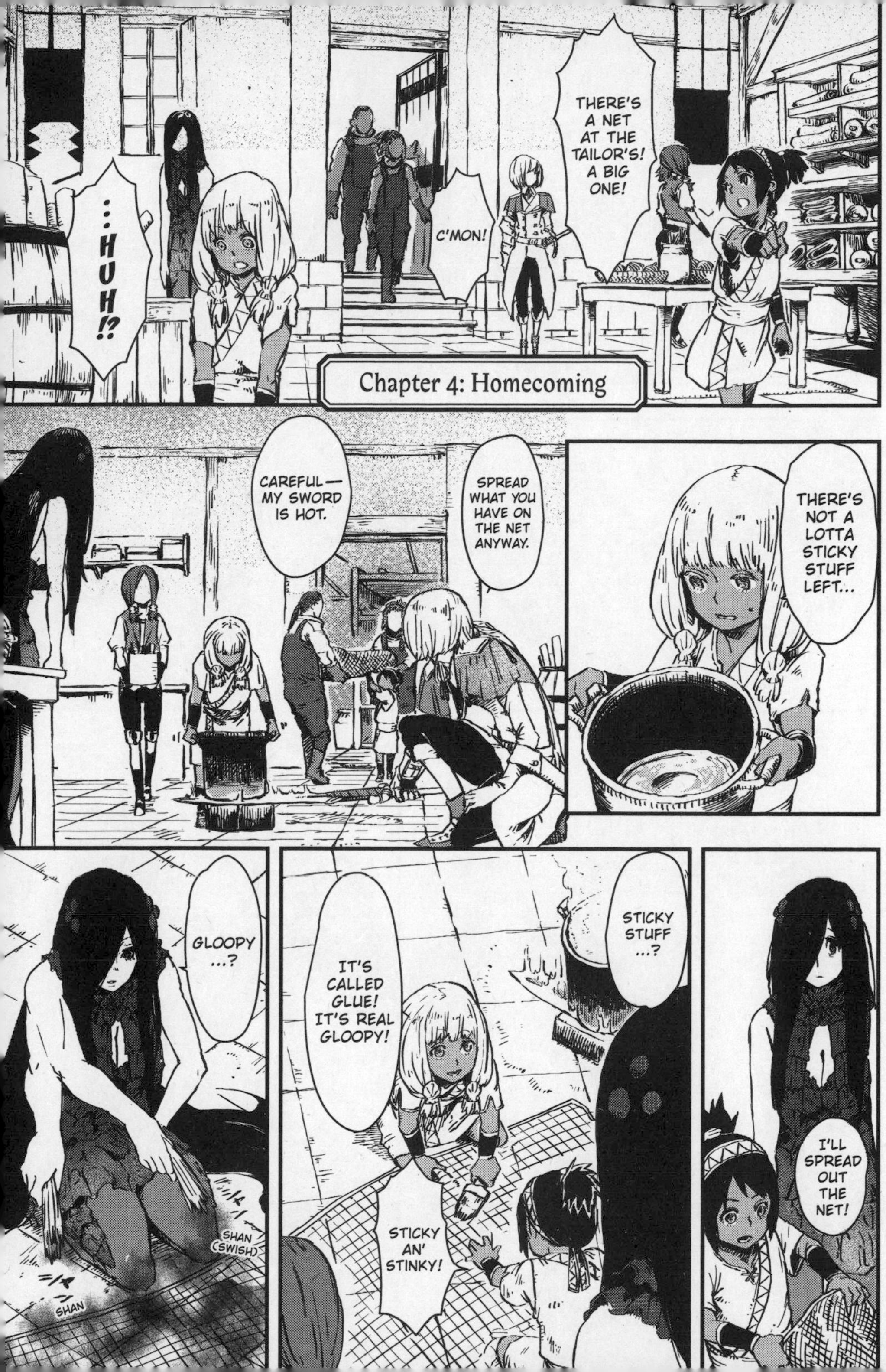

THERE'S A NET AT THE TAILOR'S! A BIG ONE!
C'MON!
...HUH!?
Chapter 4: Homecoming
THERE'S NOT A LOTTA STICKY STUFF LEFT...
SPREAD WHAT YOU HAVE ON THE NET ANYWAY.
CAREFUL— MY SWORD IS HOT.
I'LL SPREAD OUT THE NET!
STICKY STUFF ...?
IT'S CALLED GLUE! IT'S REAL GLOOPY!
STICKY AN' STINKY!
GLOOPY ...?
SHAN (SWISH)
SHAN

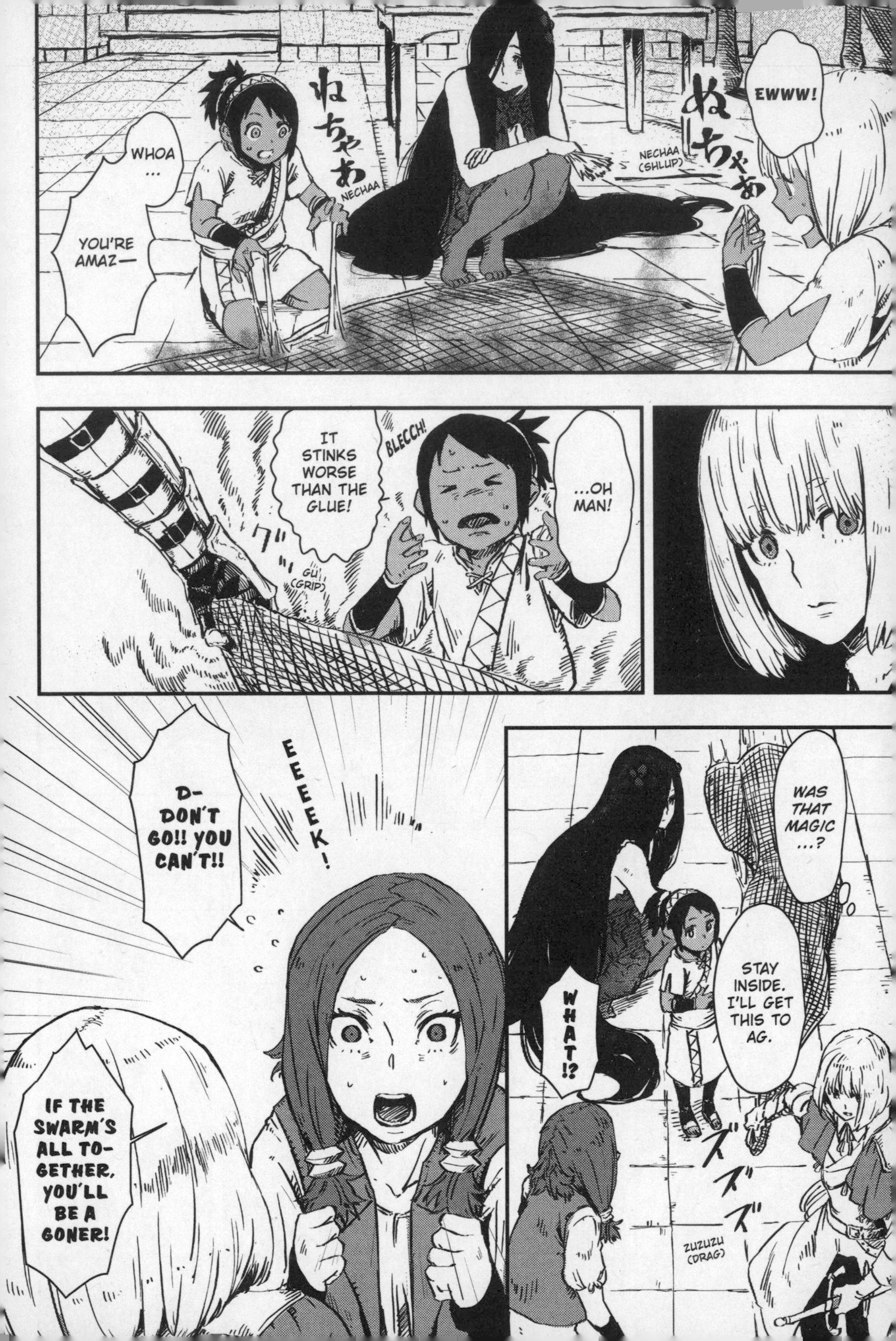
EWWW!
ぬちゃあ
NECHAA (SHLUP)
ねちゃあ
NECHAA
WHOA ...
YOU'RE AMAZ—
...OH MAN!
BLECCH!
IT STINKS WORSE THAN THE GLUE!
グッ
GU (GRIP)
WAS THAT MAGIC ...?
STAY INSIDE. I'LL GET THIS TO AG.
WHAT!?
ズズズ
ZUZUZU (DRAG)
EEEEEK!
D-DON'T GO!! YOU CAN'T!!
IF THE SWARM'S ALL TO-GETHER, YOU'LL BE A GONER!

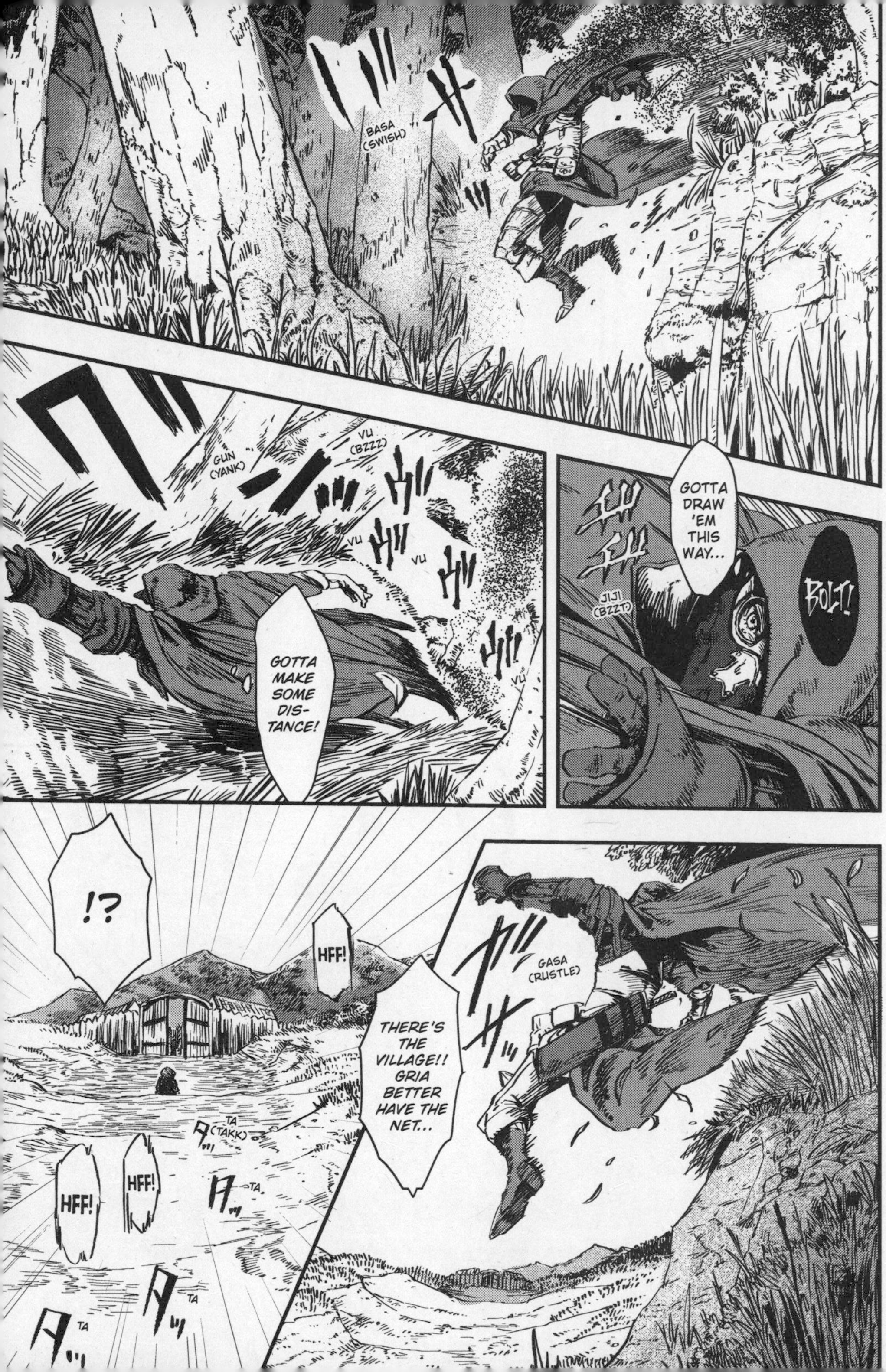
BASA (SWISH)
GOTTA DRAW 'EM THIS WAY...
JIJI (BZZT)
BOLT!
GUN (YANK)
VU (BZZZ)
VU
VU
VU
GOTTA MAKE SOME DIS-TANCE!
GASA (RUSTLE)
THERE'S THE VILLAGE!! GRIA BETTER HAVE THE NET...
!?
HFF!
TA (TAKK)
HFF!
HFF!
TA
TA
TA

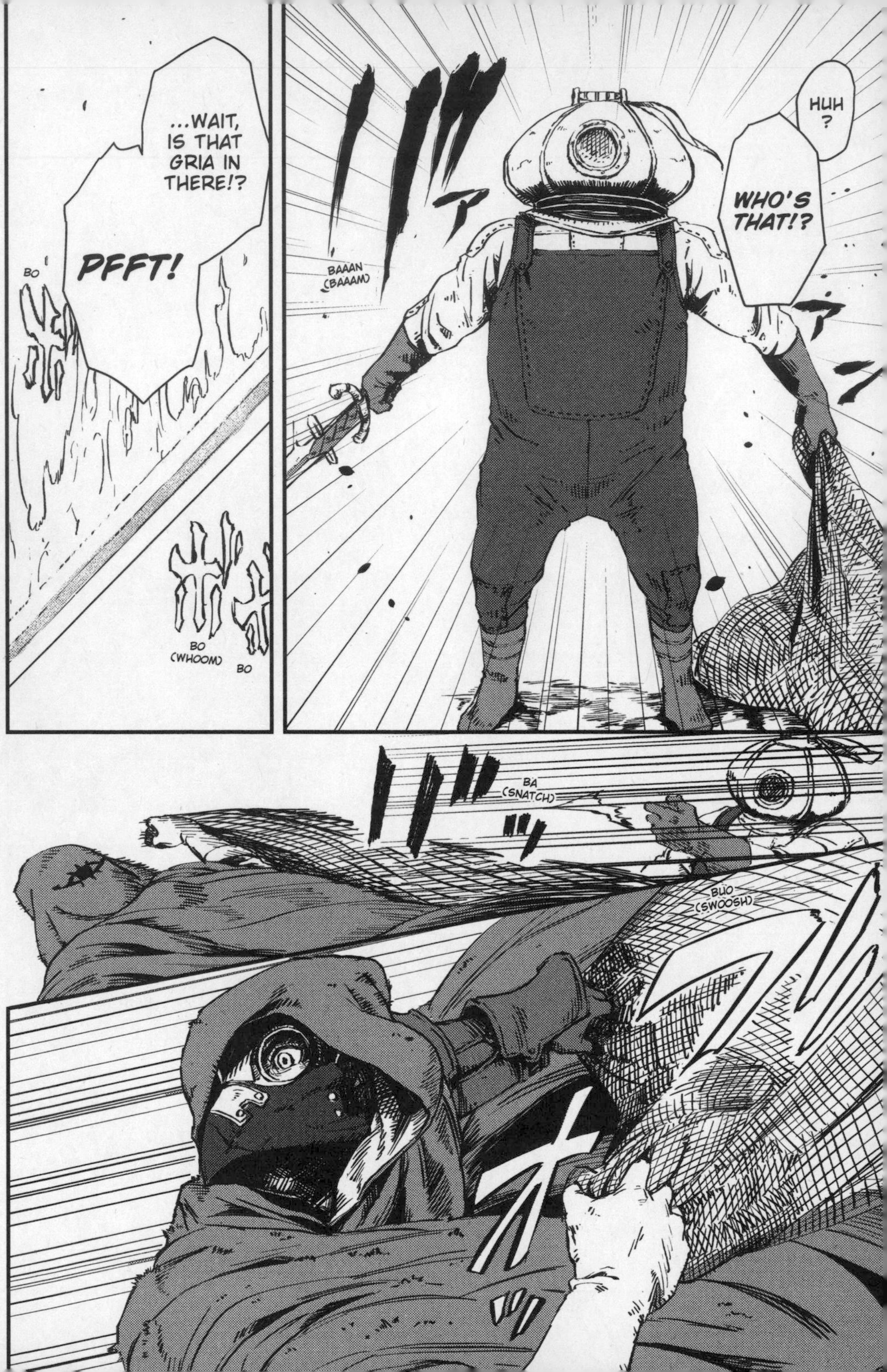
HUH?
WHO'S THAT!?
BAAAN (BAAAM)
...WAIT, IS THAT GRIA IN THERE!?
PFFT!
BO
BO (WHOOM)
BO
BA (SNATCH)
BUO (SWOOSH)

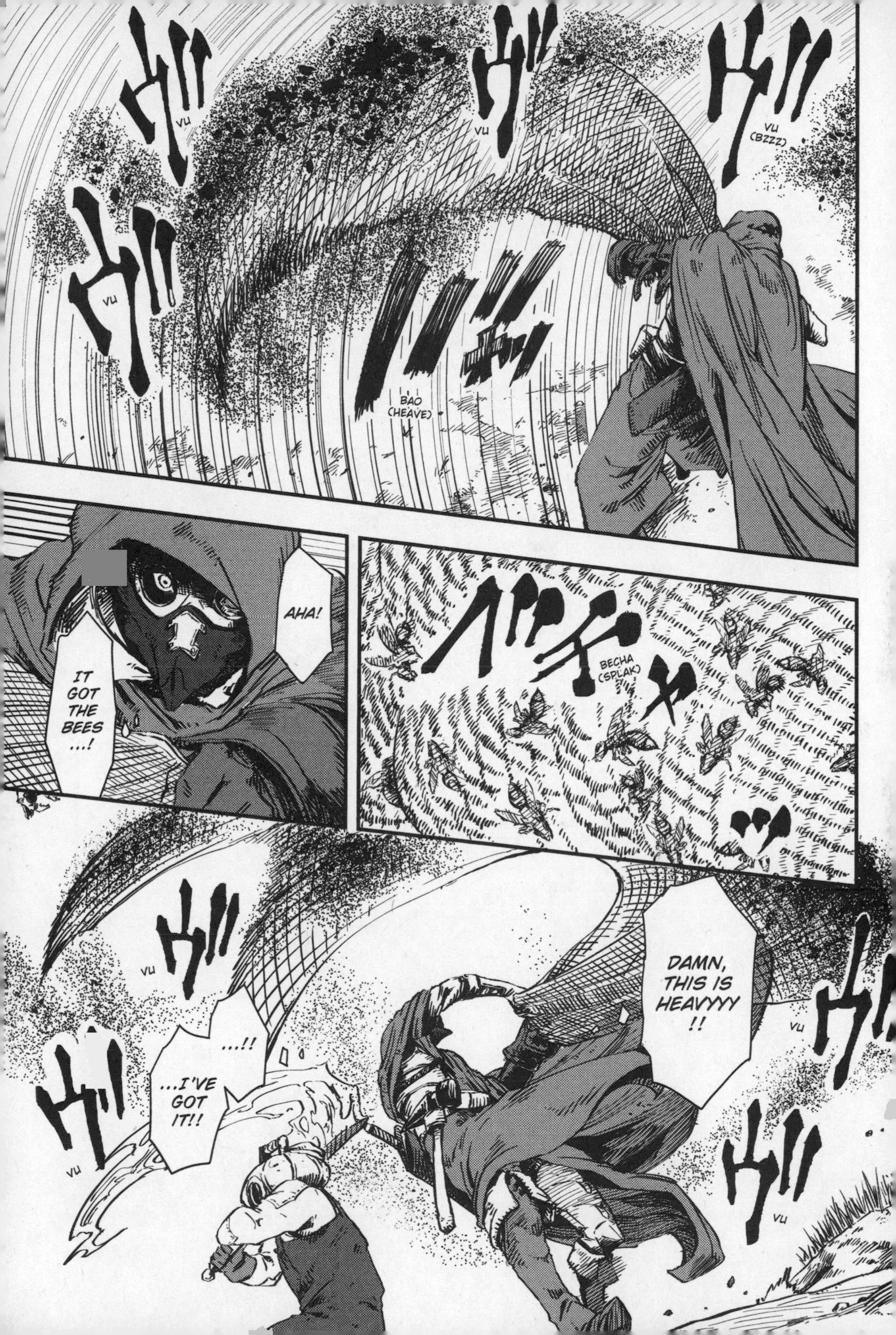
VU (BZZZ)
VU
VU
VU
BAO (HEAVE)
BECHA (SPLAK)
AHA!
IT GOT THE BEES ...!
DAMN, THIS IS HEAVYYY !!
VU
VU
...!!
...I'VE GOT IT!!
VU
VU

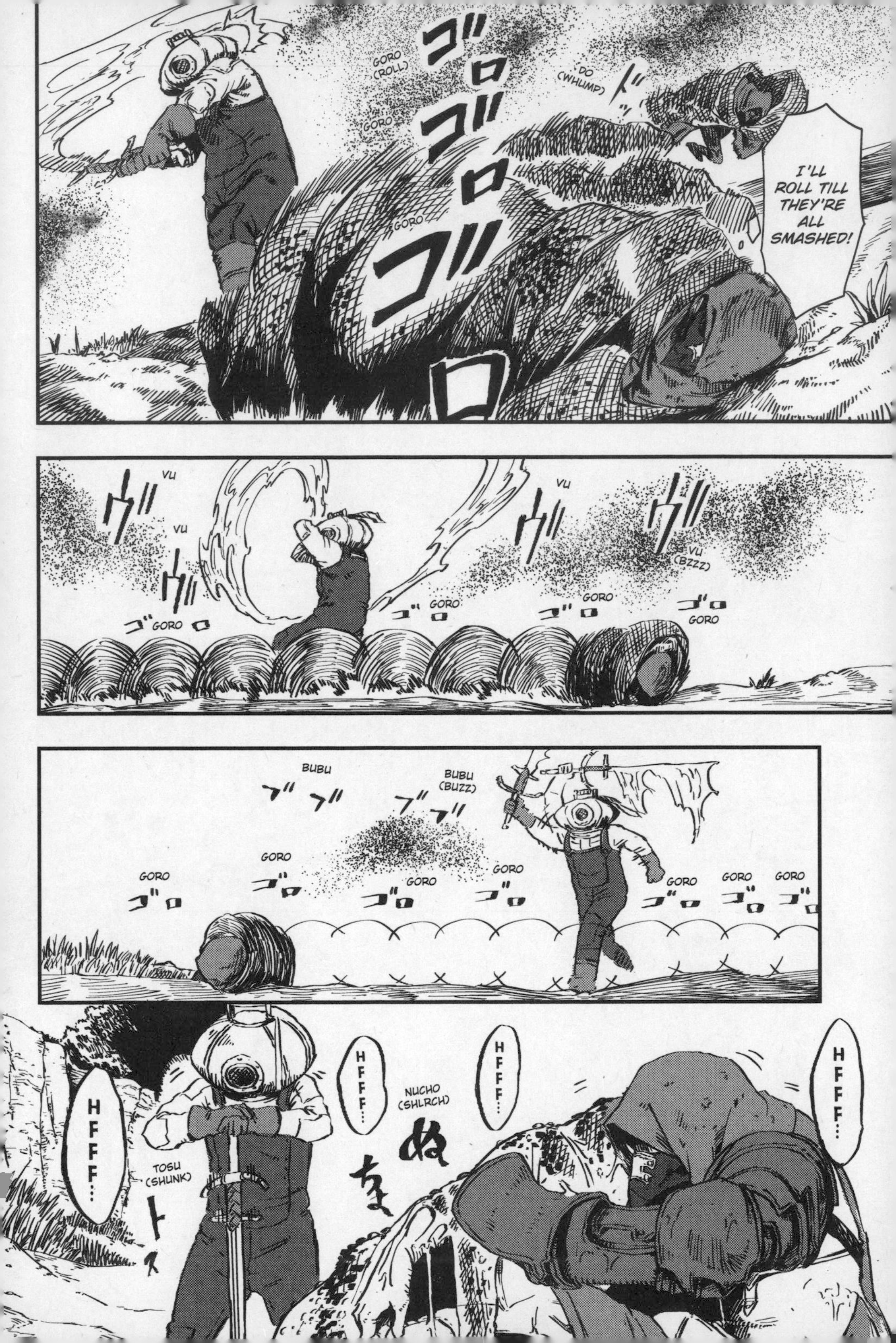
I'LL ROLL TILL THEY'RE ALL SMASHED!
DO (WHUMP)
GORO (ROLL)
GORO
GORO
VU (BZZZ)
GORO
GORO
VU
GORO
VU
VU
GORO
GORO
GORO
GORO
GORO
BUBU (BUZZ)
GORO
BUBU
GORO
GORO
HFFF...
HFFF...
NUCHO (SHLRCH)
HFFF...
TOSU (SHUNK)
HFFF...

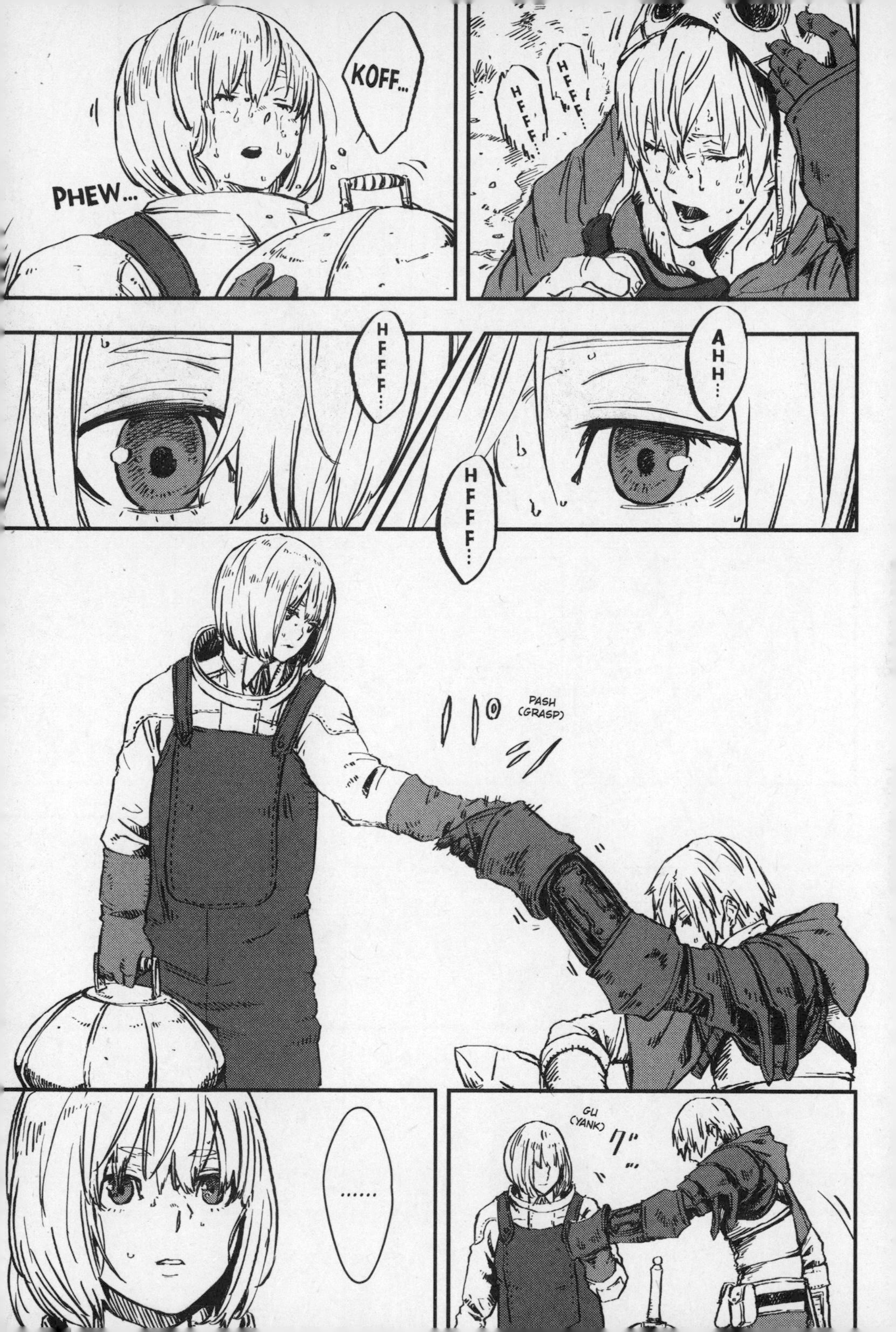
HFFFF...
HFFFF...
KOFF...
PHEW...
AHH...
HFFF...
HFFF...
PASH
(GRASP)
GU
(YANK)
......

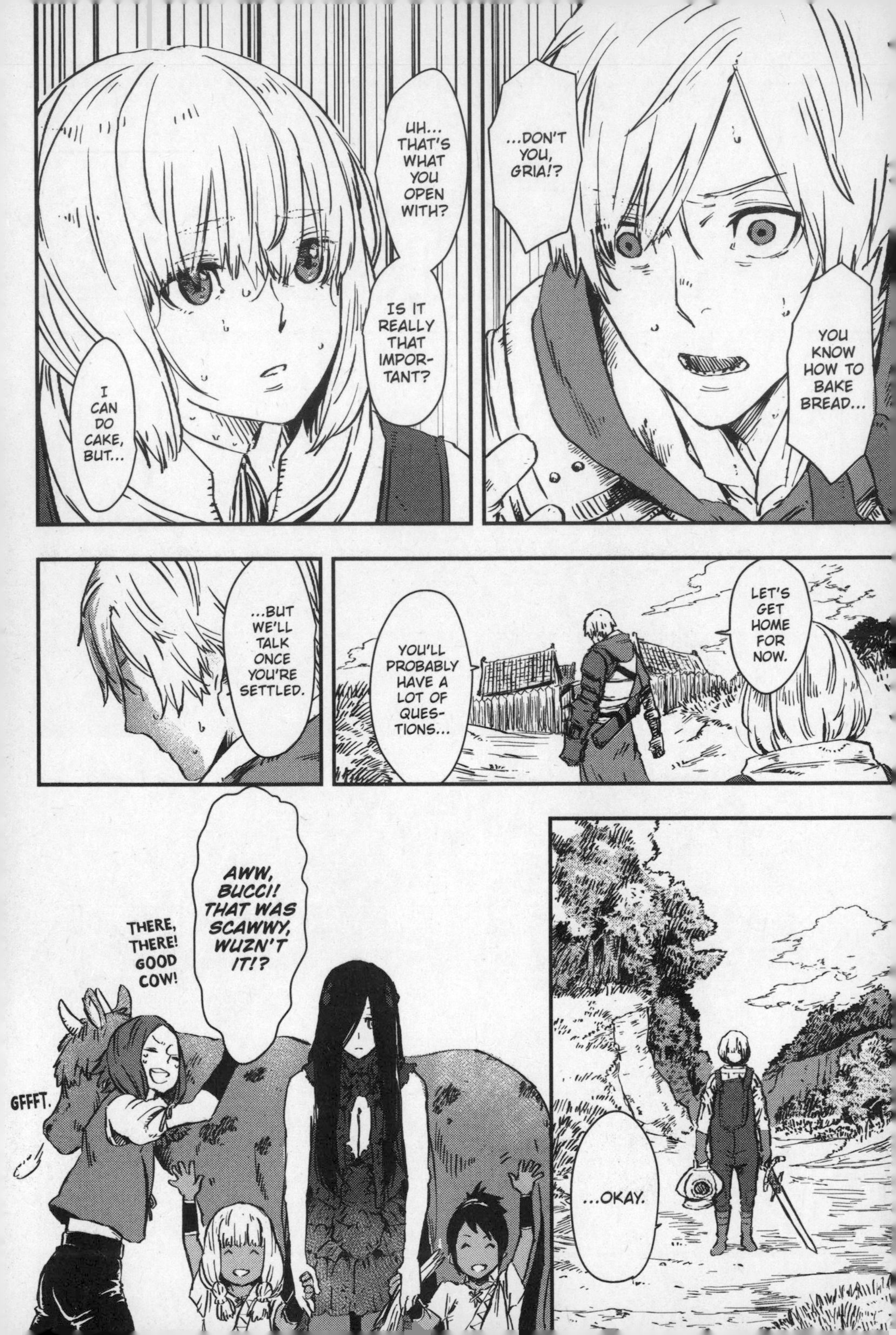
YOU KNOW HOW TO BAKE BREAD...
...DON'T YOU, GRIA!?
UH... THAT'S WHAT YOU OPEN WITH?
IS IT REALLY THAT IMPORTANT?
I CAN DO CAKE, BUT...
LET'S GET HOME FOR NOW.
YOU'LL PROBABLY HAVE A LOT OF QUES-TIONS...
...BUT WE'LL TALK ONCE YOU'RE SETTLED.
...OKAY.
AWW, BUCCI! THAT WAS SCAWWY, WUZN'T IT!?
THERE, THERE! GOOD COW!
GFFFT.

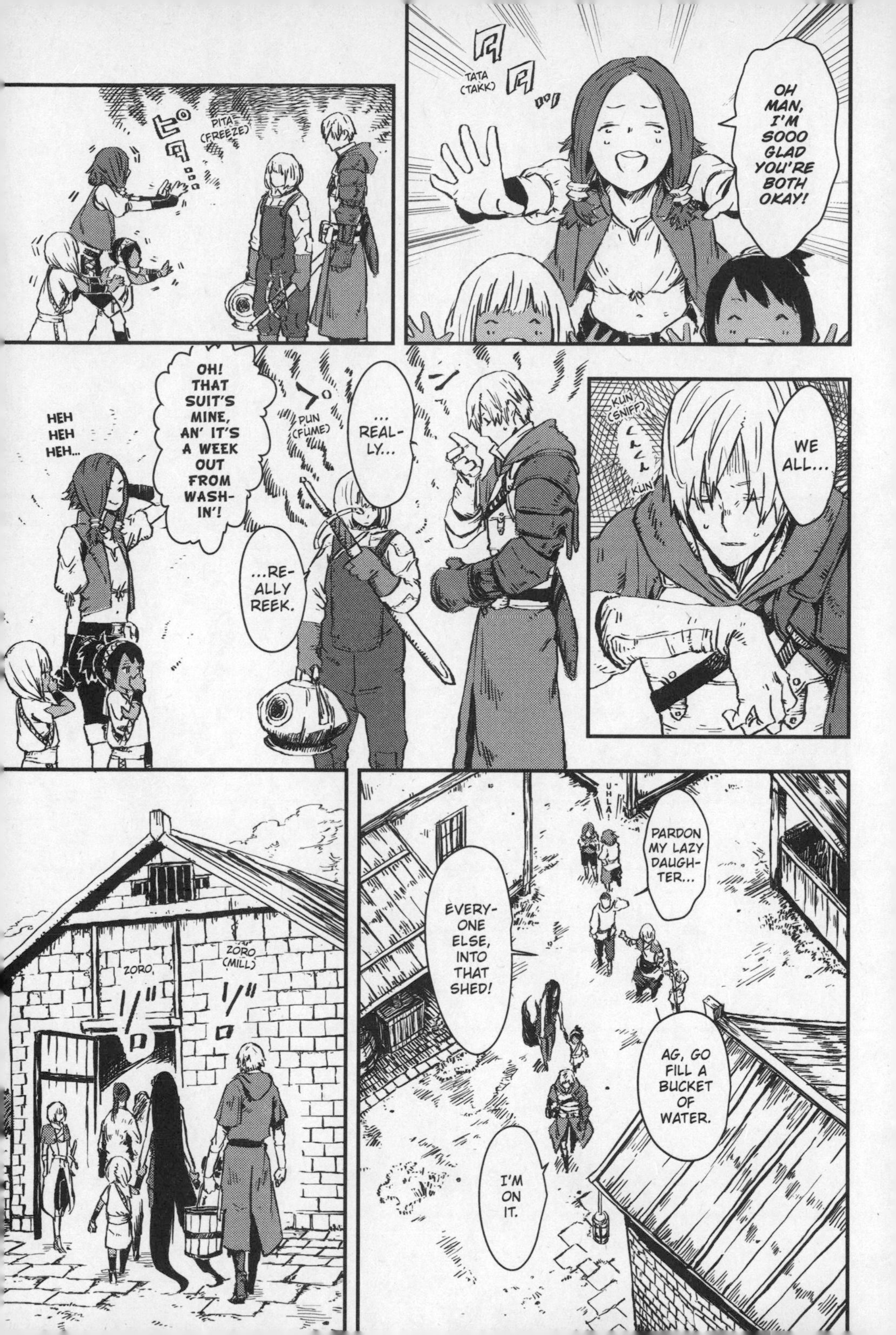
TATA (TAKK)
OH MAN, I'M SOOO GLAD YOU'RE BOTH OKAY!
PITA (FREEZE)
KUN (SNIFF)
KUN
WE ALL...
...REAL-LY...
PUN (FUME)
...RE-ALLY REEK.
OH! THAT SUIT'S MINE, AN' IT'S A WEEK OUT FROM WASH-IN'!
HEH HEH HEH...
UHLA!
PARDON MY LAZY DAUGH-TER...
EVERY-ONE ELSE, INTO THAT SHED!
AG, GO FILL A BUCKET OF WATER.
I'M ON IT.
ZORO (MILL)
ZORO

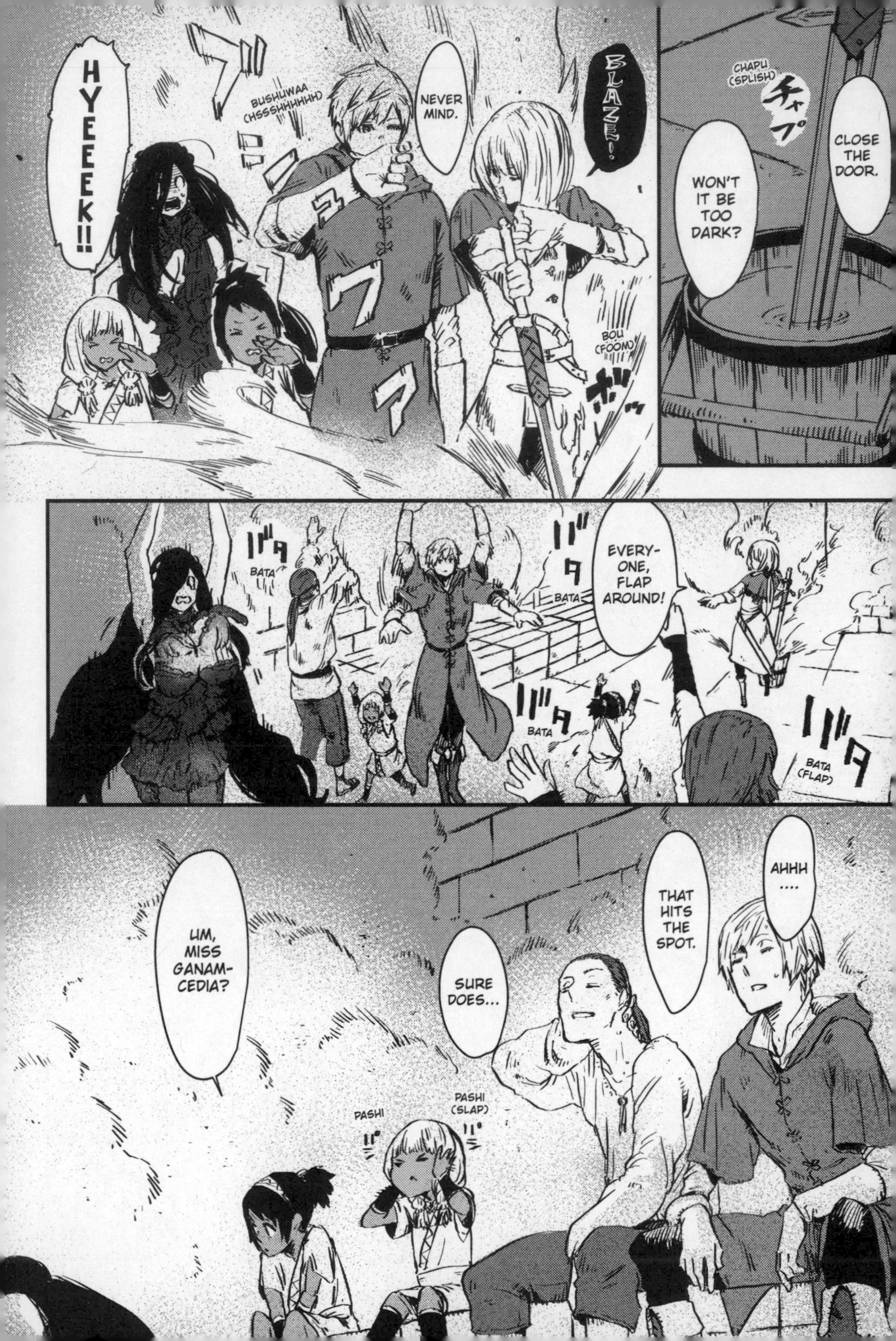

CLOSE THE DOOR.
WON'T IT BE TOO DARK?
CHAPU (SPLISH)
BLAZE!
BOU (FOOM)
NEVER MIND.
BUSHUWAA (HSSSHHHHHH)
HYEEEK!!
EVERY-ONE, FLAP AROUND!
BATA
BATA
BATA
BATA (FLAP)
AHHH....
THAT HITS THE SPOT.
SURE DOES...
UM, MISS GANAM-CEDIA?
PASHI (SLAP)
PASHI

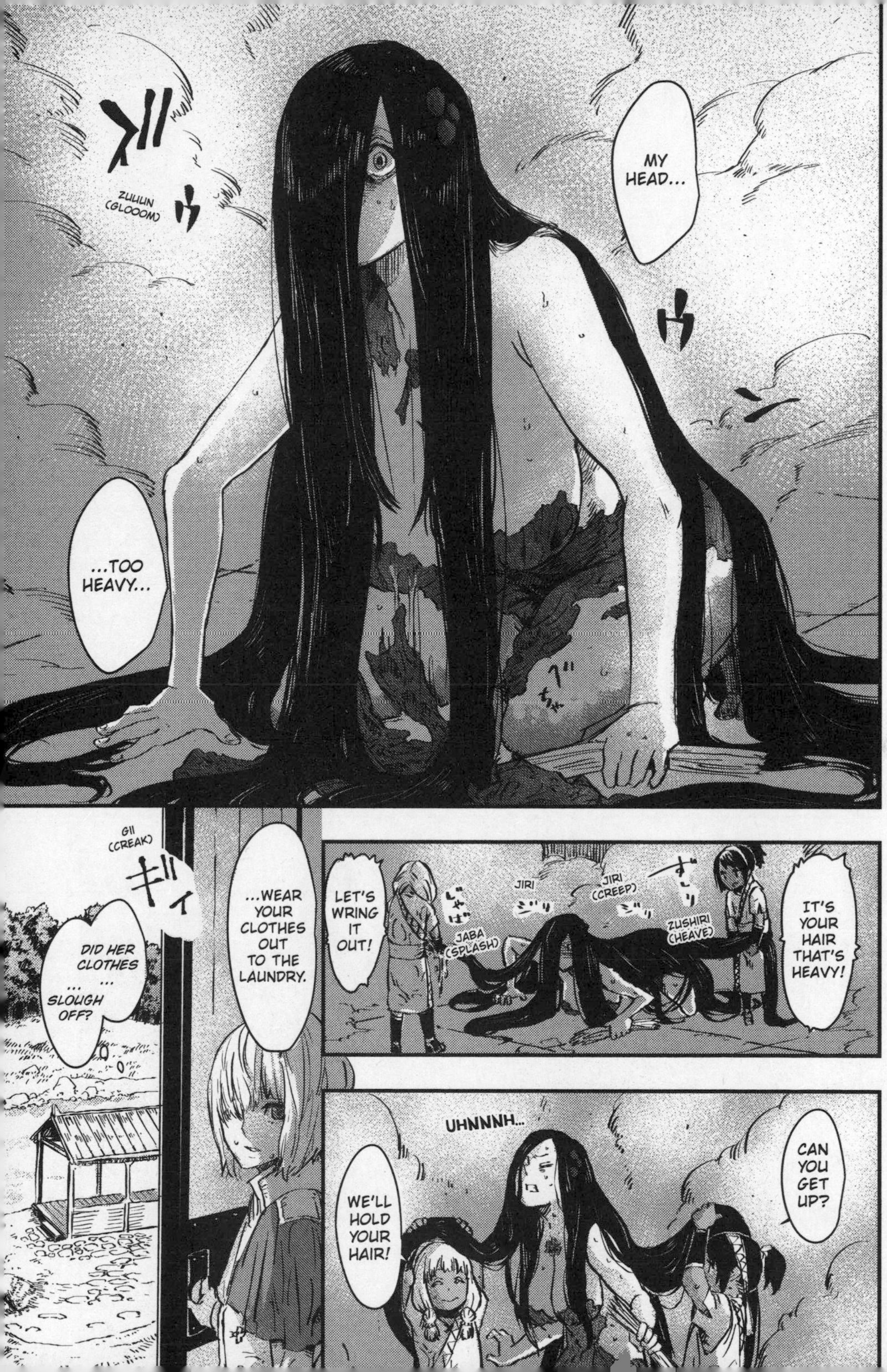
MY HEAD...
ZULUUN (GLOOOM)
...TOO HEAVY...
IT'S YOUR HAIR THAT'S HEAVY!
ZUSHIRI (HEAVE)
JIRI (CREEP)
JIRI
JABA (SPLASH)
LET'S WRING IT OUT!
CAN YOU GET UP?
UHNNNH...
WE'LL HOLD YOUR HAIR!
...WEAR YOUR CLOTHES OUT TO THE LAUNDRY.
GII (CREAK)
DID HER CLOTHES ... SLOUGH OFF?

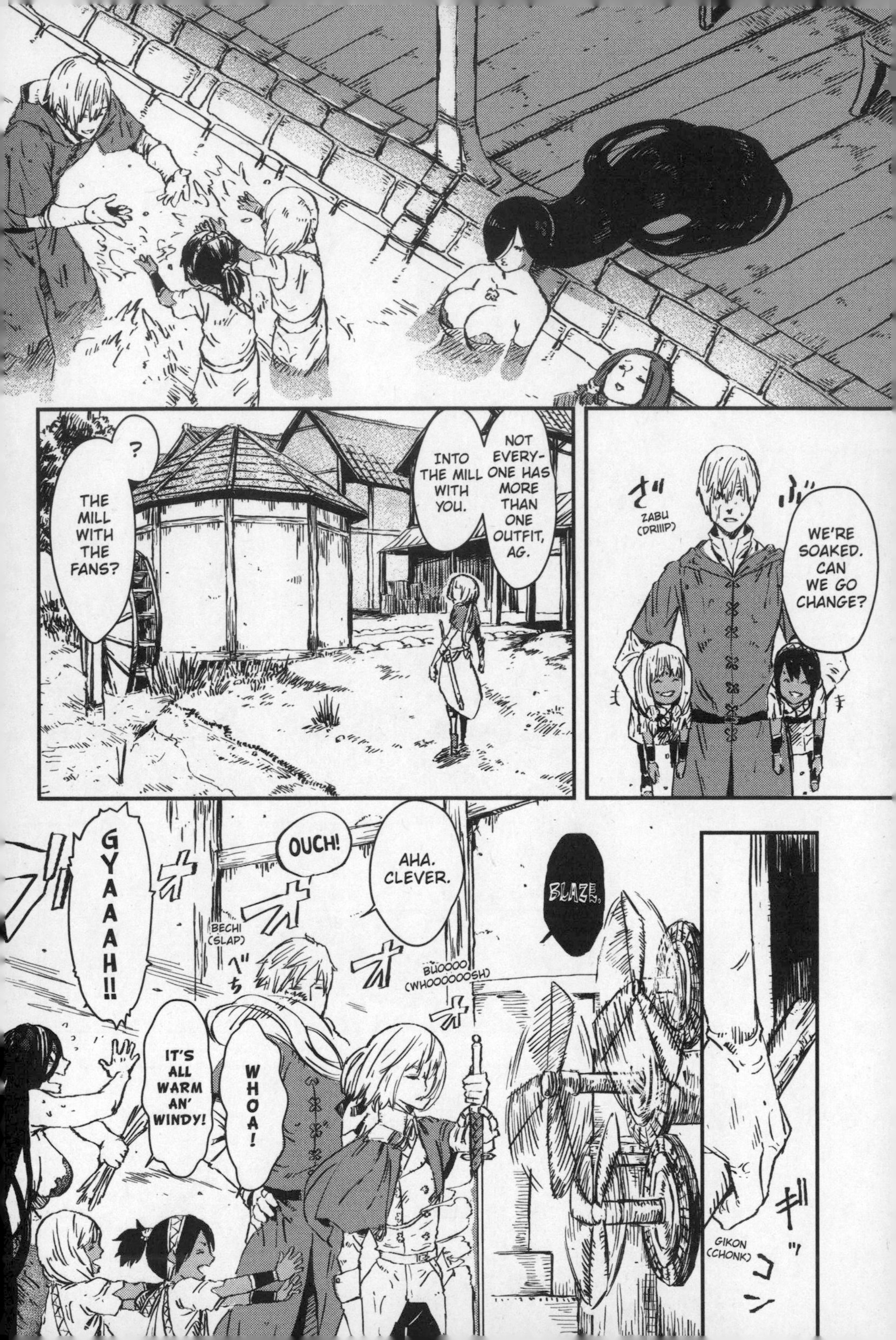
ざぶ
ZABU (DRIIIP)
WE'RE SOAKED. CAN WE GO CHANGE?
NOT EVERY-ONE HAS MORE THAN ONE OUTFIT, AG.
INTO THE MILL WITH YOU.
?
THE MILL WITH THE FANS?
ギコン
GIKON (CHONK)
BLAZE.
AHA. CLEVER.
BUOOOO (WHOOOOOOSH)
オオオオ
OUCH!
BECHI (SLAP)
べち
GYAAAAH!!
WHOA!
IT'S ALL WARM AN' WINDY!

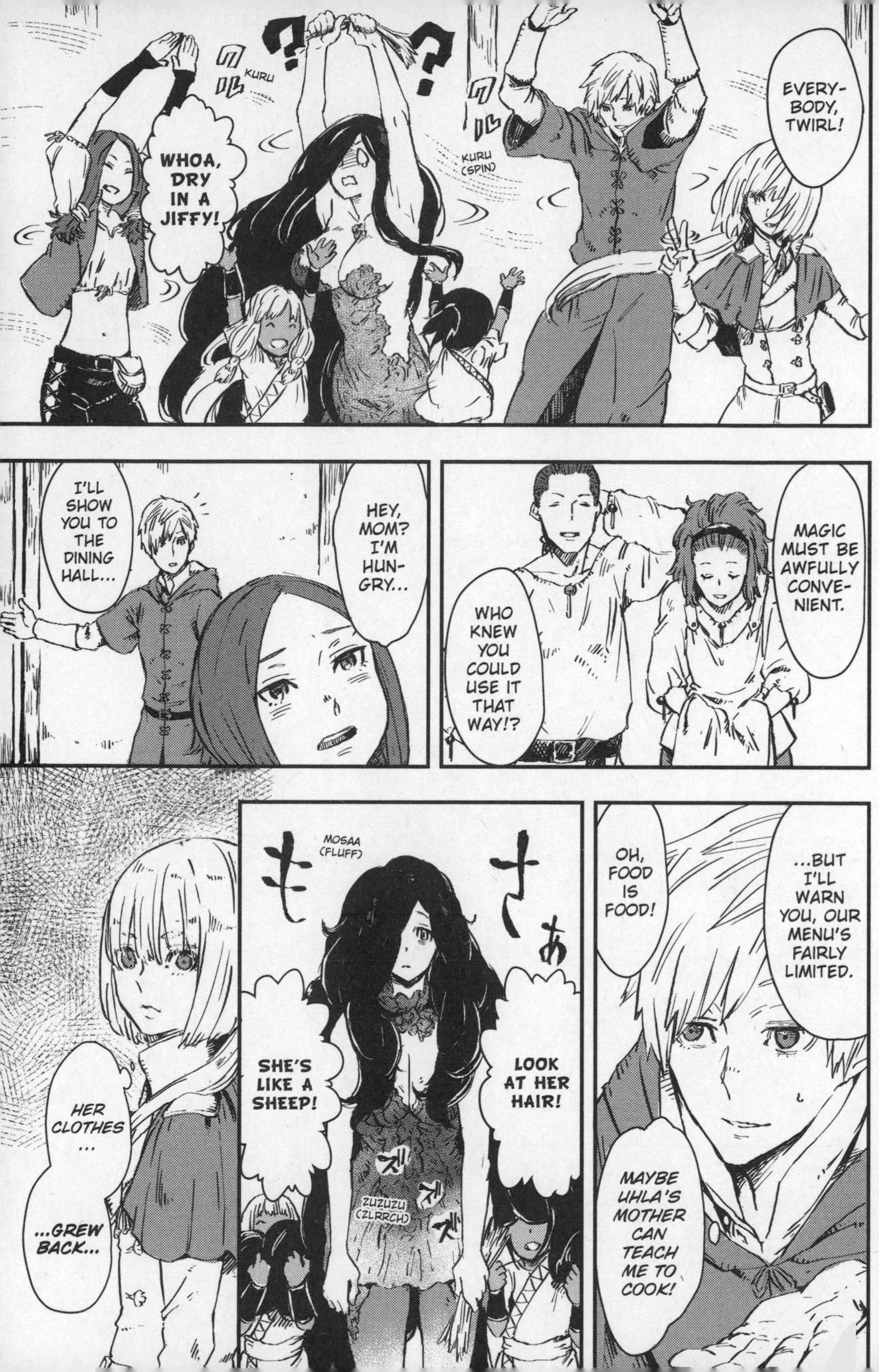
EVERY-BODY, TWIRL!
KURU (SPIN)
KURU
WHOA, DRY IN A JIFFY!
MAGIC MUST BE AWFULLY CONVE-NIENT.
WHO KNEW YOU COULD USE IT THAT WAY!?
HEY, MOM? I'M HUN-GRY...
I'LL SHOW YOU TO THE DINING HALL...
...BUT I'LL WARN YOU, OUR MENU'S FAIRLY LIMITED.
OH, FOOD IS FOOD!
MAYBE UHLA'S MOTHER CAN TEACH ME TO COOK!
MOSAA (FLUFF)
LOOK AT HER HAIR!
SHE'S LIKE A SHEEP!
ZUZUZU (ZLRRCH)
HER CLOTHES ...
...GREW BACK...

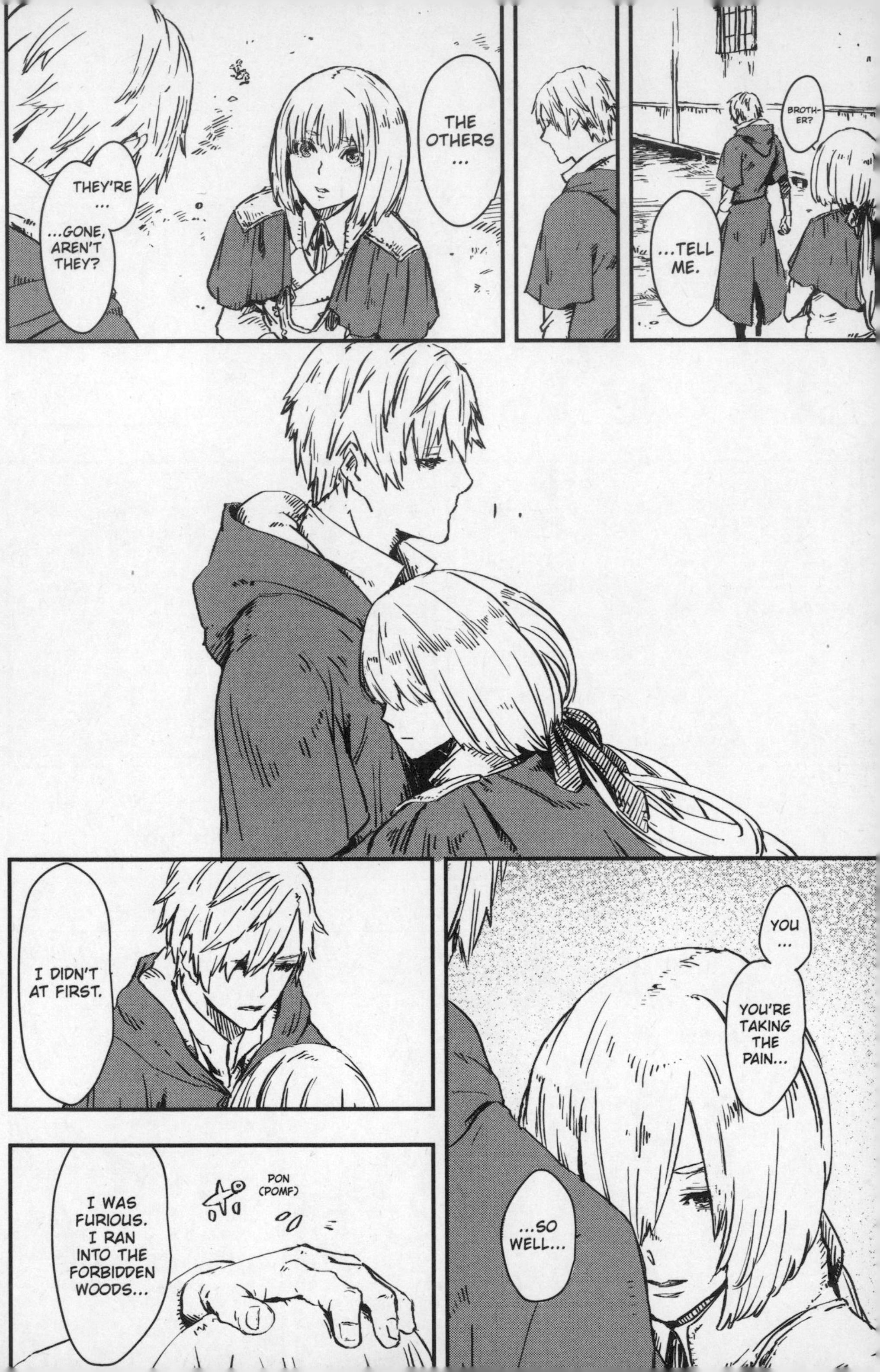
BROTHER?
...TELL ME.
THE OTHERS ...
THEY'RE ... ...GONE, AREN'T THEY?
YOU ...
YOU'RE TAKING THE PAIN...
...SO WELL...
I DIDN'T AT FIRST.
I WAS FURIOUS. I RAN INTO THE FORBIDDEN WOODS...
PON (POMF)

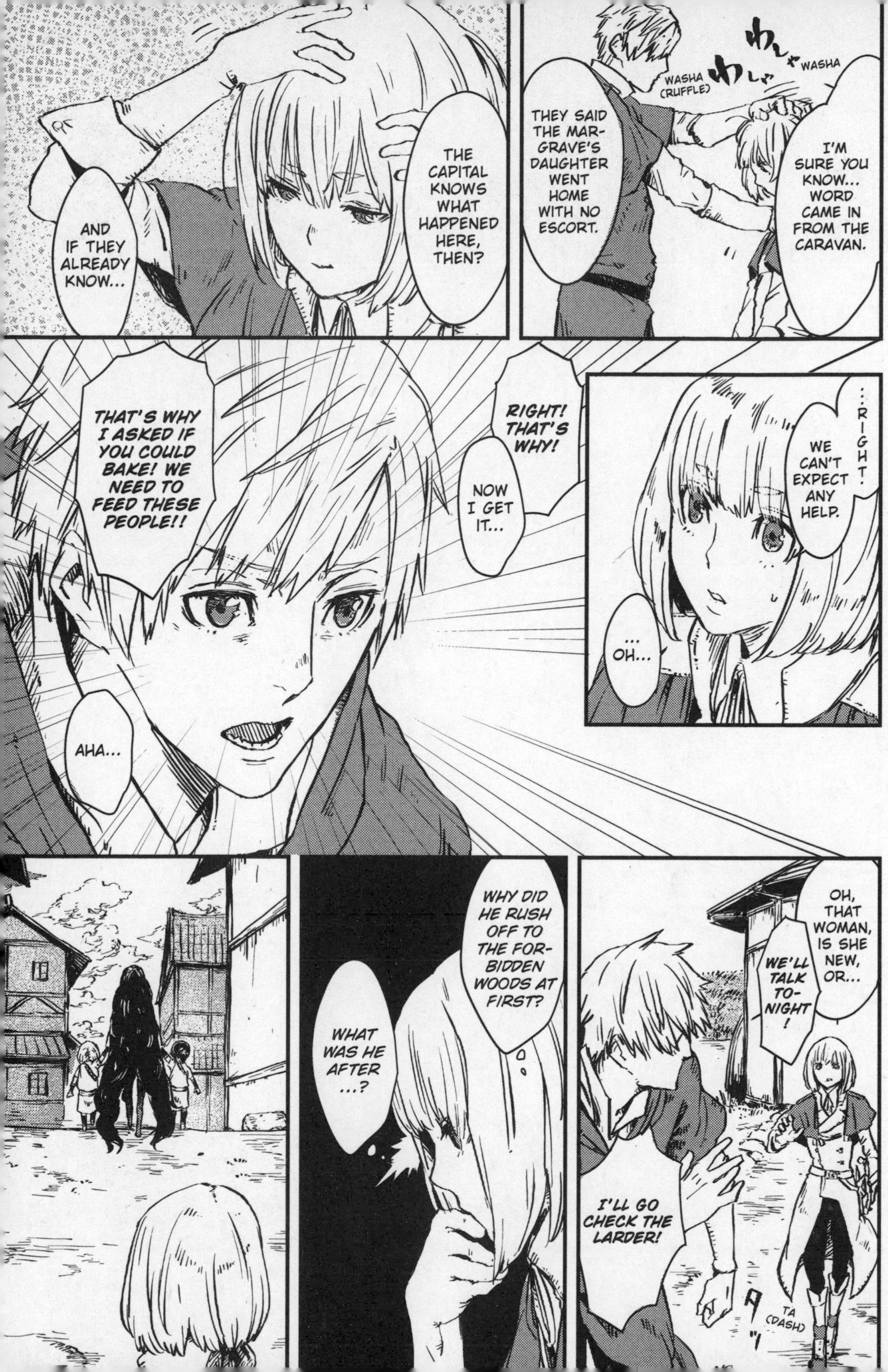
I'M SURE YOU KNOW... WORD CAME IN FROM THE CARAVAN.
WASHA WASHA (RUFFLE)
THEY SAID THE MARGRAVE'S DAUGHTER WENT HOME WITH NO ESCORT.
THE CAPITAL KNOWS WHAT HAPPENED HERE, THEN?
AND IF THEY ALREADY KNOW...
...RIGHT.
WE CAN'T EXPECT ANY HELP.
...OH...
RIGHT! THAT'S WHY!
NOW I GET IT...
THAT'S WHY I ASKED IF YOU COULD BAKE! WE NEED TO FEED THESE PEOPLE!!
AHA...
OH, THAT WOMAN, IS SHE NEW, OR...
WE'LL TALK TONIGHT!
I'LL GO CHECK THE LARDER!
TA (DASH)
WHY DID HE RUSH OFF TO THE FORBIDDEN WOODS AT FIRST?
WHAT WAS HE AFTER...?

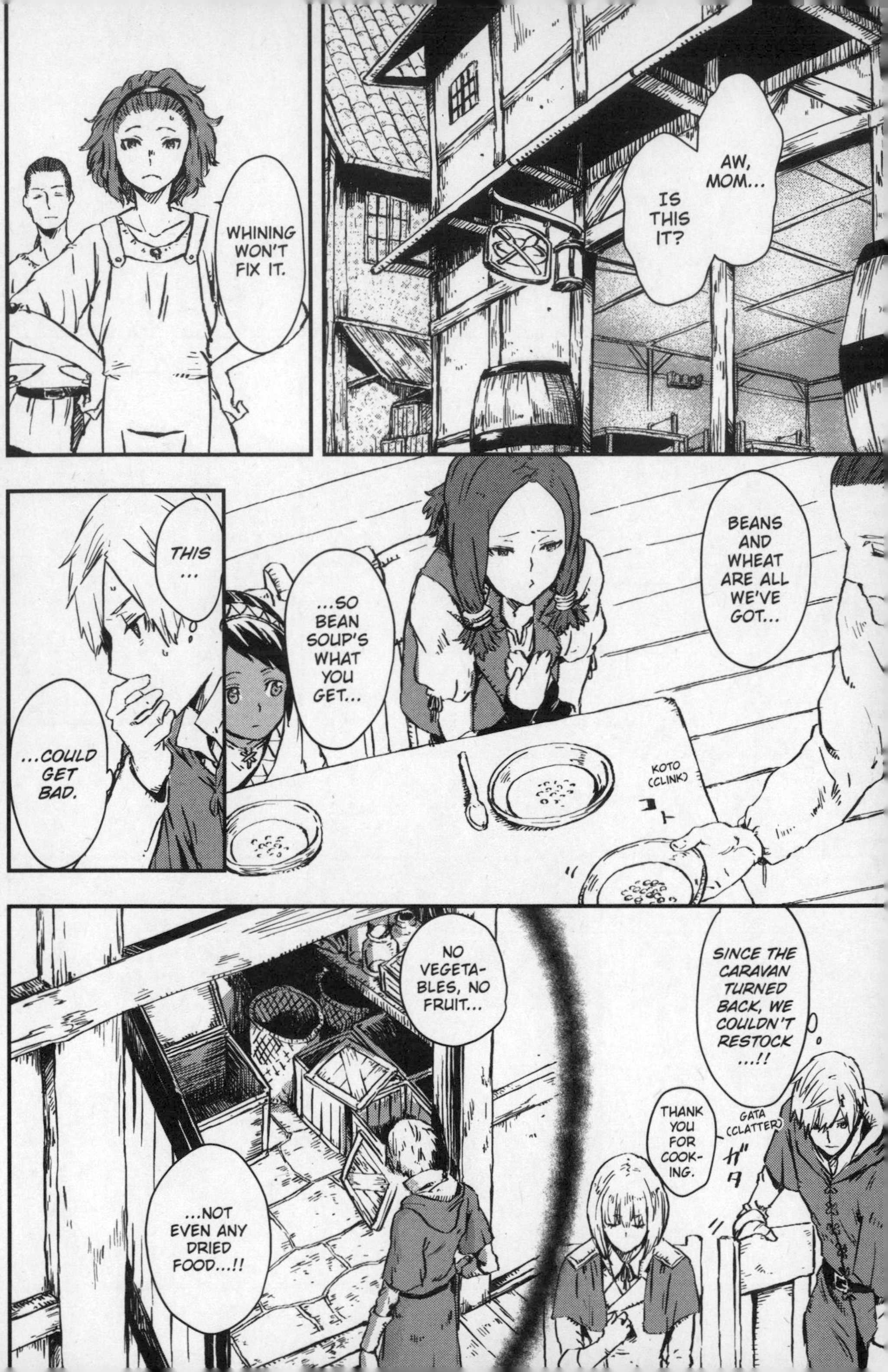
AW, MOM... IS THIS IT?
WHINING WON'T FIX IT.
BEANS AND WHEAT ARE ALL WE'VE GOT...
...SO BEAN SOUP'S WHAT YOU GET...
KOTO (CLINK)
THIS ...
...COULD GET BAD.
SINCE THE CARAVAN TURNED BACK, WE COULDN'T RESTOCK ...!!
GATA (CLATTER)
THANK YOU FOR COOK-ING.
NO VEGETA-BLES, NO FRUIT...
...NOT EVEN ANY DRIED FOOD...!!

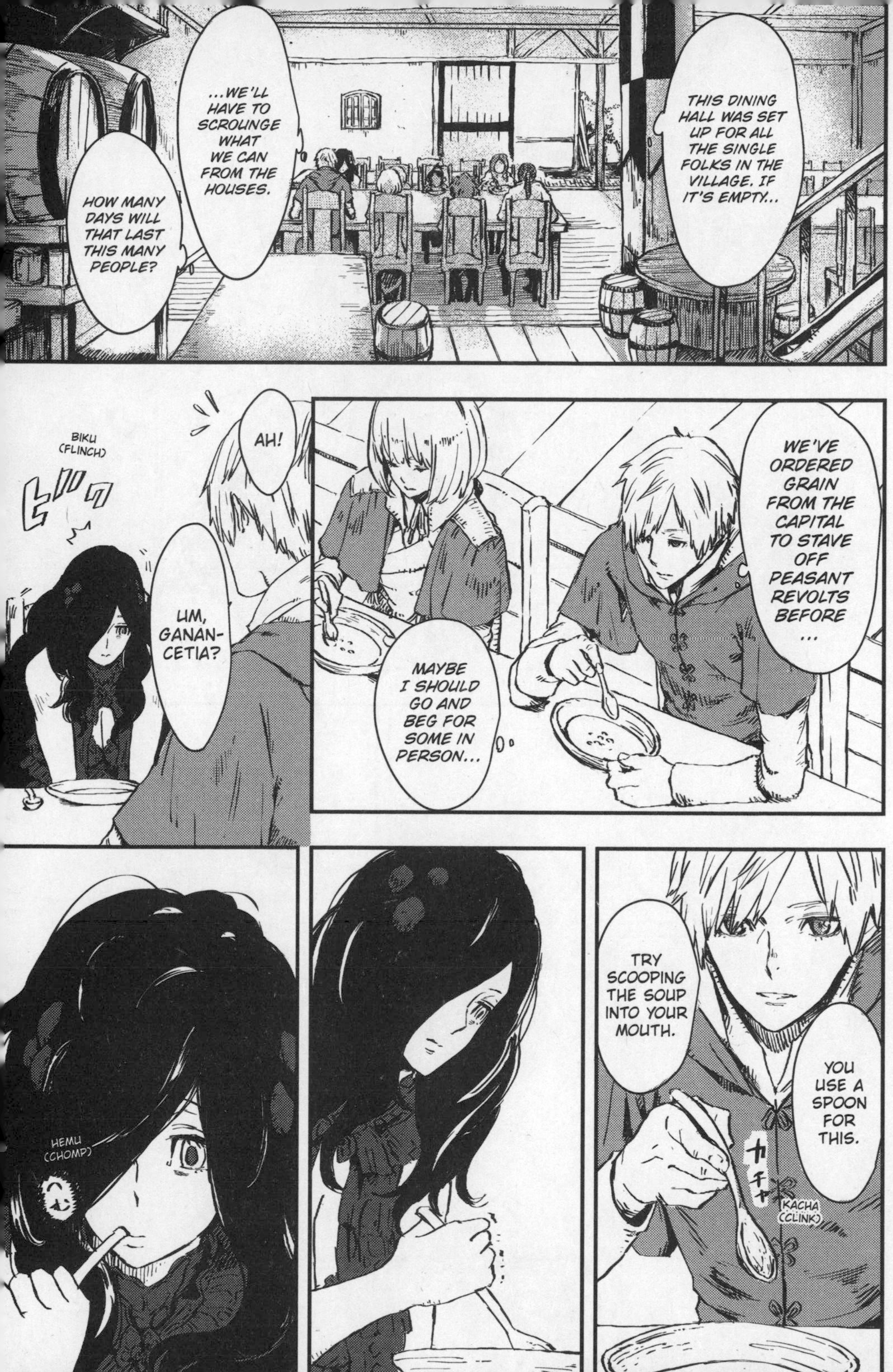
THIS DINING HALL WAS SET UP FOR ALL THE SINGLE FOLKS IN THE VILLAGE. IF IT'S EMPTY...
...WE'LL HAVE TO SCROUNGE WHAT WE CAN FROM THE HOUSES.
HOW MANY DAYS WILL THAT LAST THIS MANY PEOPLE?
WE'VE ORDERED GRAIN FROM THE CAPITAL TO STAVE OFF PEASANT REVOLTS BEFORE ...
MAYBE I SHOULD GO AND BEG FOR SOME IN PERSON...
AH!
BIKU (FLINCH)
UM, GANAN-CETIA?
TRY SCOOPING THE SOUP INTO YOUR MOUTH.
YOU USE A SPOON FOR THIS.
KACHA (CLINK)
HEMU (CHOMP)

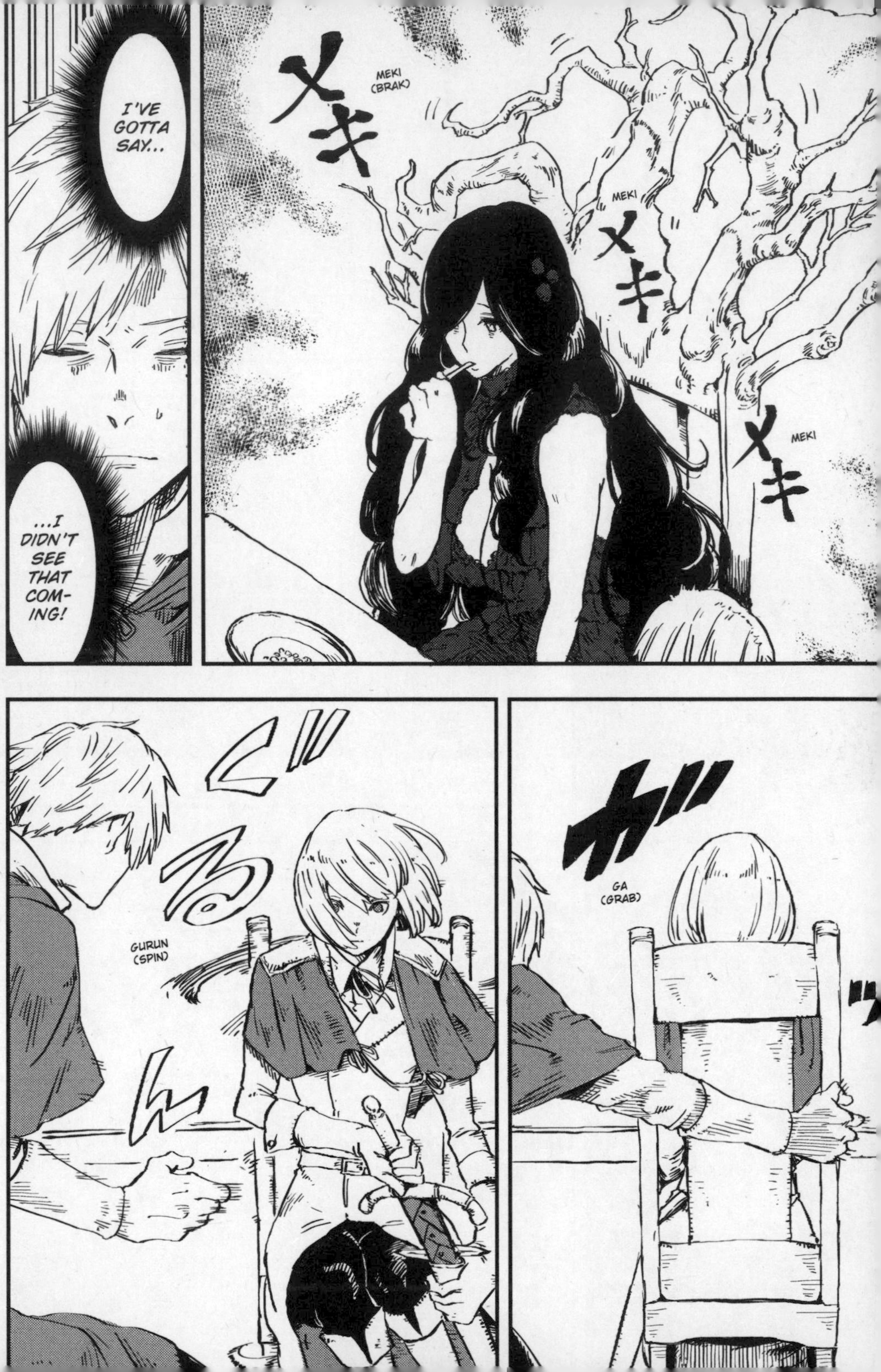
MEKI (BRAK)
MEKI
MEKI
I'VE GOTTA SAY...
...I DIDN'T SEE THAT COMING!
GA (GRAB)
GURUN (SPIN)

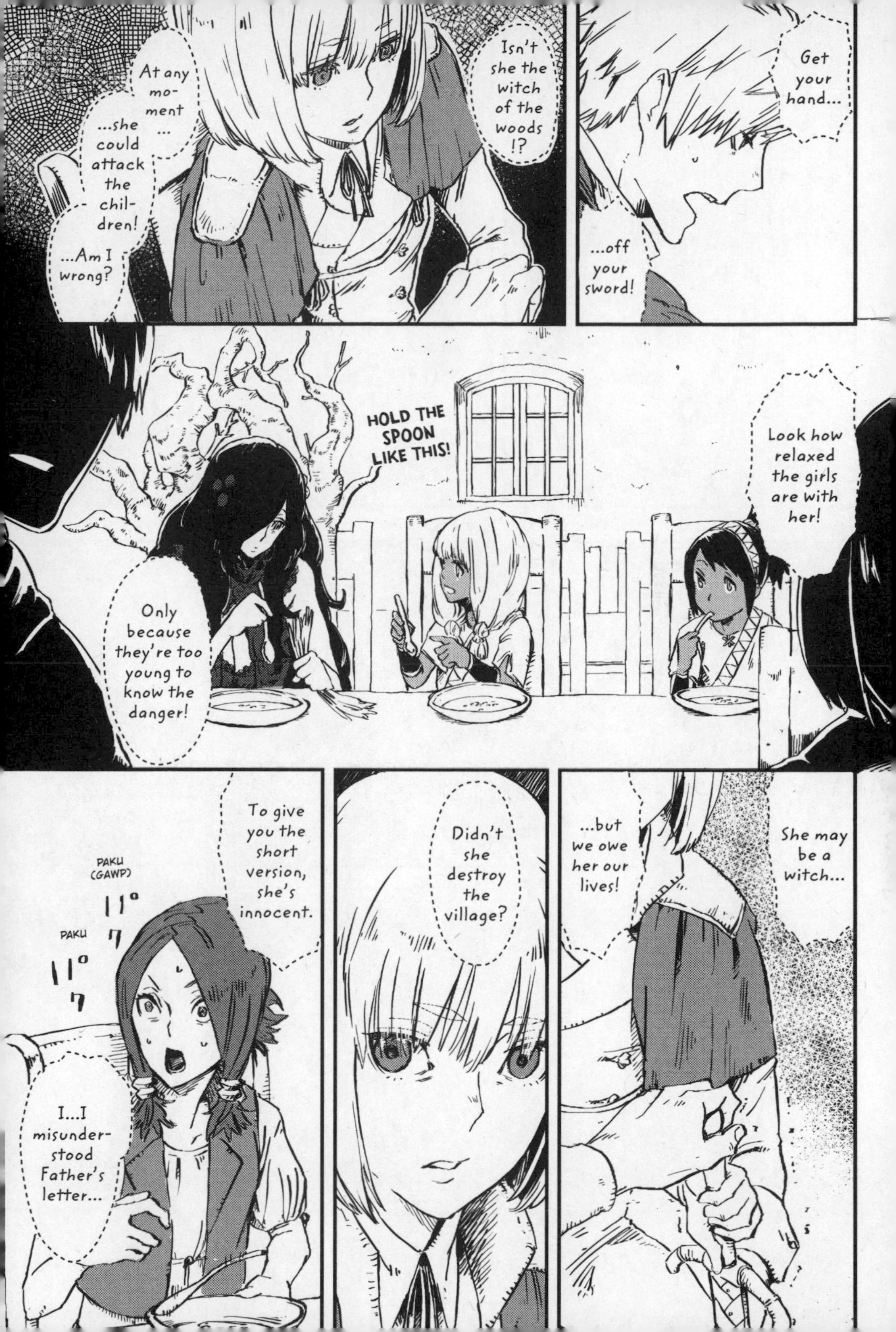
Get your hand...
...off your sword!
Isn't she the witch of the woods !?
At any moment ...
...she could attack the children!
...Am I wrong?
Look how relaxed the girls are with her!
HOLD THE SPOON LIKE THIS!
Only because they're too young to know the danger!
She may be a witch...
...but we owe her our lives!
Didn't she destroy the village?
To give you the short version, she's innocent.
PAKU (GAWP)
PAKU
I...I misunderstood Father's letter...

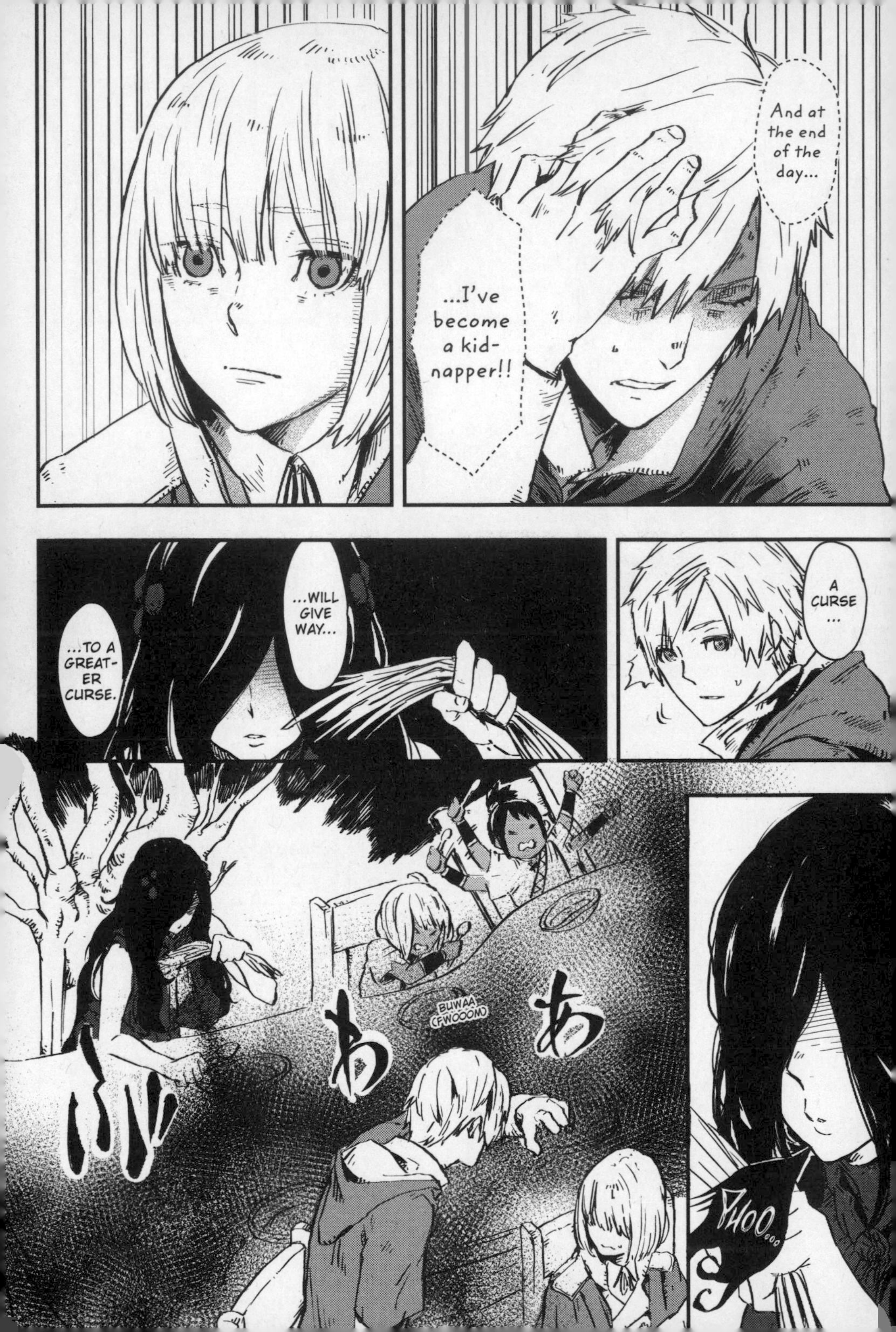

And at the end of the day...
...I've become a kid-napper!!
A CURSE ...
...WILL GIVE WAY...
...TO A GREAT-ER CURSE.
PHOO...
BUWAA (FWOOOM)
あ
あ

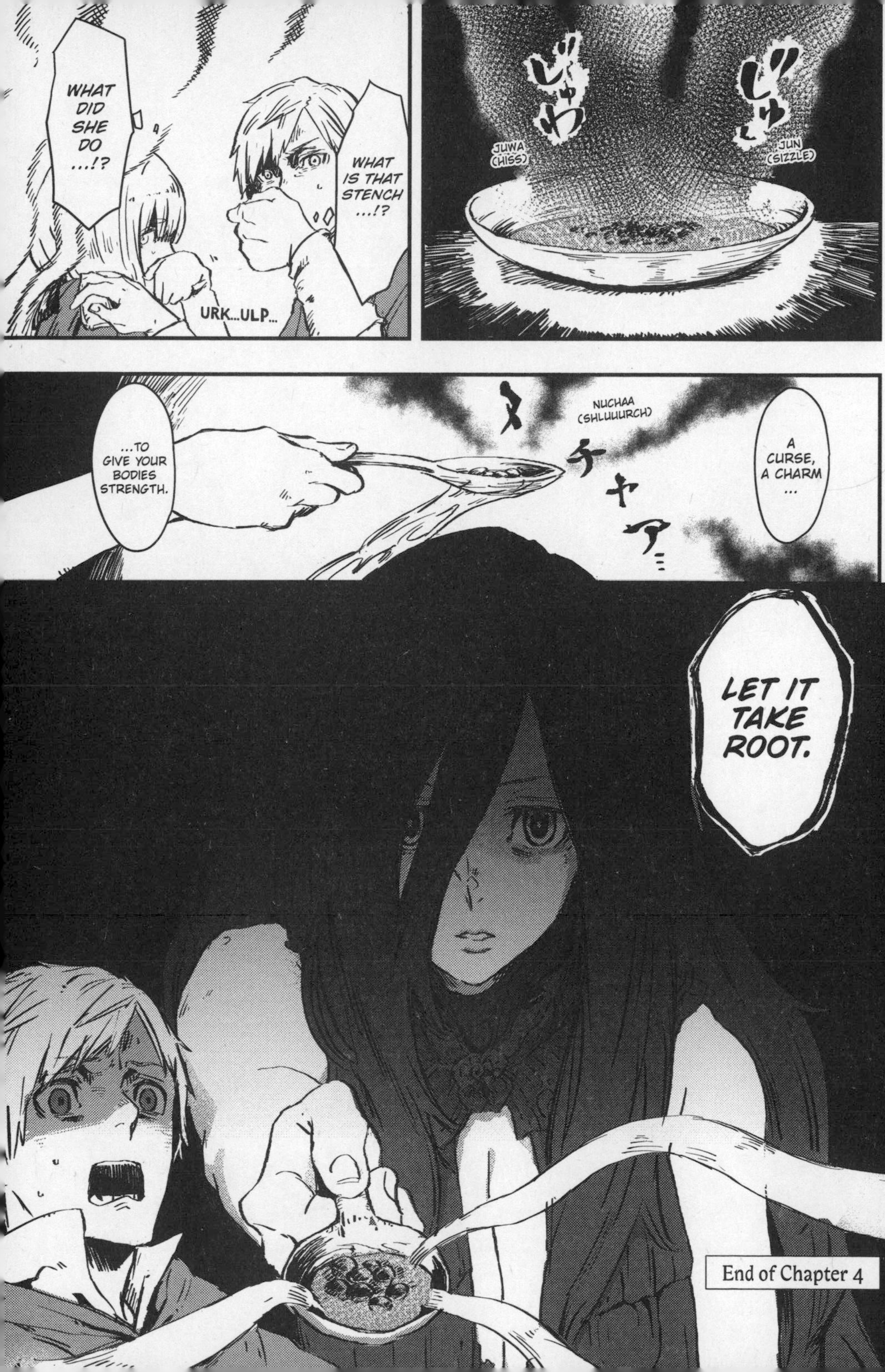
じゅん
JUN (SIZZLE)
じゅわ
JUWA (HISS)
WHAT IS THAT STENCH ...!?
WHAT DID SHE DO ...!?
URK...ULP...
A CURSE, A CHARM ...
NUCHAA (SHLUUURCH)
ヌチャア
...TO GIVE YOUR BODIES STRENGTH.
LET IT TAKE ROOT.
End of Chapter 4

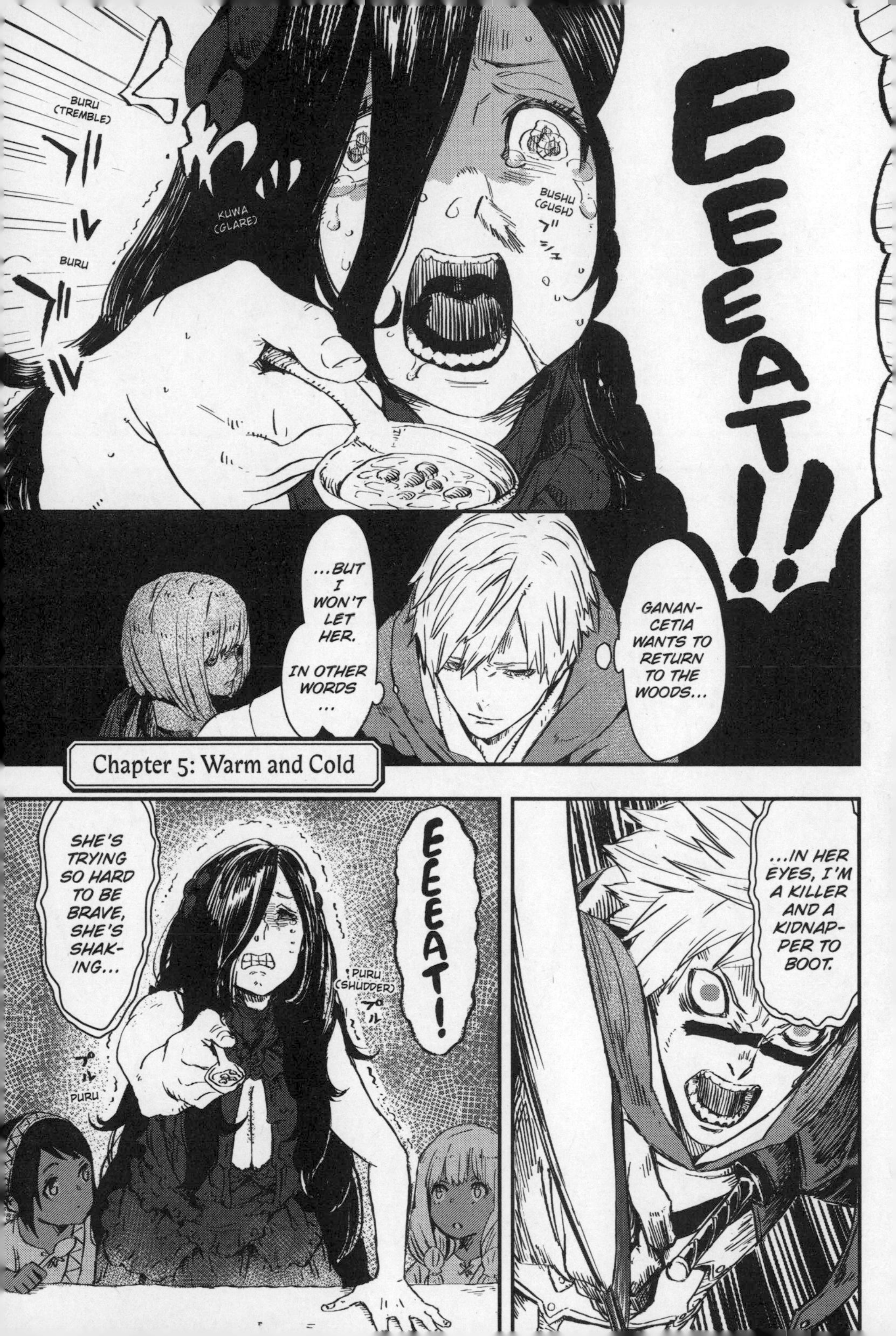
EEEEAT!!
BURU (TREMBLE)
KUWA (GLARE)
BUSHU (GUSH)
BURU
GANAN-CETIA WANTS TO RETURN TO THE WOODS...
...BUT I WON'T LET HER.
IN OTHER WORDS...
Chapter 5: Warm and Cold
...IN HER EYES, I'M A KILLER AND A KIDNAP-PER TO BOOT.
EEEAT!
PURU (SHUDDER)
SHE'S TRYING SO HARD TO BE BRAVE, SHE'S SHAK-ING...
PURU

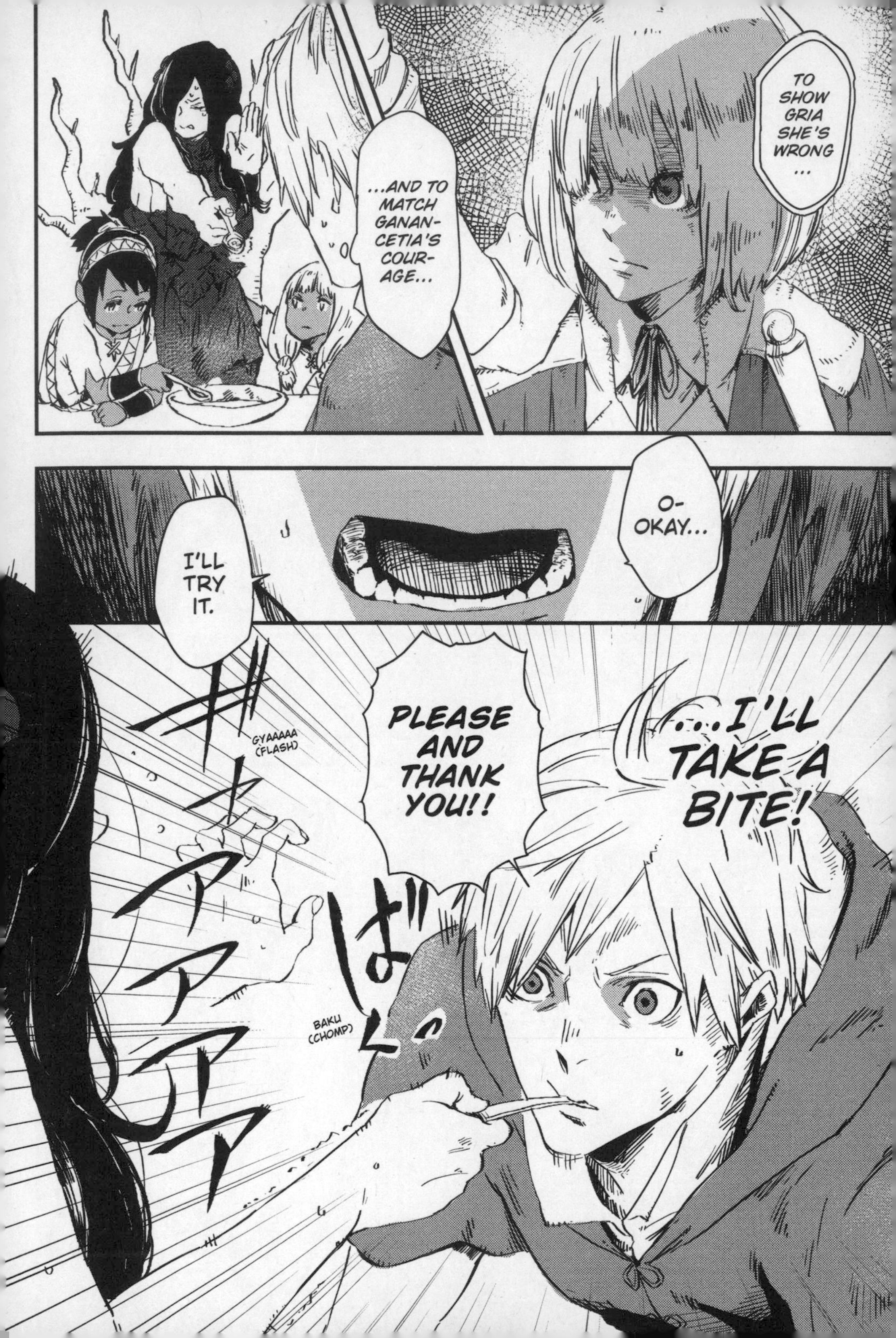
TO SHOW GRIA SHE'S WRONG...
...AND TO MATCH GANANCETIA'S COURAGE...
O-OKAY...
I'LL TRY IT.
...I'LL TAKE A BITE!
PLEASE AND THANK YOU!!
GYAAAAA (FLASH)
BAKU (CHOMP)

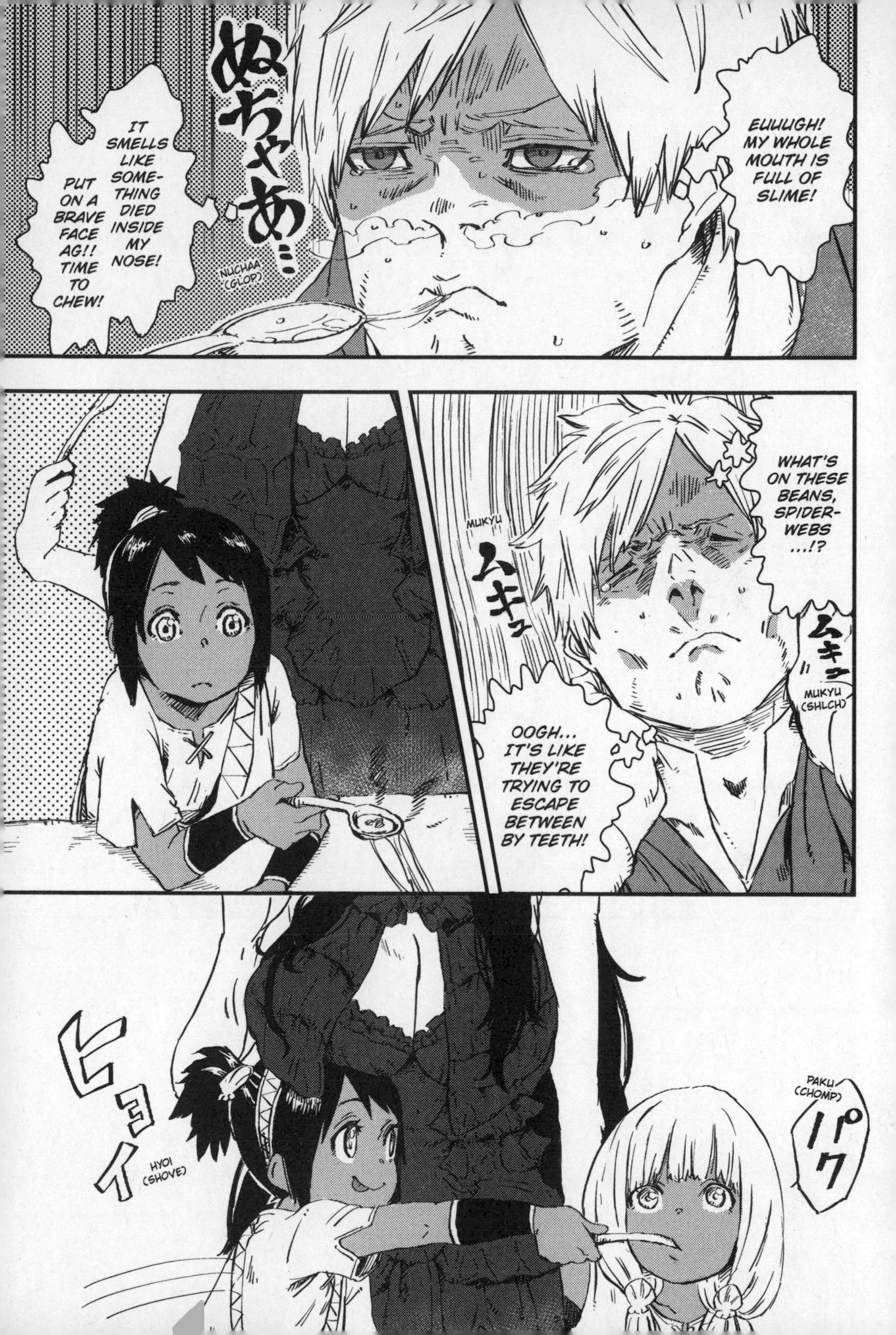
EUUUGH! MY WHOLE MOUTH IS FULL OF SLIME!
ぬちゃあ
NUCHAA (GLOP)
IT SMELLS LIKE SOME-THING DIED INSIDE MY NOSE!
PUT ON A BRAVE FACE AG!! TIME TO CHEW!
WHAT'S ON THESE BEANS, SPIDER-WEBS ...!?
ムキュ
MUKYU (SHLCH)
ムキュ
MUKYU
OOGH... IT'S LIKE THEY'RE TRYING TO ESCAPE BETWEEN BY TEETH!
パク
PAKU (CHOMP)
ヒョイ
HYOI (SHOVE)

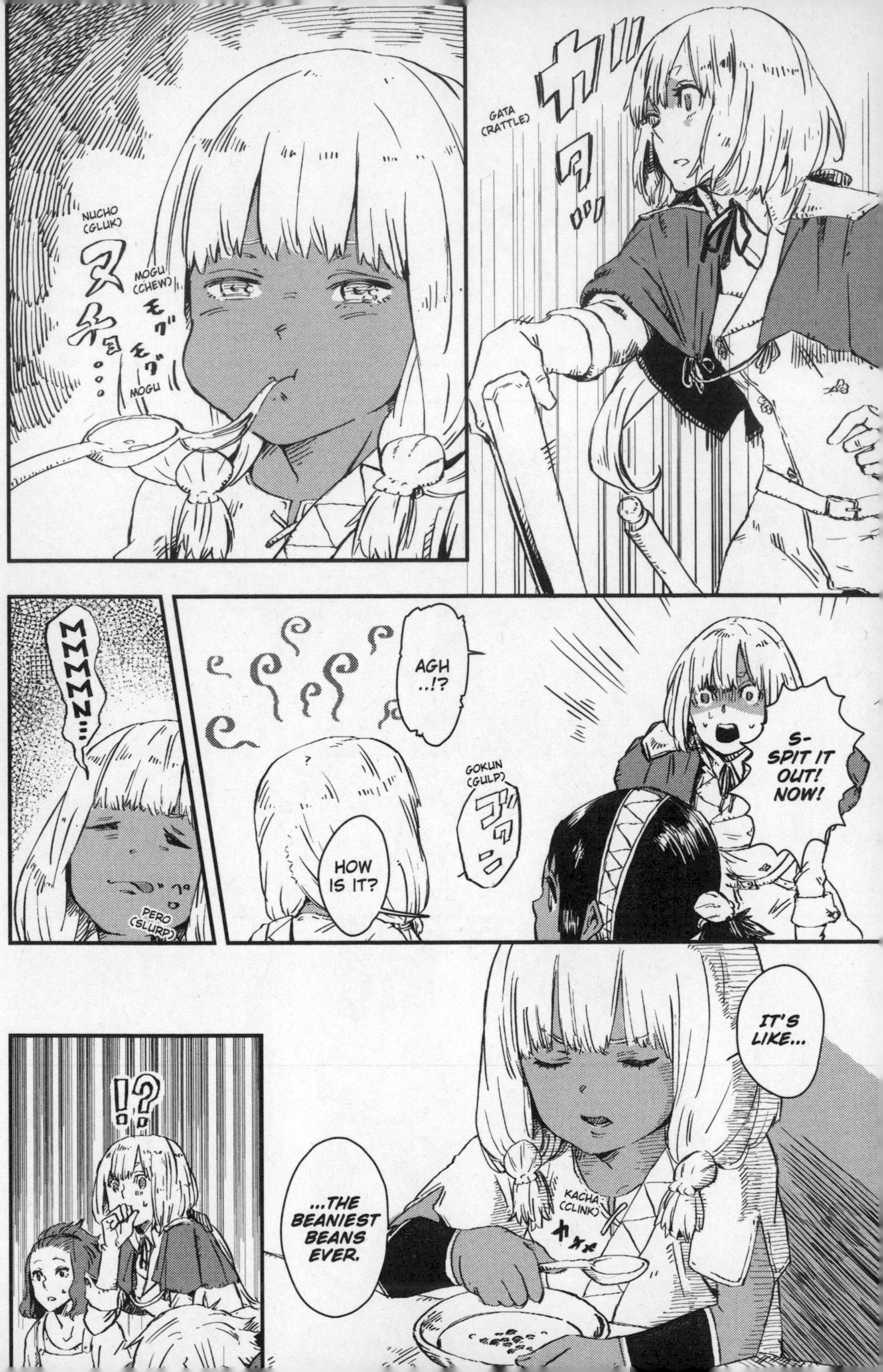
GATA (RATTLE)
NUCHO (GLUK)
MOGU (CHEW)
MOGU
AGH ..!?
S-SPIT IT OUT! NOW!
GOKUN (GULP)
HOW IS IT?
MMMMN...!
PERO (SLURP)
IT'S LIKE...
KACHA (CLINK)
...THE BEANIEST BEANS EVER.
!?

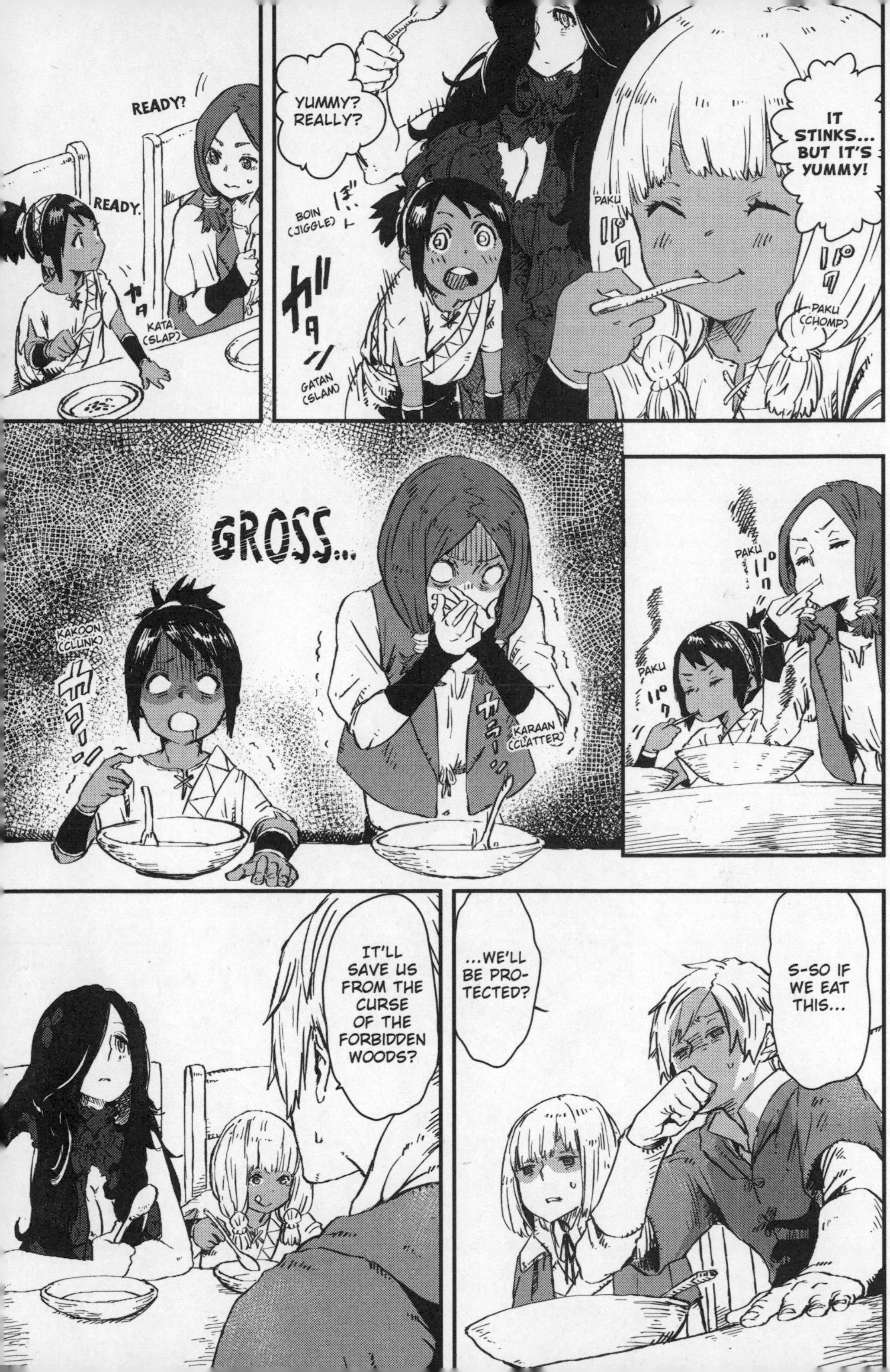
IT STINKS... BUT IT'S YUMMY!
PAKU
PAKU (CHOMP)
YUMMY? REALLY?
BOIN (JIGGLE)
GATAN (SLAM)
READY?
READY.
KATA (SLAP)
PAKU
PAKU
GROSS...
KARAAN (CLATTER)
KAKOON (CLUNK)
S-SO IF WE EAT THIS...
...WE'LL BE PRO-TECTED?
IT'LL SAVE US FROM THE CURSE OF THE FORBIDDEN WOODS?

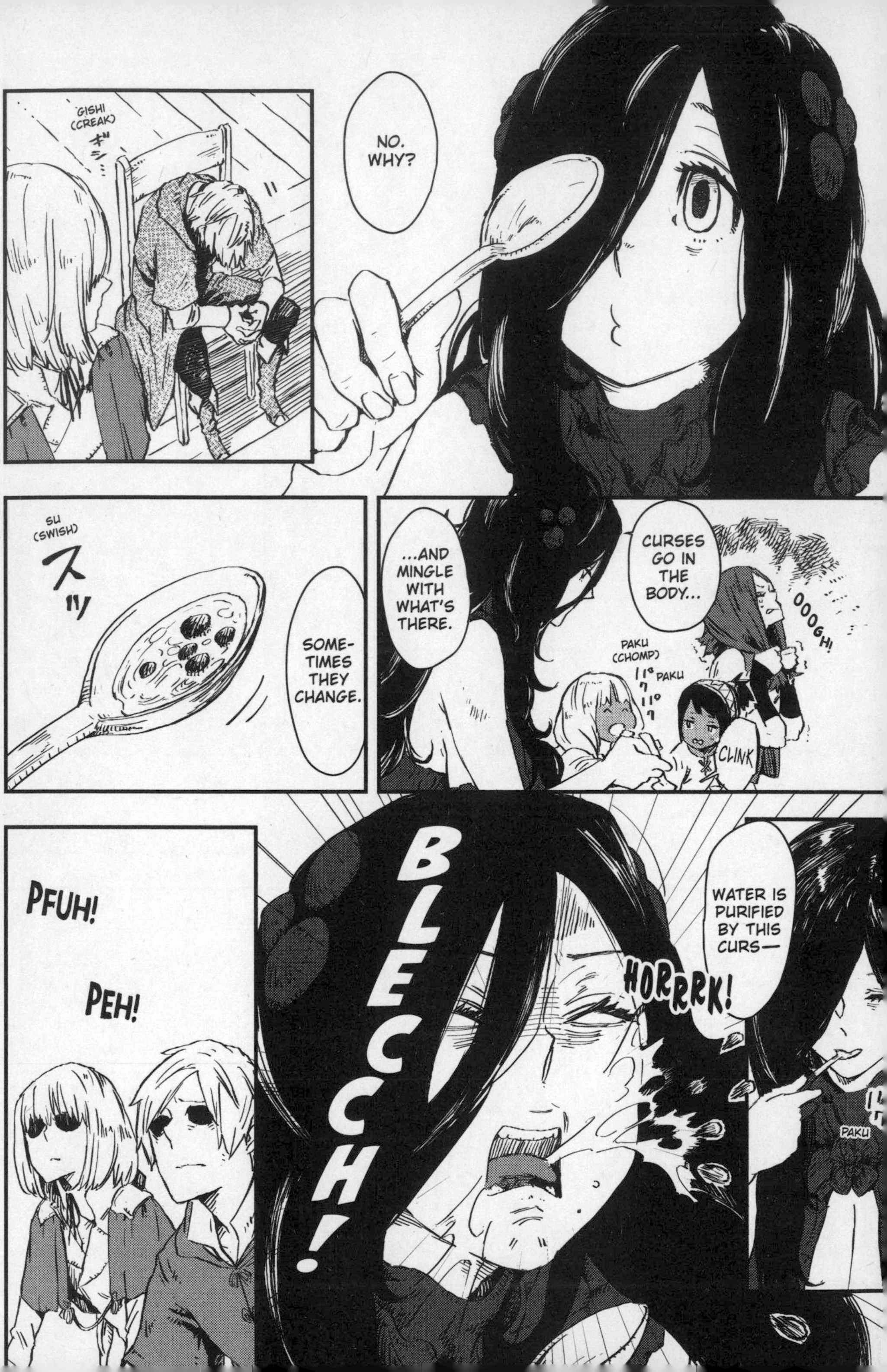
NO. WHY?
GISHI (CREAK)
ギシ
CURSES GO IN THE BODY...
...AND MINGLE WITH WHAT'S THERE.
OOOGH!
PAKU (CHOMP)
PAKU
CLINK
SU (SWISH)
ス
SOME-TIMES THEY CHANGE.
WATER IS PURIFIED BY THIS CURS—
PAKU
HORRRK!
BLEECH!
PFUH!
PEH!

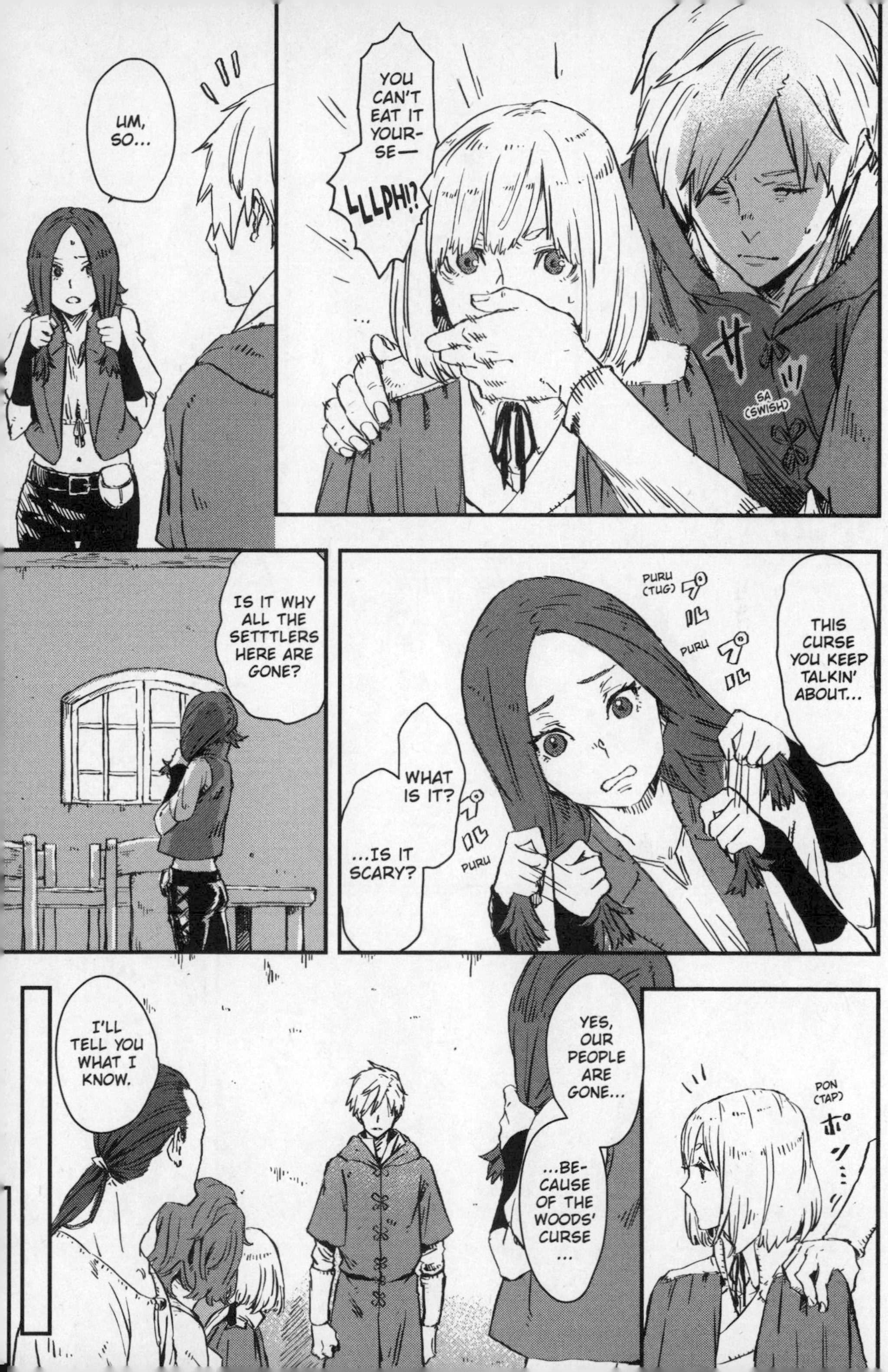
YOU CAN'T EAT IT YOURSE—
LLLPH!?
...
SA (SWISH)
UM, SO...
THIS CURSE YOU KEEP TALKIN' ABOUT...
PURU (TUG)
PURU
WHAT IS IT?
...IS IT SCARY?
PURU
IS IT WHY ALL THE SETTTLERS HERE ARE GONE?
PON (TAP)
YES, OUR PEOPLE ARE GONE...
...BECAUSE OF THE WOODS' CURSE...
I'LL TELL YOU WHAT I KNOW.

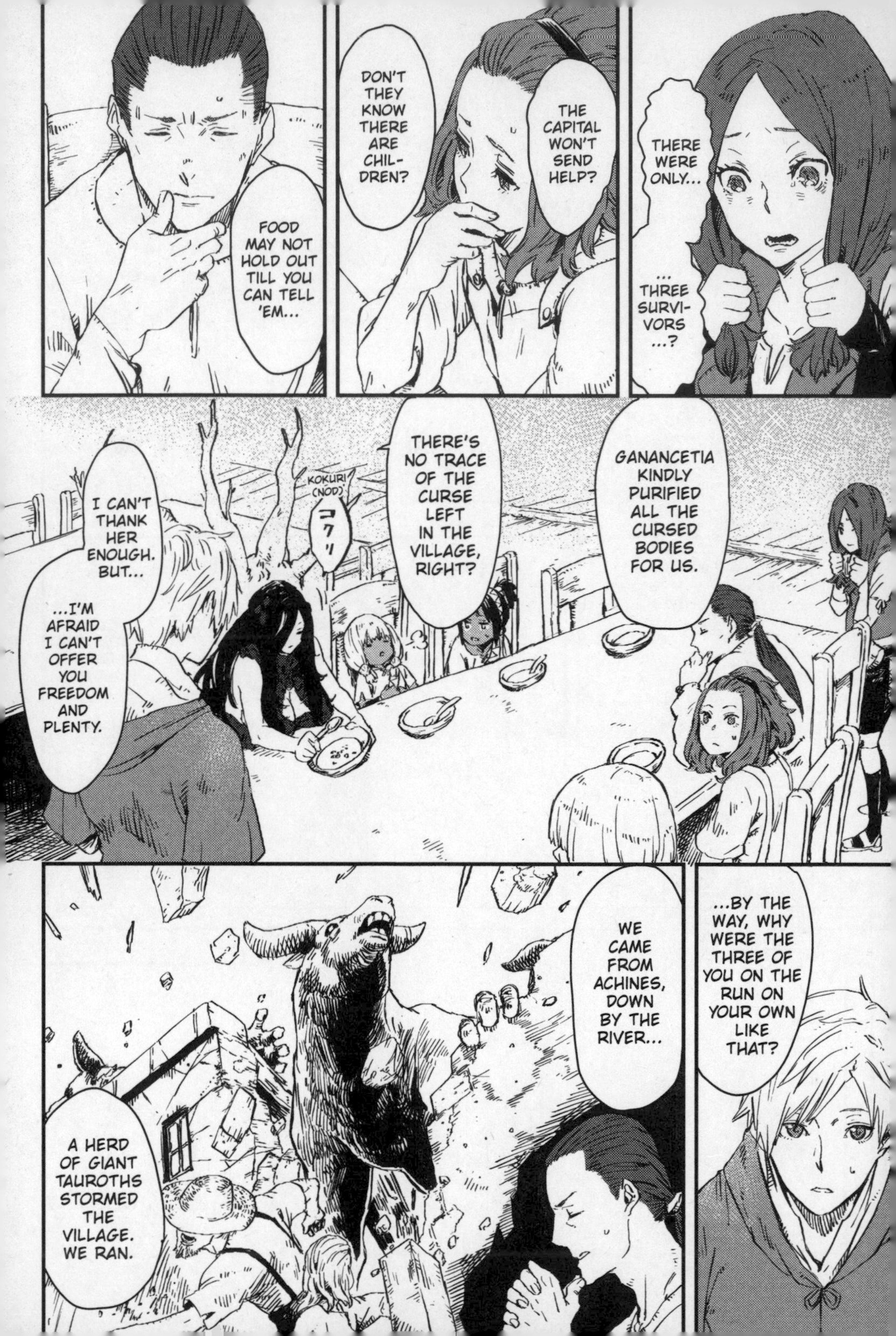
THERE WERE ONLY...
...THREE SURVIVORS...?
THE CAPITAL WON'T SEND HELP?
DON'T THEY KNOW THERE ARE CHILDREN?
FOOD MAY NOT HOLD OUT TILL YOU CAN TELL 'EM...
GANANCETIA KINDLY PURIFIED ALL THE CURSED BODIES FOR US.
THERE'S NO TRACE OF THE CURSE LEFT IN THE VILLAGE, RIGHT?
KOKURI (NOD)
コクリ
I CAN'T THANK HER ENOUGH. BUT...
...I'M AFRAID I CAN'T OFFER YOU FREEDOM AND PLENTY.
...BY THE WAY, WHY WERE THE THREE OF YOU ON THE RUN ON YOUR OWN LIKE THAT?
WE CAME FROM ACHINES, DOWN BY THE RIVER...
A HERD OF GIANT TAUROTHS STORMED THE VILLAGE. WE RAN.

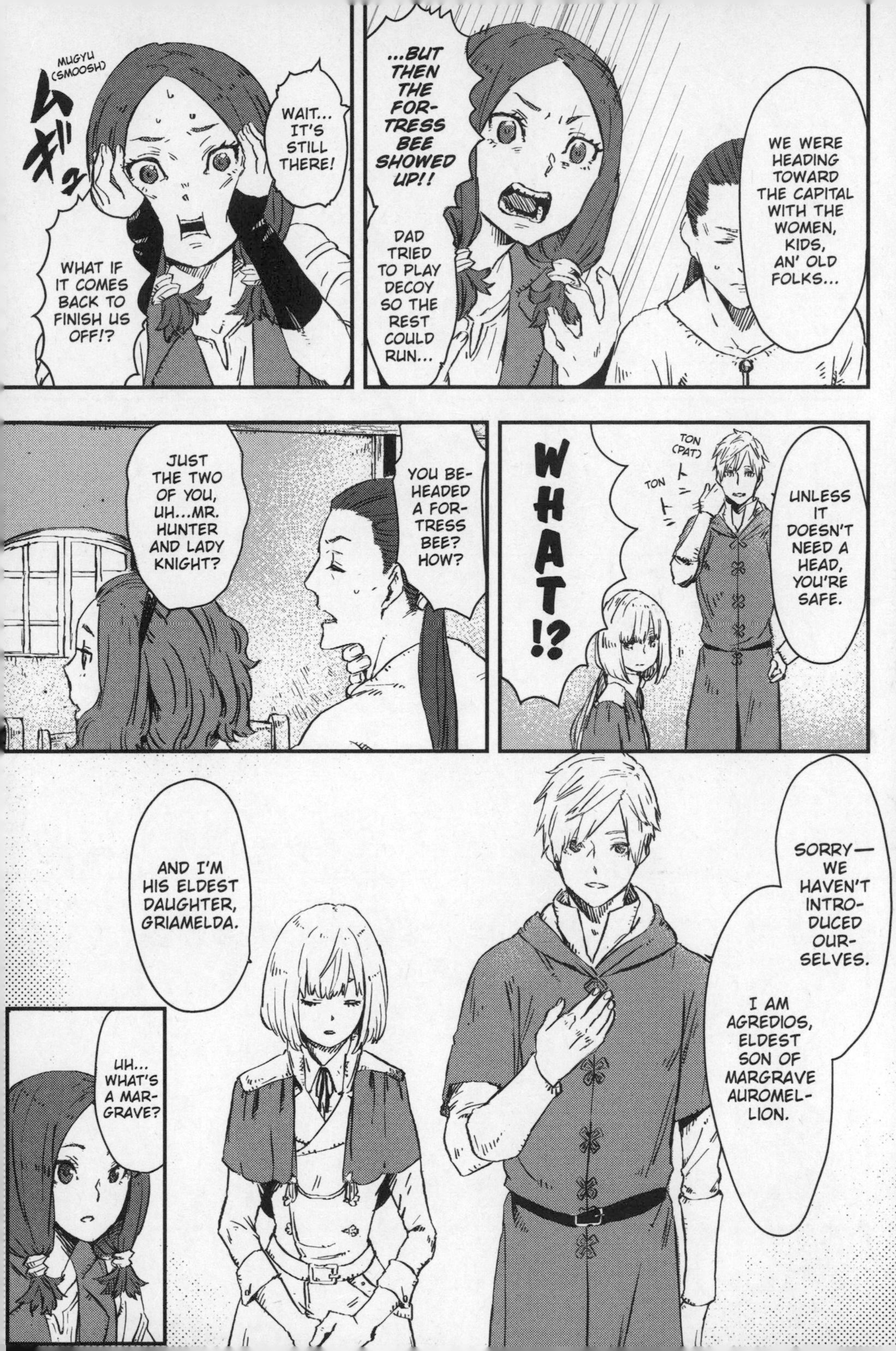
WE WERE HEADING TOWARD THE CAPITAL WITH THE WOMEN, KIDS, AN' OLD FOLKS...
...BUT THEN THE FORTRESS BEE SHOWED UP!!
DAD TRIED TO PLAY DECOY SO THE REST COULD RUN...
WAIT... IT'S STILL THERE!
MUGYU (SMOOSH)
ムギュ
WHAT IF IT COMES BACK TO FINISH US OFF!?
TON (PAT)
TON
UNLESS IT DOESN'T NEED A HEAD, YOU'RE SAFE.
WHAT!?
YOU BEHEADED A FORTRESS BEE? HOW?
JUST THE TWO OF YOU, UH...MR. HUNTER AND LADY KNIGHT?
SORRY— WE HAVEN'T INTRODUCED OURSELVES.
I AM AGREDIOS, ELDEST SON OF MARGRAVE AUROMELLION.
AND I'M HIS ELDEST DAUGHTER, GRIAMELDA.
UH... WHAT'S A MARGRAVE?

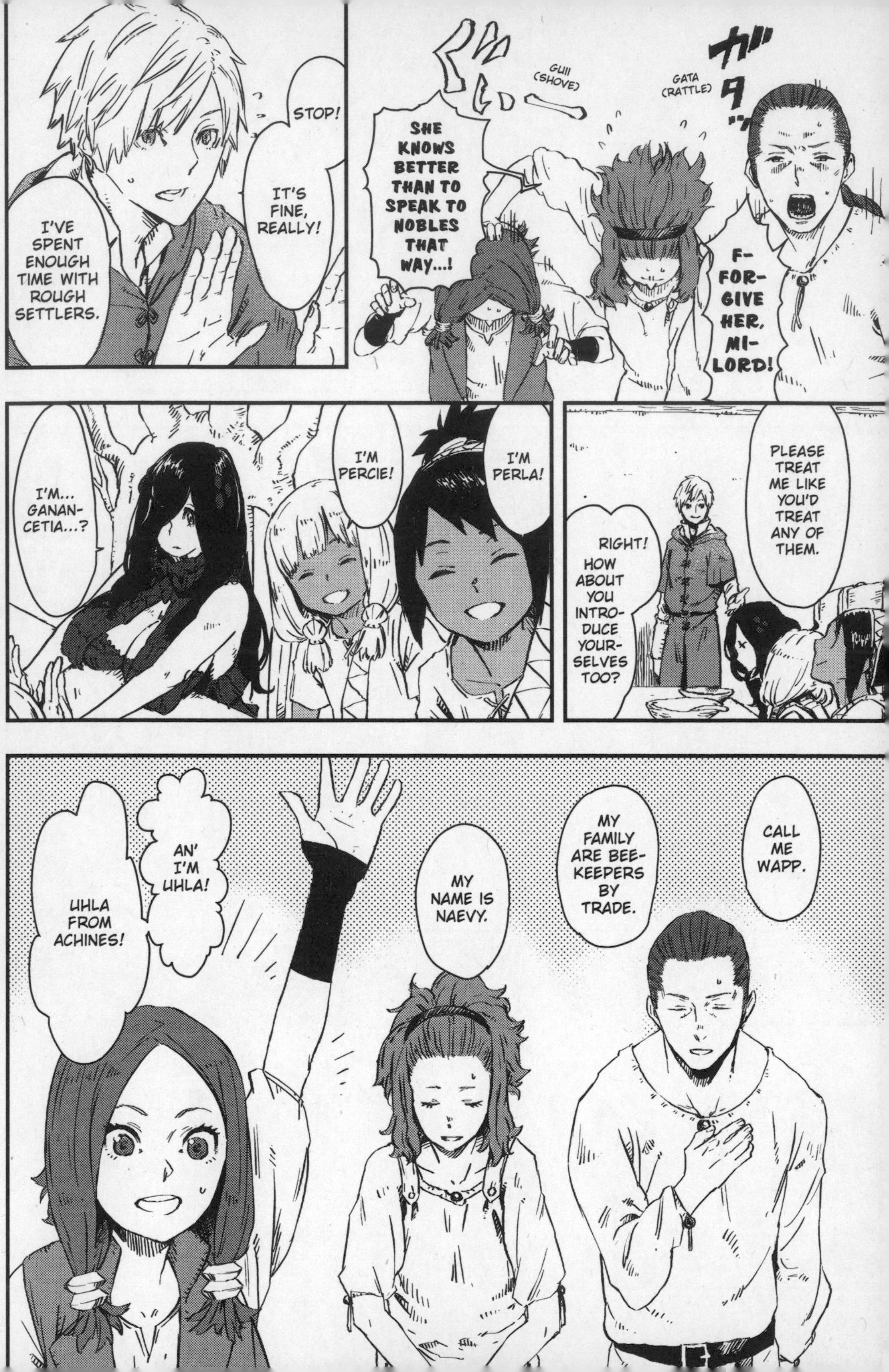
GATA (RATTLE)
GUII (SHOVE)
F-FORGIVE HER, MILORD!
SHE KNOWS BETTER THAN TO SPEAK TO NOBLES THAT WAY...!
STOP!
IT'S FINE, REALLY!
I'VE SPENT ENOUGH TIME WITH ROUGH SETTLERS.
PLEASE TREAT ME LIKE YOU'D TREAT ANY OF THEM.
RIGHT! HOW ABOUT YOU INTRODUCE YOURSELVES TOO?
I'M PERLA!
I'M PERCIE!
I'M... GANANCETIA...?
CALL ME WAPP.
MY FAMILY ARE BEEKEEPERS BY TRADE.
MY NAME IS NAEVY.
AN' I'M UHLA!
UHLA FROM ACHINES!

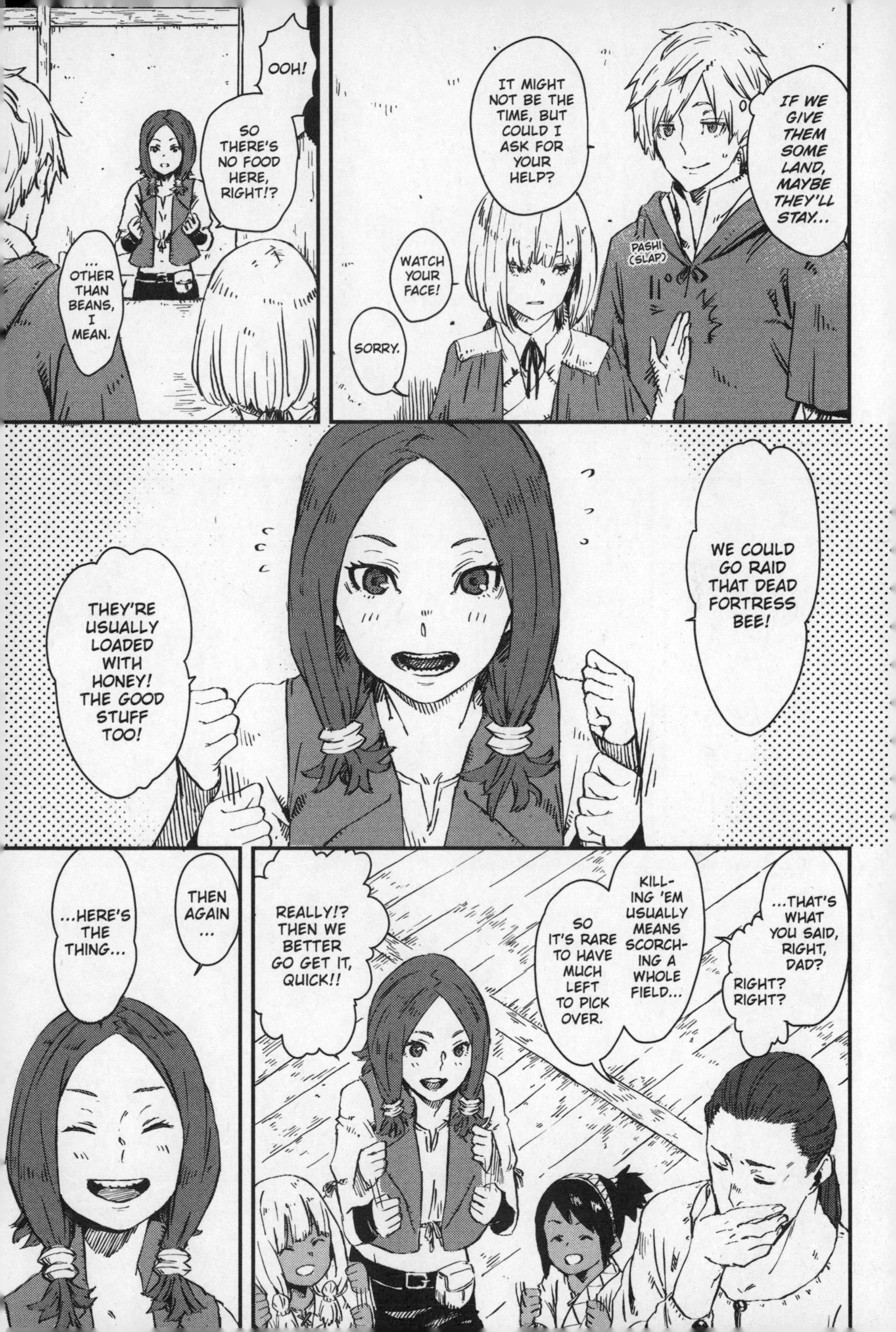
IF WE GIVE THEM SOME LAND, MAYBE THEY'LL STAY...
IT MIGHT NOT BE THE TIME, BUT COULD I ASK FOR YOUR HELP?
PASHI (SLAP)
WATCH YOUR FACE!
SORRY.
OOH!
SO THERE'S NO FOOD HERE, RIGHT!?
...OTHER THAN BEANS, I MEAN.
WE COULD GO RAID THAT DEAD FORTRESS BEE!
THEY'RE USUALLY LOADED WITH HONEY! THE GOOD STUFF TOO!
...THAT'S WHAT YOU SAID, RIGHT, DAD? RIGHT? RIGHT?
KILL-ING 'EM USUALLY MEANS SCORCH-ING A WHOLE FIELD...
SO IT'S RARE TO HAVE MUCH LEFT TO PICK OVER.
REALLY!? THEN WE BETTER GO GET IT, QUICK!!
THEN AGAIN...
...HERE'S THE THING...

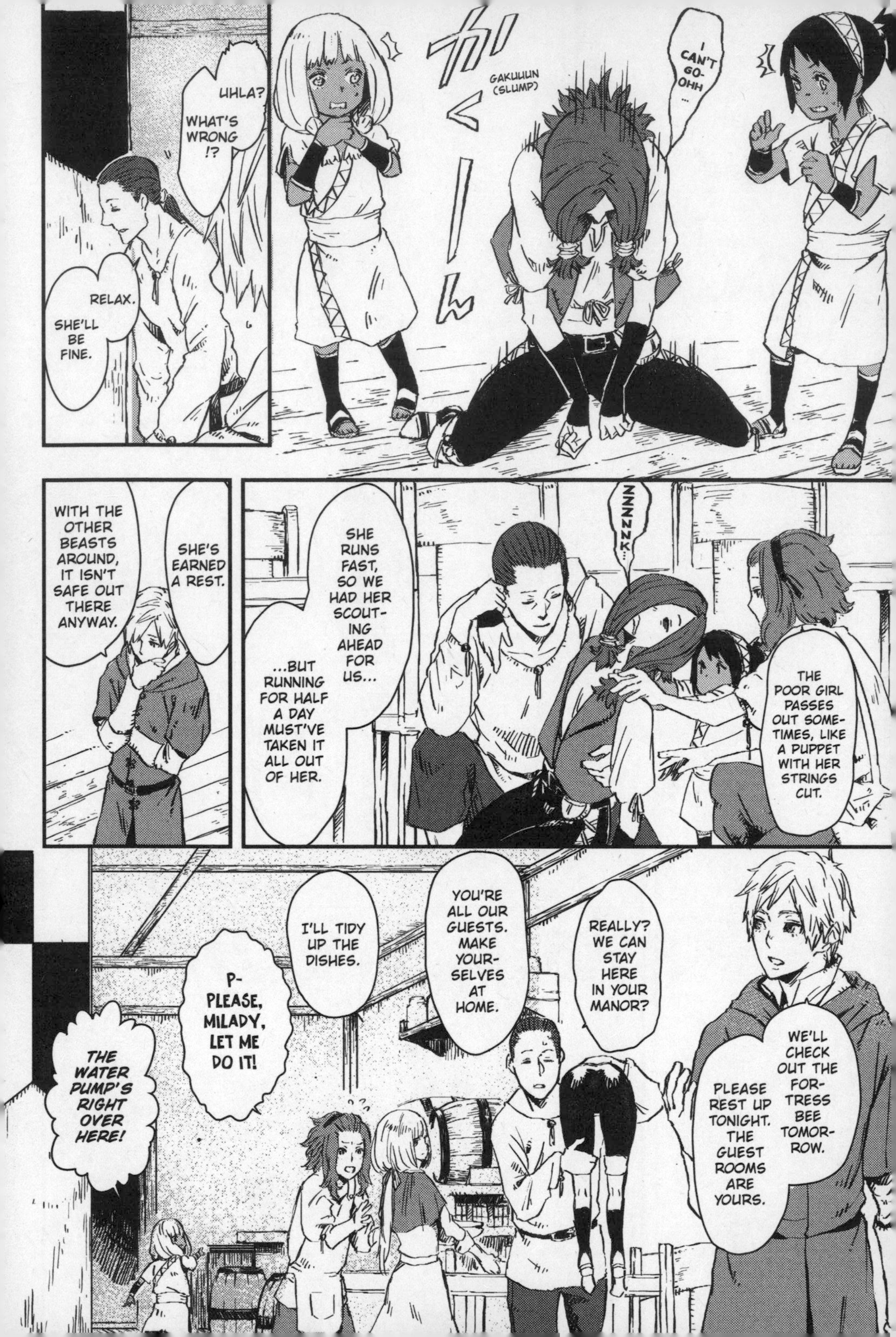
I CAN'T GO-OHH ...
GAKUUUN (SLUMP)
UHLA?
WHAT'S WRONG !?
RELAX.
SHE'LL BE FINE.
ZZZNNK...
THE POOR GIRL PASSES OUT SOMETIMES, LIKE A PUPPET WITH HER STRINGS CUT.
SHE RUNS FAST, SO WE HAD HER SCOUTING AHEAD FOR US...
...BUT RUNNING FOR HALF A DAY MUST'VE TAKEN IT ALL OUT OF HER.
SHE'S EARNED A REST.
WITH THE OTHER BEASTS AROUND, IT ISN'T SAFE OUT THERE ANYWAY.
WE'LL CHECK OUT THE FORTRESS BEE TOMORROW.
PLEASE REST UP TONIGHT. THE GUEST ROOMS ARE YOURS.
REALLY? WE CAN STAY HERE IN YOUR MANOR?
YOU'RE ALL OUR GUESTS. MAKE YOURSELVES AT HOME.
I'LL TIDY UP THE DISHES.
P-PLEASE, MILADY, LET ME DO IT!
THE WATER PUMP'S RIGHT OVER HERE!

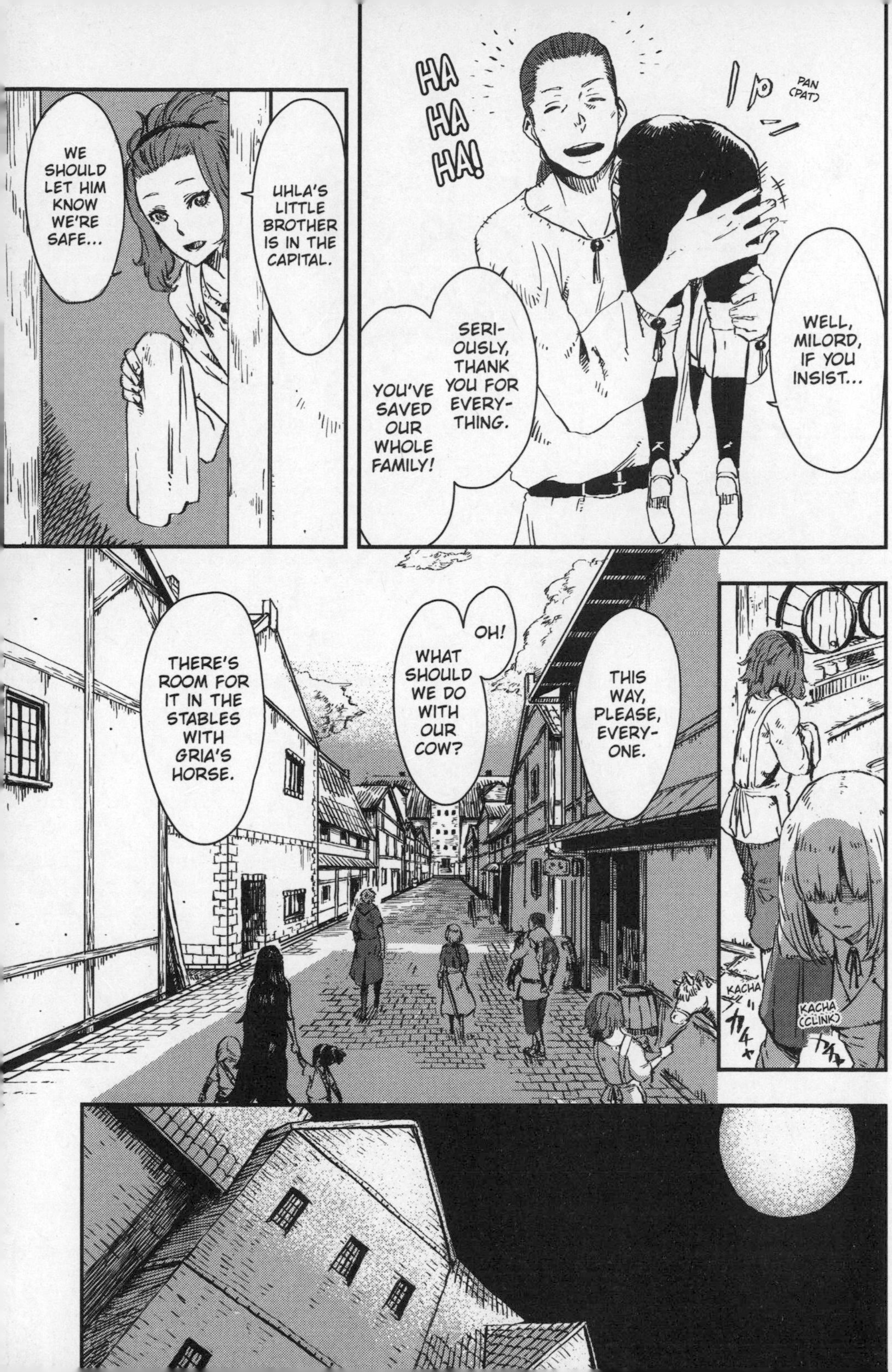
PAN (PAT)
HA HA HA!
WELL, MILORD, IF YOU INSIST...
SERIOUSLY, THANK YOU FOR EVERYTHING.
YOU'VE SAVED OUR WHOLE FAMILY!
UHLA'S LITTLE BROTHER IS IN THE CAPITAL.
WE SHOULD LET HIM KNOW WE'RE SAFE...
KACHA (CLINK)
KACHA
THIS WAY, PLEASE, EVERYONE.
OH!
WHAT SHOULD WE DO WITH OUR COW?
THERE'S ROOM FOR IT IN THE STABLES WITH GRIA'S HORSE.

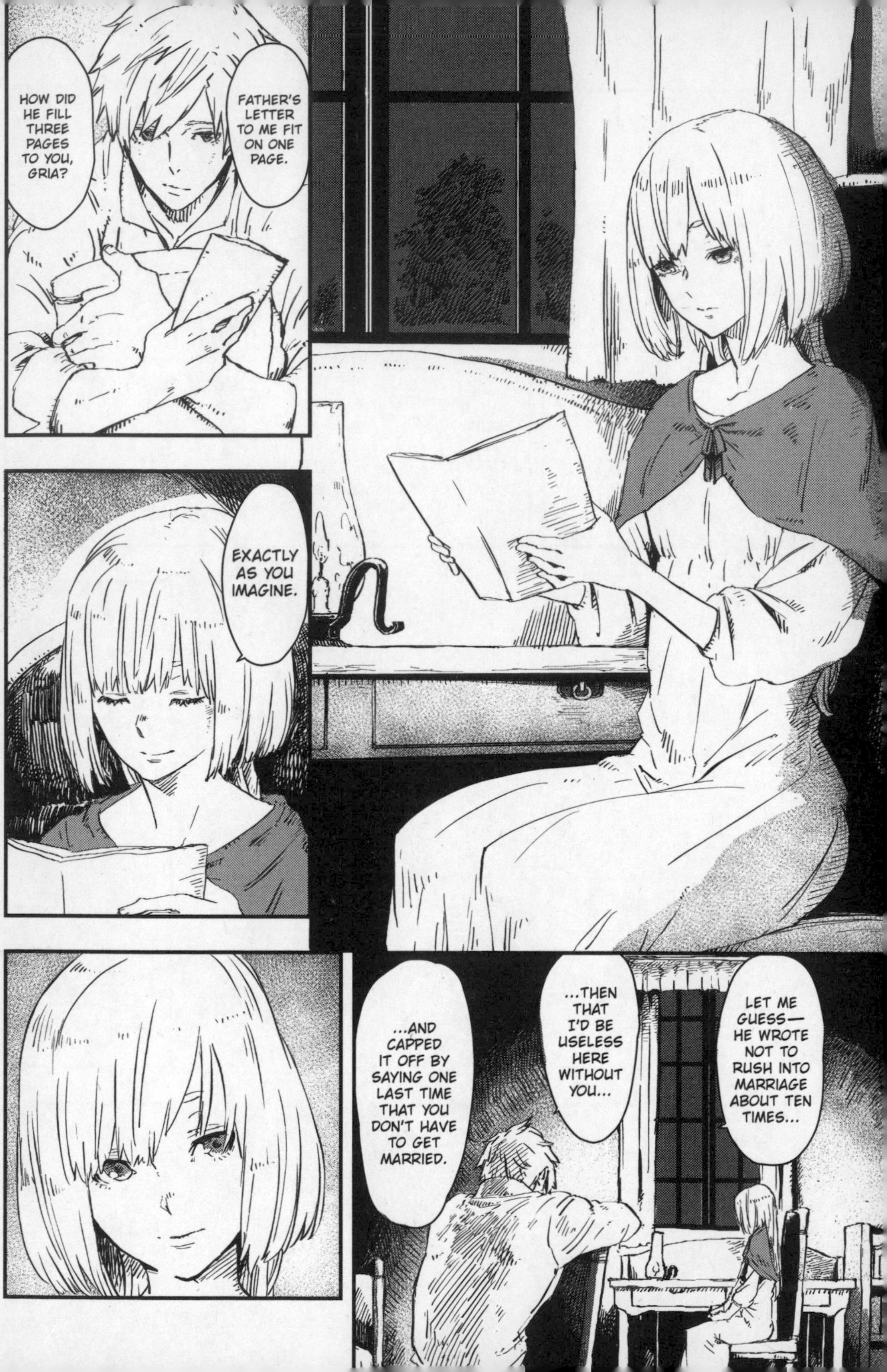
FATHER'S LETTER TO ME FIT ON ONE PAGE.
HOW DID HE FILL THREE PAGES TO YOU, GRIA?
EXACTLY AS YOU IMAGINE.
LET ME GUESS— HE WROTE NOT TO RUSH INTO MARRIAGE ABOUT TEN TIMES...
...THEN THAT I'D BE USELESS HERE WITHOUT YOU...
...AND CAPPED IT OFF BY SAYING ONE LAST TIME THAT YOU DON'T HAVE TO GET MARRIED.

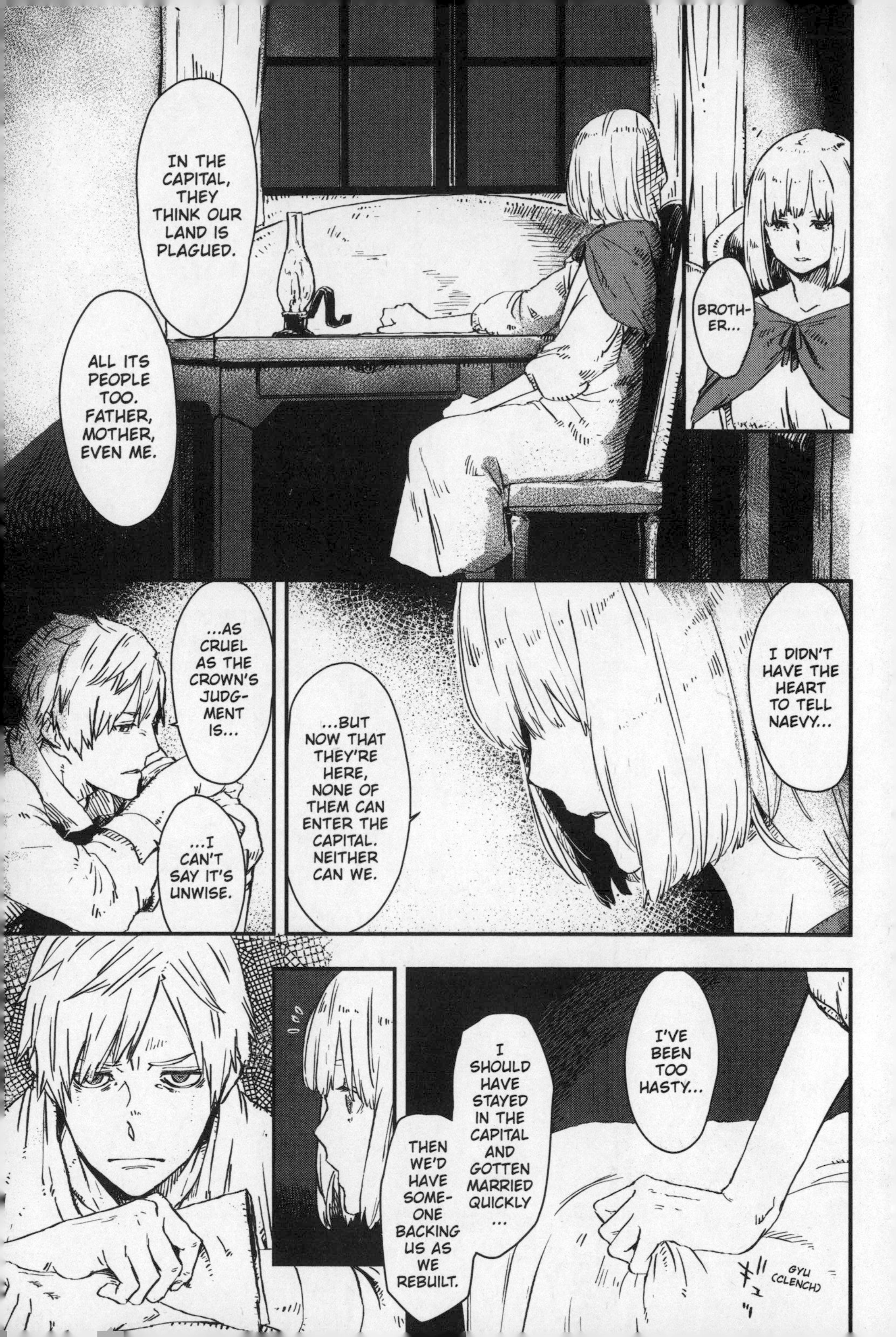
BROTHER...
IN THE CAPITAL, THEY THINK OUR LAND IS PLAGUED.
ALL ITS PEOPLE TOO. FATHER, MOTHER, EVEN ME.
I DIDN'T HAVE THE HEART TO TELL NAEVY...
...BUT NOW THAT THEY'RE HERE, NONE OF THEM CAN ENTER THE CAPITAL. NEITHER CAN WE.
...AS CRUEL AS THE CROWN'S JUDGMENT IS...
...I CAN'T SAY IT'S UNWISE.
I'VE BEEN TOO HASTY...
GYU (CLENCH)
I SHOULD HAVE STAYED IN THE CAPITAL AND GOTTEN MARRIED QUICKLY...
THEN WE'D HAVE SOMEONE BACKING US AS WE REBUILT.

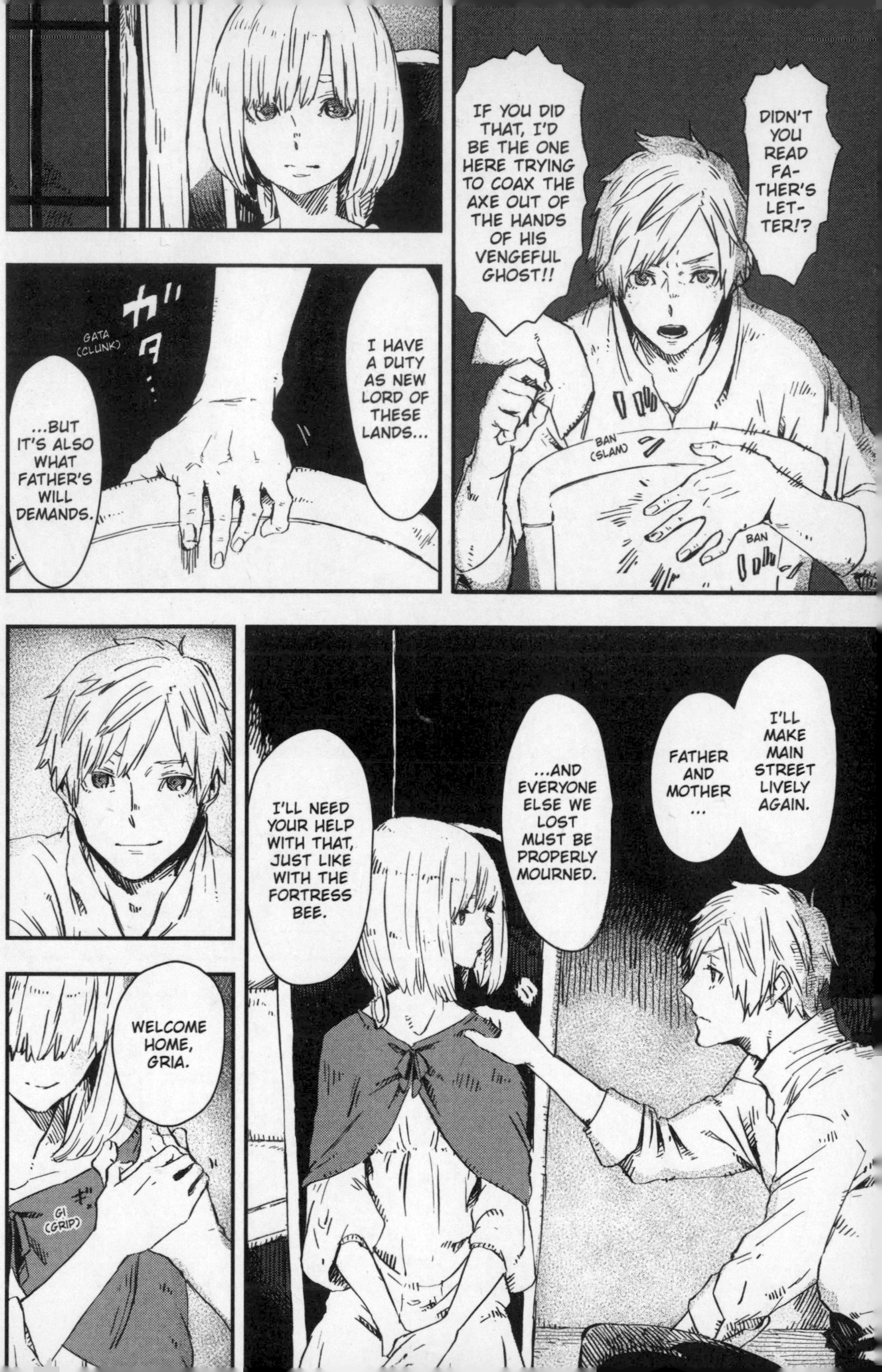
DIDN'T YOU READ FA-THER'S LET-TER!?
IF YOU DID THAT, I'D BE THE ONE HERE TRYING TO COAX THE AXE OUT OF THE HANDS OF HIS VENGEFUL GHOST!!
BAN (SLAM)
BAN
I HAVE A DUTY AS NEW LORD OF THESE LANDS...
GATA (CLUNK)
...BUT IT'S ALSO WHAT FATHER'S WILL DEMANDS.
I'LL MAKE MAIN STREET LIVELY AGAIN.
FATHER AND MOTHER...
...AND EVERYONE ELSE WE LOST MUST BE PROPERLY MOURNED.
I'LL NEED YOUR HELP WITH THAT, JUST LIKE WITH THE FORTRESS BEE.
WELCOME HOME, GRIA.
GI (GRIP)

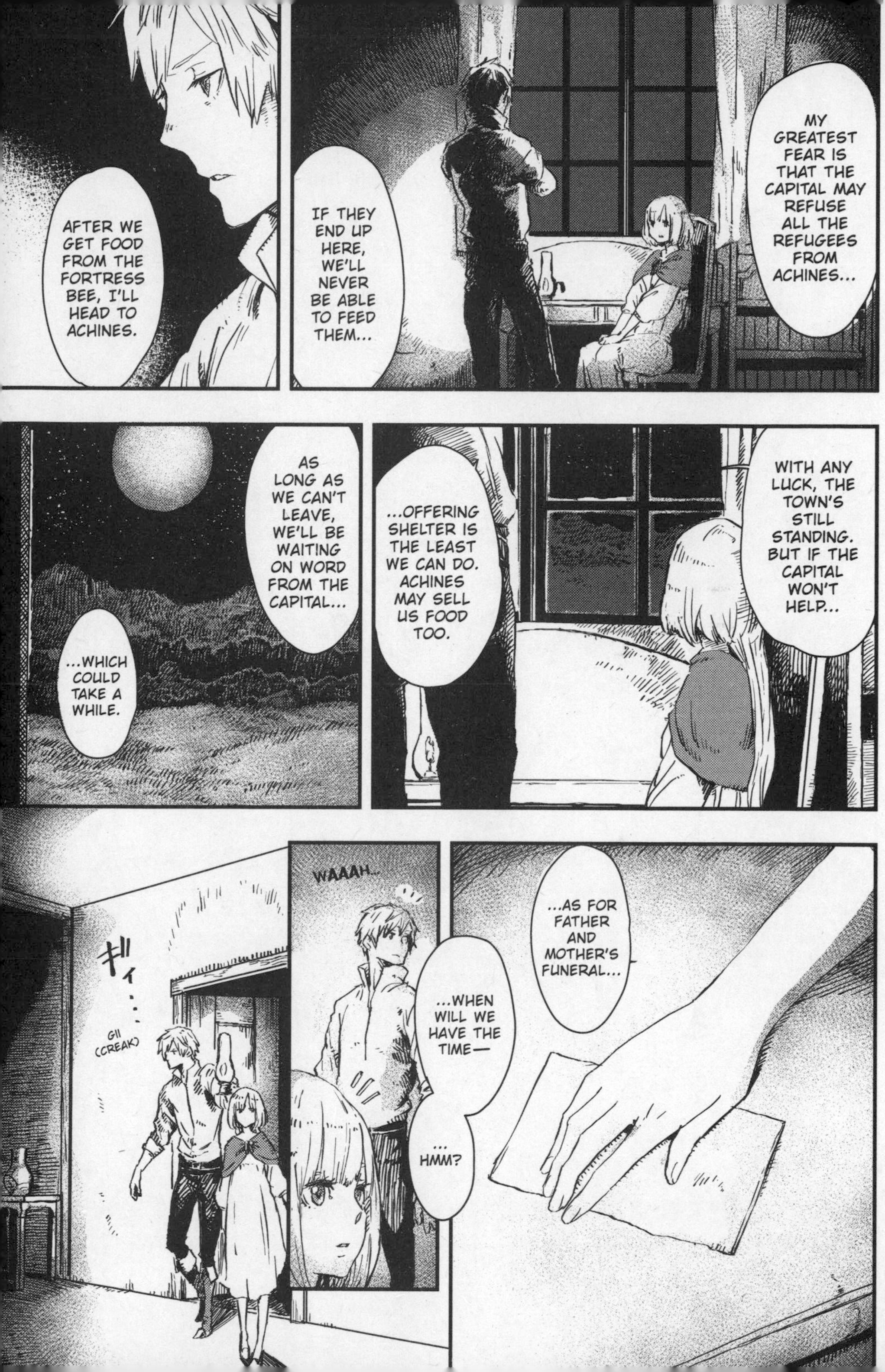
MY GREATEST FEAR IS THAT THE CAPITAL MAY REFUSE ALL THE REFUGEES FROM ACHINES...
IF THEY END UP HERE, WE'LL NEVER BE ABLE TO FEED THEM...
AFTER WE GET FOOD FROM THE FORTRESS BEE, I'LL HEAD TO ACHINES.
WITH ANY LUCK, THE TOWN'S STILL STANDING. BUT IF THE CAPITAL WON'T HELP...
...OFFERING SHELTER IS THE LEAST WE CAN DO. ACHINES MAY SELL US FOOD TOO.
AS LONG AS WE CAN'T LEAVE, WE'LL BE WAITING ON WORD FROM THE CAPITAL...
...WHICH COULD TAKE A WHILE.
...AS FOR FATHER AND MOTHER'S FUNERAL...
...WHEN WILL WE HAVE THE TIME—
WAAAH...
... HMM?
ギィ...
GII (CREAK)

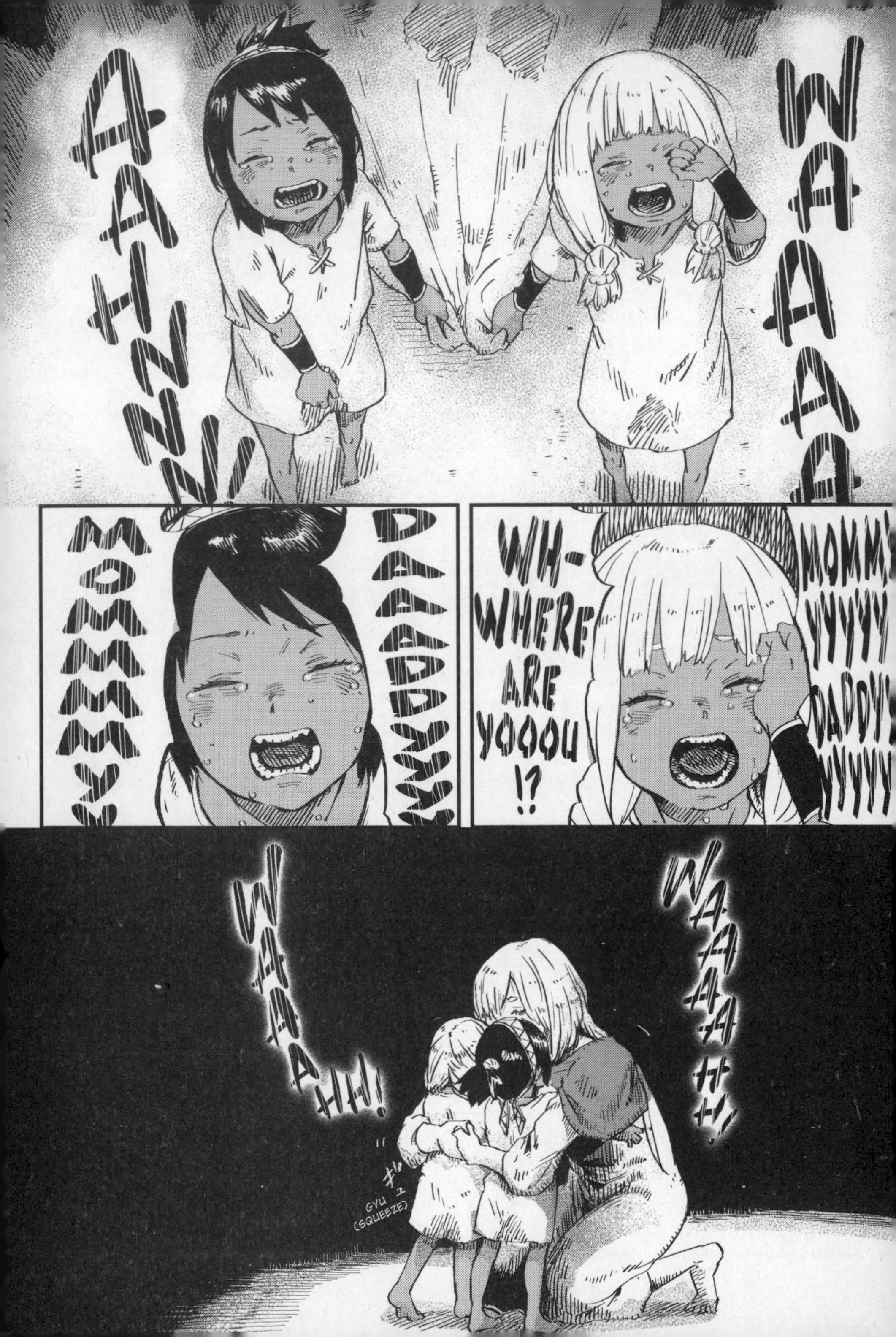
WAAAAA
AAHNNN!
WH-WHERE ARE YOOOU!?
MOMMYYYYY DADDYYYYY
DAAADDYYY
MOMMMMMY
WAAAAAHH!
WAAAAAHH!
GYU (SQUEEZE)

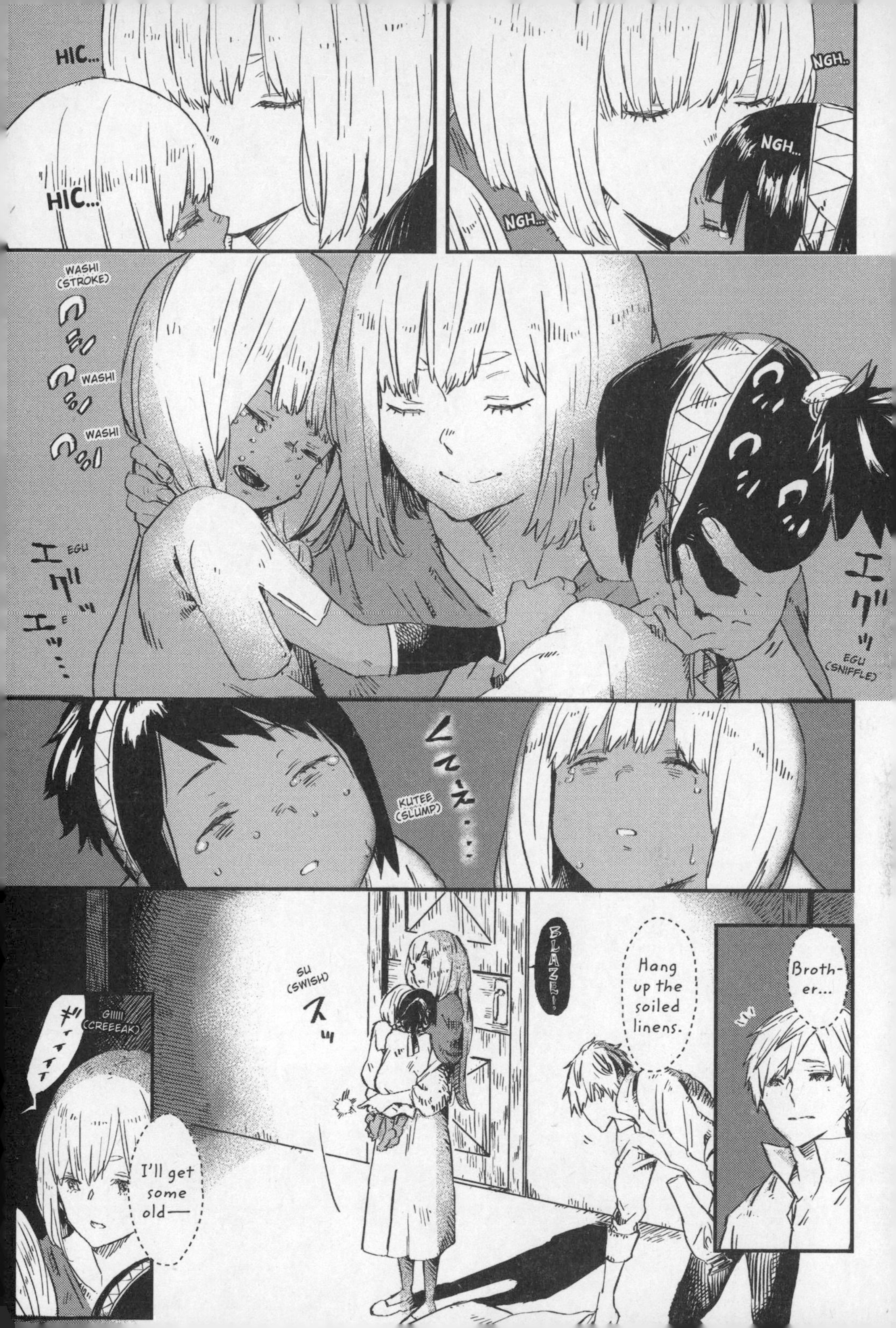
NGH..
NGH...
NGH...
HIC...
HIC...
EGU (SNIFFLE)
WASHI (STROKE)
WASHI
WASHI
EGU
E
KUTEE (SLUMP)
Brother...
Hang up the soiled linens.
BLAZE!
SU (SWISH)
GIIIII (CREEEAK)
I'll get some old—

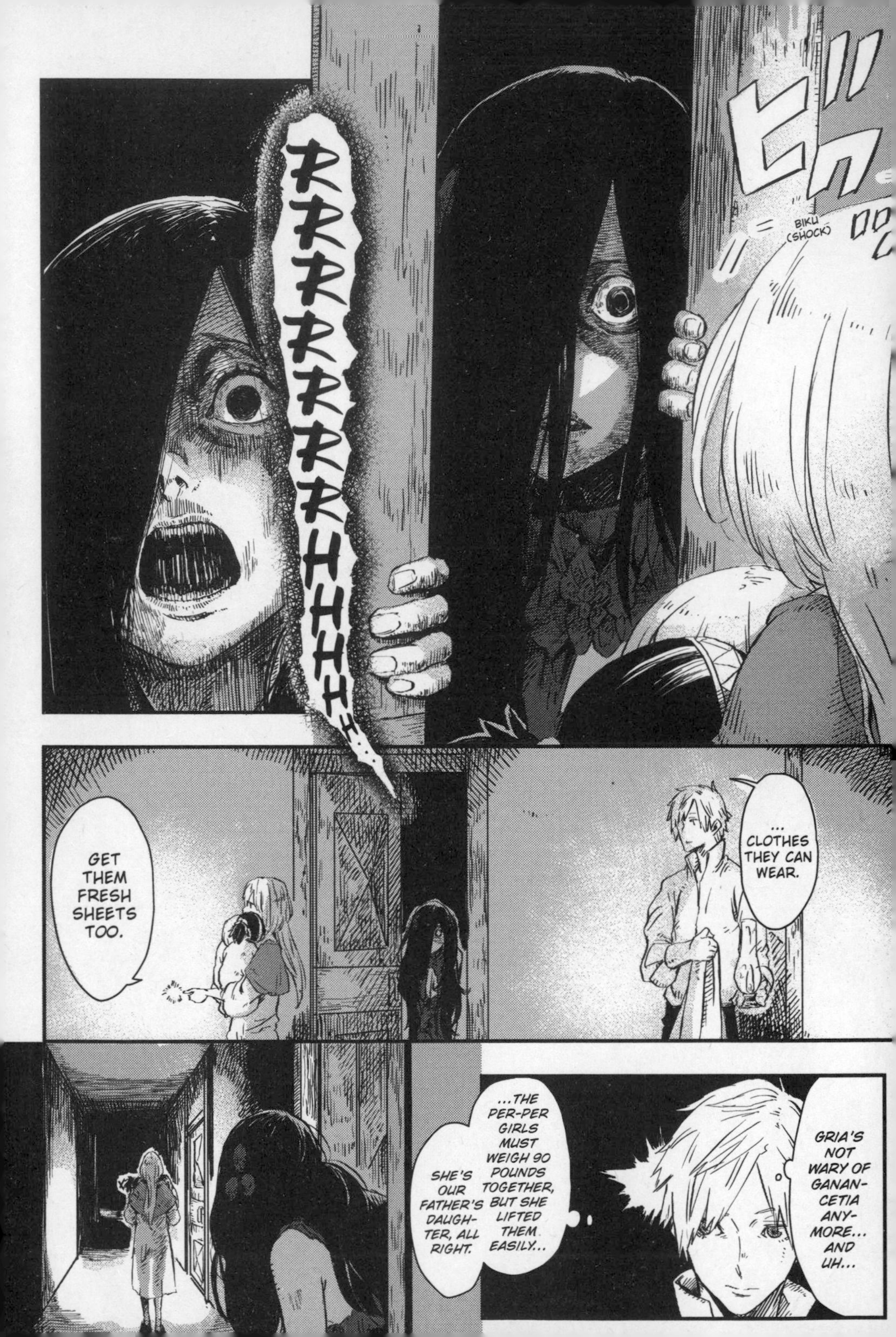
ビクッ
BIKU (SHOCK)
RRRRRRRRHHHHH...
...CLOTHES THEY CAN WEAR.
GET THEM FRESH SHEETS TOO.
GRIA'S NOT WARY OF GANAN-CETIA ANYMORE... AND UH...
...THE PER-PER GIRLS MUST WEIGH 90 POUNDS TOGETHER, BUT SHE LIFTED THEM EASILY...
SHE'S OUR FATHER'S DAUGH-TER, ALL RIGHT.

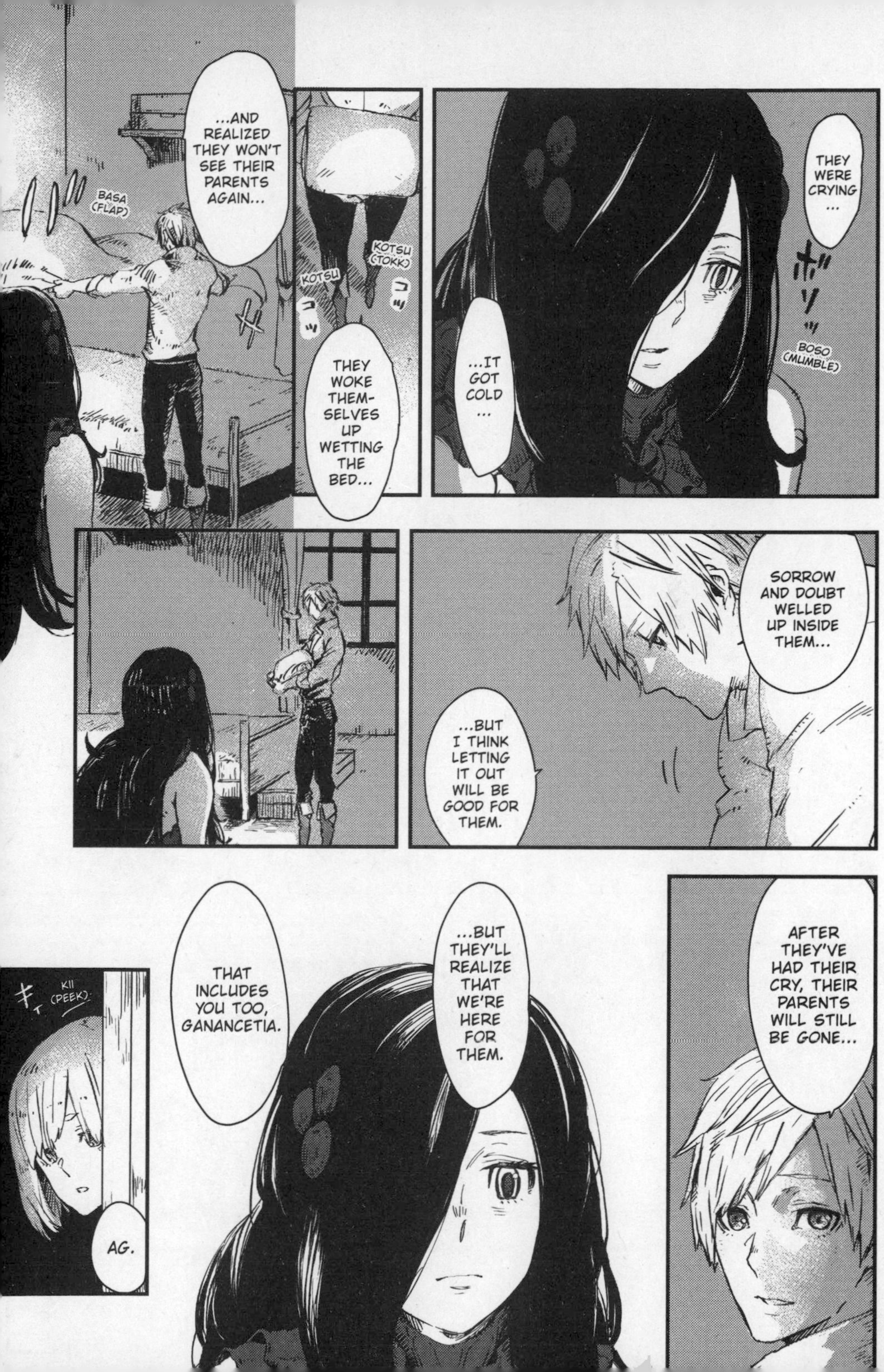
THEY WERE CRYING...
BOSO (MUMBLE)
...IT GOT COLD...
KOTSU (TOKK)
KOTSU
THEY WOKE THEM-SELVES UP WETTING THE BED...
...AND REALIZED THEY WON'T SEE THEIR PARENTS AGAIN...
BASA (FLAP)
SORROW AND DOUBT WELLED UP INSIDE THEM...
...BUT I THINK LETTING IT OUT WILL BE GOOD FOR THEM.
AFTER THEY'VE HAD THEIR CRY, THEIR PARENTS WILL STILL BE GONE...
...BUT THEY'LL REALIZE THAT WE'RE HERE FOR THEM.
THAT INCLUDES YOU TOO, GANANCETIA.
KII (PEEK)
AG.

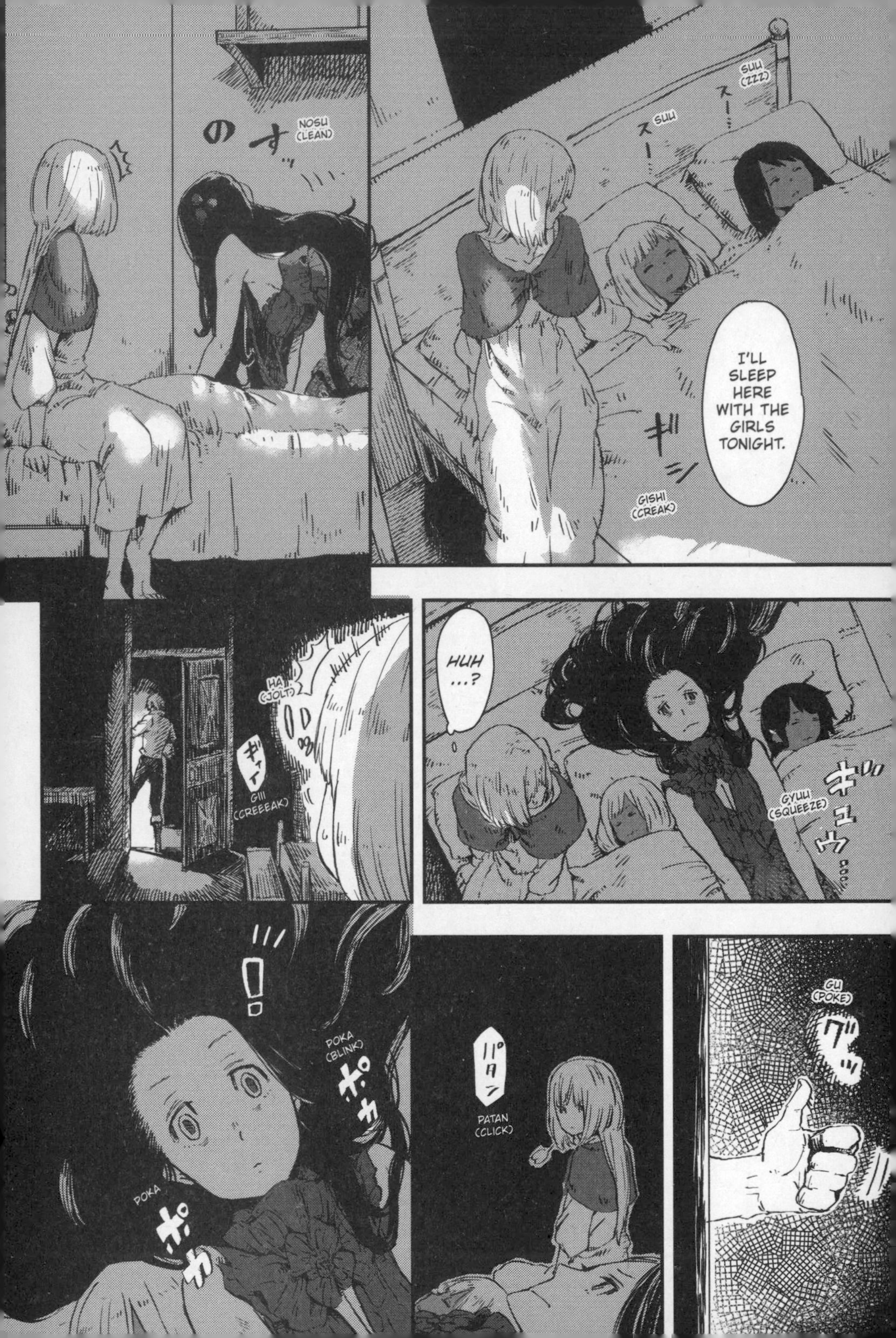
SUU (ZZZ)
SUU
I'LL SLEEP HERE WITH THE GIRLS TONIGHT.
GISHI (CREAK)
NOSU (LEAN)
HUH ...?
GYUU (SQUEEZE)
HA (JOLT)
GIII (CREEEAK)
GU (POKE)
PATAN (CLICK)
POKA (BLINK)
POKA

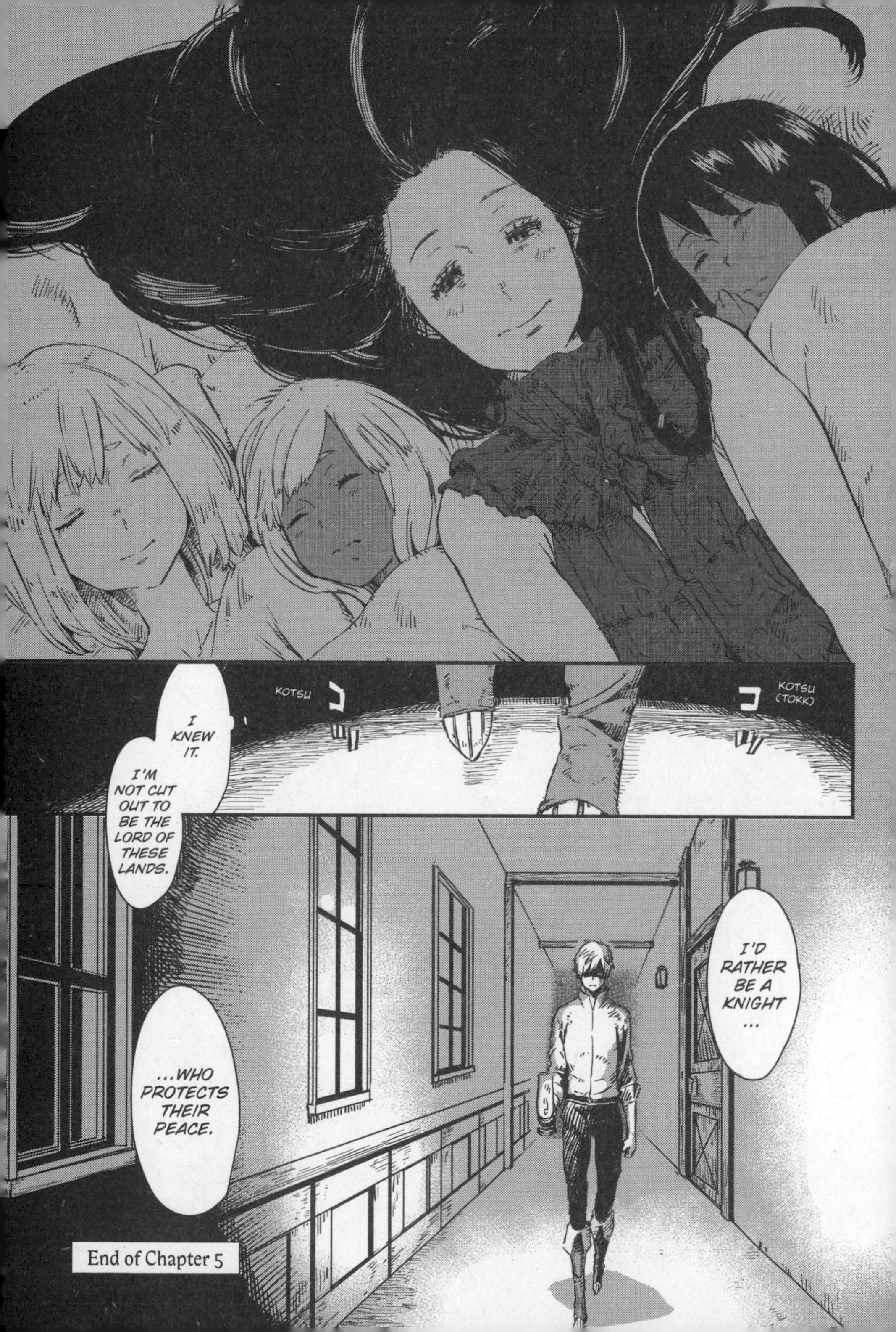

KOTSU (TOKK)
コ
KOTSU
コ
I KNEW IT.
I'M NOT CUT OUT TO BE THE LORD OF THESE LANDS.
I'D RATHER BE A KNIGHT...
...WHO PROTECTS THEIR PEACE.

End of Chapter 5

Chapter 6: The Proper Use of Fire

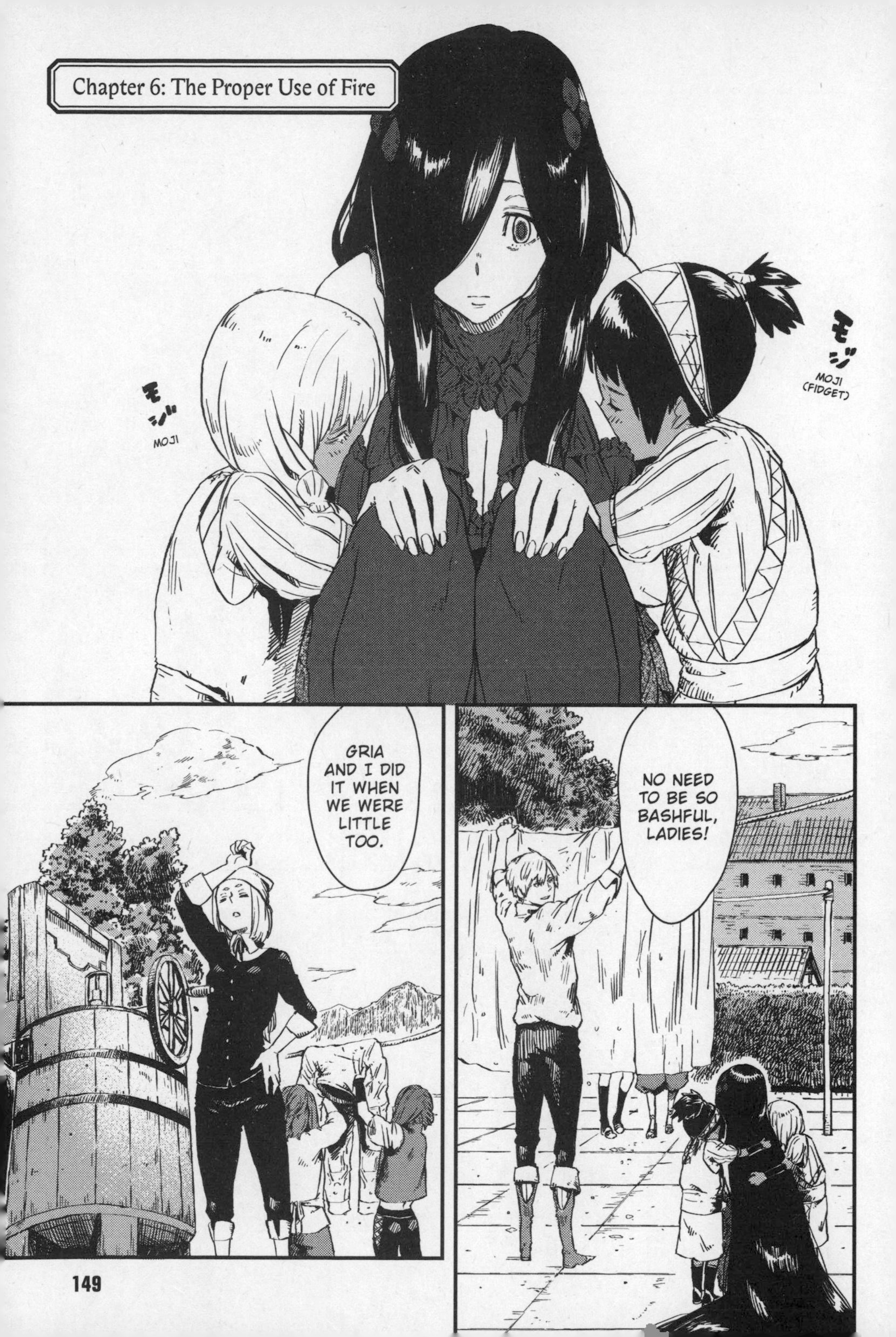

モジ
MOJI (FIDGET)
モジ
MOJI
NO NEED TO BE SO BASHFUL, LADIES!
GRIA AND I DID IT WHEN WE WERE LITTLE TOO.

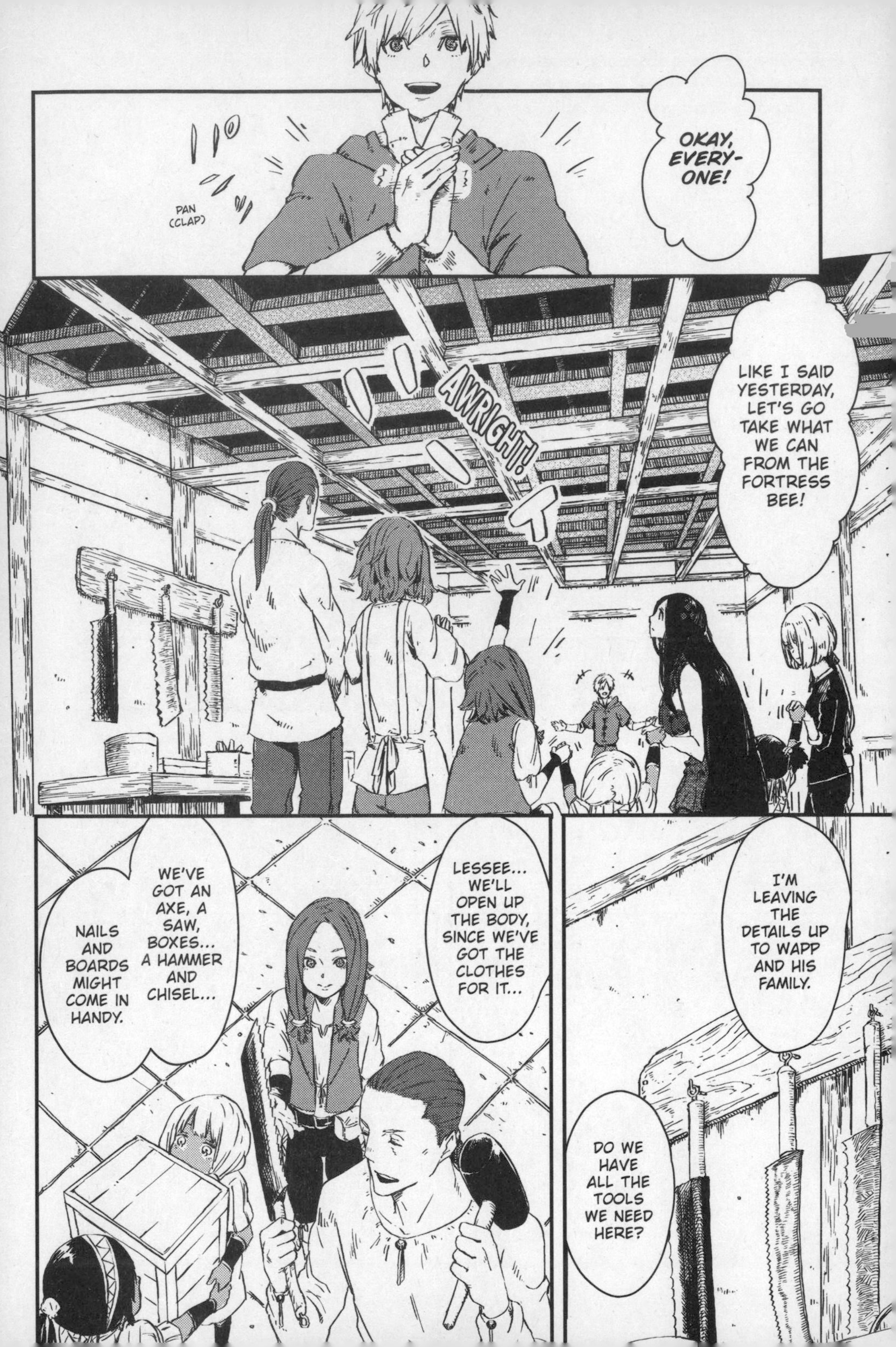
OKAY, EVERY-ONE!
PAN (CLAP)
LIKE I SAID YESTERDAY, LET'S GO TAKE WHAT WE CAN FROM THE FORTRESS BEE!
AWRIGHT!
I'M LEAVING THE DETAILS UP TO WAPP AND HIS FAMILY.
DO WE HAVE ALL THE TOOLS WE NEED HERE?
LESSEE... WE'LL OPEN UP THE BODY, SINCE WE'VE GOT THE CLOTHES FOR IT...
WE'VE GOT AN AXE, A SAW, BOXES... A HAMMER AND CHISEL...
NAILS AND BOARDS MIGHT COME IN HANDY.

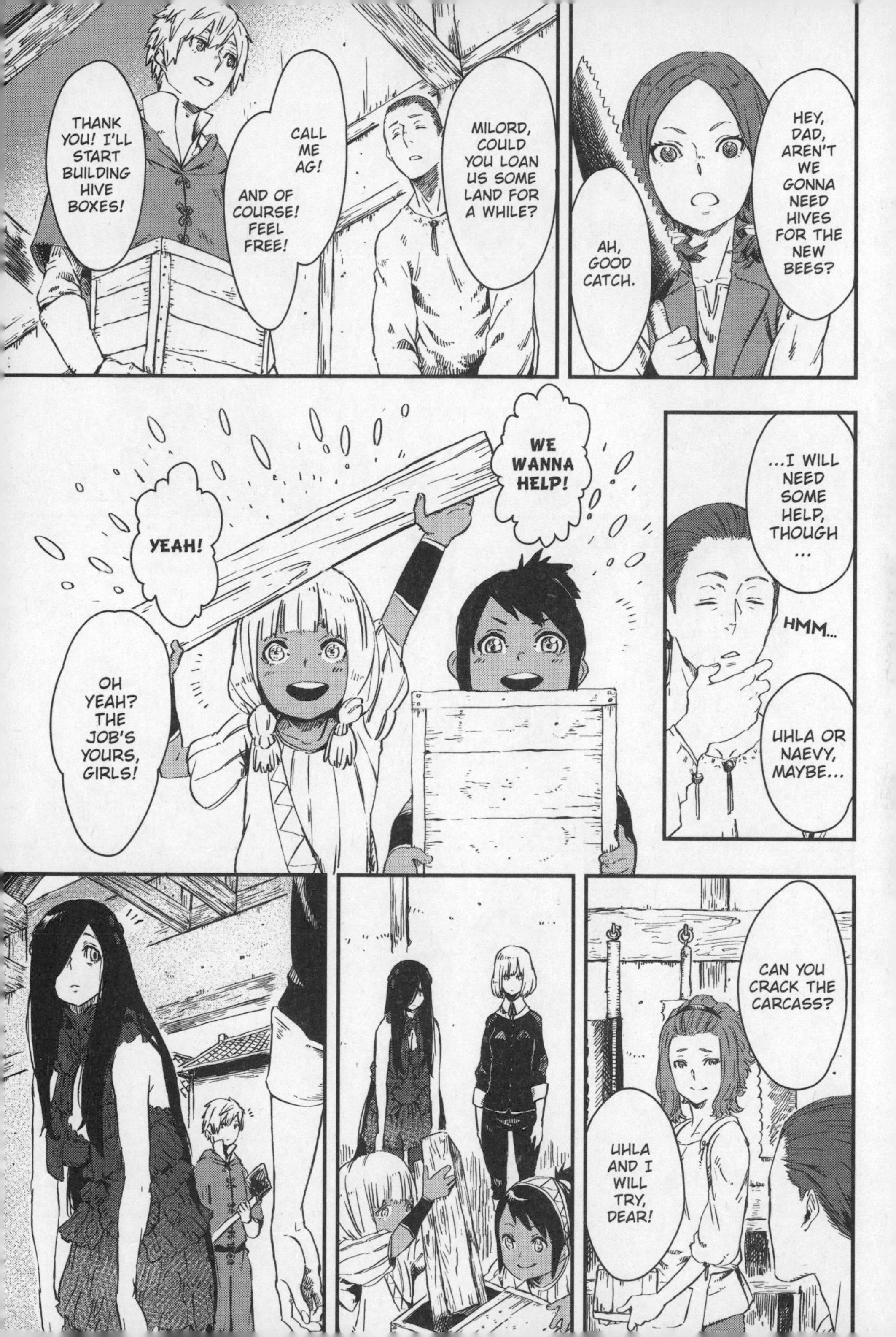
HEY, DAD, AREN'T WE GONNA NEED HIVES FOR THE NEW BEES?
AH, GOOD CATCH.
MILORD, COULD YOU LOAN US SOME LAND FOR A WHILE?
CALL ME AG!
AND OF COURSE! FEEL FREE!
THANK YOU! I'LL START BUILDING HIVE BOXES!
...I WILL NEED SOME HELP, THOUGH ...
HMM...
UHLA OR NAEVY, MAYBE...
WE WANNA HELP!
YEAH!
OH YEAH? THE JOB'S YOURS, GIRLS!
CAN YOU CRACK THE CARCASS?
UHLA AND I WILL TRY, DEAR!

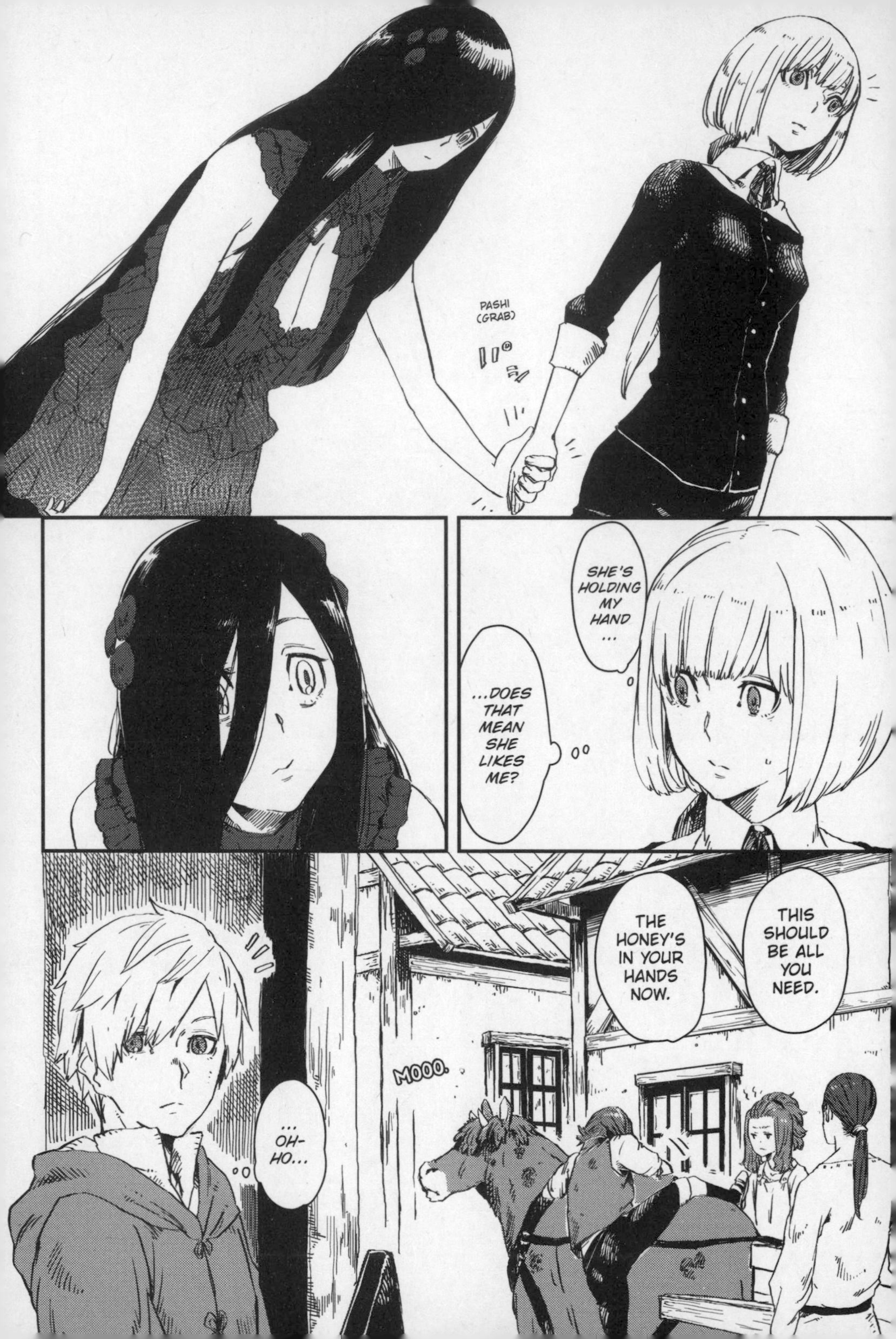
PASHI (GRAB)
SHE'S HOLDING MY HAND...
...DOES THAT MEAN SHE LIKES ME?
THIS SHOULD BE ALL YOU NEED.
THE HONEY'S IN YOUR HANDS NOW.
MOOO.
...OH-HO...

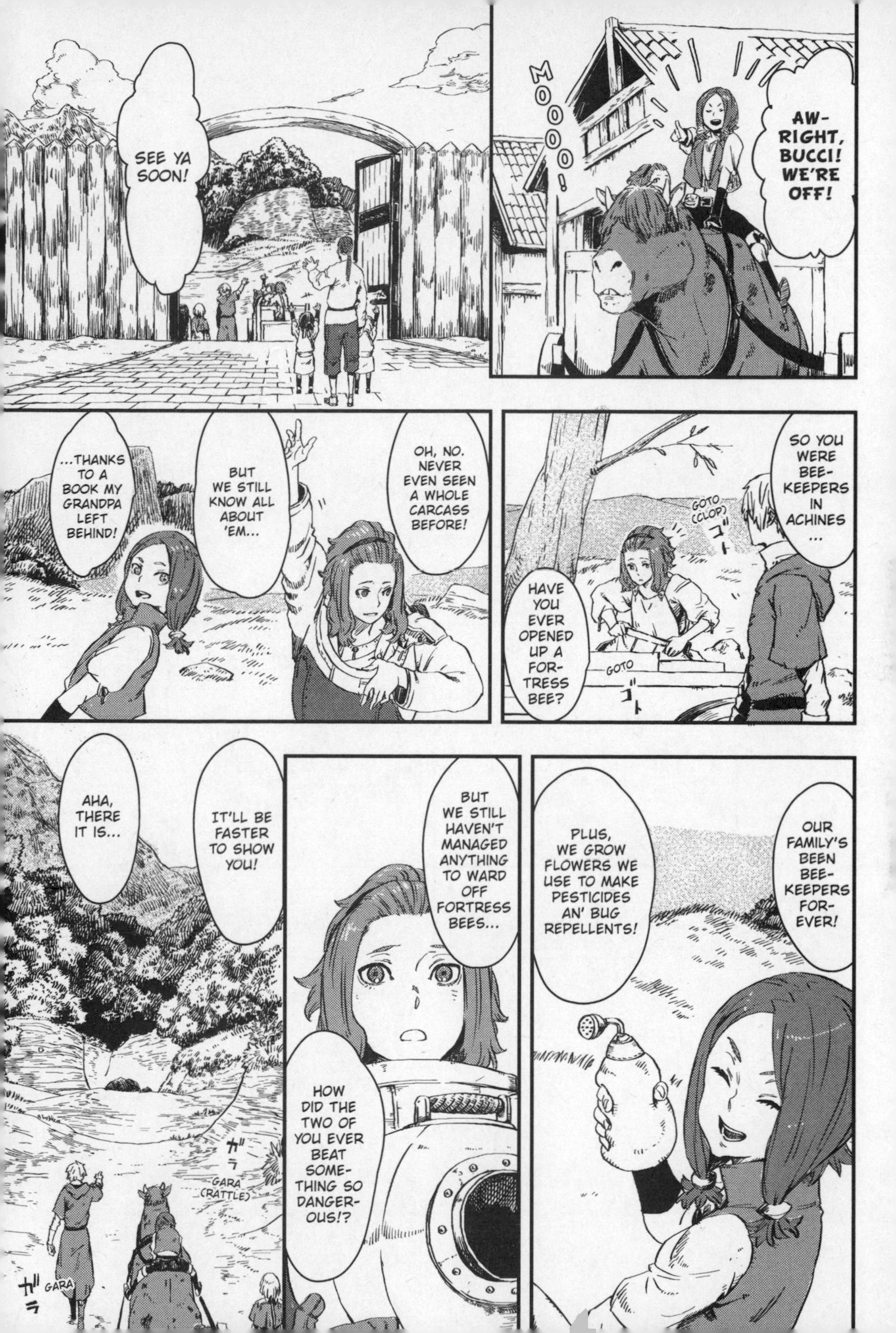
AW-RIGHT, BUCCI! WE'RE OFF!
MOOOOO!
SEE YA SOON!
SO YOU WERE BEE-KEEPERS IN ACHINES...
GOTO (CLOP)
ゴト
HAVE YOU EVER OPENED UP A FOR-TRESS BEE?
GOTO
ゴト
OH, NO. NEVER EVEN SEEN A WHOLE CARCASS BEFORE!
BUT WE STILL KNOW ALL ABOUT 'EM...
...THANKS TO A BOOK MY GRANDPA LEFT BEHIND!
OUR FAMILY'S BEEN BEE-KEEPERS FOR-EVER!
PLUS, WE GROW FLOWERS WE USE TO MAKE PESTICIDES AN' BUG REPELLENTS!
BUT WE STILL HAVEN'T MANAGED ANYTHING TO WARD OFF FORTRESS BEES...
HOW DID THE TWO OF YOU EVER BEAT SOME-THING SO DANGER-OUS!?
IT'LL BE FASTER TO SHOW YOU!
AHA, THERE IT IS...
ガラ
GARA (RATTLE)
ガラ
GARA

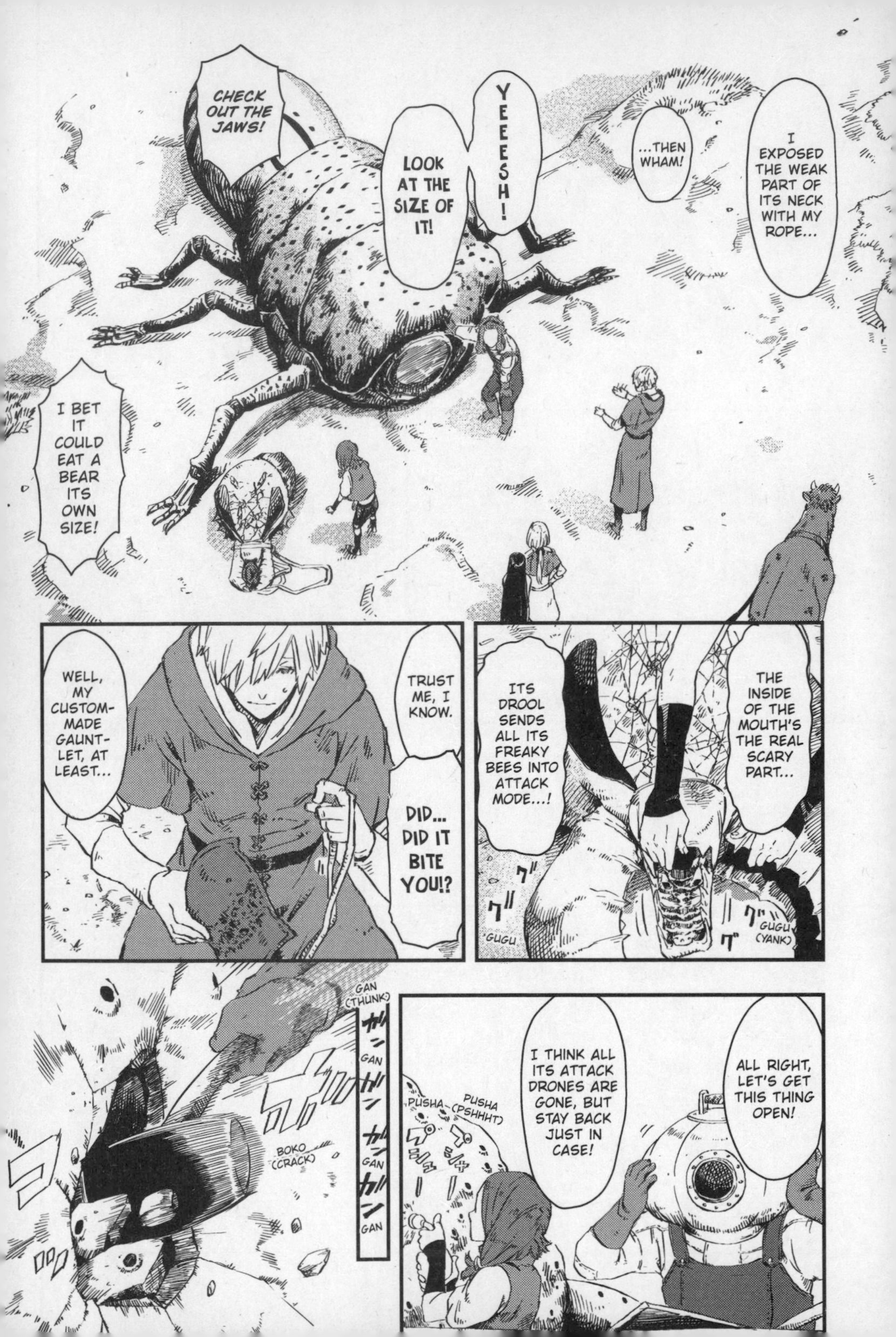
I EXPOSED THE WEAK PART OF ITS NECK WITH MY ROPE...
...THEN WHAM!
YEEESH!
LOOK AT THE SIZE OF IT!
CHECK OUT THE JAWS!
I BET IT COULD EAT A BEAR ITS OWN SIZE!
THE INSIDE OF THE MOUTH'S THE REAL SCARY PART...
ITS DROOL SENDS ALL ITS FREAKY BEES INTO ATTACK MODE...!
GUGU (YANK)
GUGU
TRUST ME, I KNOW.
DID... DID IT BITE YOU!?
WELL, MY CUSTOM-MADE GAUNTLET, AT LEAST...
ALL RIGHT, LET'S GET THIS THING OPEN!
I THINK ALL ITS ATTACK DRONES ARE GONE, BUT STAY BACK JUST IN CASE!
PUSHA (PSHHHT)
PUSHA
GAN (THUNK)
GAN
GAN
GAN
BOKO (CRACK)

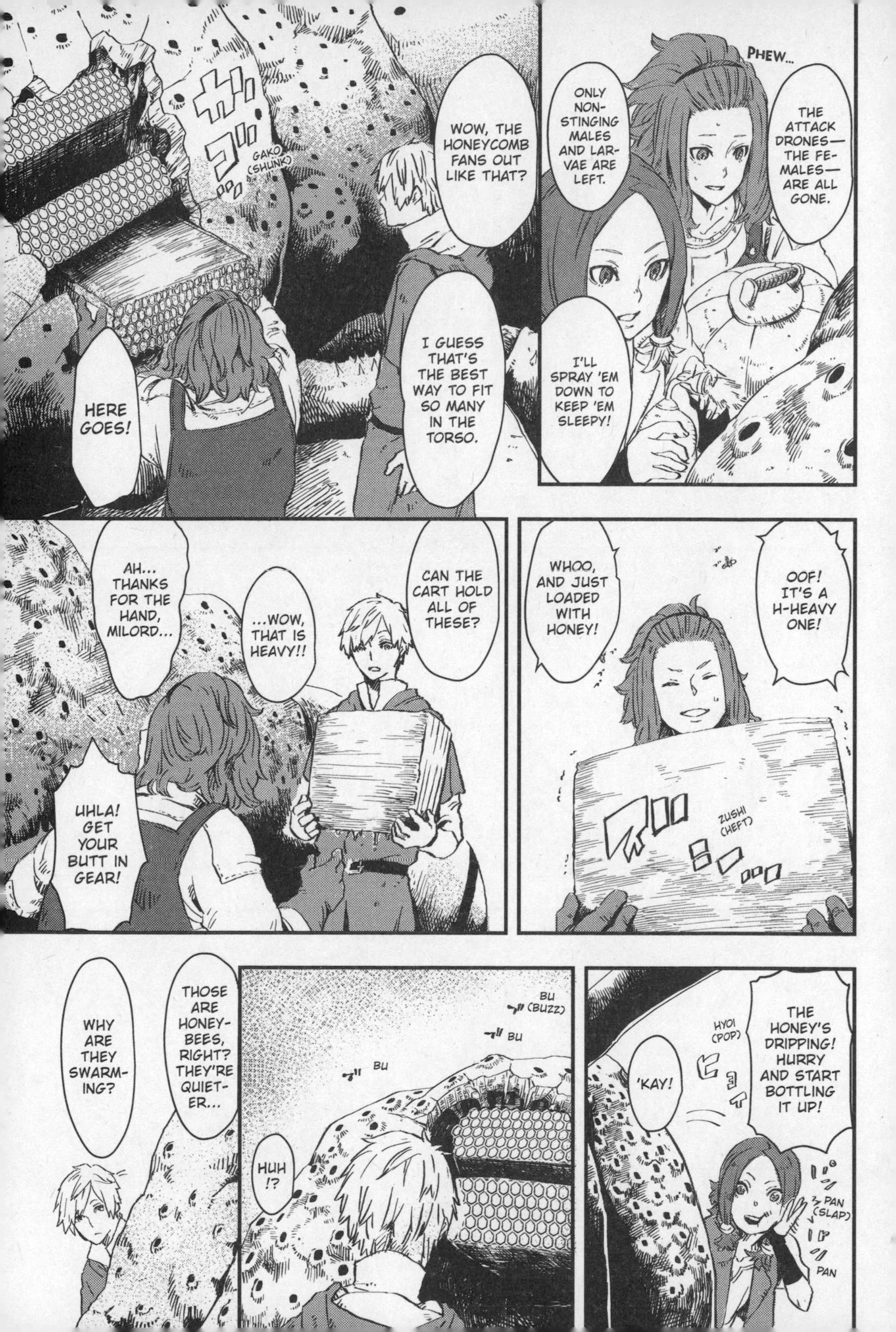
PHEW...
THE ATTACK DRONES— THE FEMALES— ARE ALL GONE.
ONLY NON-STINGING MALES AND LARVAE ARE LEFT.
I'LL SPRAY 'EM DOWN TO KEEP 'EM SLEEPY!
WOW, THE HONEYCOMB FANS OUT LIKE THAT?
GAKO (SHUNK)
I GUESS THAT'S THE BEST WAY TO FIT SO MANY IN THE TORSO.
HERE GOES!
OOF! IT'S A H-HEAVY ONE!
WHOO, AND JUST LOADED WITH HONEY!
ZUSHI (HEFT)
CAN THE CART HOLD ALL OF THESE?
...WOW, THAT IS HEAVY!!
AH... THANKS FOR THE HAND, MILORD...
UHLA! GET YOUR BUTT IN GEAR!
THE HONEY'S DRIPPING! HURRY AND START BOTTLING IT UP!
HYOI (POP)
'KAY!
PAN (SLAP)
PAN
BU (BUZZ)
BU
BU
HUH!?
THOSE ARE HONEYBEES, RIGHT? THEY'RE QUIETER...
WHY ARE THEY SWARMING?

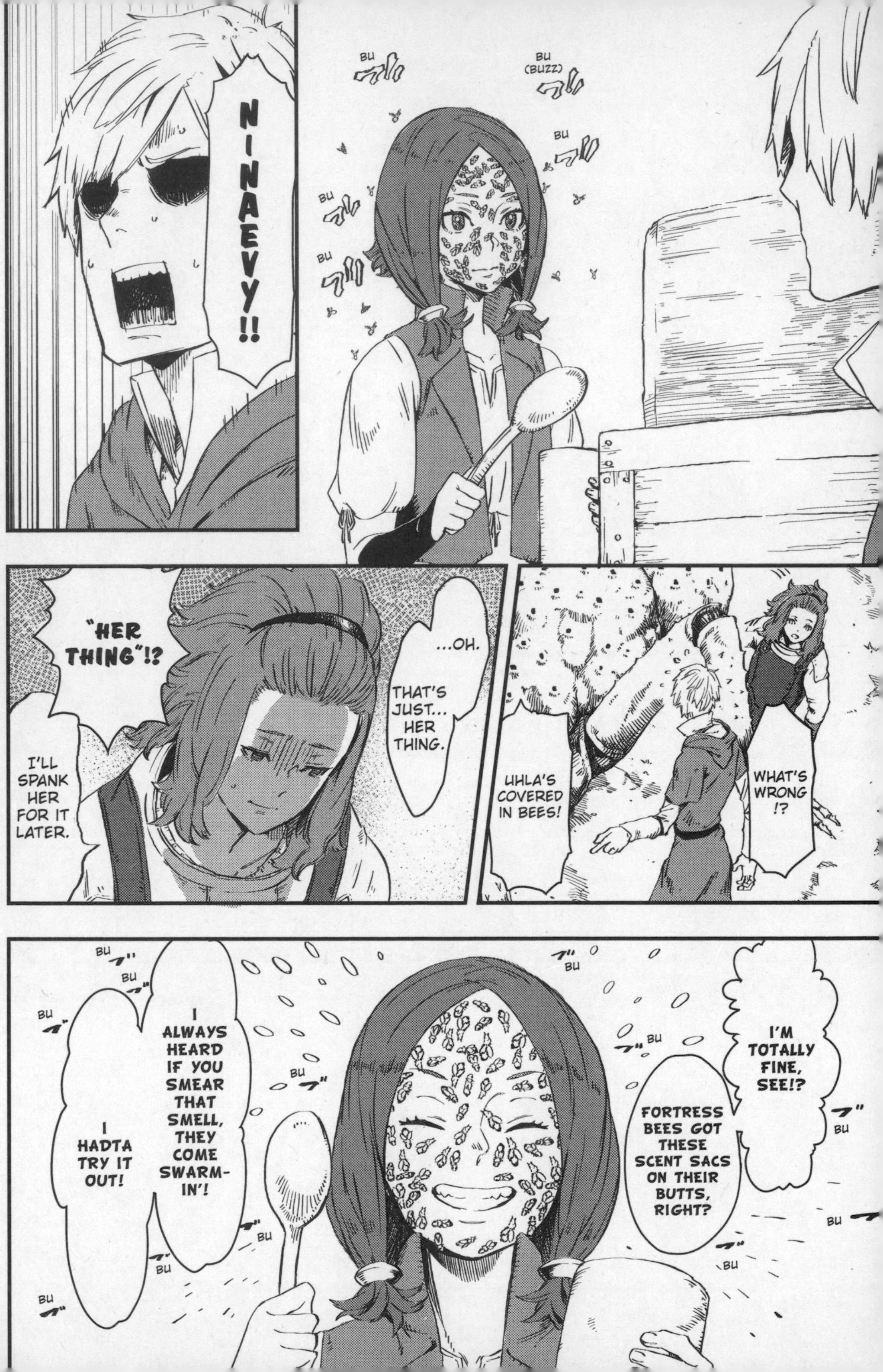
BU
BU (BUZZ)
BU
BU
BU
NINAEVY!!
WHAT'S WRONG !?
UHLA'S COVERED IN BEES!
...OH.
THAT'S JUST... HER THING.
"HER THING"!?
I'LL SPANK HER FOR IT LATER.
BU
I'M TOTALLY FINE, SEE!?
BU
FORTRESS BEES GOT THESE SCENT SACS ON THEIR BUTTS, RIGHT?
BU
BU
I ALWAYS HEARD IF YOU SMEAR THAT SMELL, THEY COME SWARM-IN'!
I HADTA TRY IT OUT!
BU
BU
BU
BU

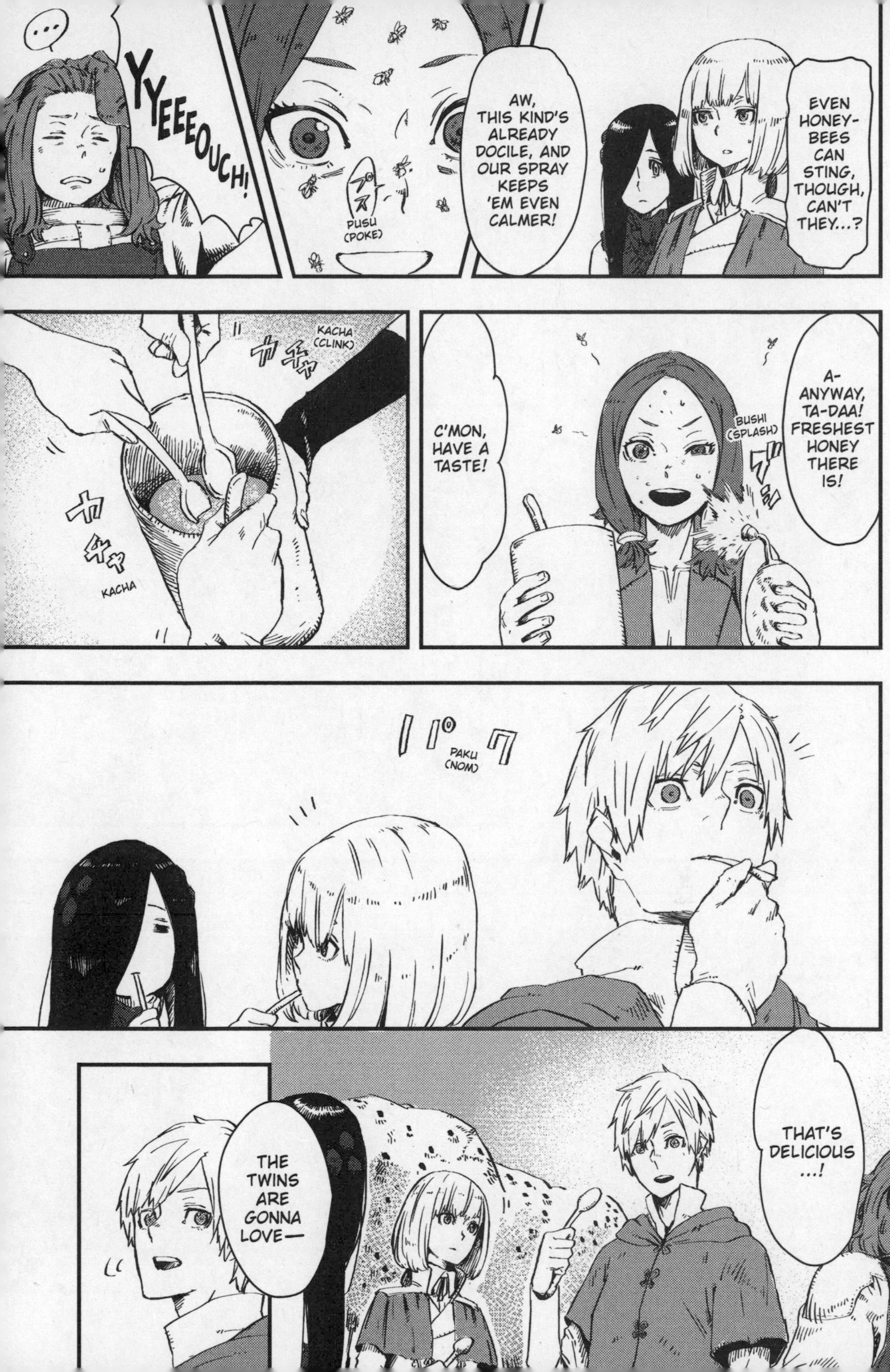
EVEN HONEY-BEES CAN STING, THOUGH, CAN'T THEY...?
AW, THIS KIND'S ALREADY DOCILE, AND OUR SPRAY KEEPS 'EM EVEN CALMER!
PUSU (POKE)
YYEEEOUCH!
...
A-ANYWAY, TA-DAA! FRESHEST HONEY THERE IS!
BUSHI (SPLASH)
C'MON, HAVE A TASTE!
KACHA (CLINK)
KACHA
PAKU (NOM)
THAT'S DELICIOUS...!
THE TWINS ARE GONNA LOVE—

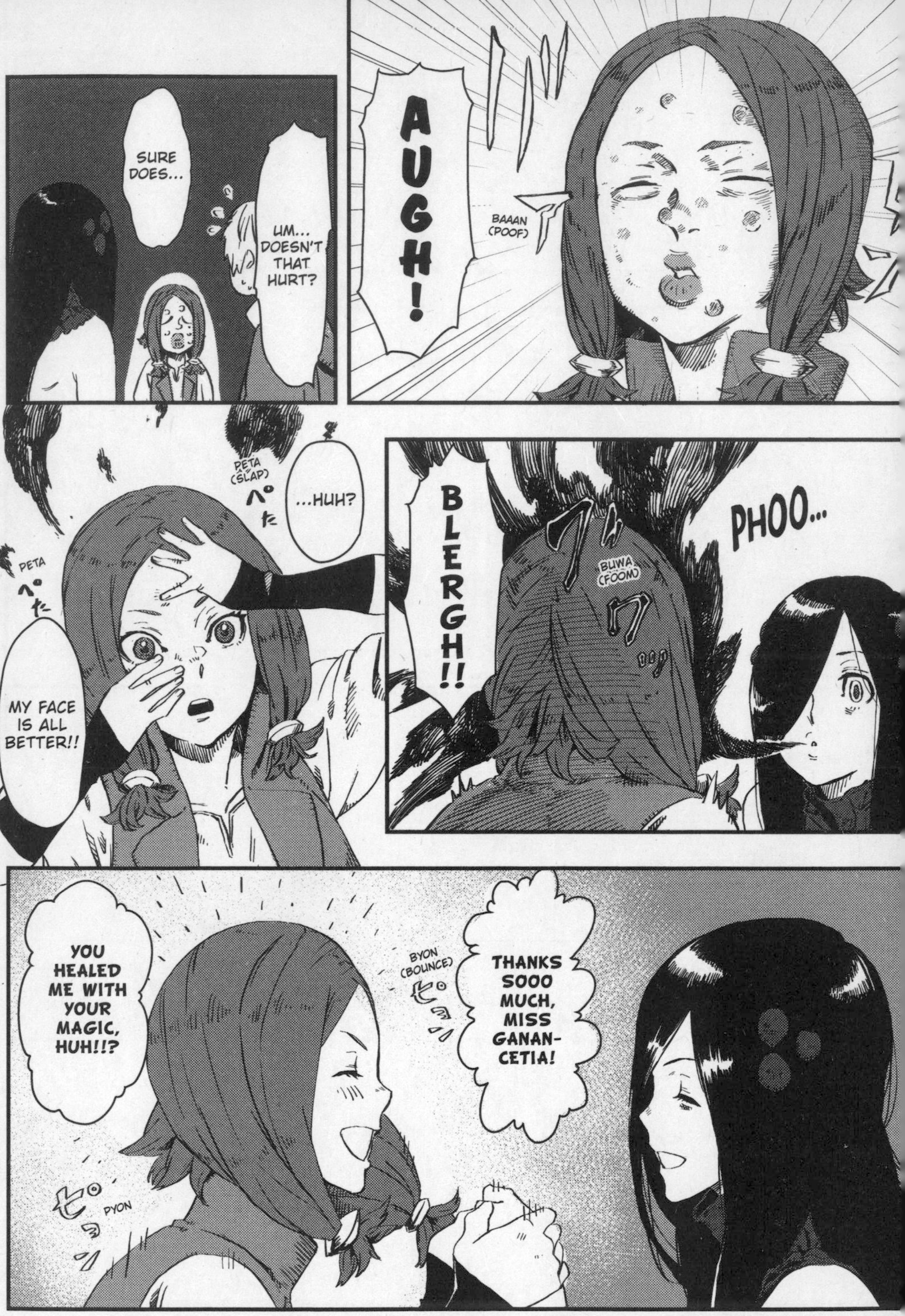
AUGH!
BAAAN (POOF)
UM... DOESN'T THAT HURT?
SURE DOES...
PHOO...
BLERGH!!
BUWA (FOOM)
...HUH?
PETA (SLAP)
ぺた
PETA
ぺた
MY FACE IS ALL BETTER!!
THANKS SOOO MUCH, MISS GANAN-CETIA!
BYON (BOUNCE)
ぴょ
YOU HEALED ME WITH YOUR MAGIC, HUH!!?
ぴょ
PYON

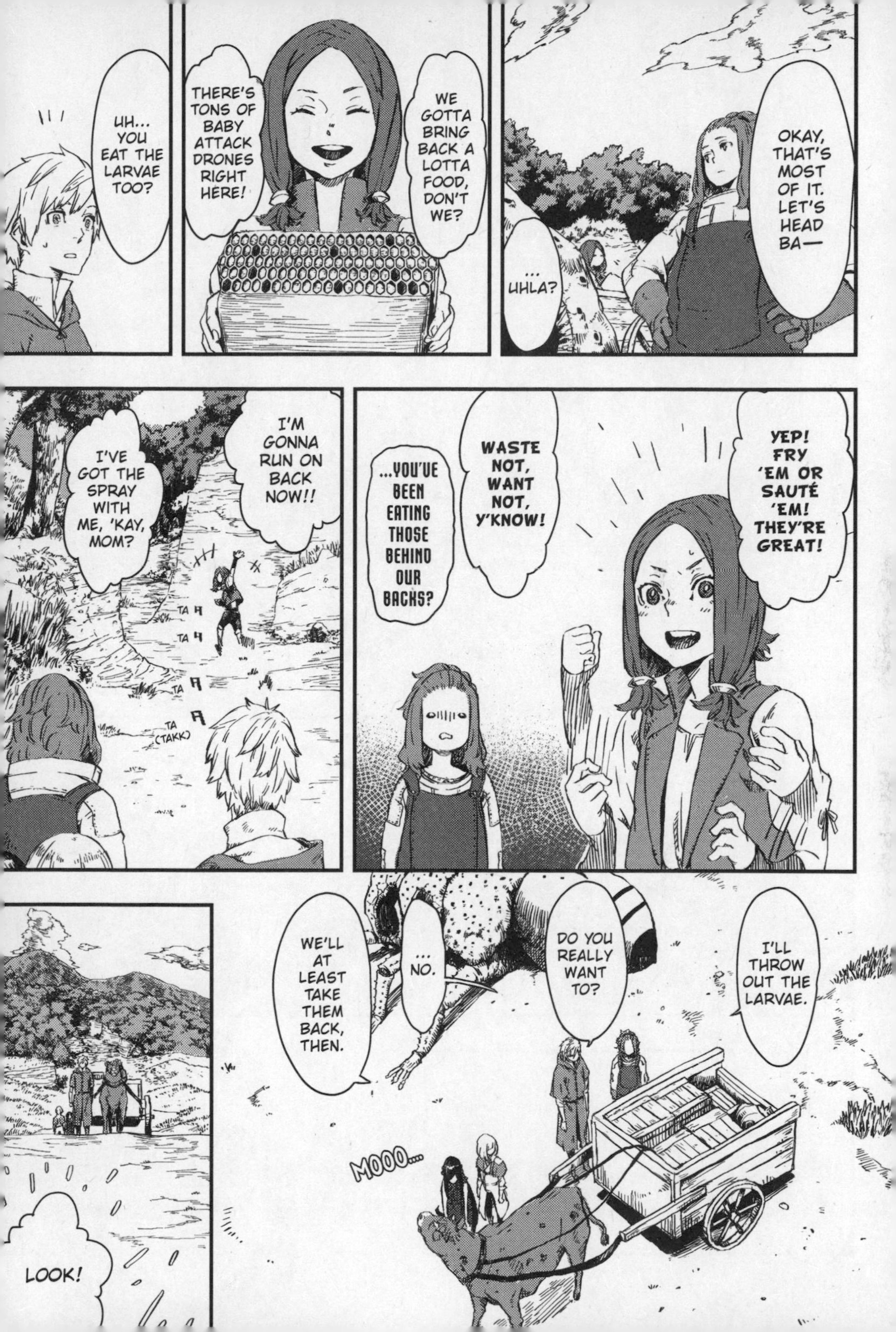
OKAY, THAT'S MOST OF IT. LET'S HEAD BA—
...UHLA?
WE GOTTA BRING BACK A LOTTA FOOD, DON'T WE?
THERE'S TONS OF BABY ATTACK DRONES RIGHT HERE!
UH... YOU EAT THE LARVAE TOO?
YEP! FRY 'EM OR SAUTÉ 'EM! THEY'RE GREAT!
WASTE NOT, WANT NOT, Y'KNOW!
...YOU'VE BEEN EATING THOSE BEHIND OUR BACKS?
I'M GONNA RUN ON BACK NOW!!
I'VE GOT THE SPRAY WITH ME, 'KAY, MOM?
TA TA TA TA (TAKK)
I'LL THROW OUT THE LARVAE.
DO YOU REALLY WANT TO?
...NO.
WE'LL AT LEAST TAKE THEM BACK, THEN.
MOOO...
LOOK!

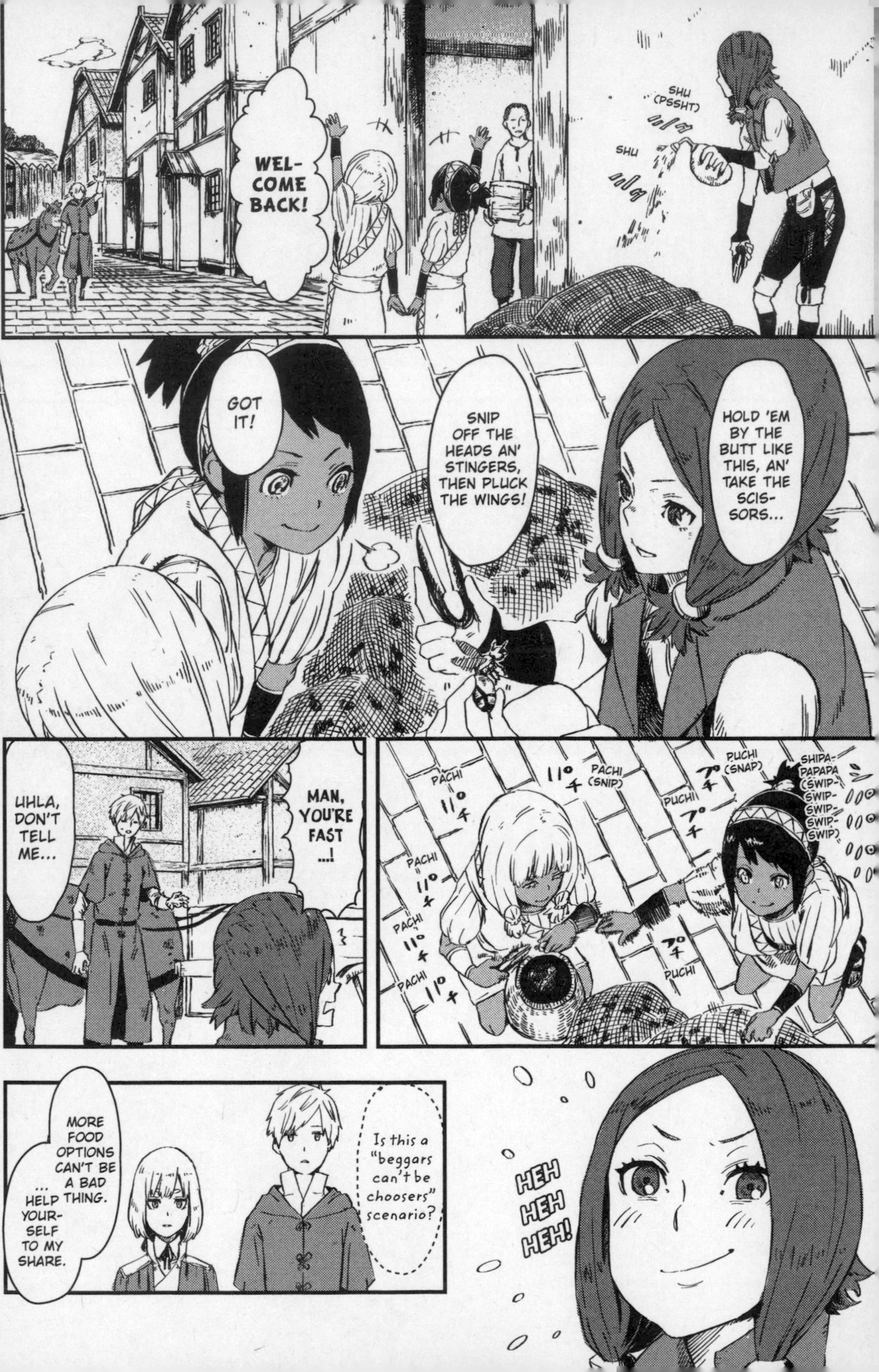
SHU (PSSHT)
SHU
WEL-COME BACK!
HOLD 'EM BY THE BUTT LIKE THIS, AN' TAKE THE SCIS-SORS...
SNIP OFF THE HEADS AN' STINGERS, THEN PLUCK THE WINGS!
GOT IT!
SHIPA-PAPAPA (SWIP-SWIP-SWIP-SWIP-SWIP)
PUCHI (SNAP)
PUCHI
PUCHI
PACHI (SNIP)
PACHI
PACHI
PACHI
PACHI
MAN, YOU'RE FAST ...!
UHLA, DON'T TELL ME...
HEH HEH HEH!
Is this a "beggars can't be choosers" scenario?
MORE FOOD OPTIONS CAN'T BE A BAD THING.
... HELP YOUR-SELF TO MY SHARE.

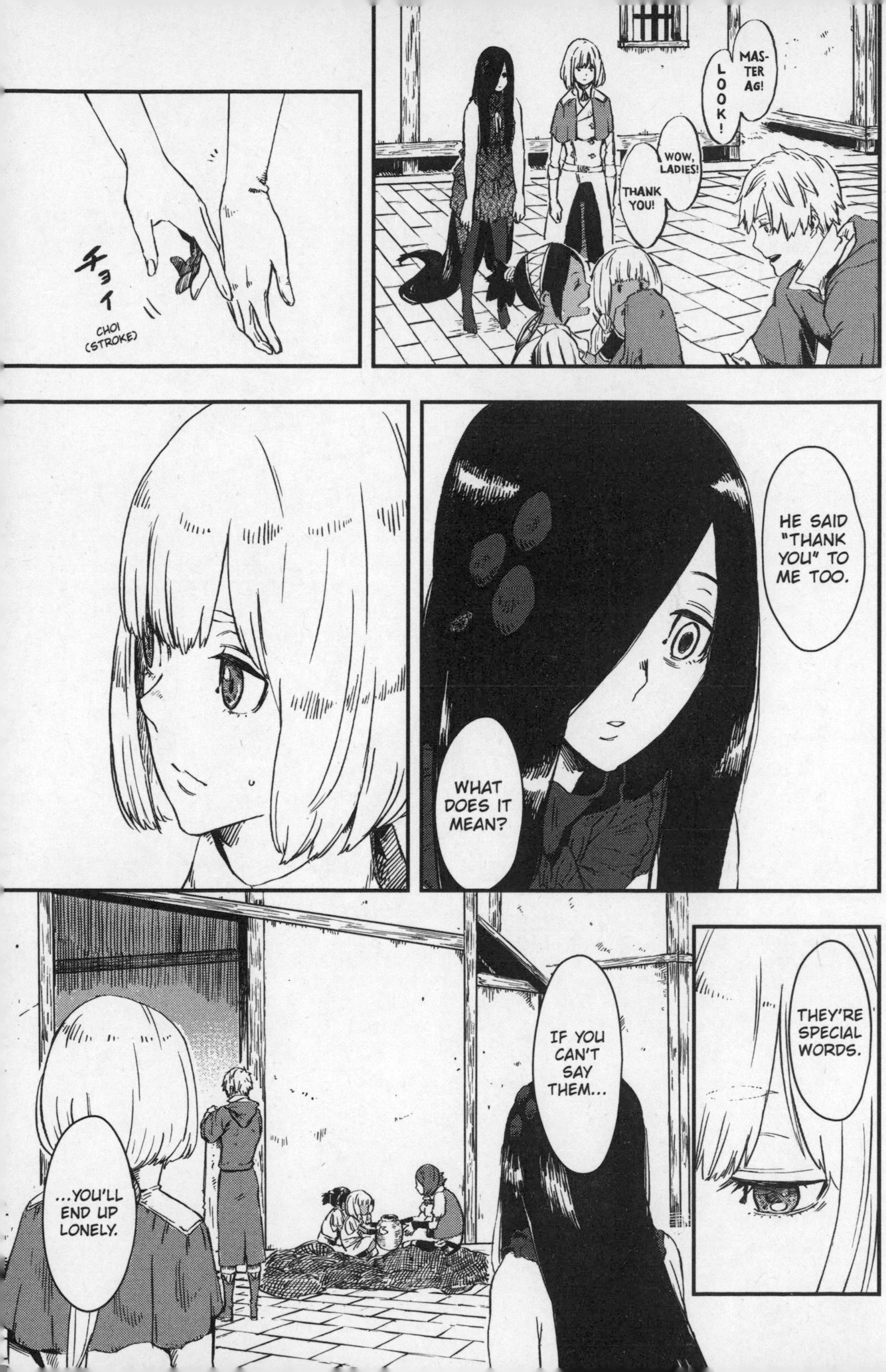
MAS-TER AG!
LOOK!
WOW, LADIES!
THANK YOU!
チョイ
CHOI (STROKE)
HE SAID "THANK YOU" TO ME TOO.
WHAT DOES IT MEAN?
THEY'RE SPECIAL WORDS.
IF YOU CAN'T SAY THEM...
...YOU'LL END UP LONELY.

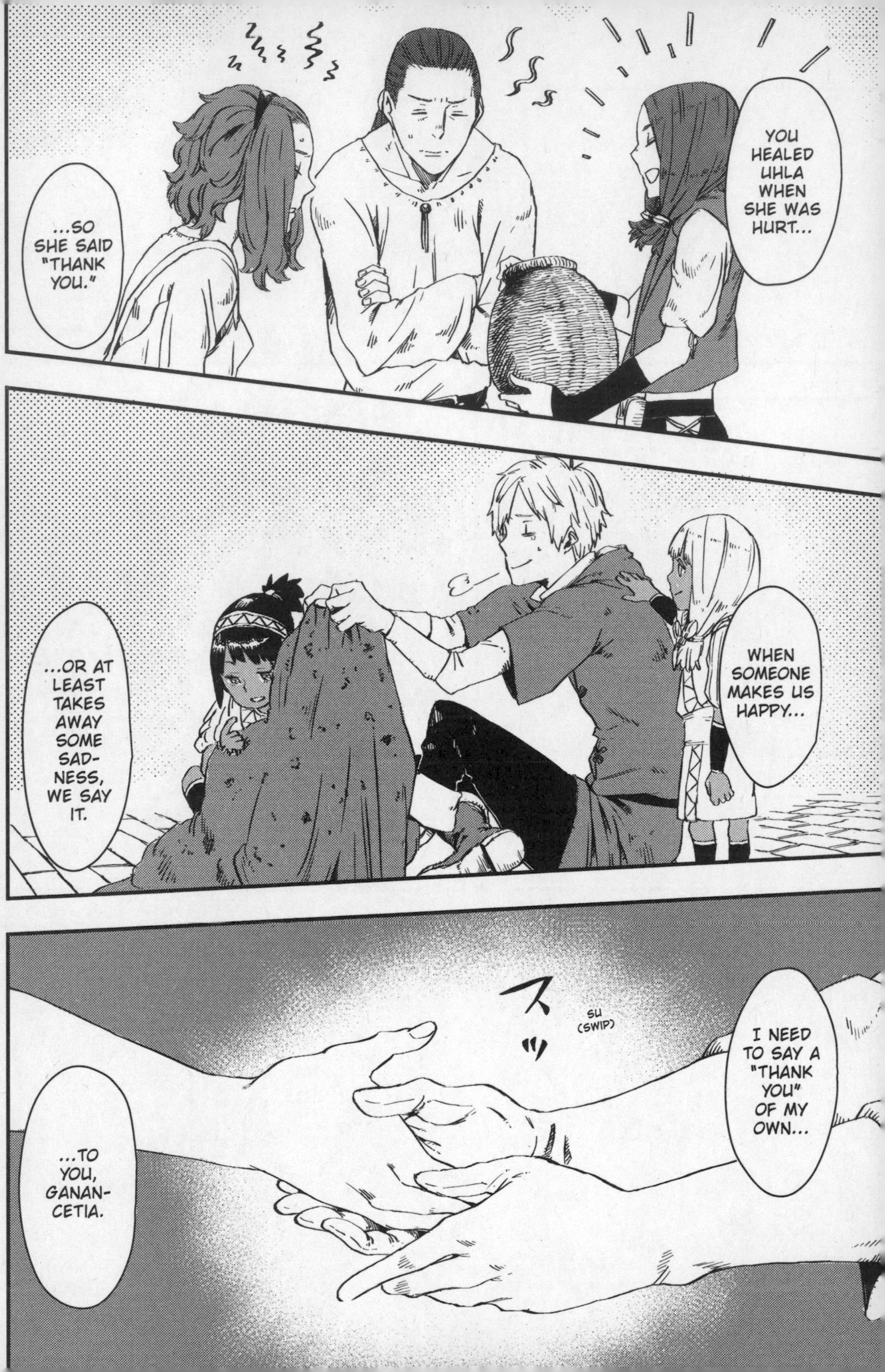
YOU HEALED UHLA WHEN SHE WAS HURT...
...SO SHE SAID "THANK YOU."
WHEN SOMEONE MAKES US HAPPY...
...OR AT LEAST TAKES AWAY SOME SAD-NESS, WE SAY IT.
ス ッ
SU (SWIP)
I NEED TO SAY A "THANK YOU" OF MY OWN...
...TO YOU, GANAN-CETIA.

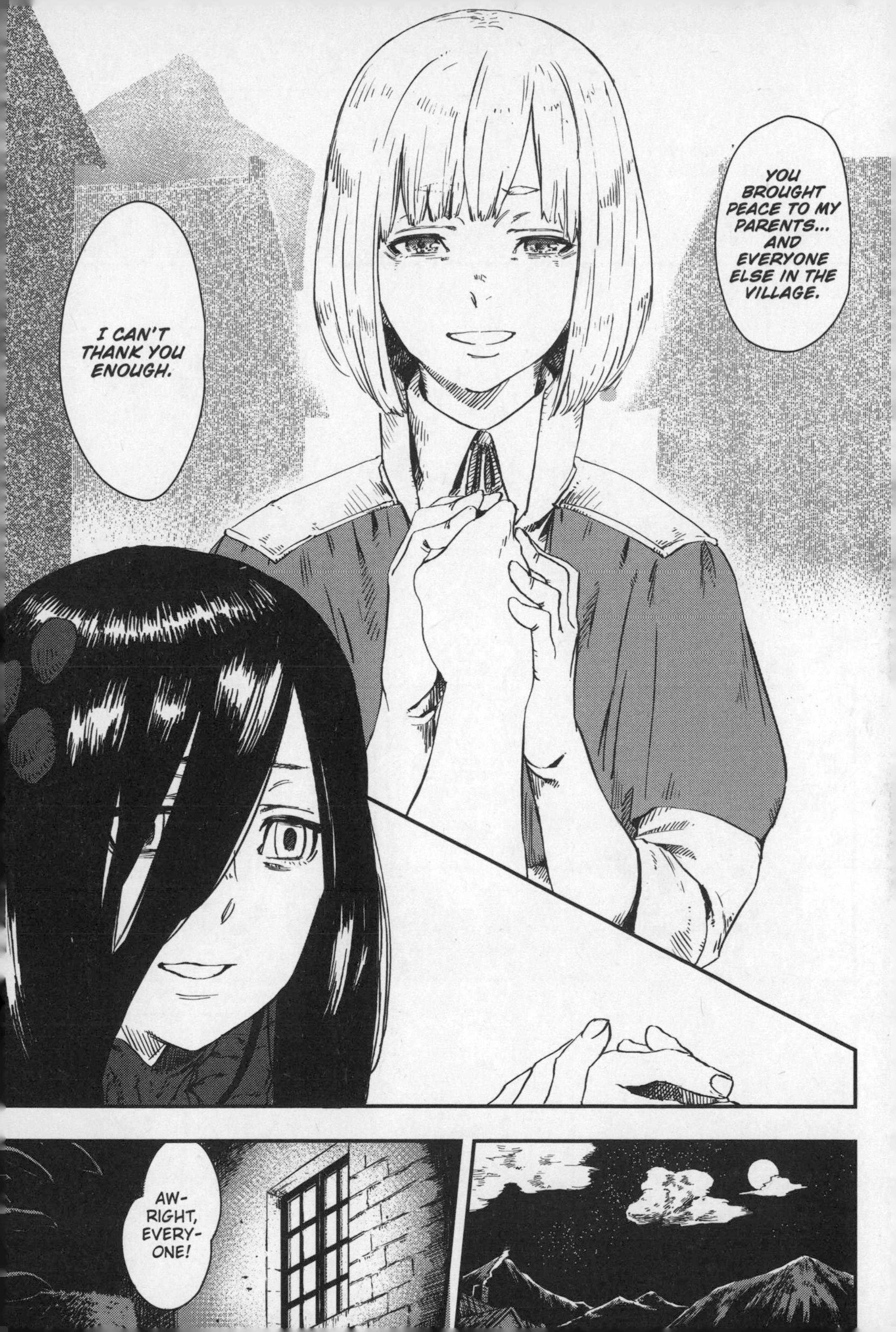
YOU BROUGHT PEACE TO MY PARENTS... AND EVERYONE ELSE IN THE VILLAGE.
I CAN'T THANK YOU ENOUGH.
AW-RIGHT, EVERY-ONE!

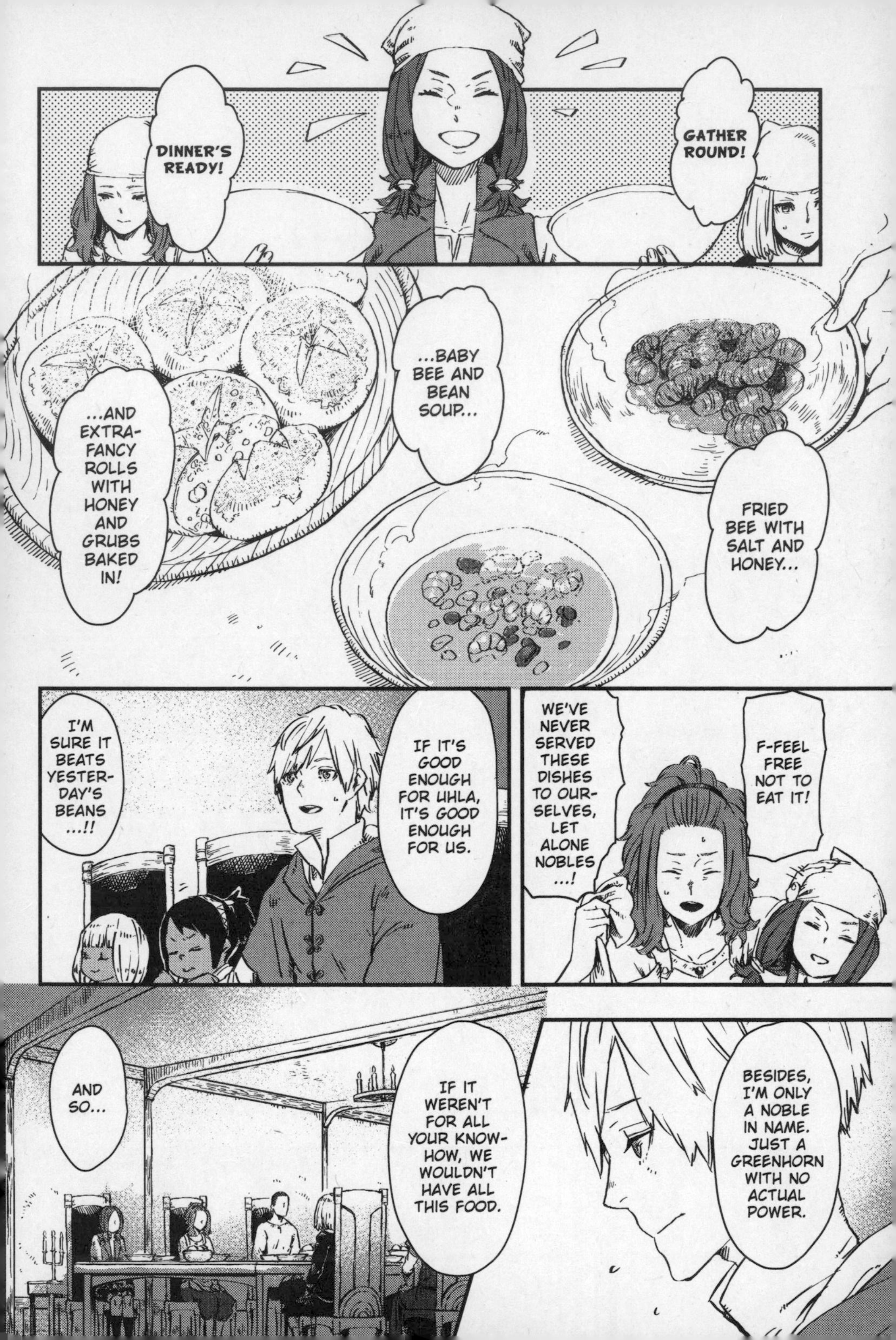
GATHER ROUND!
DINNER'S READY!
FRIED BEE WITH SALT AND HONEY...
...BABY BEE AND BEAN SOUP...
...AND EXTRA-FANCY ROLLS WITH HONEY AND GRUBS BAKED IN!
F-FEEL FREE NOT TO EAT IT!
WE'VE NEVER SERVED THESE DISHES TO OURSELVES, LET ALONE NOBLES...!
IF IT'S GOOD ENOUGH FOR UHLA, IT'S GOOD ENOUGH FOR US.
I'M SURE IT BEATS YESTERDAY'S BEANS...!!
BESIDES, I'M ONLY A NOBLE IN NAME. JUST A GREENHORN WITH NO ACTUAL POWER.
IF IT WEREN'T FOR ALL YOUR KNOW-HOW, WE WOULDN'T HAVE ALL THIS FOOD.
AND SO...

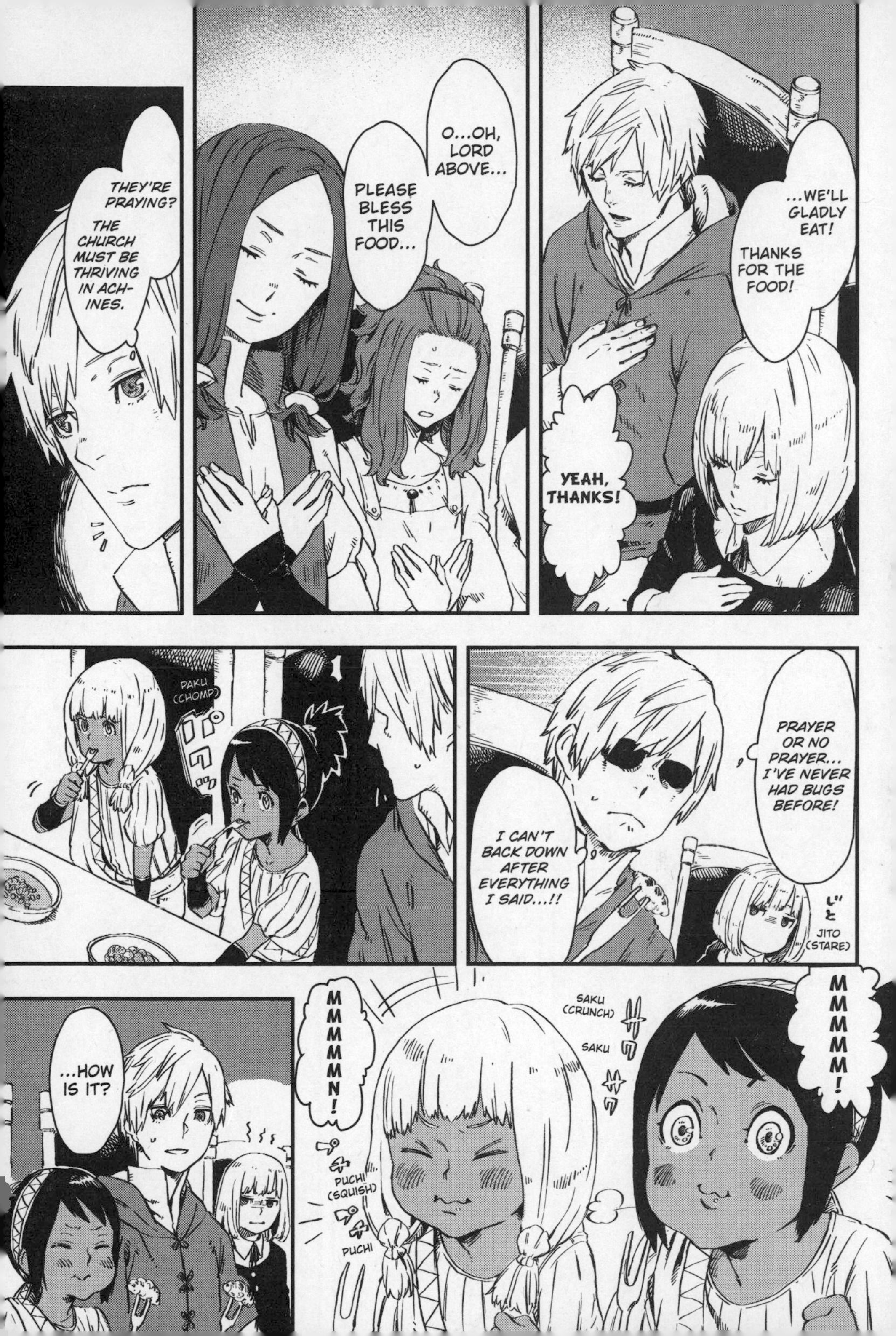
...WE'LL GLADLY EAT!
THANKS FOR THE FOOD!
YEAH, THANKS!
O...OH, LORD ABOVE...
PLEASE BLESS THIS FOOD...
THEY'RE PRAYING?
THE CHURCH MUST BE THRIVING IN ACH-INES.
PRAYER OR NO PRAYER... I'VE NEVER HAD BUGS BEFORE!
I CAN'T BACK DOWN AFTER EVERYTHING I SAID...!!
じと
JITO (STARE)
PAKU (CHOMP)
MMMMM!
SAKU (CRUNCH)
SAKU
MMMMMN!
PUCHI (SQUISH)
PUCHI
...HOW IS IT?

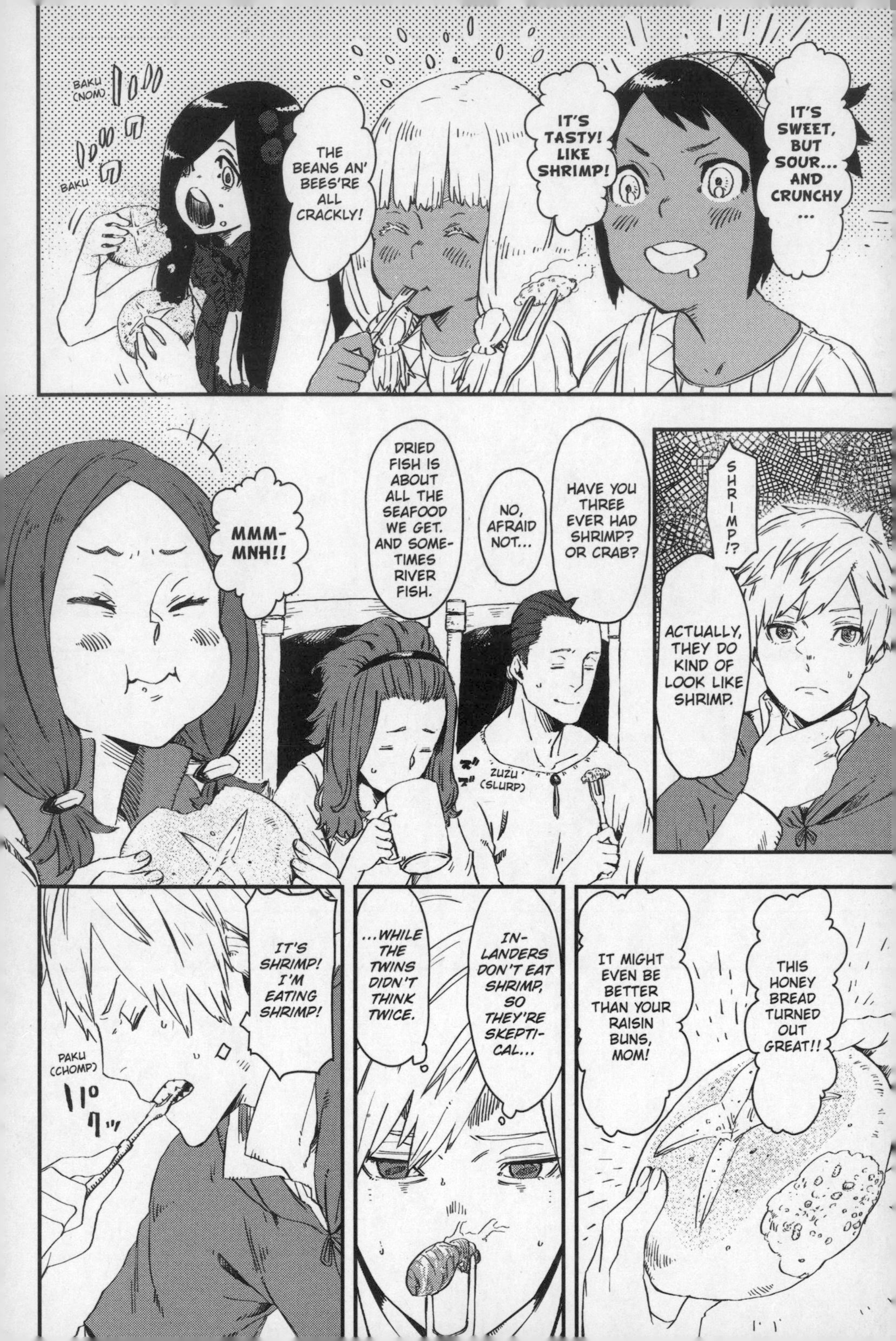
IT'S SWEET, BUT SOUR... AND CRUNCHY...
IT'S TASTY! LIKE SHRIMP!
THE BEANS AN' BEES'RE ALL CRACKLY!
BAKU (NOM)
BAKU
SHRIMP!?
ACTUALLY, THEY DO KIND OF LOOK LIKE SHRIMP.
HAVE YOU THREE EVER HAD SHRIMP? OR CRAB?
NO, AFRAID NOT...
DRIED FISH IS ABOUT ALL THE SEAFOOD WE GET. AND SOMETIMES RIVER FISH.
MMM-MNH!!
ZUZU (SLURP)
THIS HONEY BREAD TURNED OUT GREAT!!
IT MIGHT EVEN BE BETTER THAN YOUR RAISIN BUNS, MOM!
INLANDERS DON'T EAT SHRIMP, SO THEY'RE SKEPTICAL...
...WHILE THE TWINS DIDN'T THINK TWICE.
IT'S SHRIMP! I'M EATING SHRIMP!
PAKU (CHOMP)

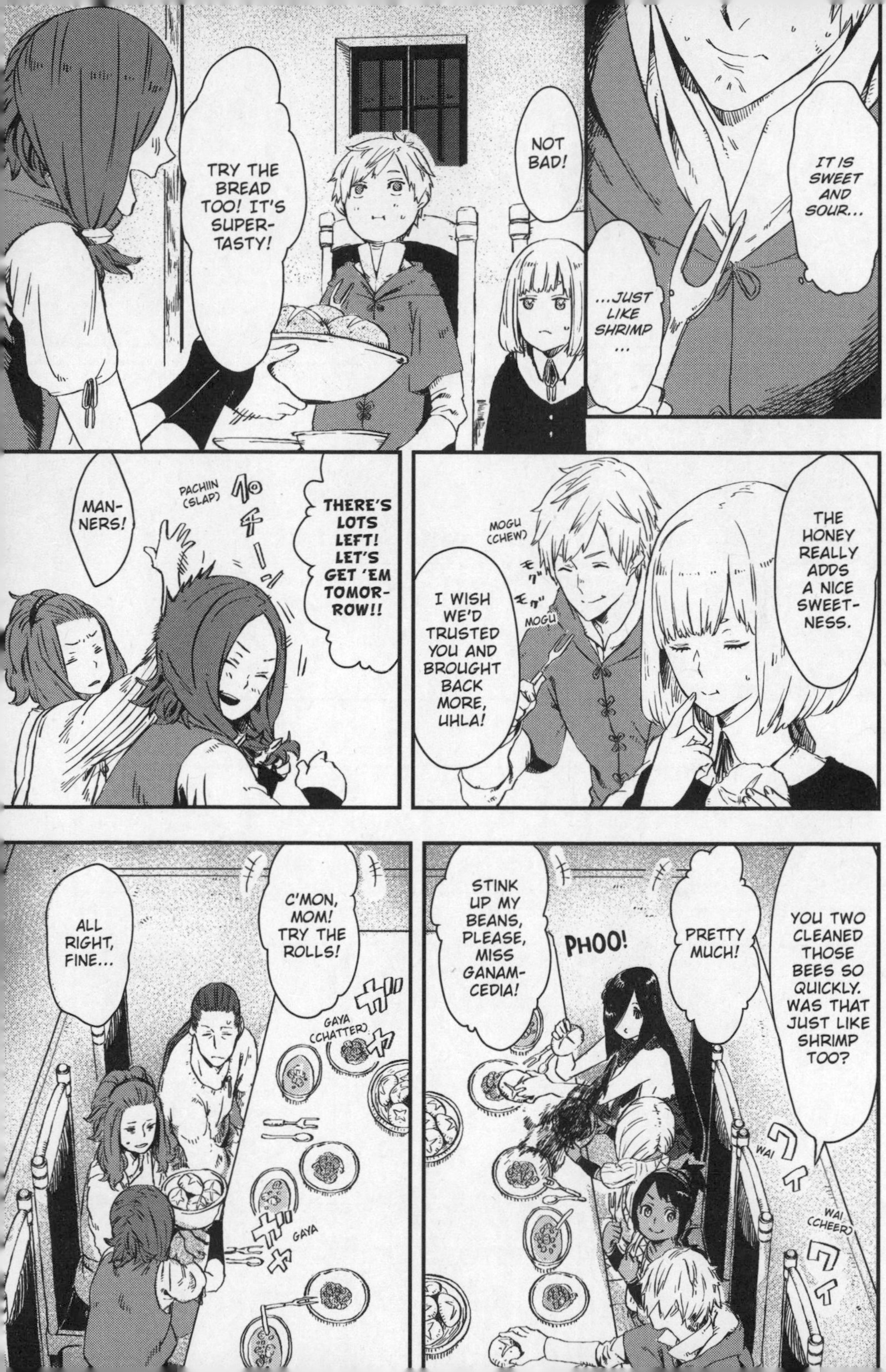
IT IS SWEET AND SOUR...
...JUST LIKE SHRIMP...
NOT BAD!
TRY THE BREAD TOO! IT'S SUPER-TASTY!
THE HONEY REALLY ADDS A NICE SWEETNESS.
MOGU (CHEW)
MOGU
I WISH WE'D TRUSTED YOU AND BROUGHT BACK MORE, UHLA!
THERE'S LOTS LEFT! LET'S GET 'EM TOMORROW!!
PACHIIN (SLAP)
MANNERS!
YOU TWO CLEANED THOSE BEES SO QUICKLY. WAS THAT JUST LIKE SHRIMP TOO?
PRETTY MUCH!
PHOO!
STINK UP MY BEANS, PLEASE, MISS GANAMCEDIA!
WAI
WAI (CHEER)
C'MON, MOM! TRY THE ROLLS!
GAYA (CHATTER)
ALL RIGHT, FINE...
GAYA

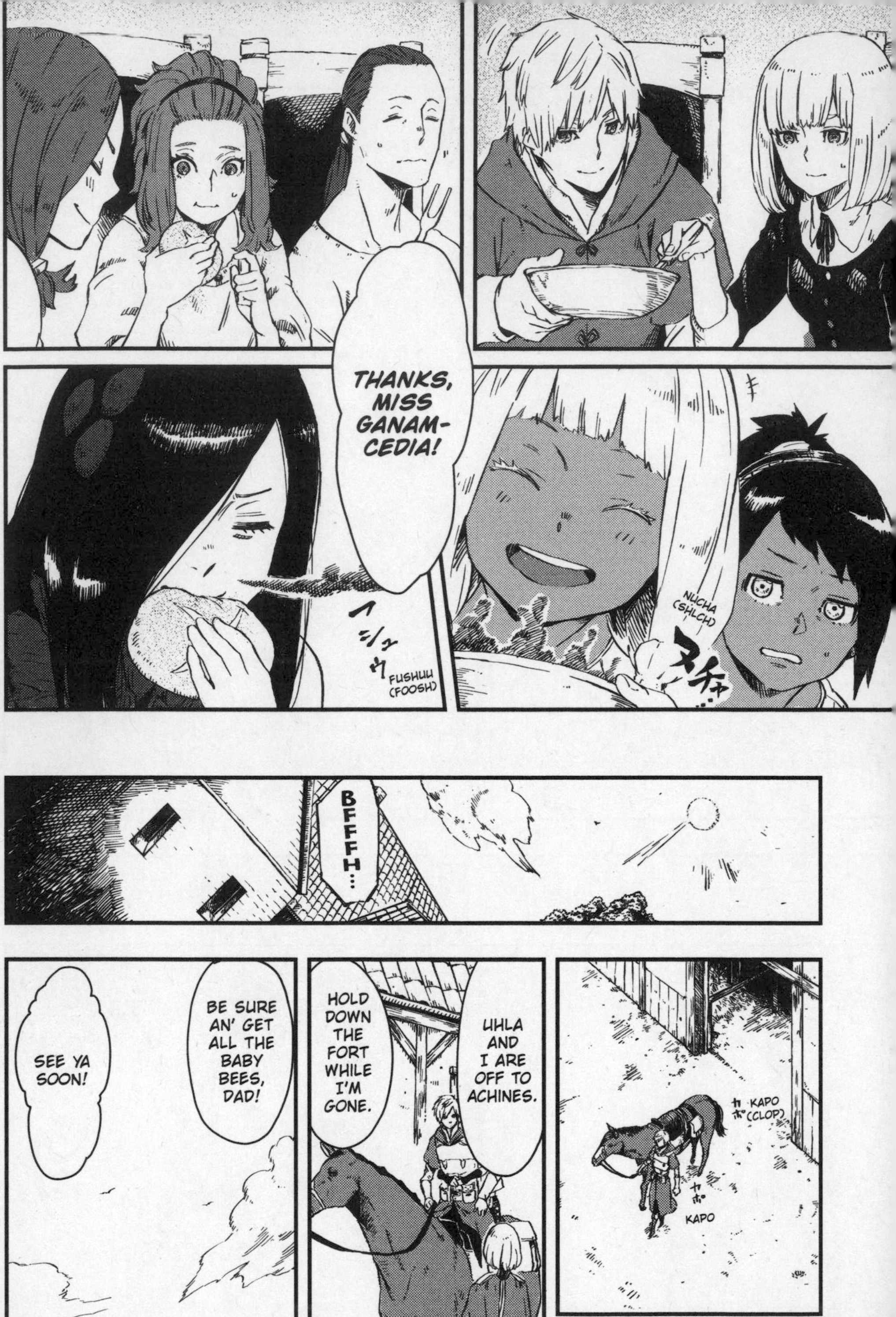

THANKS, MISS GANAM-CEDIA!
ヌチャ
NUCHA (SHLCH)
フシュウ
FUSHUU (FOOSH)
BFFFH...
カポ
KAPO (CLOP)
カポ
KAPO
UHLA AND I ARE OFF TO ACHINES.
HOLD DOWN THE FORT WHILE I'M GONE.
BE SURE AN' GET ALL THE BABY BEES, DAD!
SEE YA SOON!

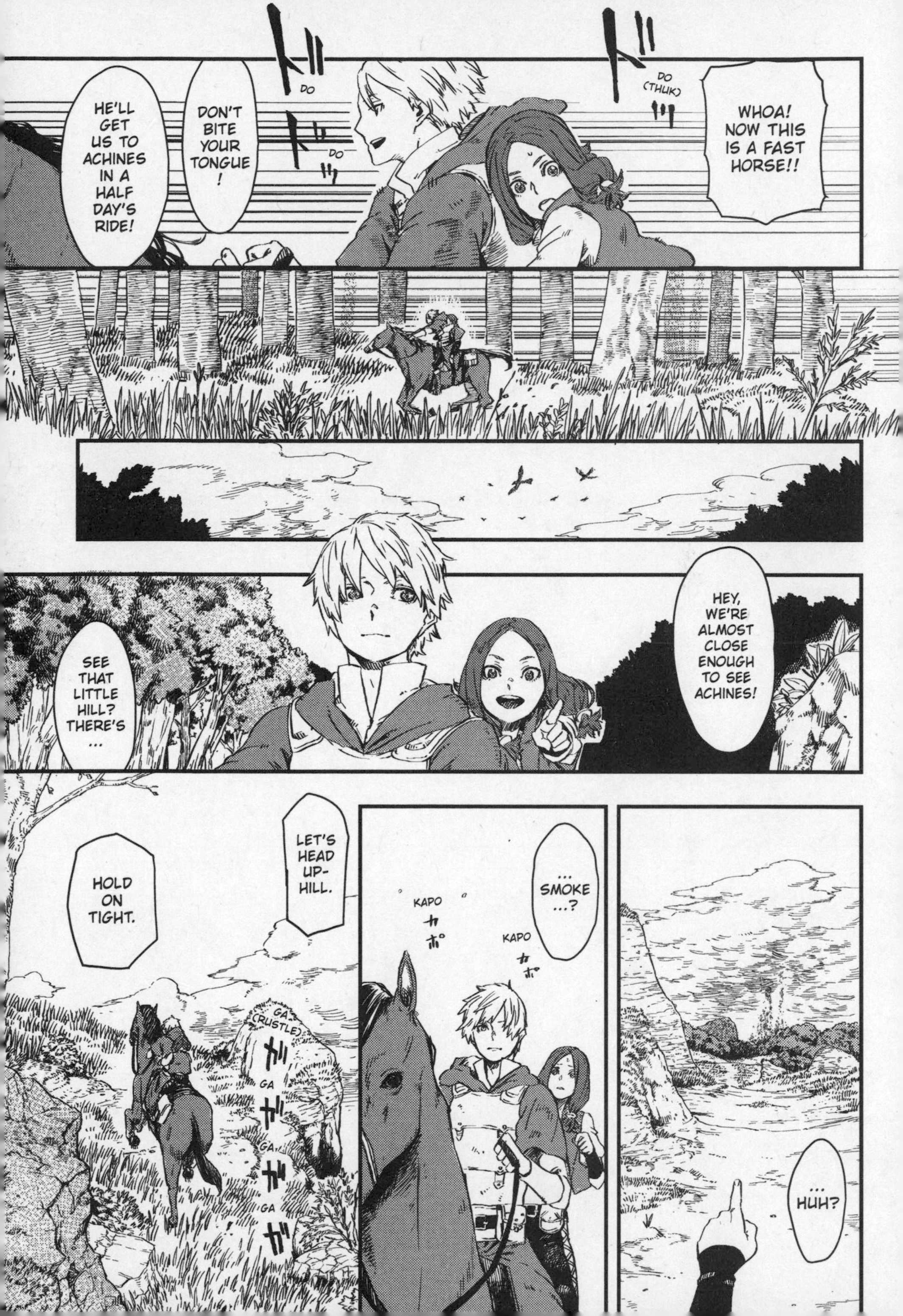
WHOA! NOW THIS IS A FAST HORSE!!
DO (THUK)
DO
DON'T BITE YOUR TONGUE!
DO
HE'LL GET US TO ACHINES IN A HALF DAY'S RIDE!
HEY, WE'RE ALMOST CLOSE ENOUGH TO SEE ACHINES!
SEE THAT LITTLE HILL? THERE'S ...
... HUH?
... SMOKE ...?
KAPO
KAPO
LET'S HEAD UP-HILL.
HOLD ON TIGHT.
GA (RUSTLE)
GA
GA
GA

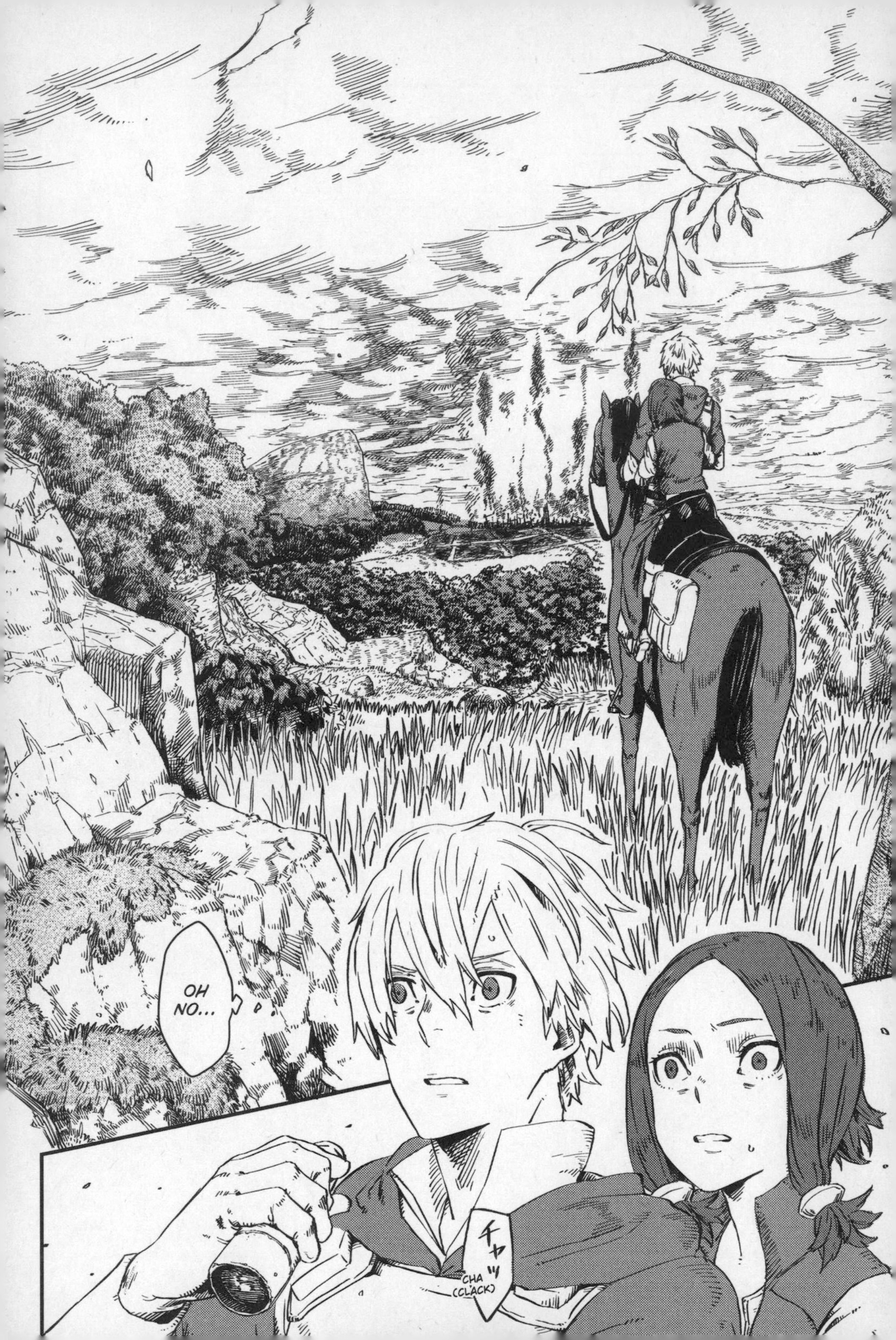
OH NO...
チャッ
CHA (CLACK)

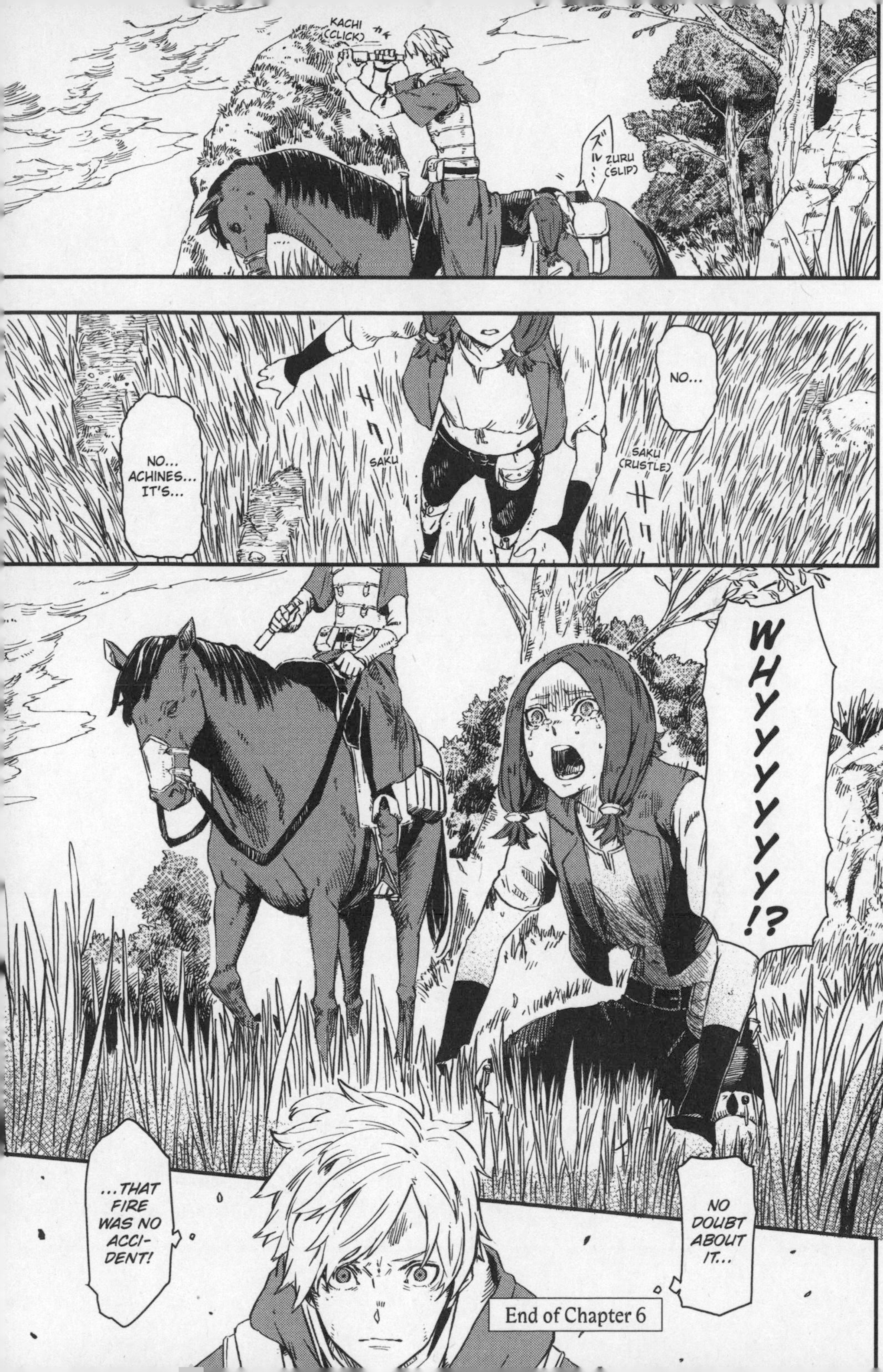
ズル
ZURU (SLIP)
KACHI (CLICK)
NO...
SAKU (RUSTLE)
SAKU
NO... ACHINES... IT'S...
WHYYYYYY!?
NO DOUBT ABOUT IT...
...THAT FIRE WAS NO ACCI-DENT!
End of Chapter 6

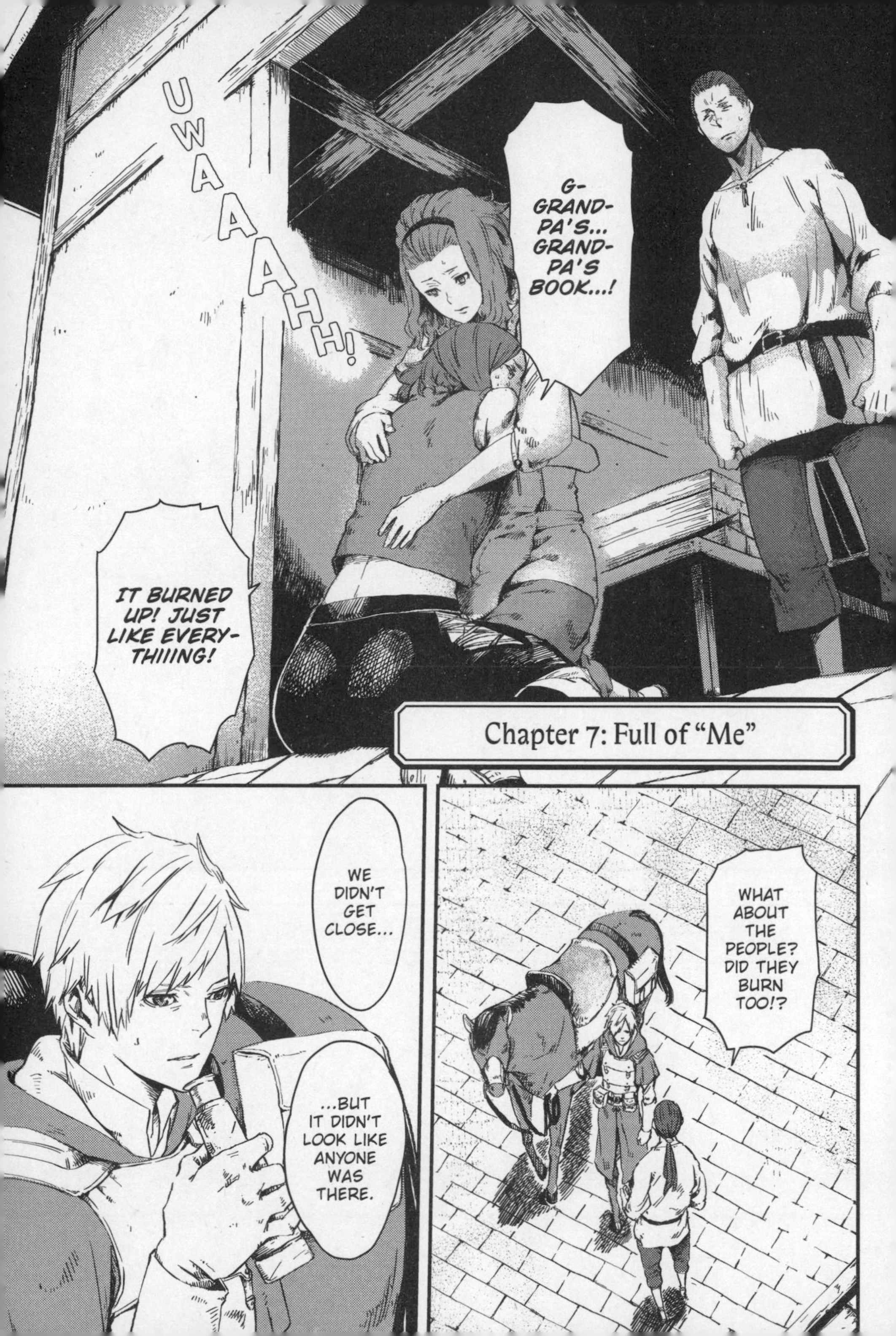
G-GRANDPA'S... GRANDPA'S BOOK...!
UWAAAAHH!
IT BURNED UP! JUST LIKE EVERYTHIIING!
Chapter 7: Full of "Me"
WHAT ABOUT THE PEOPLE? DID THEY BURN TOO!?
WE DIDN'T GET CLOSE...
...BUT IT DIDN'T LOOK LIKE ANYONE WAS THERE.

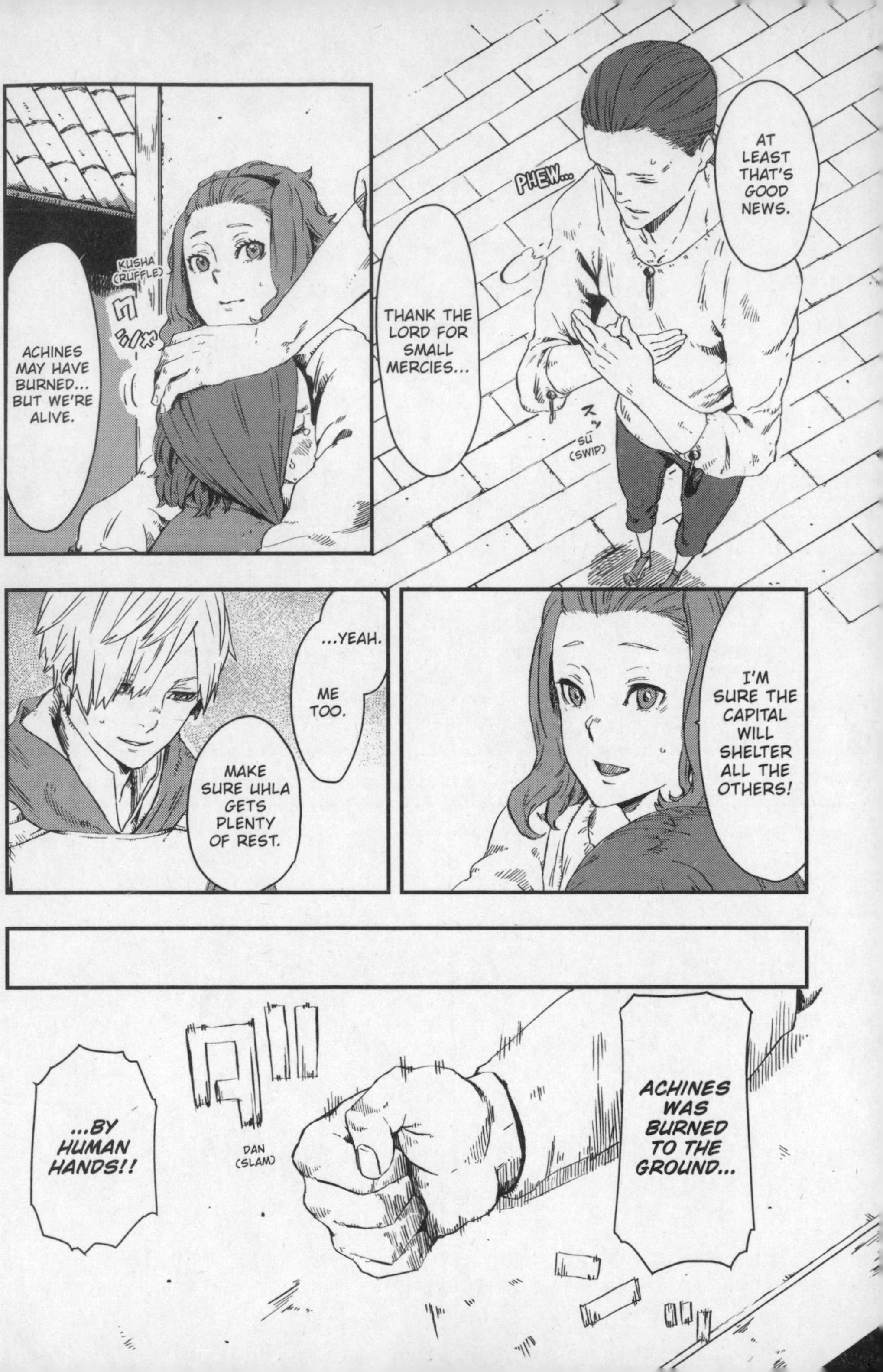
AT LEAST THAT'S GOOD NEWS.
PHEW...
THANK THE LORD FOR SMALL MERCIES...
スッ
SŪ (SWIP)
KUSHA (RUFFLE)
ACHINES MAY HAVE BURNED... BUT WE'RE ALIVE.
I'M SURE THE CAPITAL WILL SHELTER ALL THE OTHERS!
...YEAH.
ME TOO.
MAKE SURE UHLA GETS PLENTY OF REST.
ACHINES WAS BURNED TO THE GROUND...
DAN (SLAM)
...BY HUMAN HANDS!!

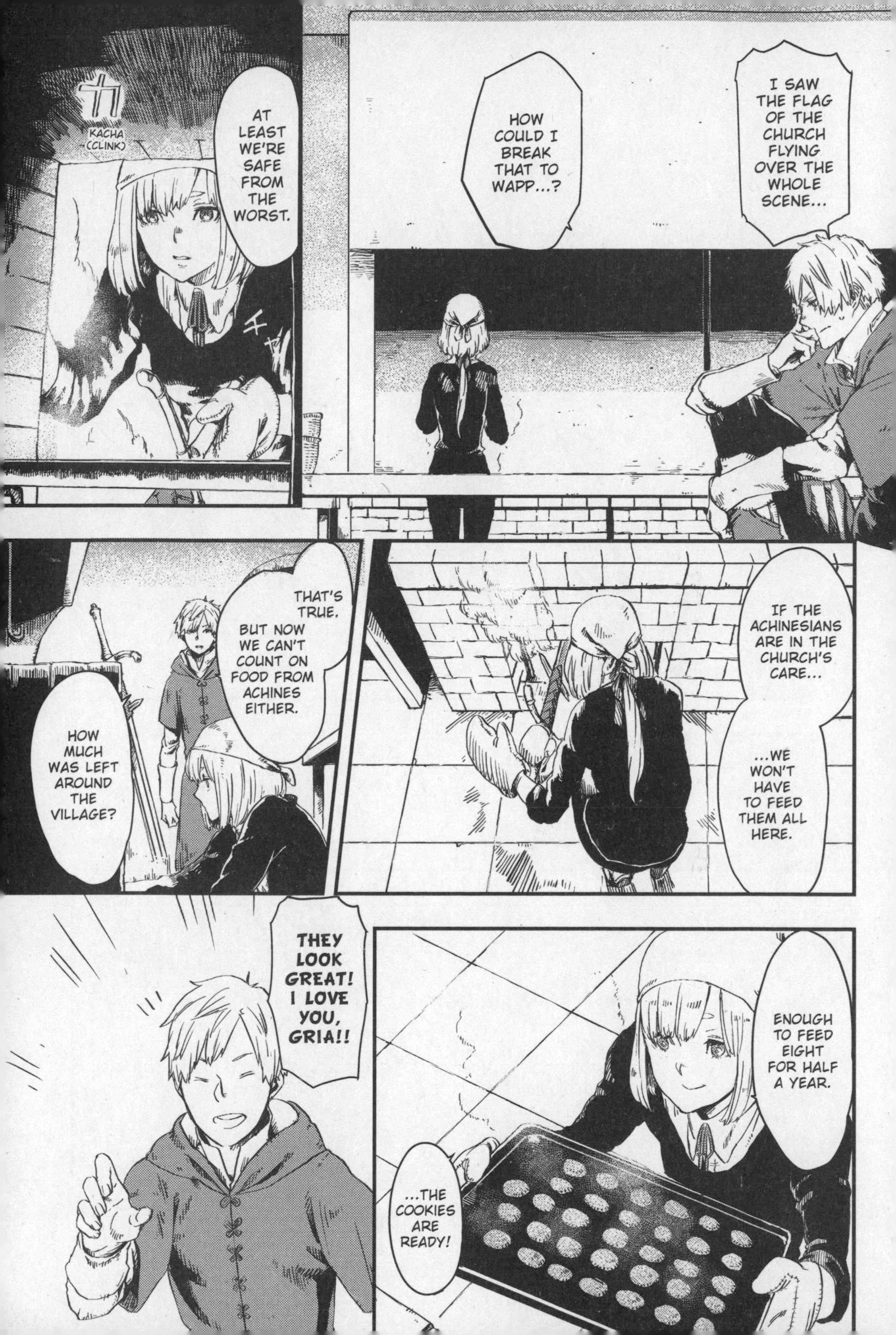
I SAW THE FLAG OF THE CHURCH FLYING OVER THE WHOLE SCENE...
HOW COULD I BREAK THAT TO WAPP...?
KACHA (CLINK)
AT LEAST WE'RE SAFE FROM THE WORST.
IF THE ACHINESIANS ARE IN THE CHURCH'S CARE...
...WE WON'T HAVE TO FEED THEM ALL HERE.
THAT'S TRUE. BUT NOW WE CAN'T COUNT ON FOOD FROM ACHINES EITHER.
HOW MUCH WAS LEFT AROUND THE VILLAGE?
ENOUGH TO FEED EIGHT FOR HALF A YEAR.
...THE COOKIES ARE READY!
THEY LOOK GREAT! I LOVE YOU, GRIA!!

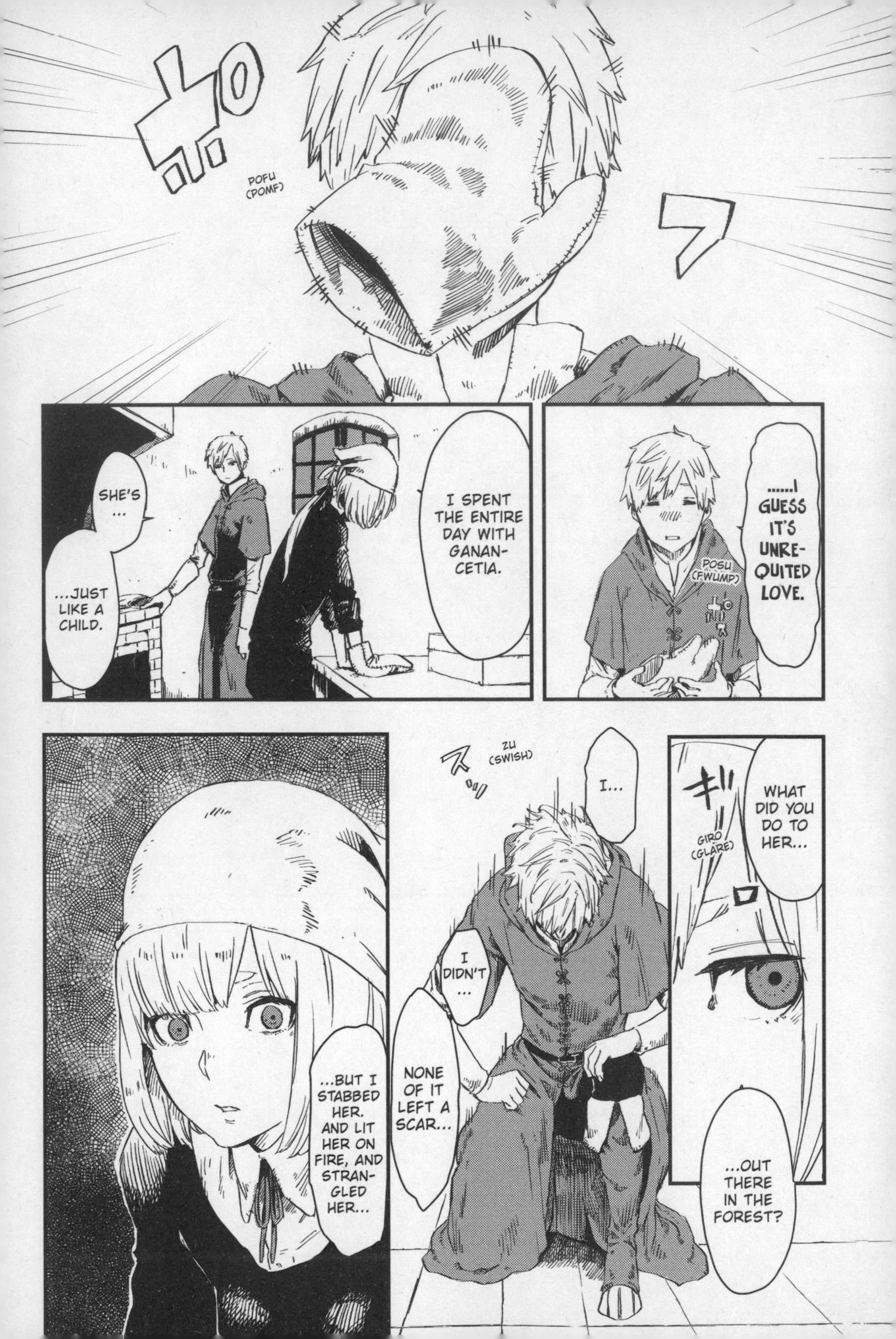
POFU (POMF)
......I GUESS IT'S UNREQUITED LOVE.
POSU (FWUMP)
I SPENT THE ENTIRE DAY WITH GANANCETIA.
SHE'S ...
...JUST LIKE A CHILD.
GIRO (GLARE)
WHAT DID YOU DO TO HER...
...OUT THERE IN THE FOREST?
ZU (SWISH)
I...
I DIDN'T ...
NONE OF IT LEFT A SCAR...
...BUT I STABBED HER. AND LIT HER ON FIRE, AND STRANGLED HER...

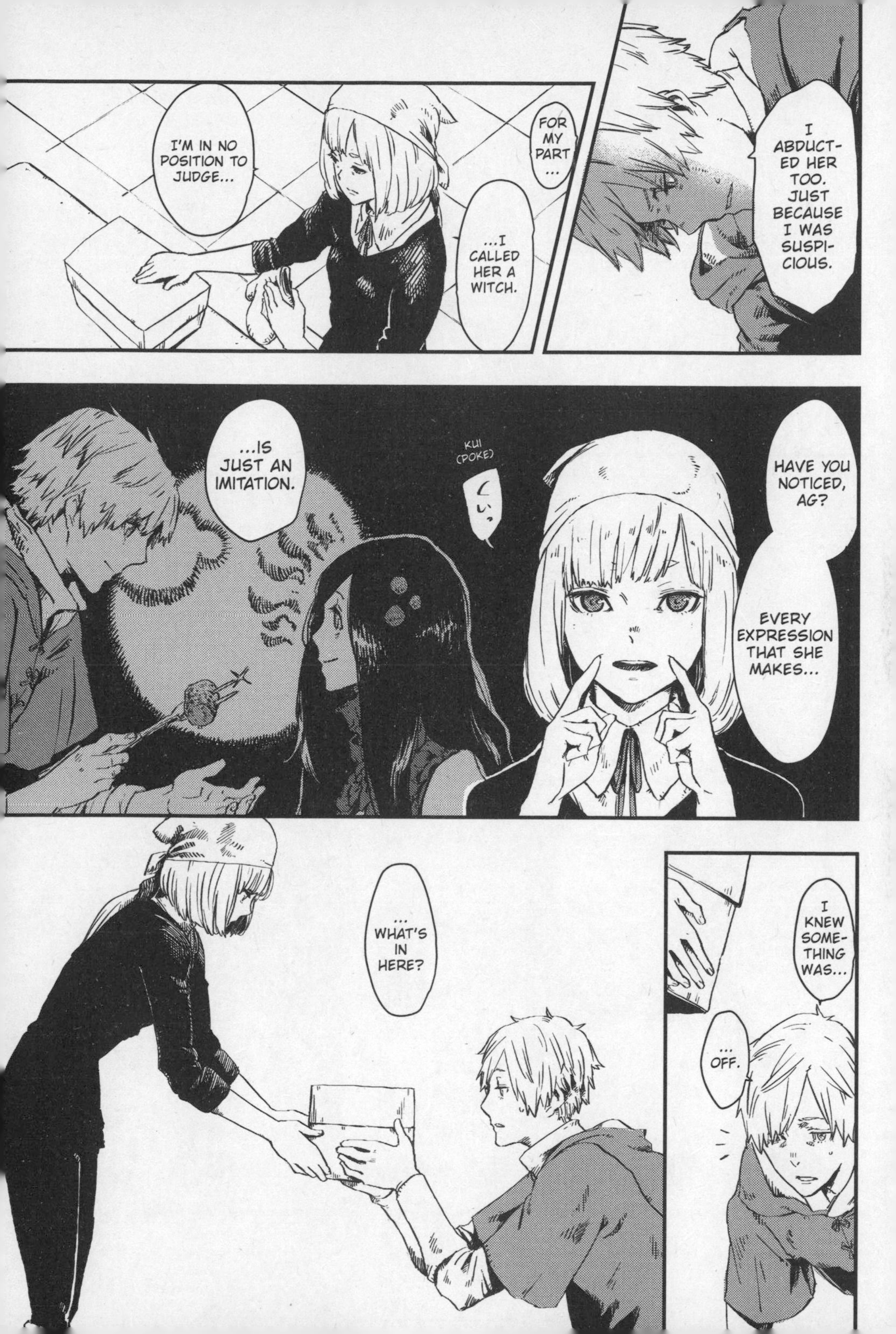
I ABDUCTED HER TOO. JUST BECAUSE I WAS SUSPICIOUS.
FOR MY PART...
...I CALLED HER A WITCH.
I'M IN NO POSITION TO JUDGE...
HAVE YOU NOTICED, AG?
EVERY EXPRESSION THAT SHE MAKES...
KUI (POKE)
くいっ
...IS JUST AN IMITATION.
I KNEW SOMETHING WAS...
...OFF.
...WHAT'S IN HERE?

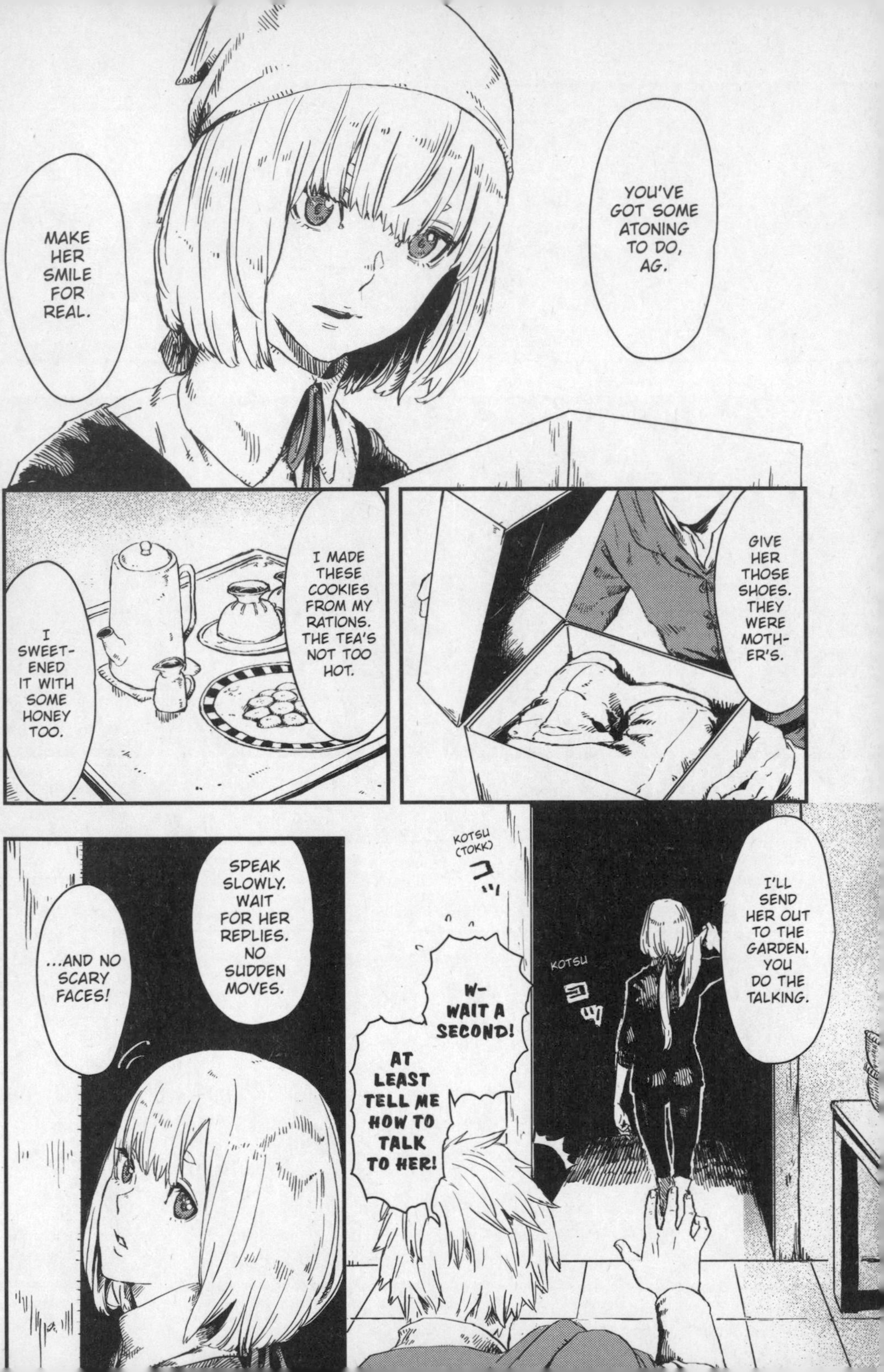
YOU'VE GOT SOME ATONING TO DO, AG.
MAKE HER SMILE FOR REAL.
GIVE HER THOSE SHOES. THEY WERE MOTHER'S.
I MADE THESE COOKIES FROM MY RATIONS. THE TEA'S NOT TOO HOT.
I SWEETENED IT WITH SOME HONEY TOO.
I'LL SEND HER OUT TO THE GARDEN. YOU DO THE TALKING.
KOTSU (TOKK)
KOTSU
W-WAIT A SECOND!
AT LEAST TELL ME HOW TO TALK TO HER!
SPEAK SLOWLY. WAIT FOR HER REPLIES. NO SUDDEN MOVES.
...AND NO SCARY FACES!

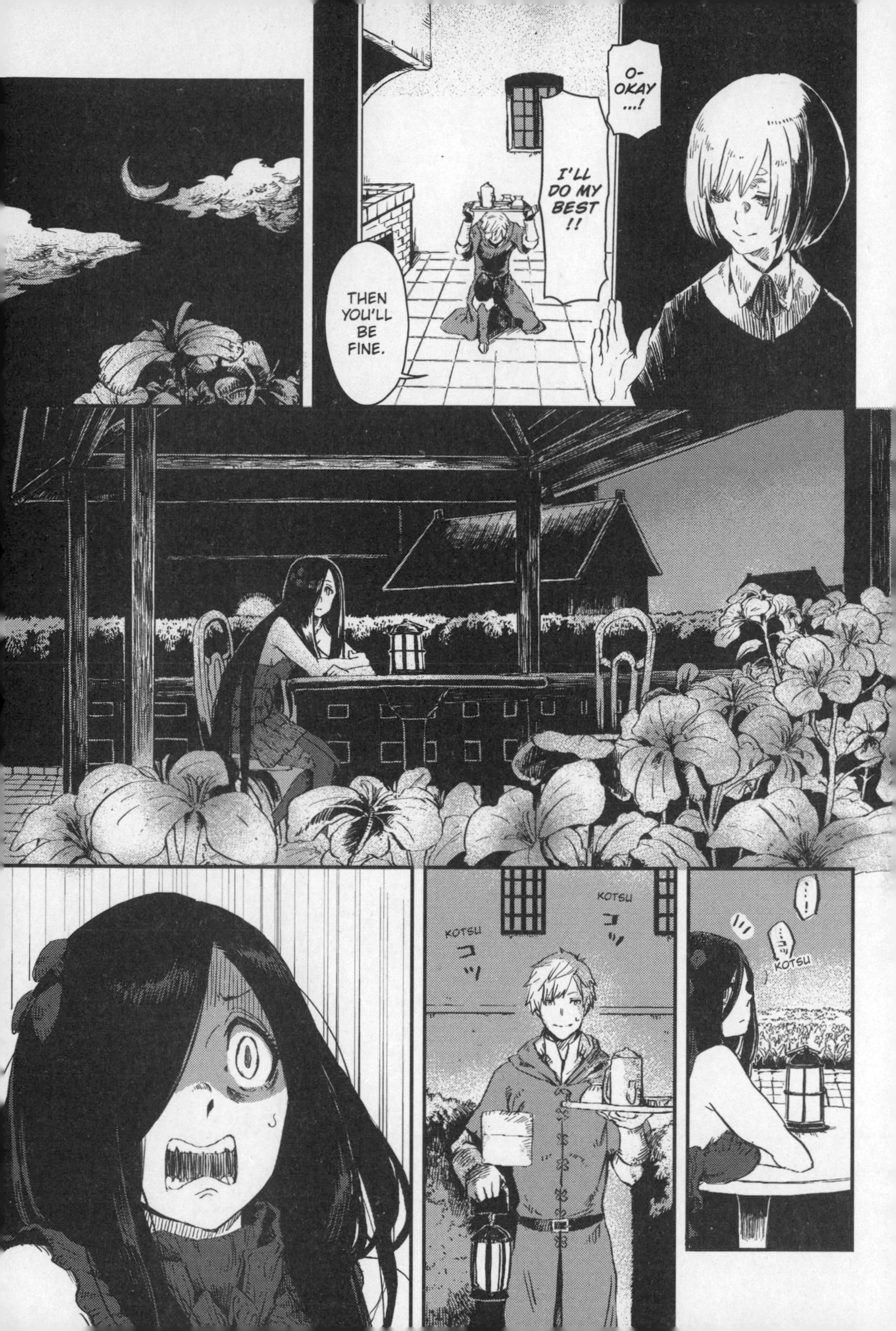
O-OKAY ...!
I'LL DO MY BEST !!
THEN YOU'LL BE FINE.
...!
...コッ
KOTSU
KOTSU
コッ
KOTSU
コッ

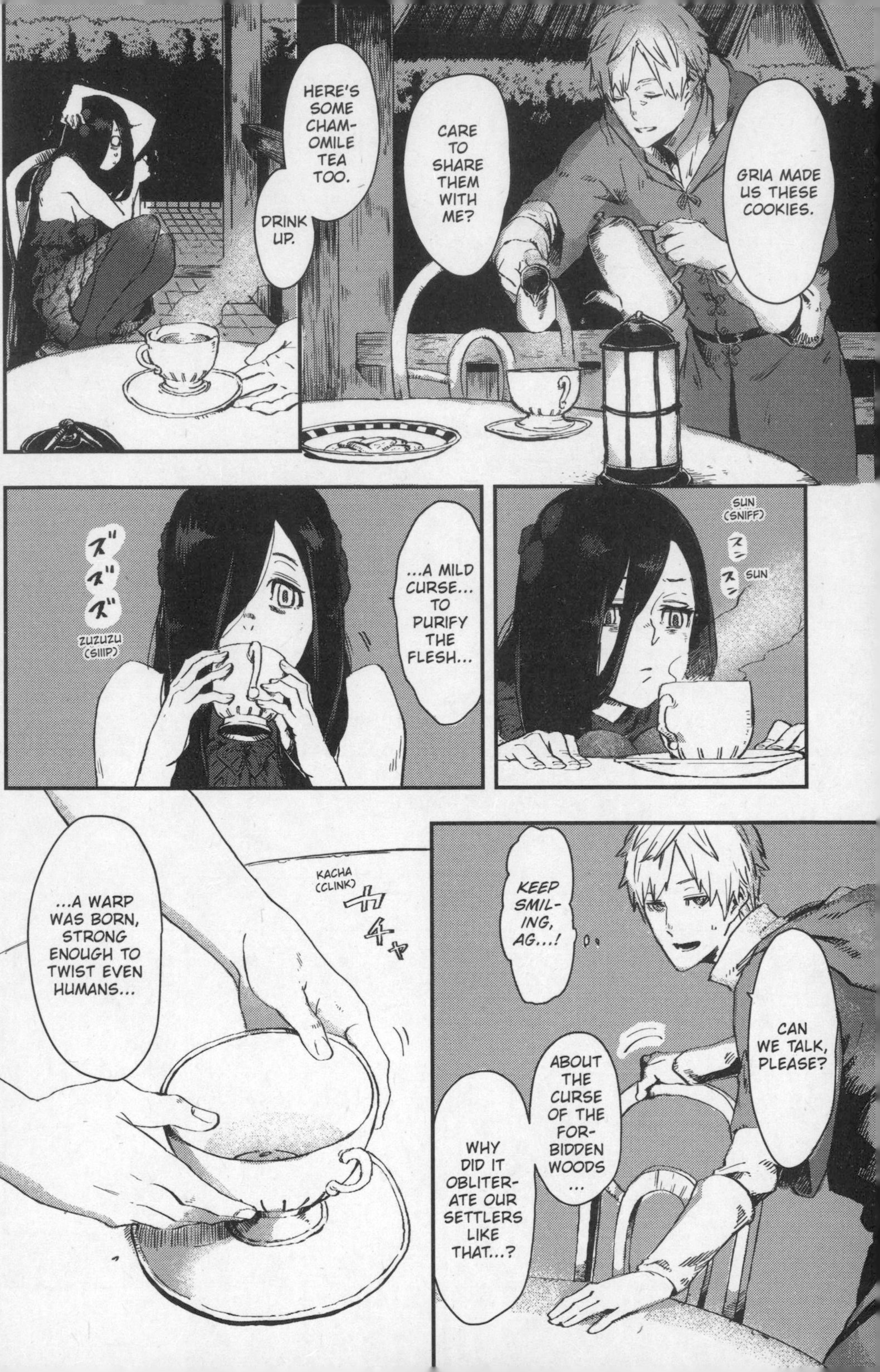

GRIA MADE US THESE COOKIES.
CARE TO SHARE THEM WITH ME?
HERE'S SOME CHAMOMILE TEA TOO.
DRINK UP.
SUN (SNIFF)
スン
スン
SUN
...A MILD CURSE... TO PURIFY THE FLESH...
ズズズ
ZUZUZU (SIIIP)
KEEP SMILING, AG...!
CAN WE TALK, PLEASE?
ABOUT THE CURSE OF THE FORBIDDEN WOODS...
WHY DID IT OBLITERATE OUR SETTLERS LIKE THAT...?
KACHA (CLINK)
カチャ
...A WARP WAS BORN, STRONG ENOUGH TO TWIST EVEN HUMANS...

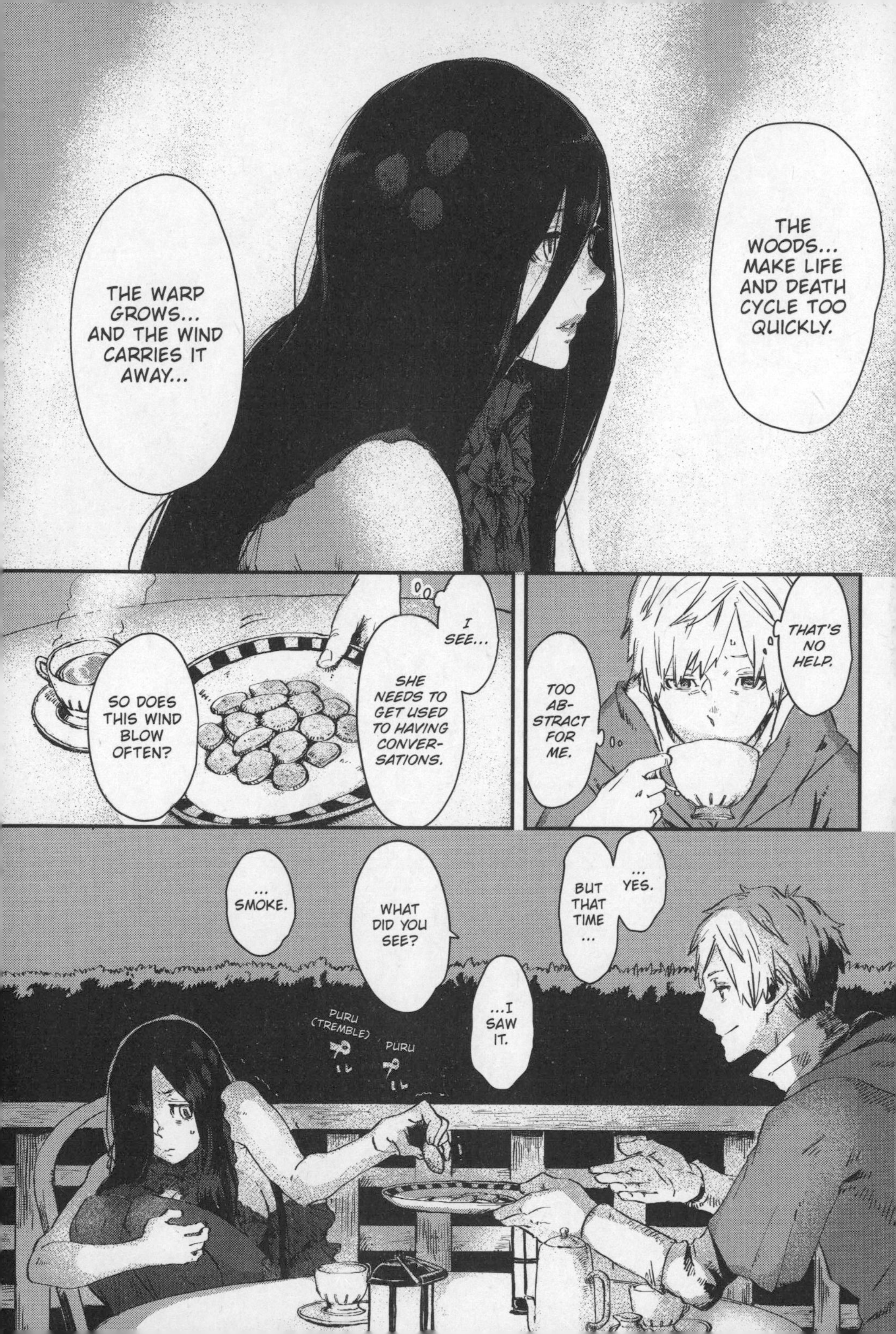
THE WOODS... MAKE LIFE AND DEATH CYCLE TOO QUICKLY.
THE WARP GROWS... AND THE WIND CARRIES IT AWAY...
THAT'S NO HELP.
TOO ABSTRACT FOR ME.
I SEE...
SHE NEEDS TO GET USED TO HAVING CONVERSATIONS.
SO DOES THIS WIND BLOW OFTEN?
... YES.
BUT THAT TIME ...
...I SAW IT.
WHAT DID YOU SEE?
... SMOKE.
PURU (TREMBLE)
PURU

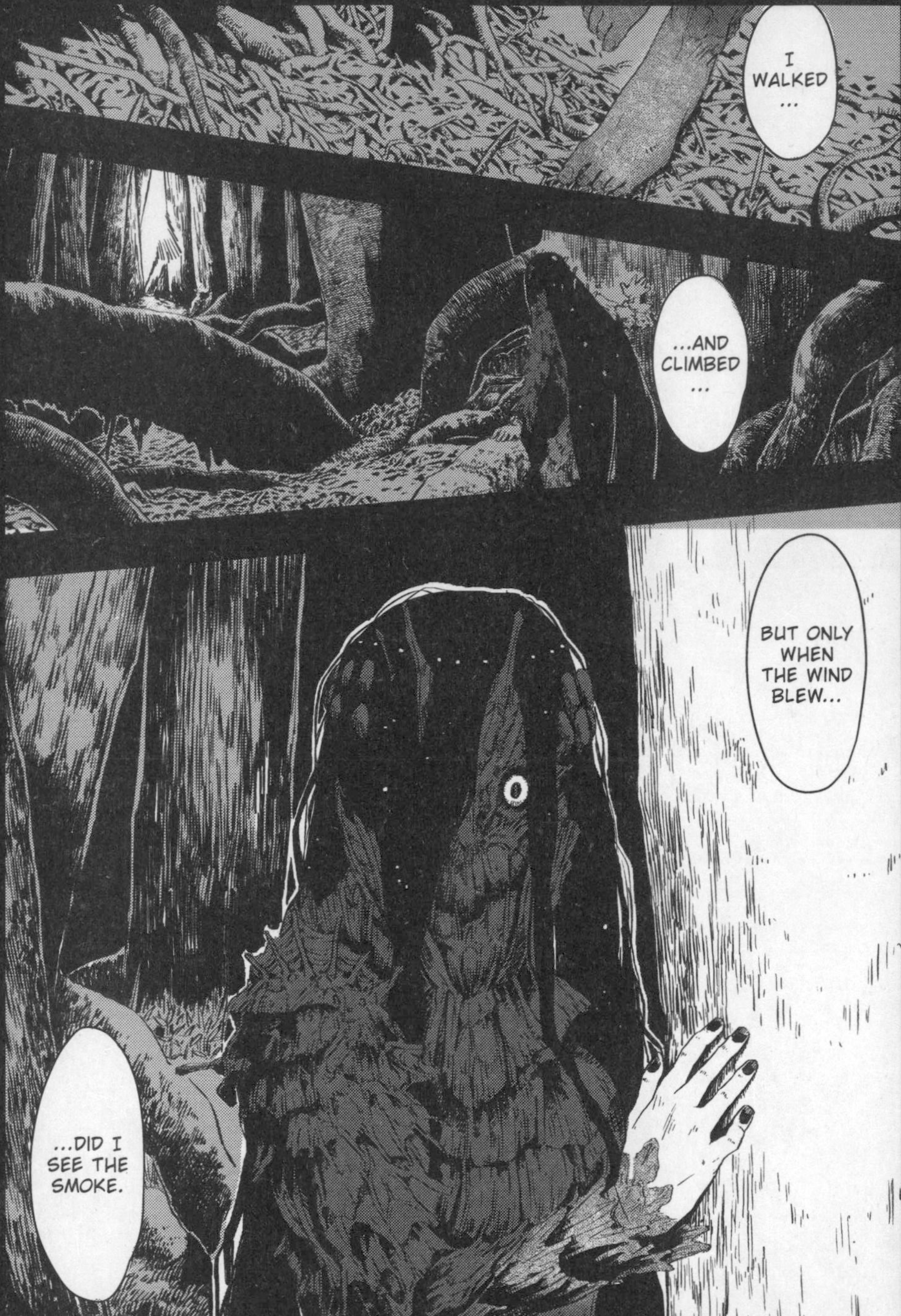

I WALKED ...
...AND CLIMBED ...
BUT ONLY WHEN THE WIND BLEW...
...
...DID I SEE THE SMOKE.

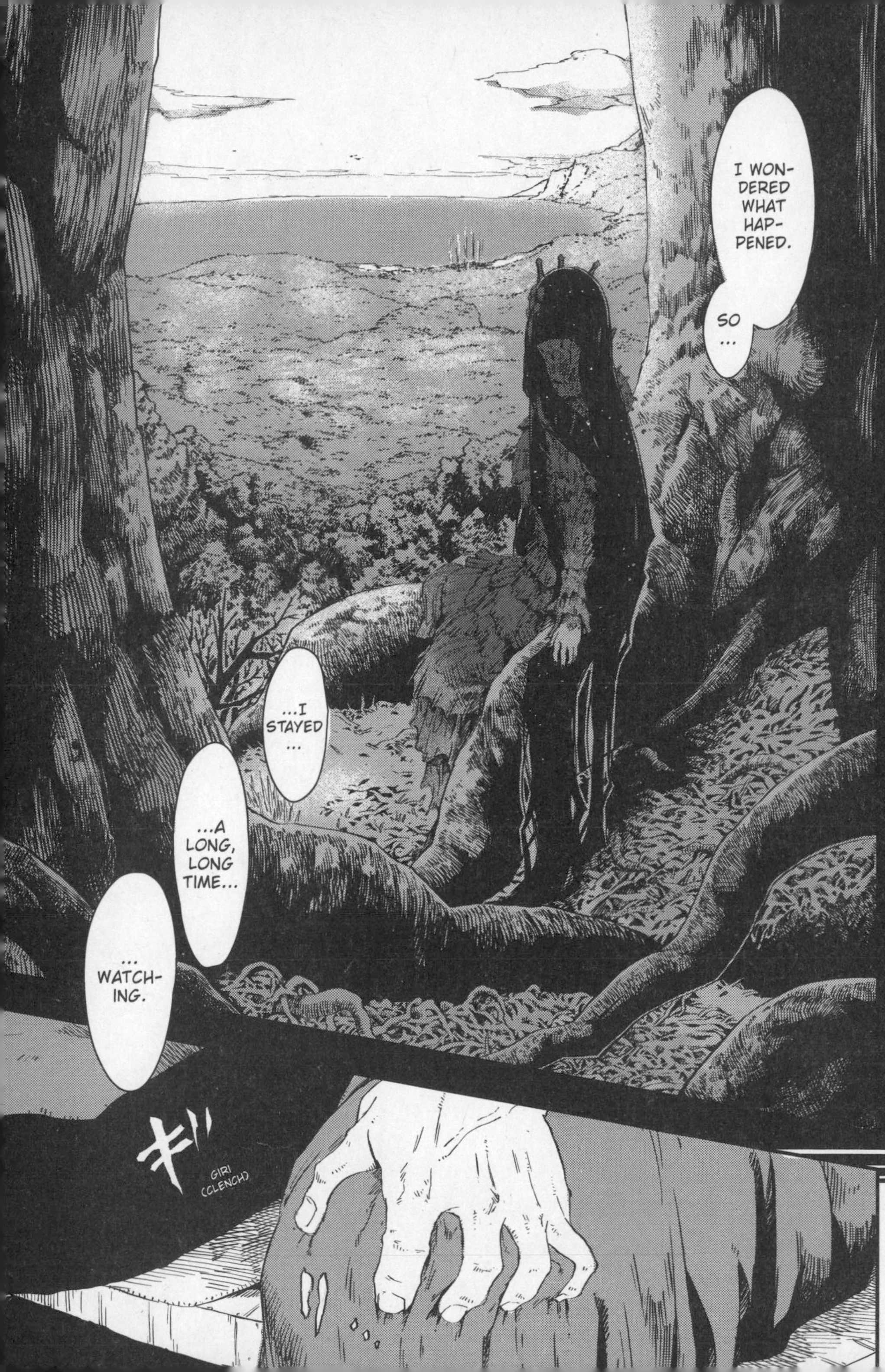
I WONDERED WHAT HAPPENED.
SO...
...I STAYED...
...A LONG, LONG TIME...
...WATCHING.
キリ
GIRI (CLENCH)

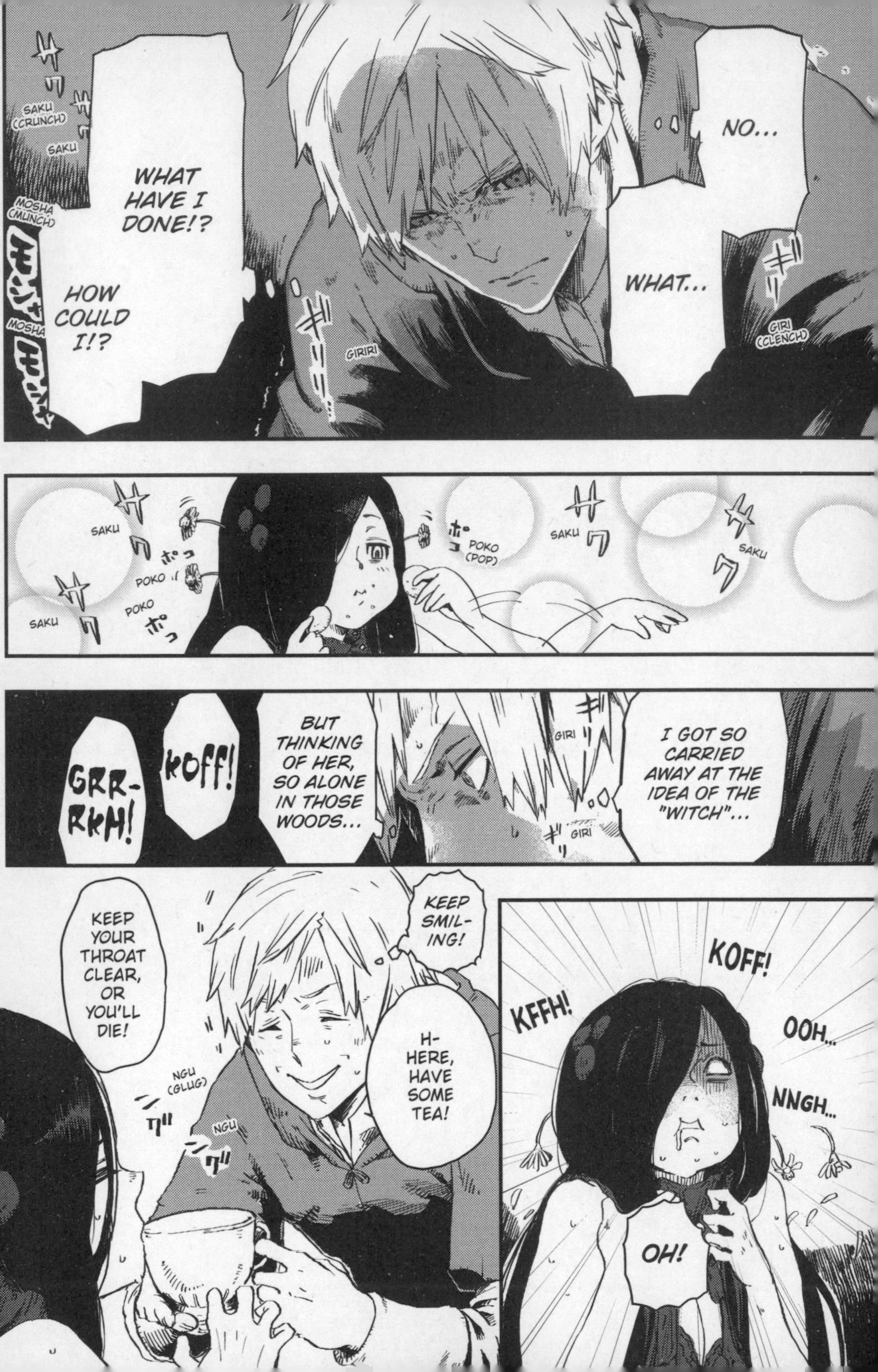
NO...
WHAT...
GIRI (CLENCH)
WHAT HAVE I DONE!?
HOW COULD I!?
GIRIRI
SAKU (CRUNCH)
SAKU
MOSHA (MUNCH)
MOSHA
SAKU
SAKU
POKO (POP)
POKO
POKO
SAKU
SAKU
I GOT SO CARRIED AWAY AT THE IDEA OF THE "WITCH"...
GIRI
GIRI
BUT THINKING OF HER, SO ALONE IN THOSE WOODS...
KOFF!
GRR-RKH!
KOFF!
KFFH!
OOH...
NNGH...
OH!
KEEP SMIL-ING!
H-HERE, HAVE SOME TEA!
KEEP YOUR THROAT CLEAR, OR YOU'LL DIE!
NGU (GLUG)
NGU

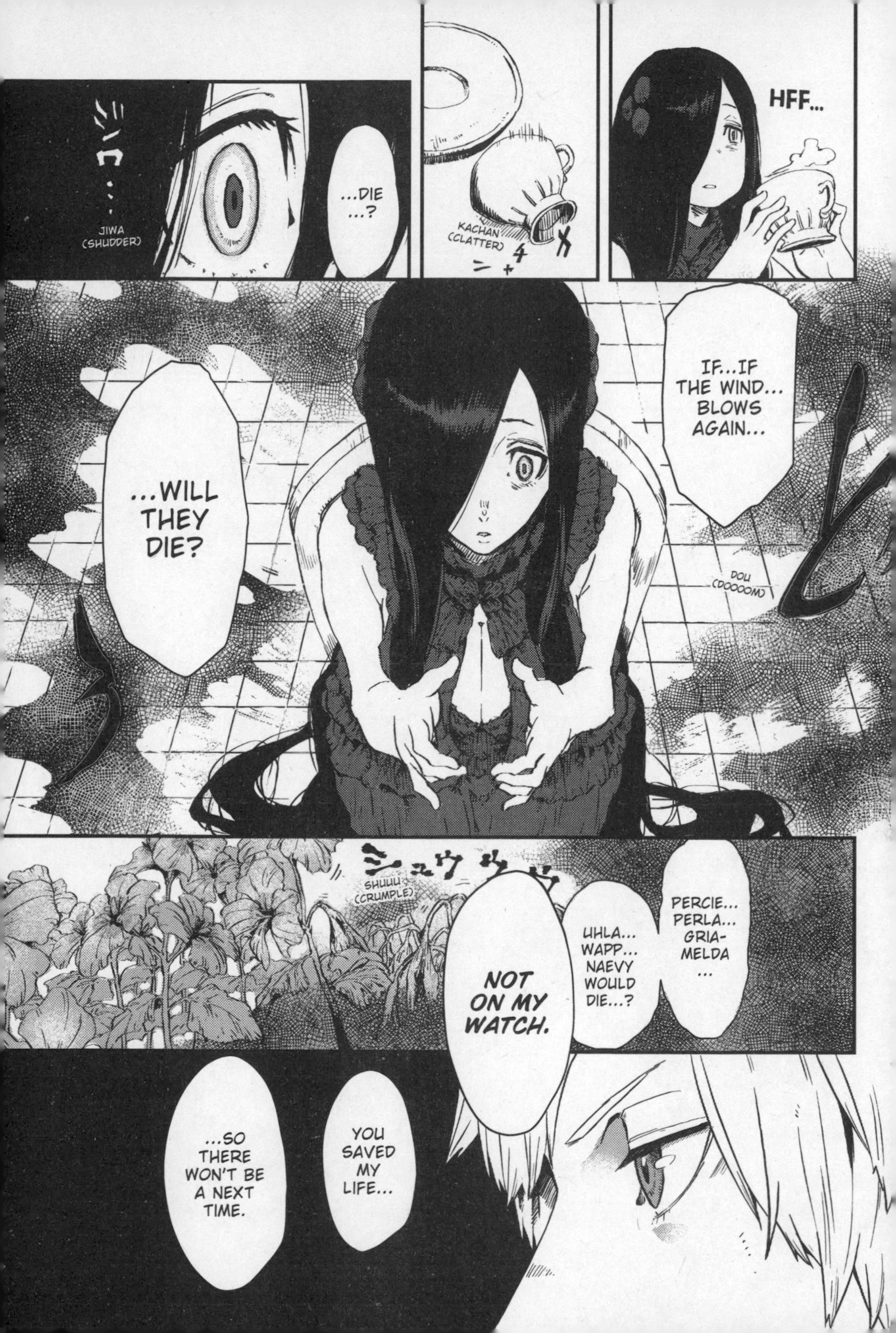
HFF...
KACHAN (CLATTER)
...DIE ...?
JIWA (SHUDDER)
IF...IF THE WIND... BLOWS AGAIN...
DOU (DOOOOM)
...WILL THEY DIE?
PERCIE... PERLA... GRIA-MELDA ...
UHLA... WAPP... NAEVY WOULD DIE...?
SHUUU (CRUMPLE)
NOT ON MY WATCH.
YOU SAVED MY LIFE...
...SO THERE WON'T BE A NEXT TIME.

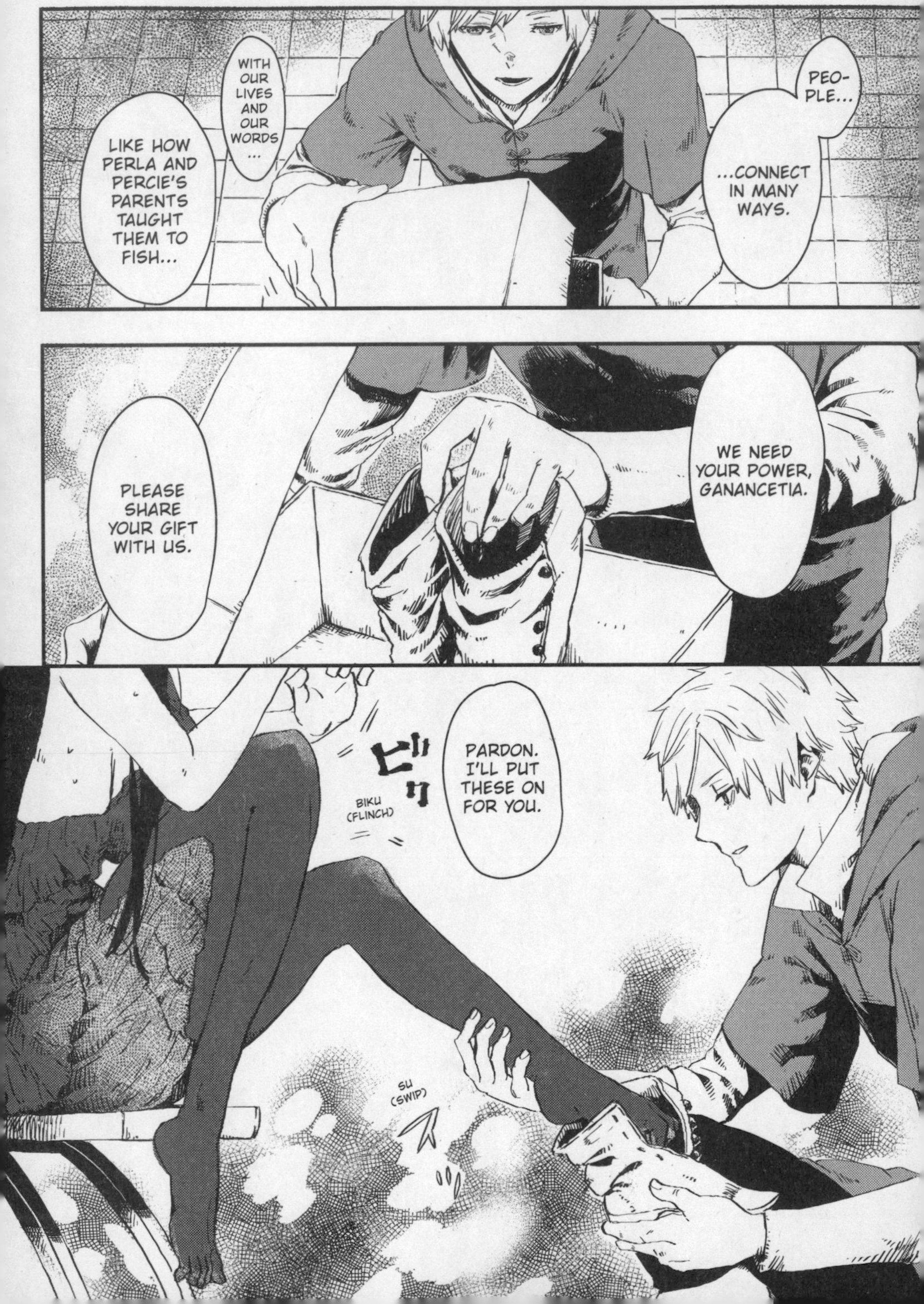
PEO-PLE...
...CONNECT IN MANY WAYS.
WITH OUR LIVES AND OUR WORDS...
LIKE HOW PERLA AND PERCIE'S PARENTS TAUGHT THEM TO FISH...
WE NEED YOUR POWER, GANANCETIA.
PLEASE SHARE YOUR GIFT WITH US.
PARDON. I'LL PUT THESE ON FOR YOU.
ビク
BIKU (FLINCH)
SU (SWIP)

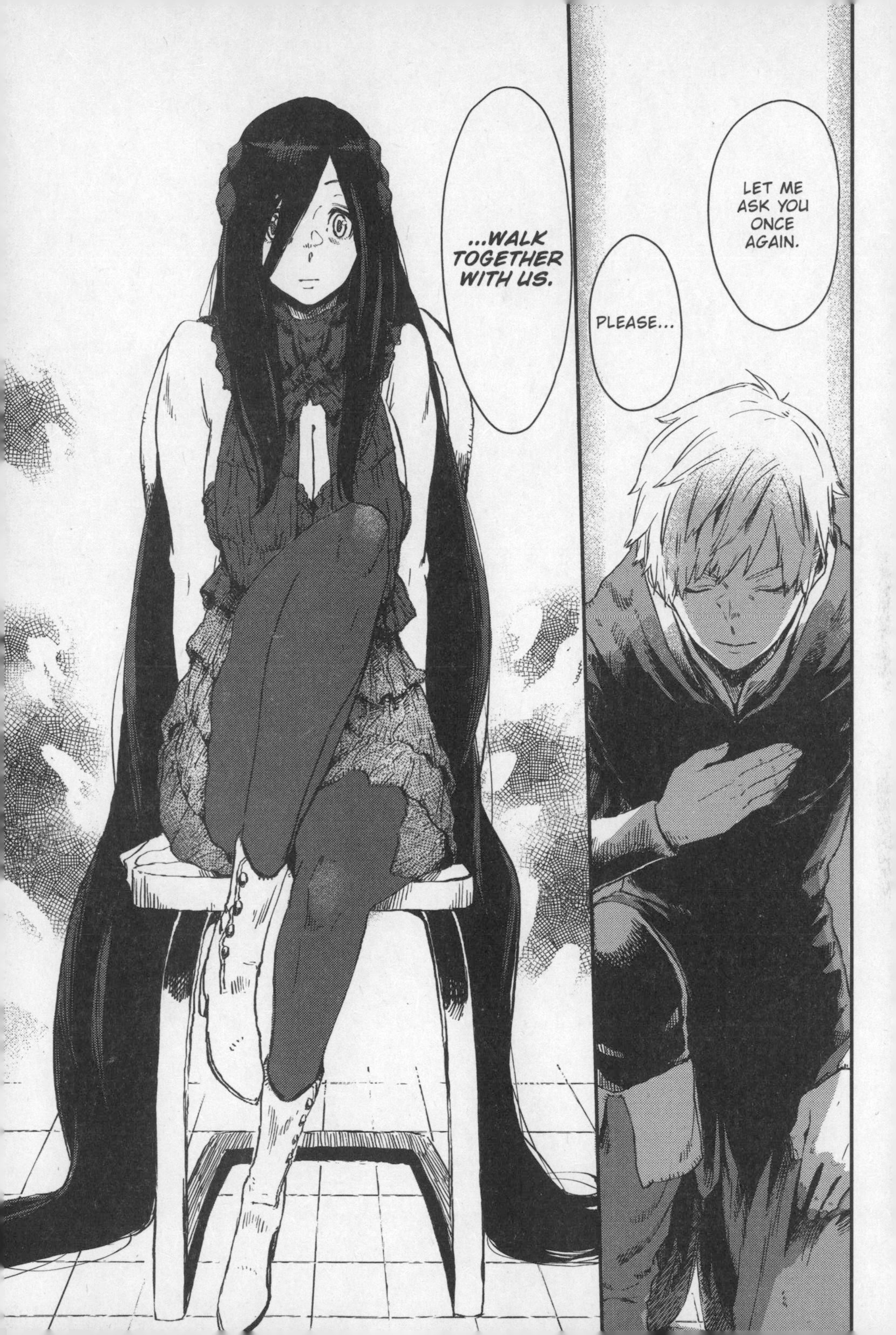
LET ME ASK YOU ONCE AGAIN.
PLEASE...
...WALK TOGETHER WITH US.

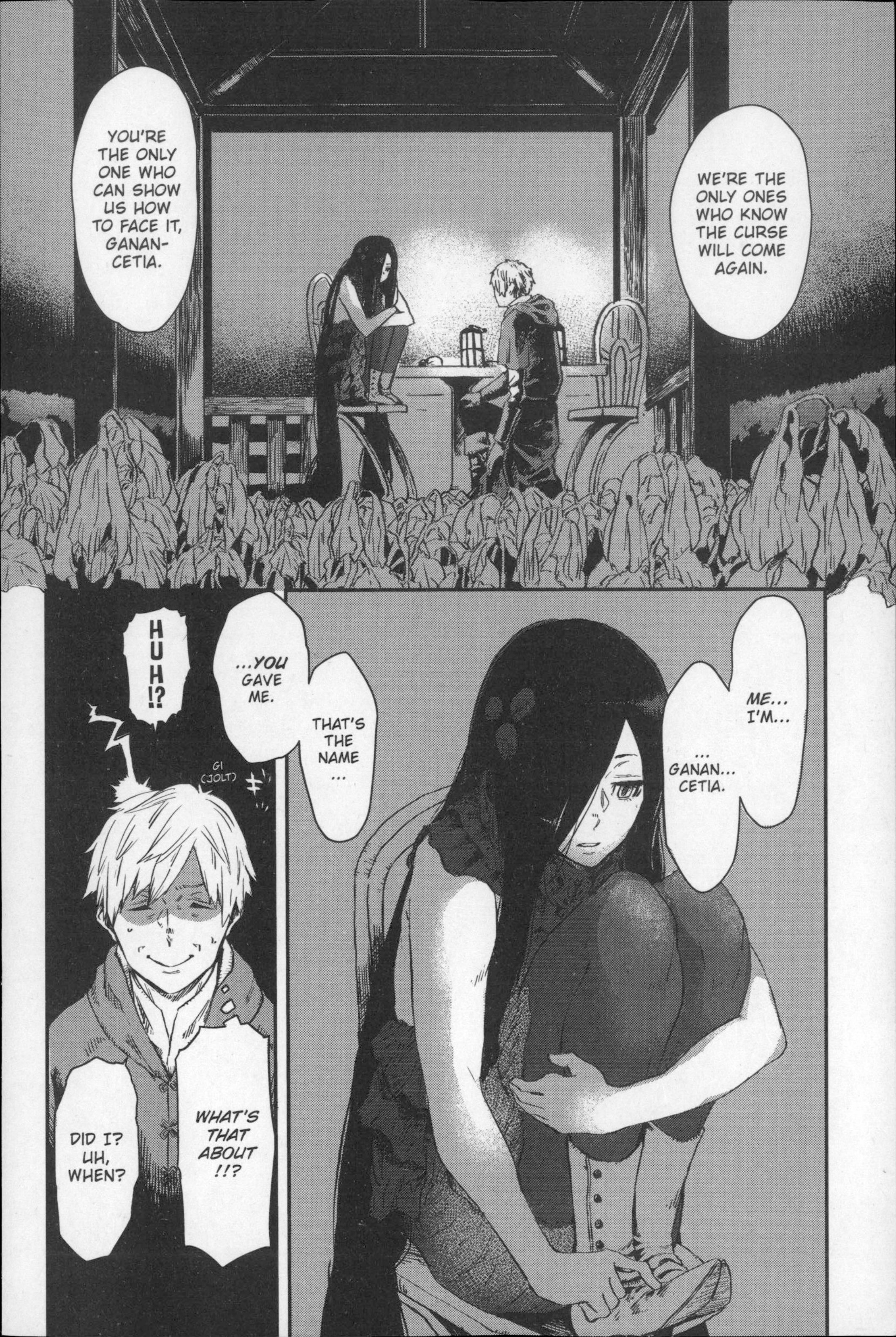
WE'RE THE ONLY ONES WHO KNOW THE CURSE WILL COME AGAIN.
YOU'RE THE ONLY ONE WHO CAN SHOW US HOW TO FACE IT, GANAN-CETIA.
ME... I'M...
...GANAN... CETIA.
...YOU GAVE ME.
THAT'S THE NAME...
HUH!?
GI (JOLT)
WHAT'S THAT ABOUT!!?
DID I? UH, WHEN?

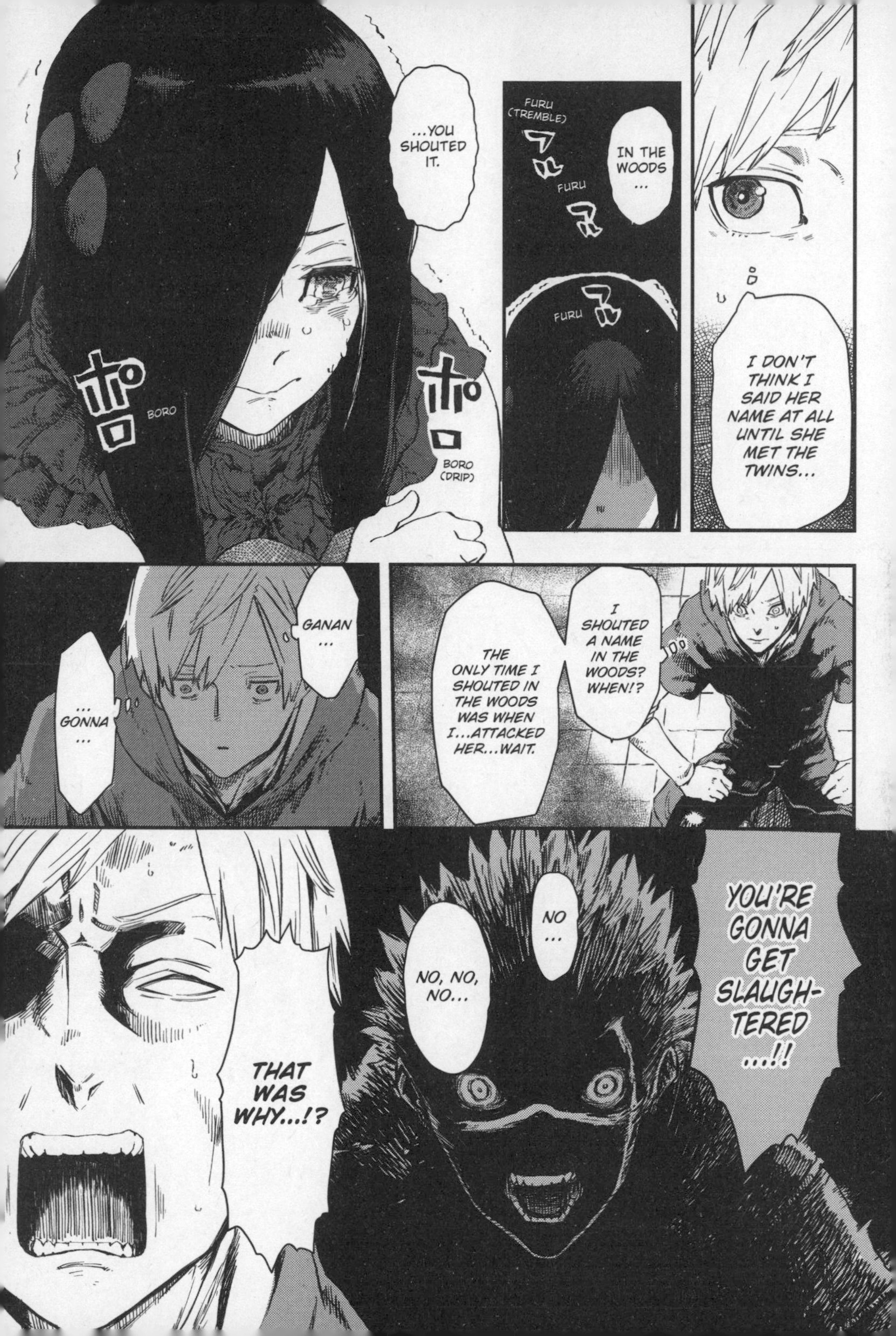

I DON'T THINK I SAID HER NAME AT ALL UNTIL SHE MET THE TWINS...
IN THE WOODS ...
フル
FURU (TREMBLE)
フル
FURU
フル
FURU
...YOU SHOUTED IT.
ポロ
BORO (DRIP)
ポロ
BORO
I SHOUTED A NAME IN THE WOODS? WHEN!?
THE ONLY TIME I SHOUTED IN THE WOODS WAS WHEN I...ATTACKED HER...WAIT.
GANAN ...
... GONNA ...
YOU'RE GONNA GET SLAUGHTERED ...!!
NO ...
NO, NO, NO...
THAT WAS WHY...!?

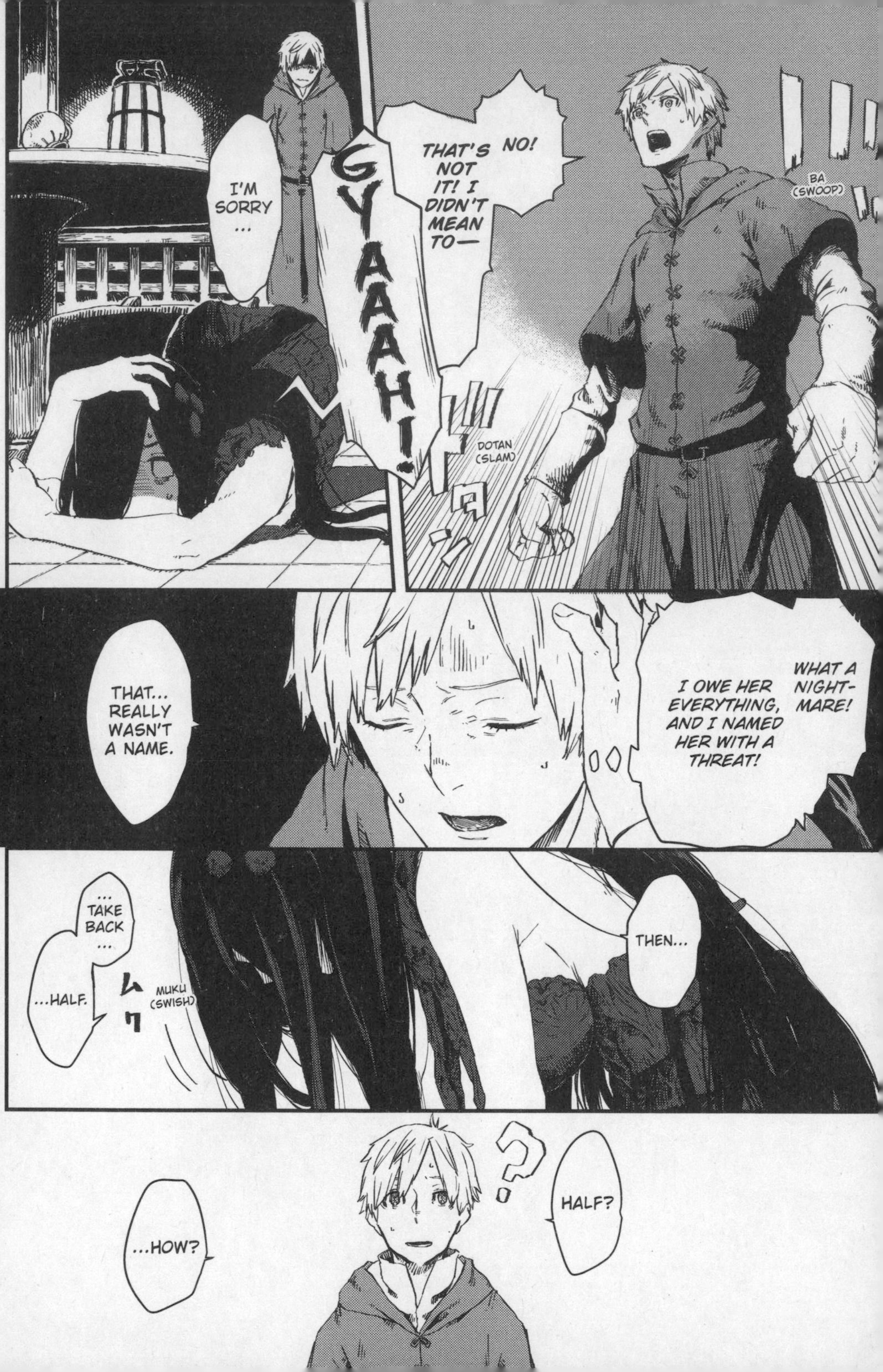
NO!
THAT'S NOT IT! I DIDN'T MEAN TO—
BA (SWOOP)
DOTAN (SLAM)
GYAAAH!
I'M SORRY...
WHAT A NIGHT-MARE!
I OWE HER EVERYTHING, AND I NAMED HER WITH A THREAT!
THAT... REALLY WASN'T A NAME.
THEN...
...TAKE BACK...
...HALF.
MUKU (SWISH)
HALF?
...HOW?

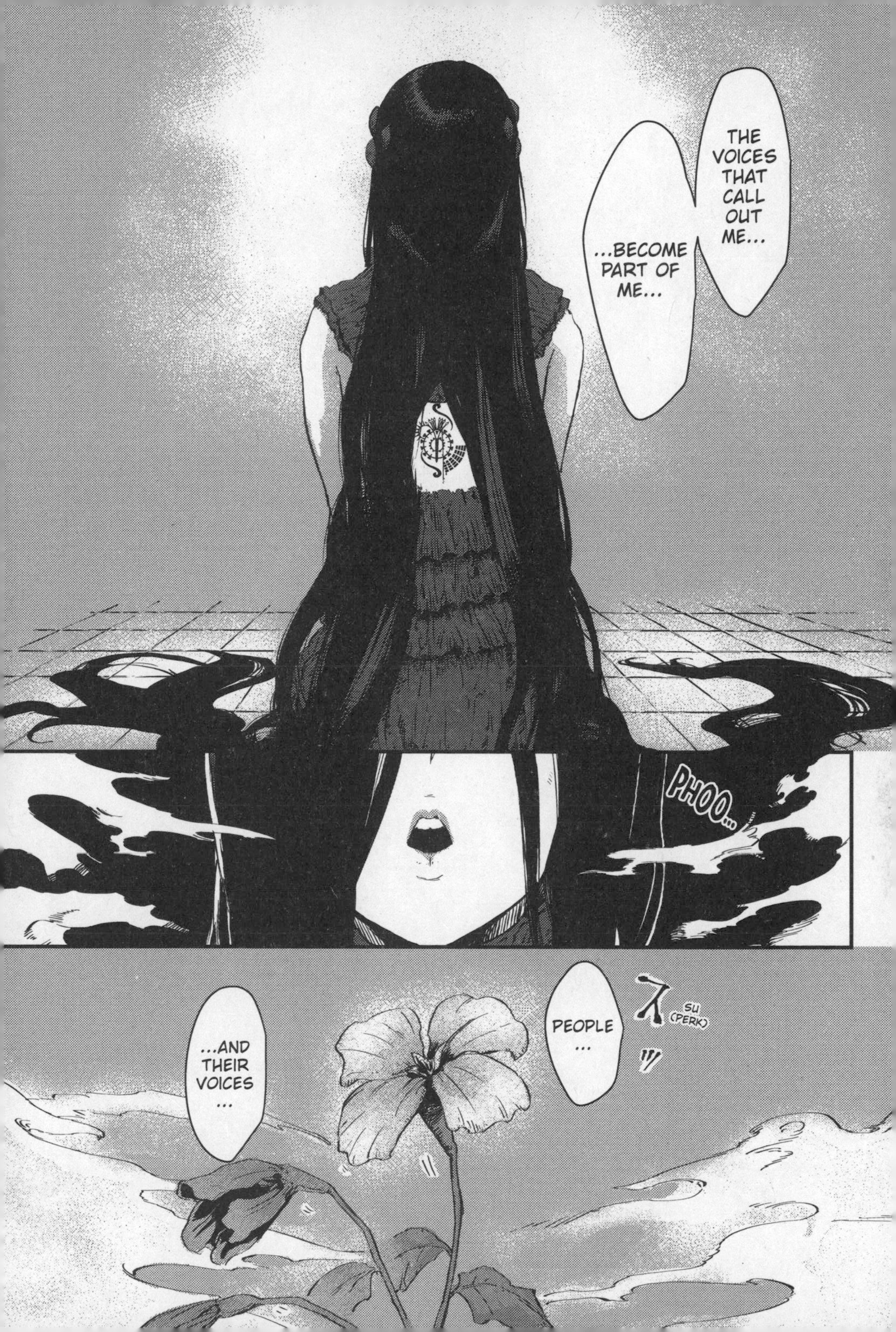
THE VOICES THAT CALL OUT ME...
...BECOME PART OF ME...
PHOO...
SU (PERK)
PEOPLE ...
...AND THEIR VOICES ...

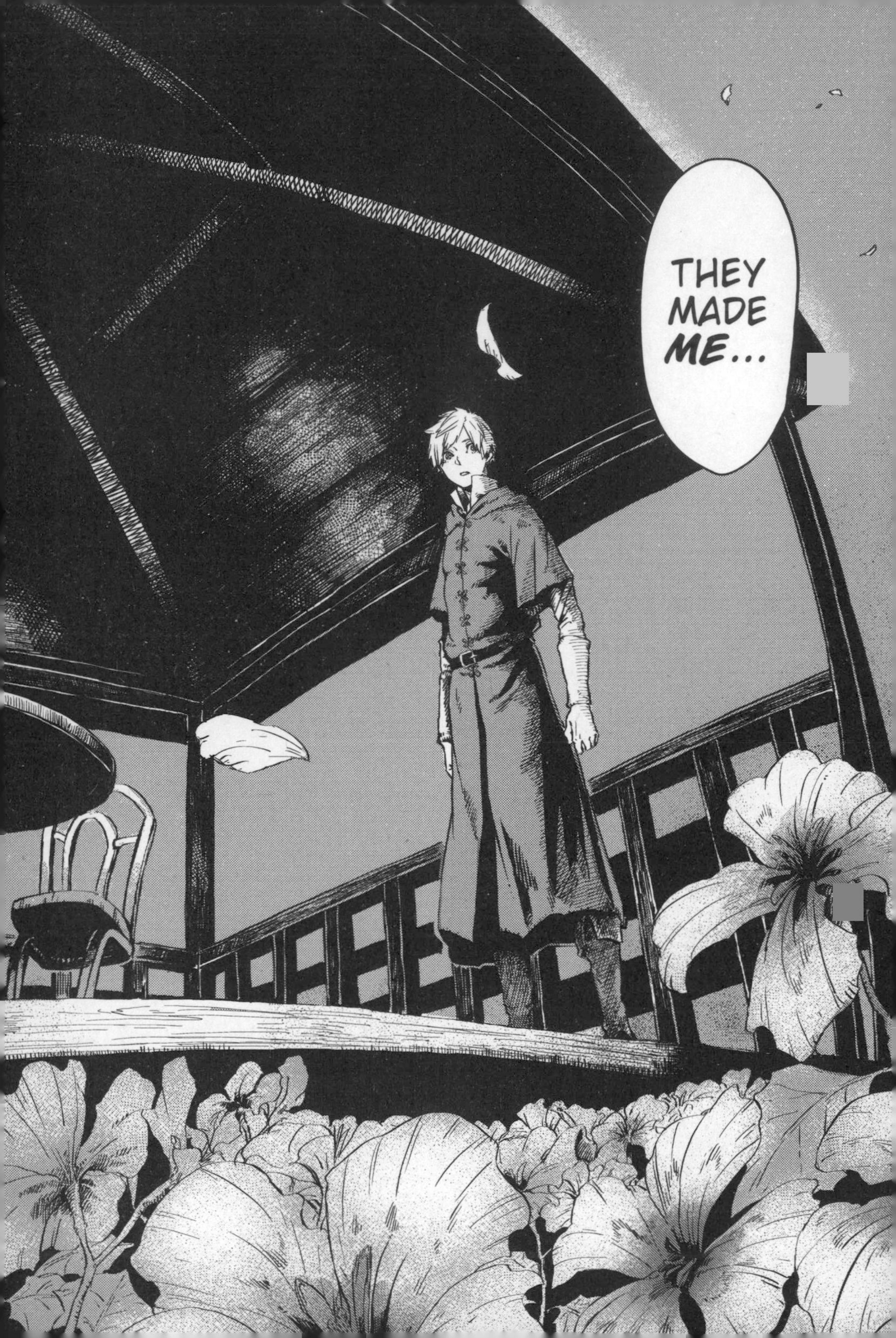
THEY MADE ME...

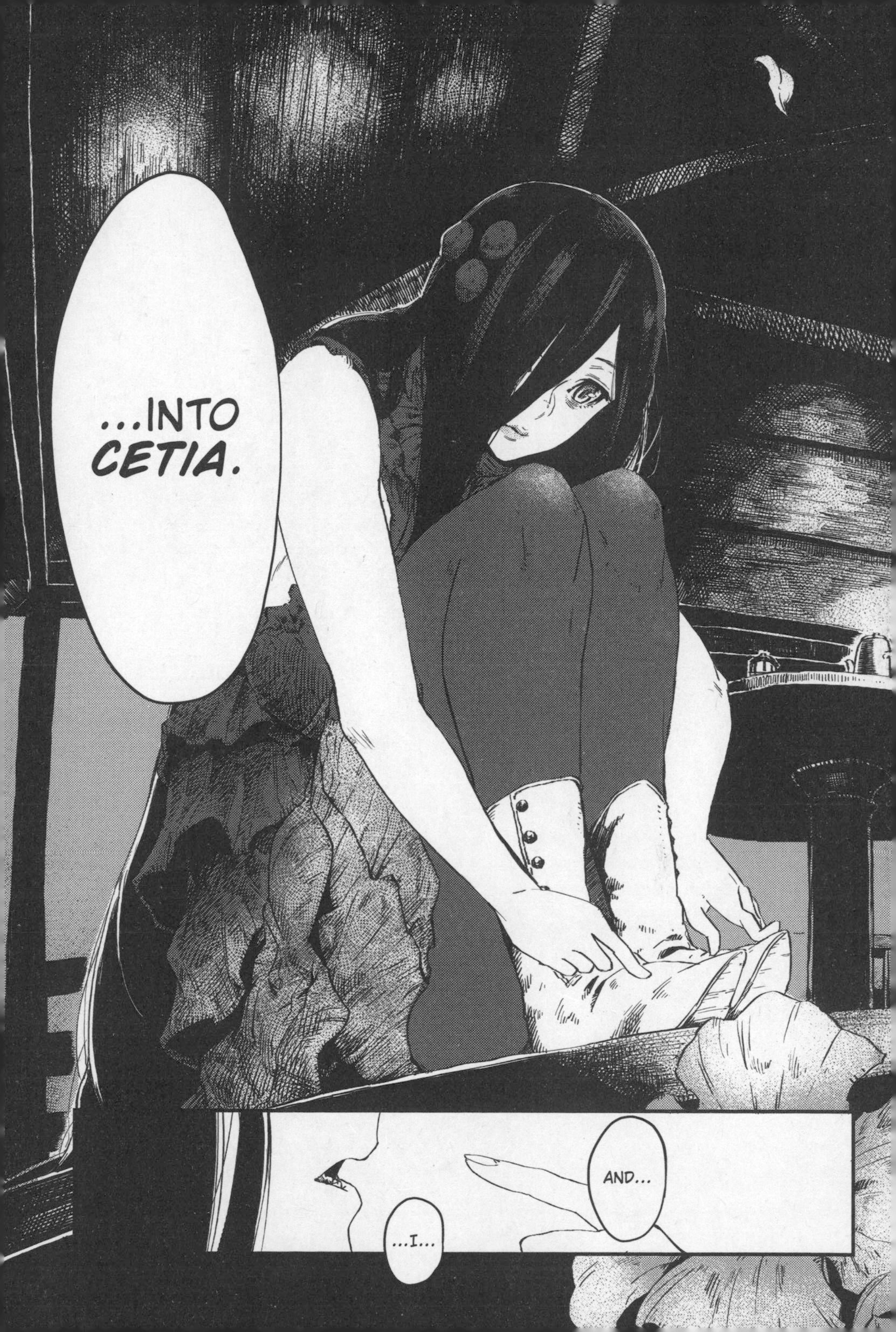

...INTO CETIA.
AND...
...I...

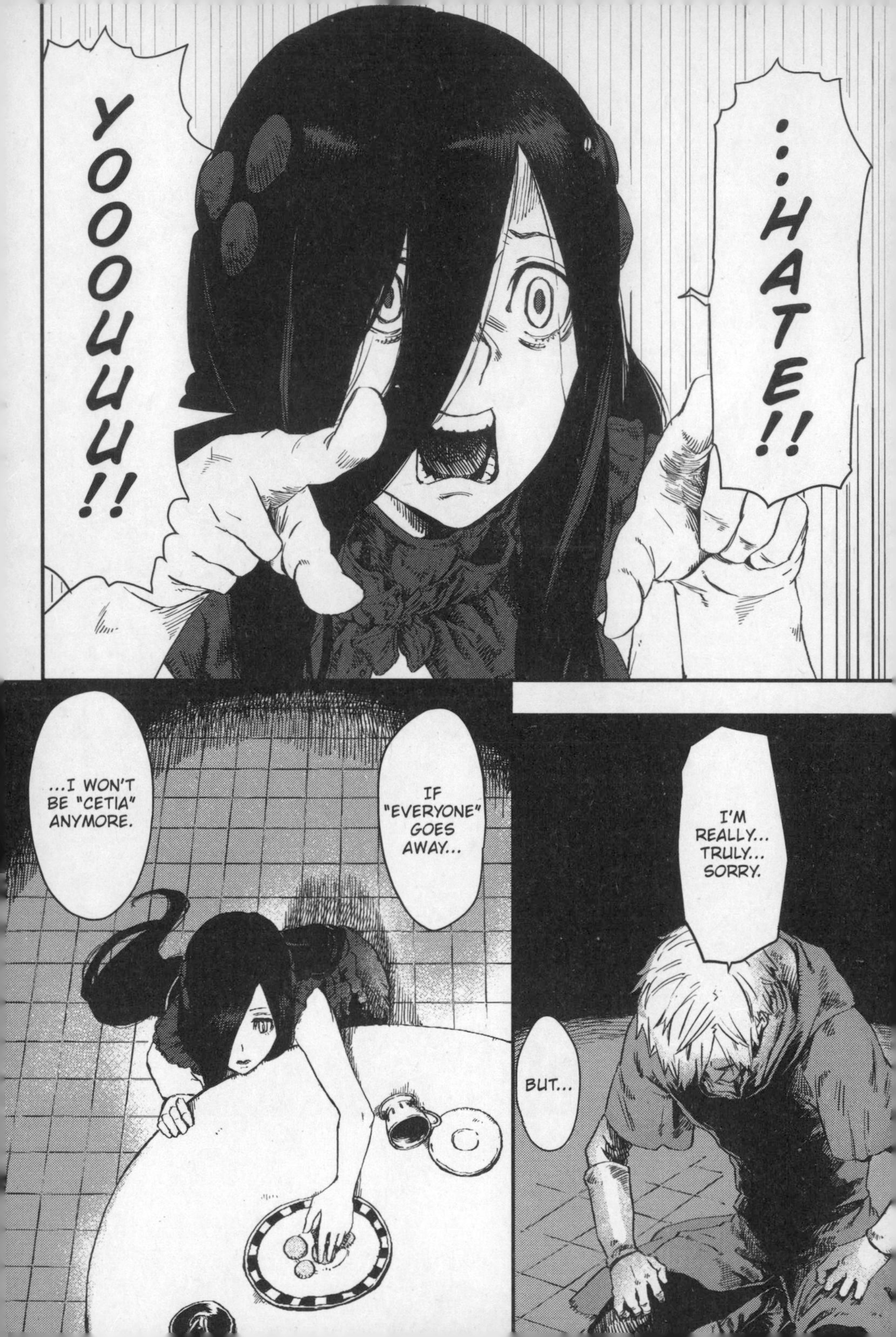
...HATE!!
YOOOUUU!!
I'M REALLY... TRULY... SORRY.
BUT...
IF "EVERYONE" GOES AWAY...
...I WON'T BE "CETIA" ANYMORE.

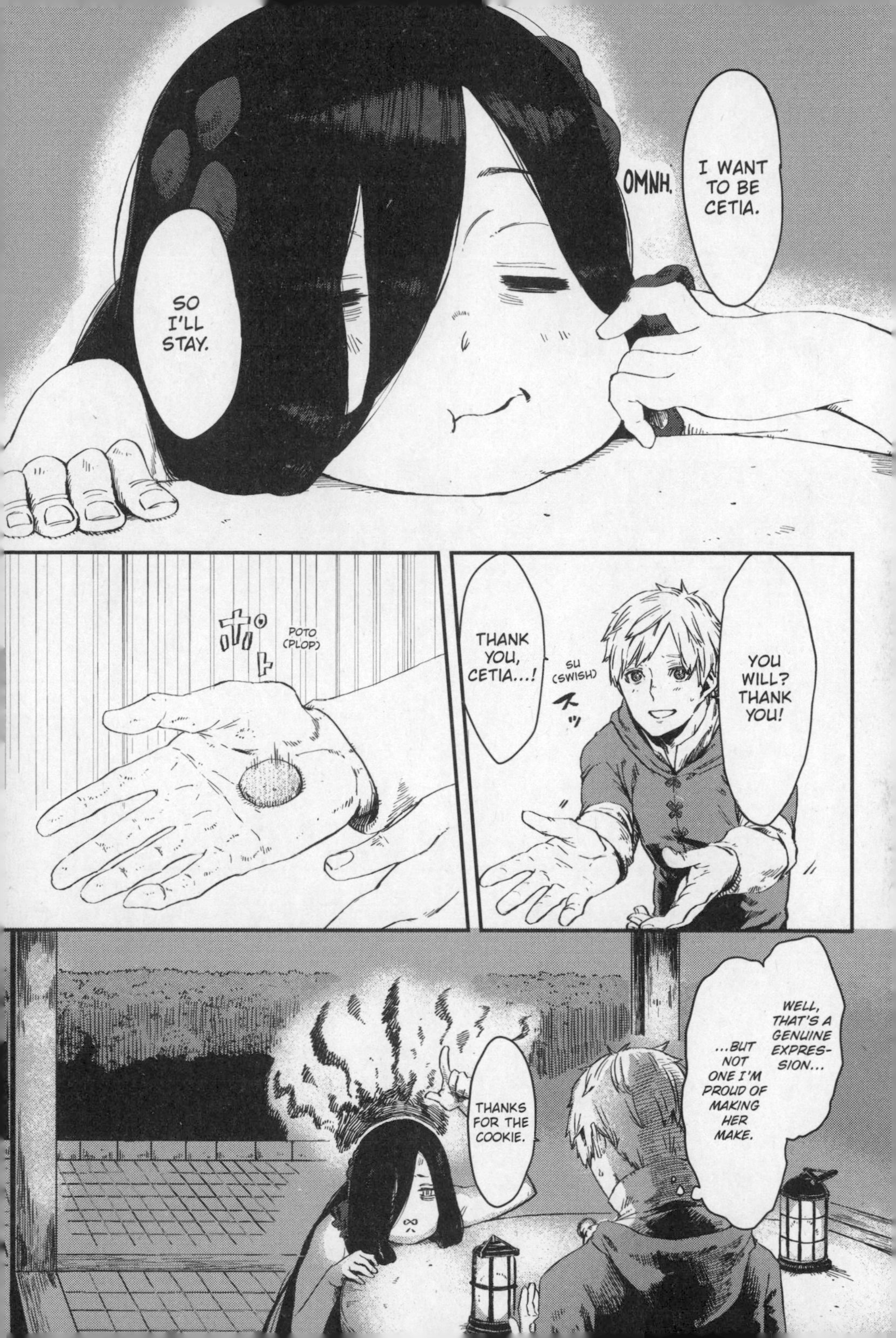
I WANT TO BE CETIA.
OMNH.
SO I'LL STAY.
YOU WILL? THANK YOU!
スッ
SU (SWISH)
THANK YOU, CETIA...!
ポト
POTO (PLOP)
WELL, THAT'S A GENUINE EXPRES-SION...
...BUT NOT ONE I'M PROUD OF MAKING HER MAKE.
THANKS FOR THE COOKIE.

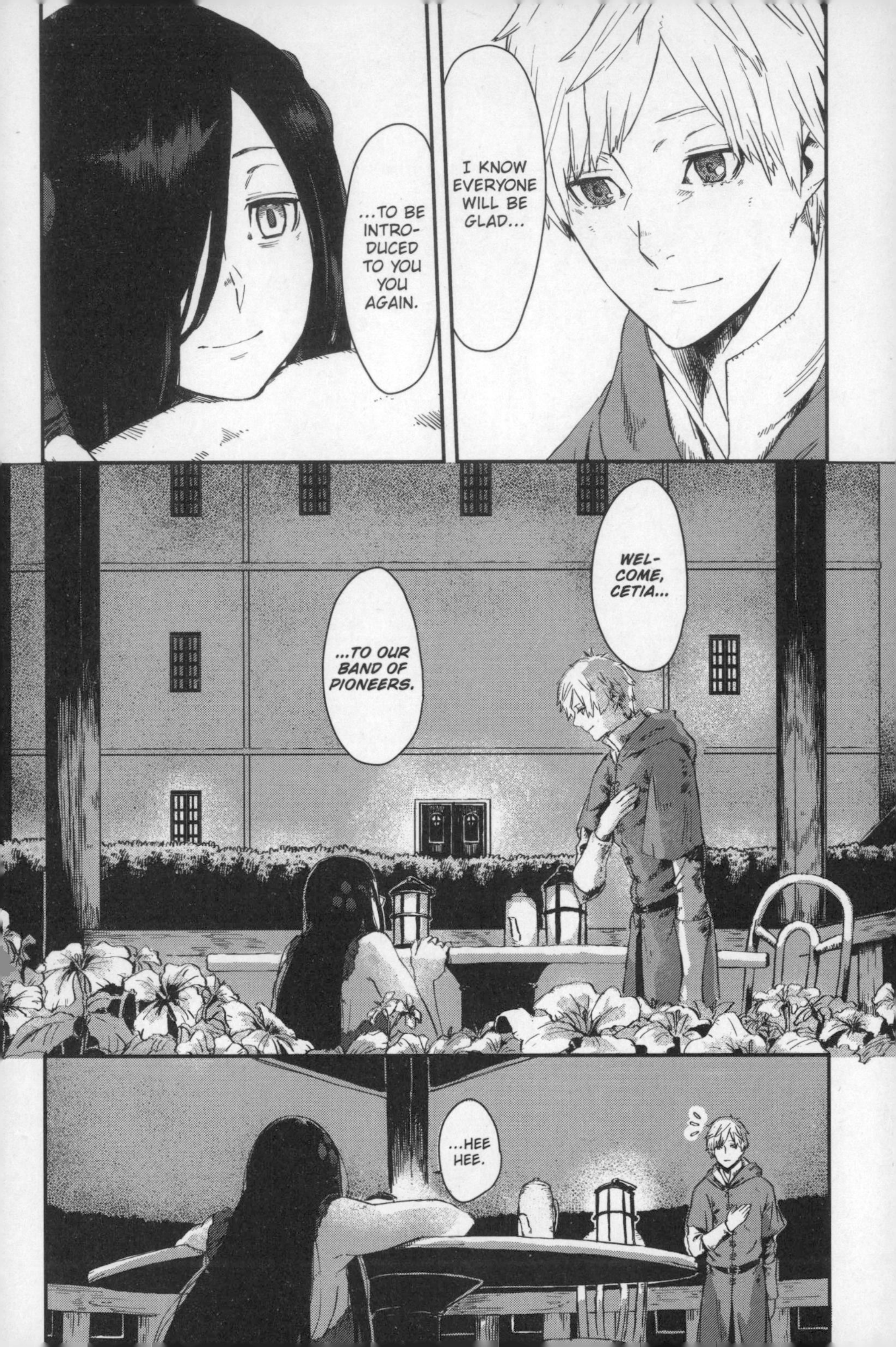
I KNOW EVERYONE WILL BE GLAD...
...TO BE INTRO-DUCED TO YOU YOU AGAIN.
WEL-COME, CETIA...
...TO OUR BAND OF PIONEERS.
...HEE HEE.

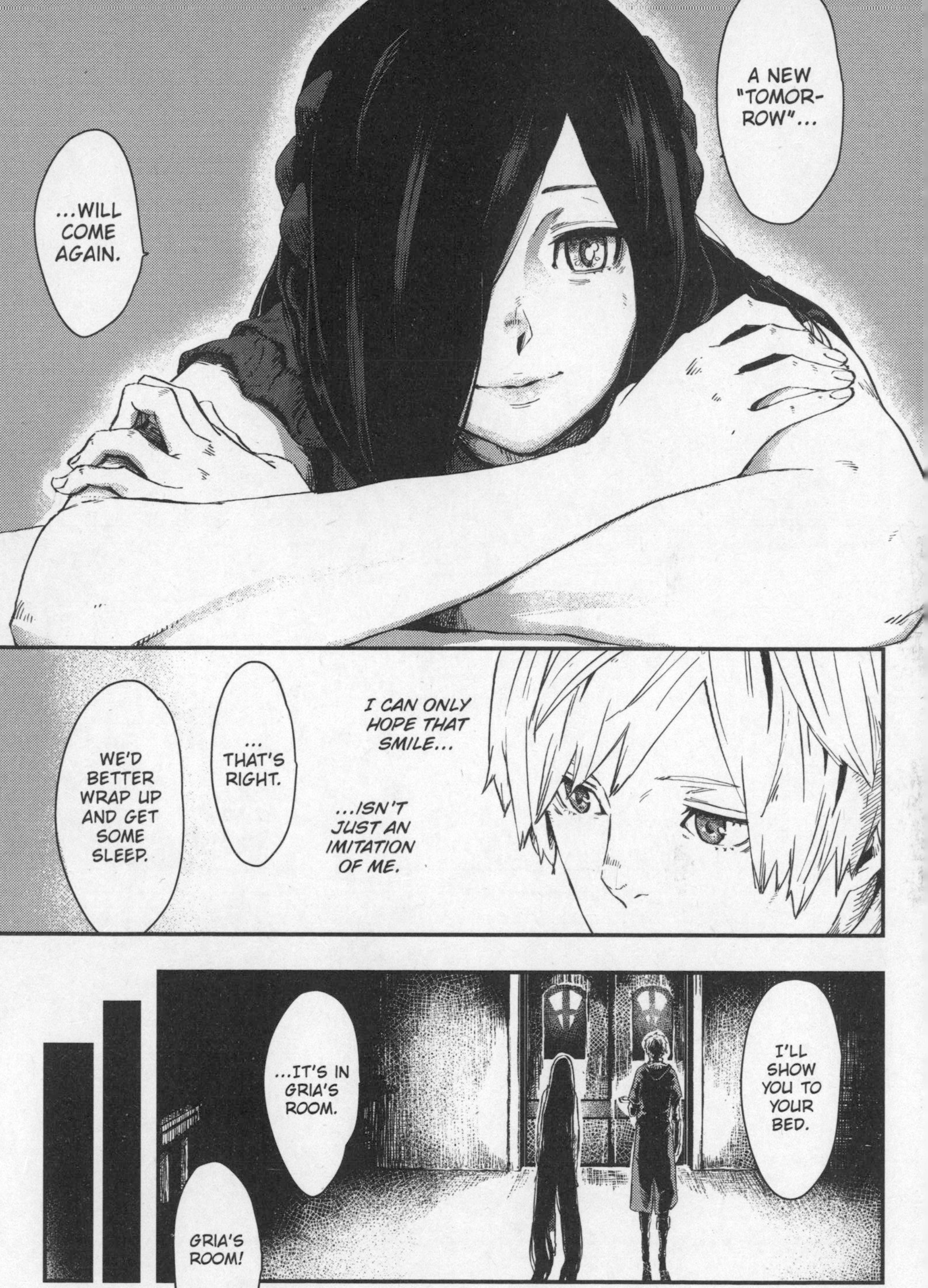
A NEW "TOMOR-ROW"...
...WILL COME AGAIN.
I CAN ONLY HOPE THAT SMILE...
...ISN'T JUST AN IMITATION OF ME.
... THAT'S RIGHT.
WE'D BETTER WRAP UP AND GET SOME SLEEP.
I'LL SHOW YOU TO YOUR BED.
...IT'S IN GRIA'S ROOM.
GRIA'S ROOM!

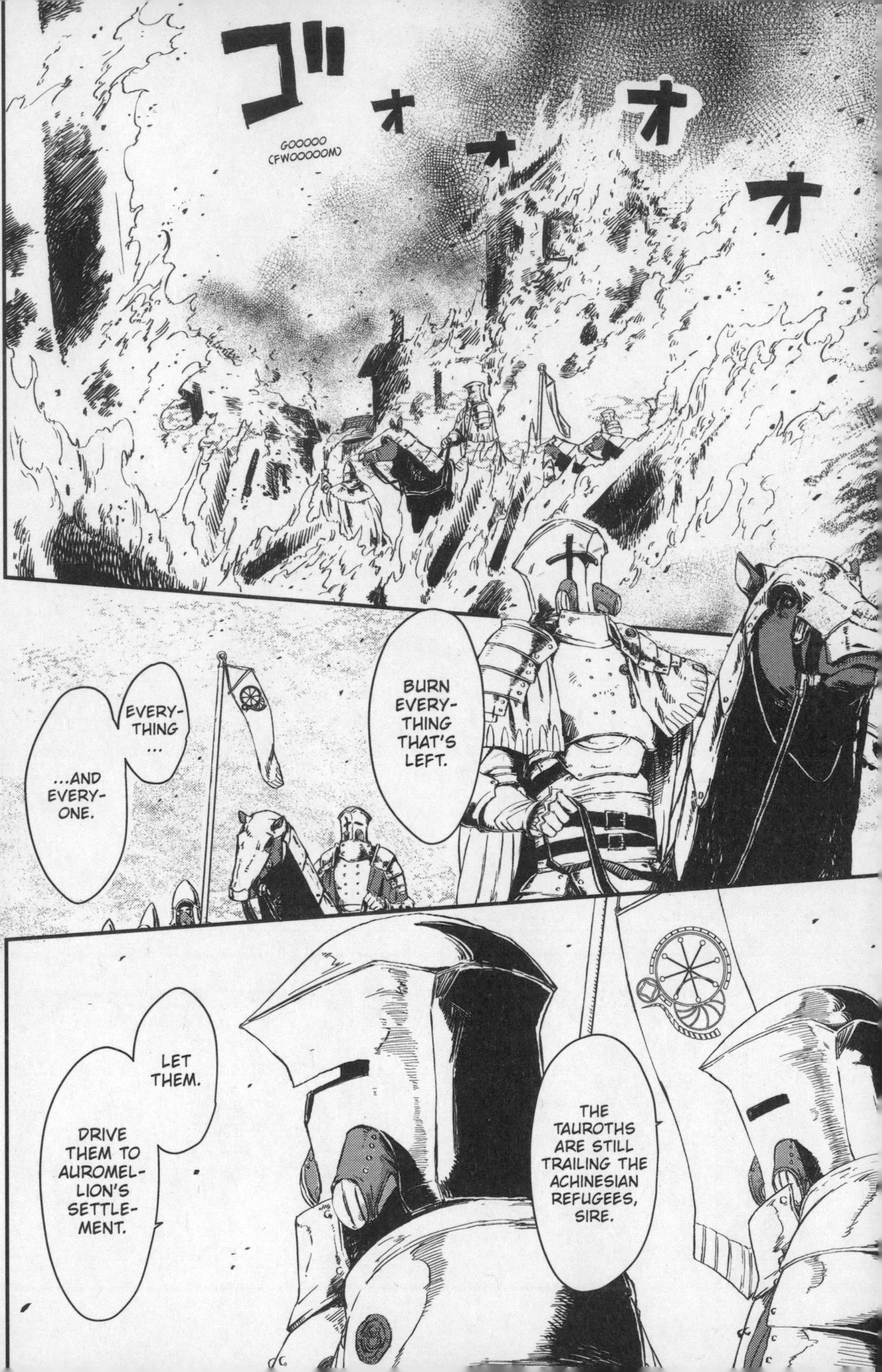
ゴォオオオ
GOOOOO (FWOOOOOM)
BURN EVERY-THING THAT'S LEFT.
EVERY-THING ...
...AND EVERY-ONE.
THE TAUROTHS ARE STILL TRAILING THE ACHINESIAN REFUGEES, SIRE.
LET THEM.
DRIVE THEM TO AUROMEL-LION'S SETTLE-MENT.

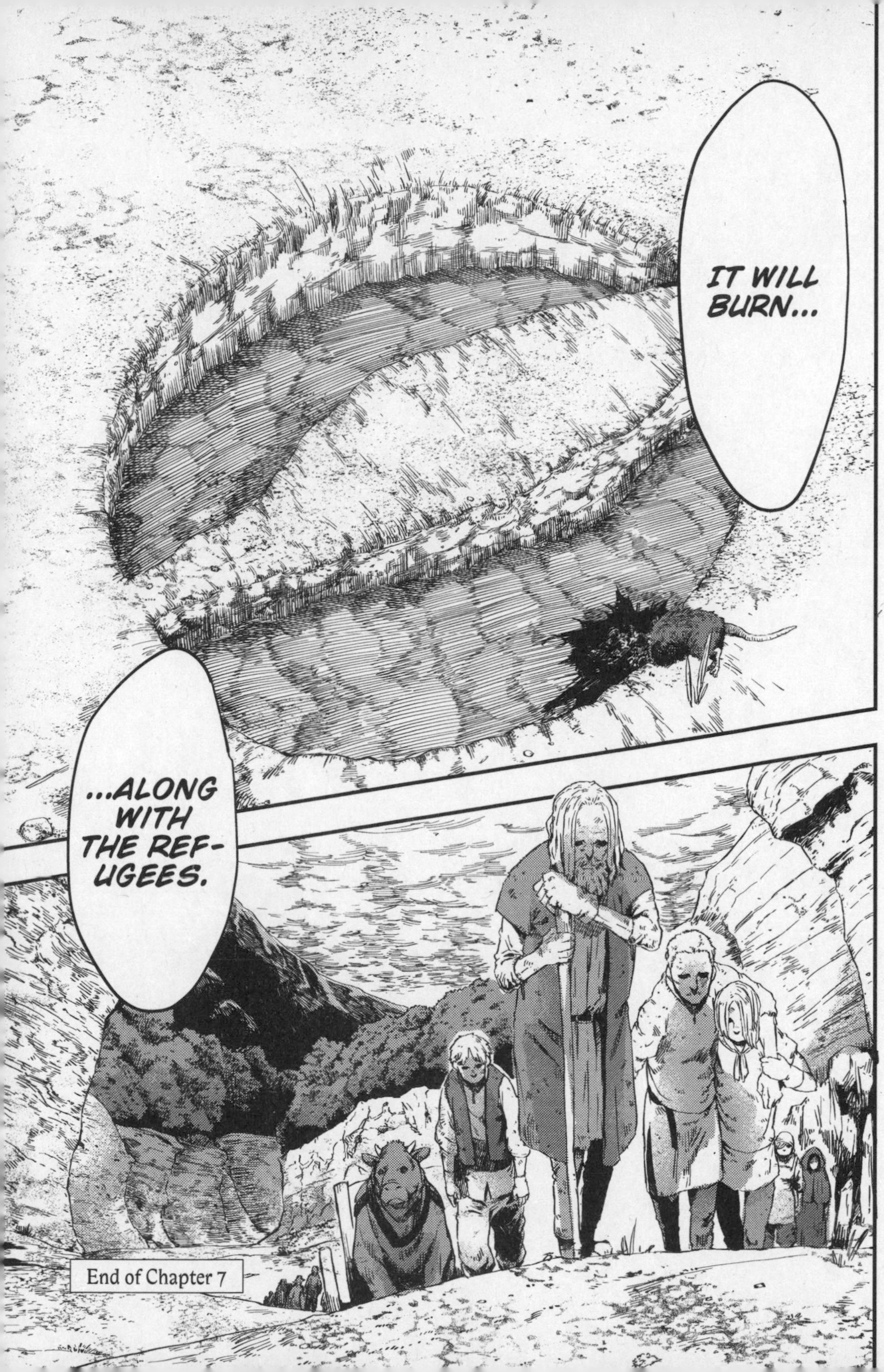
IT WILL BURN...
...ALONG WITH THE REF- UGEES.
End of Chapter 7

The Witch and the Knight Will Survive – Initial Designs

AGREDIOS

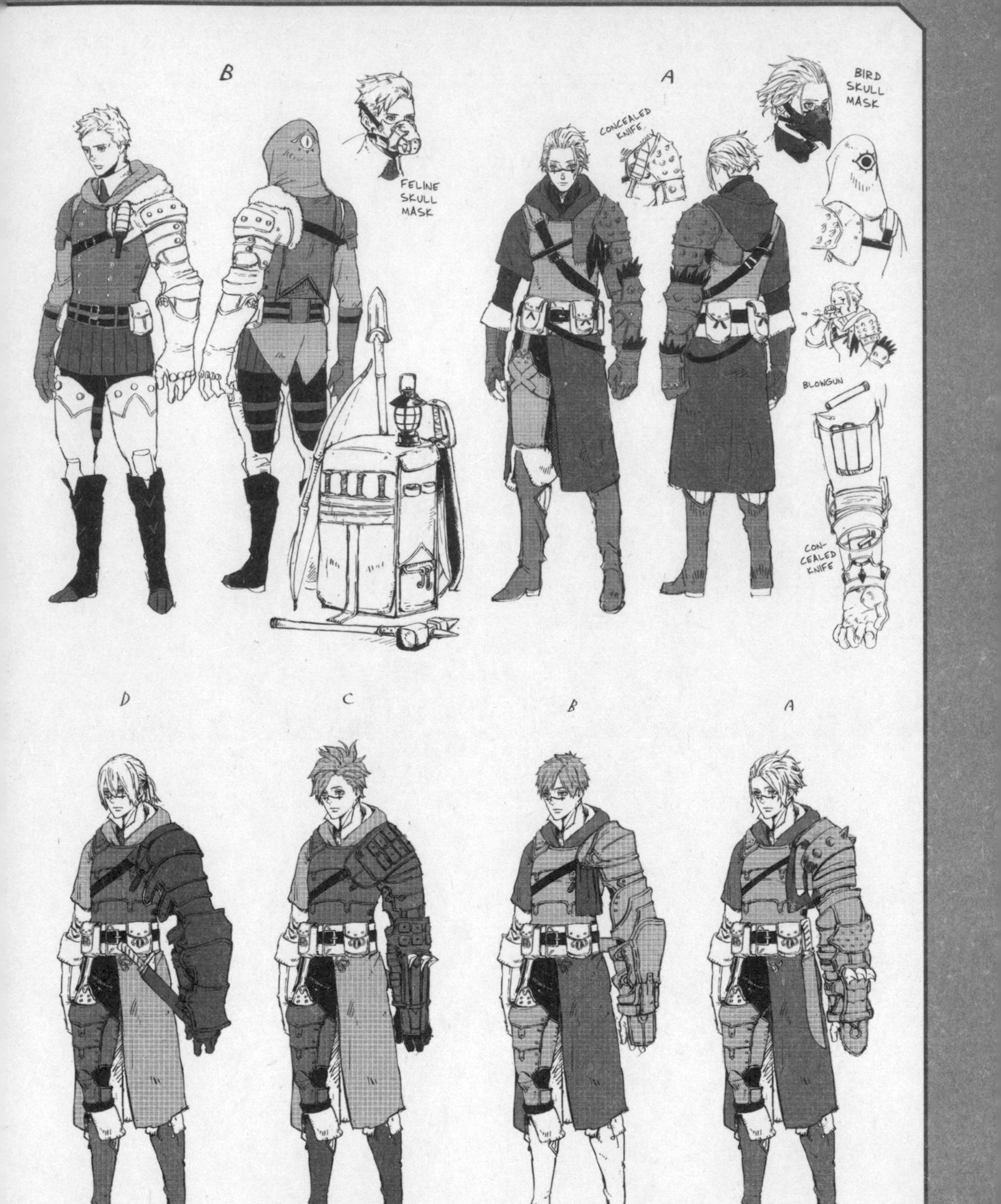
B
FELINE SKULL MASK
A
CONCEALED KNIFE
BIRD SKULL MASK
BLOWGUN
CON-CEALED KNIFE
D
C
B
A

CETIA

β
A
SHE COULD HOLD THIS STAFF LIKE A GUITAR.
ROCK YOU!
CUNEIFORM-STYLE TATTOO
IT HAS THE POWER TO HOLD BOTH TIME AND THE FOREST IN PLACE. MAYBE AN IMPORTANT CHARACTER PUT IT ON HER SKIN? MIGHT NOT BE NECESSARY.
STAFF ADORNED WITH WOODEN BELLS... ...OR MAYBE
CASTA-NETS!
FLAMENCO!

PERLA

PERCIE

β
A

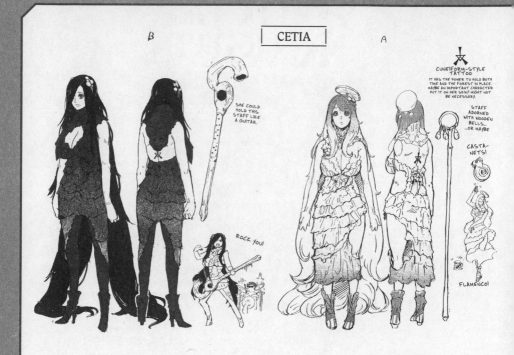

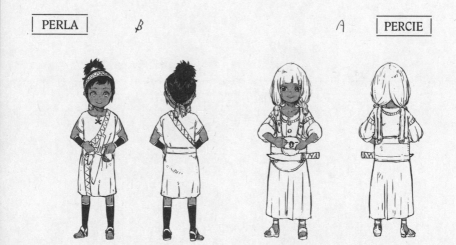